THE AIRFIELDS OF BRITAIN

THE AIRFIELDS OF BRITAIN

Volume 1 A-Bur

KENNETH P. BANNERMAN

ISE

First published in 1994.

IS Enterprises,
PO Box 379, Clarkston, Glasgow G76 8AD
(for communications)

© Kenneth P. Bannerman, 1994

All rights reserved

British Library Cataloguing in Publication Data

Bannerman, Kenneth P.
The Airfields of Britain – Volume 1: A-Bur
I. Title
387.7360941

ISBN 0-9516298-1-6

Printed in Great Britain by McCorquodale (Scotland) Limited, Glasgow.
Phototypeset by Newtext Composition Limited, Glasgow.

Dedicated to the special memory
of my greatly missed father
WILLIAM LOVE BANNERMAN
1921-1992
Always there, never forgotten

Contents

Introduction and Acknowledgements	9
Terminology	14
The Airfields of Britain	19
Other British Airfields	372
Alternative Airfield Names	392

Introduction and Acknowledgements

Airfields have been treated in the same way as men and equipment after any war since the time of Queen Elizabeth I. When not in need, they are left to rot or do the best they can on their own. The exact and most emotive comment yet made in appreciation of the book that, despite all the odds, has blasted its way into the national conscience.

A Towering Control has inspired a vast number of people, like this gentleman living in Leeds, to privately write in about Britain's top historical stars. There is unequivocal agreement with the sentiments expressed, repeated remembrance of happy times past and present, and constant anger about how our airfields – active and disused – are still being treated. The people have spoken: quite remarkable for a book launched with hardly any publicity and written by a complete unknown.

The British public know what they want, and this new book plus other volumes to come will certainly give it to them with both barrels. Forget past books, some of them so bad it is almost criminal they were published, for this is the most comprehensive home airfield history ever written. Apart from one or two types which should not be counted as true airfields, every site is included: the superstars, airfields known in your area but not nationally, or the most obscure ones imaginable. Civil airfields are given as much attention as their military brethren. Not given anywhere near as much prominence are the frequently utterly trivial and always overwhelming facts and figures bogging down other books to make way for readable histories put forward in a simple but totally co-ordinated format.

If already committed enthusiasts are becoming worried, do not despair. Although *The Airfields of Britain* series will not go into the most minute details, there are still plenty of factual notes – and correct notes at that – about airfield dates, architecture and usage. Research has shown how the ordinary person simply wants to know when an airfield opened and closed, what happened there, what it comprised of and what remains. He or she does not want to be told about every last unit movement, for example, right down to each small detachment which arrived and departed as boredom would soon set in. Certain big name airfields would require a book to themselves if every detail was squeezed in and become a writer's nightmare.

As with *A Towering Control,* this complementary book and subsequent volumes will break new ground and styles. The same forceful tone and emphasis on our airfields' social impact remain as before. Illustrated in depth are their non-stop success, fascinating quirks and intricate connections proving that the airfields of Britain form one big family. At the end of each history is quoted an Ordnance Survey map reference and travel directions should you wish to visit a site. Terminology is again kept down to an absolute minimum too as in *A Towering Control.*

Three particularly novel features are worth mentioning. Perhaps least obvious is the slightly greater attention proportionately given towards less noted airfields. Famous places such as Biggin Hill are naturally heavily described in all their glory but a more unknown airfield does not necessarily have a more uninteresting history; as alternative books tend to neglect them, all the more reason for giving less hailed sites a marginal advantage.

Unfortunately, not every airfield possesses such a detailed life, and this is why an additional section is placed at the end of the book. Here are mentioned more historically vague or occasionally less important airfields.

The other feature which may well strike you as different is a massively heavy reliance upon modern photographs. What about all those old views dating right back in time? Consideration was given at great length to this point but the increasing conclusion became that most past photographs are now fairly familiar and really say nothing new. By employing current views primarily showing airfields – not aircraft and, dare one say it, not even people – one can only enhance the increasing public outrage at the all too often atrocious treatment they are now receiving.

A huge amount of research has gone into this book. The whole enterprise has proved a most fascinating and exciting experience, whether trawling through less obvious documents or gleaning just that little bit of extra information from people who are genuinely interested. So much is known and yet still so little as airfields somehow combine to become neighbours and strangers at the same time. We discover, for example, how the then reigning monarch's visit to Bircham Newton on May 24 1934 is the first such official trip to a British service

INTRODUCTION & ACKNOWLEDGEMENTS

airfield since World War One. Stately residence Sandringham, you might be interested to know, happens to stand less than twelve miles away to only make matters even worse: talk about a real royal scandal. Stories concerning submarines lying in a shallow stream and the possibility of radar devices sterilising anyone who dared drive down Bishops Court's main runway conversely illustrate how fantasy can easily interfere with fact!

Airfields matter: of that there is not a shadow of doubt. But you would not think so on seeing the almighty barrage of trivia and flippancy today. Losers win and are admired, winners lose and are slapped down at every opportunity. 'This base must never, never close,' said Winston Churchill in 1940 of Biggin Hill, but it now has in a military capacity. Long-term socially benevolent achievement is also sacrificed for short-term selfish gain with military and civil general aviation airfields being under constant attack, privatisation now incredibly infesting the RAF, former service accommodation such as at Binbrook almost being given away and defence spending slashed when the world is patently a more unstable place. Disused airfields meanwhile succumb to tacky yuppie housing, golf courses and supermarkets or still more God-awful small-minded environmental and pacifist pressure groups. The moral in this tale is that whether you are Biggin Hill or Benny Hill, try and be a big winner in Britain and see how far you can get. Maybe the rest of the world greatly admires you but the snipers will always be waiting back home.

One thought the occasion when a certain major media organisation cancelled a radio interview with the author because yours truly was '...not a celebrity' surpassed all belief and could not be topped. Why bother with promoting a book which could create tens of thousands of jobs and unlock vast new reserves of urgently needed income for Britain when we presumably must hear at all costs the latest garbage about soap operas, royalty and minor trendy or politically correct social issues? But now has arisen a story about a farmer who not only refuses the body of a Battle of Britain pilot to be exhumed from his land but even forbids this hero's relatives to enter the field to simply place flowers at the site. Shocking, absolutely shocking – and if scum like this can take such an attitude towards a human being, any airfield does not stand a chance.

Public support for Britain's airfields however reaches ever greater peaks if the reaction to *A Towering Control* is taken as a yardstick. Thanks for all the material and highly favourable comment received already, such as the letter from our friend in Leeds, and now read about these uniquely different places

THE AIRFIELDS OF BRITAIN: VOLUME 1

called airfields which have so phenomenally altered life in this country. One correspondent has told me that 25 per cent of the British Heritage budget is allocated each year to solely maintain the royal houses: an alarming thought, and just morally wrong. The powers that be must start saving their real history instead – and fast, or else another party will do it for them. Until that happens, the fair society our airfields fought to preserve will continue to remain a myth.

Kenneth P. Bannerman.

The author would like to thank the following concerns and individuals for their assistance with providing information and/or photographs:

Public Record Office, Royal Air Force Museum, Imperial War Museum, Fleet Air Arm Museum.

Regional Record Offices: Bedfordshire (Nigel Lutt), Coventry City (David Rimmer), Hampshire (Stephen Edwards), Northamptonshire (Rachel Watson), Suffolk/Bury St Edmunds (E.P. Button), Suffolk/Lowestoft (David Wright), West Sussex (Patricia Gill), Warwickshire (R.J. Chamberlaine-Brothers), Wiltshire (Steven D. Hobbs).

Libraries: Alloa (Ian Murray), Alness (Mrs L. Lawson), Altrincham (Valerie Freeman), Balderton (Miss A. Renton), Bangor, Bedford Central (Barry Stephenson), Birkenhead Central (David Thompson), Birmingham Central, Blackburn Central (N.L. Monks), Bridlington, Brighton Reference (Mary Laney), Burford, Burscough (Margaret Bracegirdle), Chesterfield Central (L. Greaves), Colchester Central (Jane Dansie), Halifax Central (C. Kearns and J.R. Jebson), High Wycombe (M. Rickard), Hoddesdon (J. Wetherill), Humberside/Beverley Group HQ (J.G.W. Roberts), Inverness (Miss C.A. Goodfellow), Luton Central (Michael Perl), Middlesbrough Central (N. Moorsom and D. Tyrell), North East of Scotland Library Service (G. Moore), North Eastern Education and Library Board (Claire McReynolds), Pwllheli (M. Hughes), South Eastern Education and Library Board (Joan Magee), Southend (Martin Palmer), Telford (Helen Brooks), Torquay Central (P.J. Bottrill), West Glamorgan/Swansea (Brian Thomas).

ADT-Blackbushe Airport 85 Limited (J.S. Marshall), Airports UK Limited/Biggin Hill Airport (Peter Mirams), Airways Aero Associations Limited (David Lewry), Alderney Airport

INTRODUCTION & ACKNOWLEDGEMENTS

(Keith Webster), Automobile Association, Beechwood Park School (G.J.C. Williams), Benbecula Airport (R. Stewart), Bircham Newton Training Centre, Border Parachute Centre, British International Helicopters/Beccles Heliport (Joe West), City of Dundee District Council, Cumbria County Council (David Marsden), DRE Aberporth, East Kent Packers Limited (R. Bell), Ford Motorsport, Glasgow Flying Club, HQ Air Cadets/RAF Newton, Highlands and Islands Airports Limited (Callum B. Smith), Hull Aero Club, Leicestershire County Council (A.W. Stevenson), Loganair Limited (Tom Meikle), London Luton Airport (David Ellis), Luton Museum Service (Dr Stephen Bunker), Martin-Baker Aircraft Co Ltd, National Air Traffic Services (J. Hume), North Down Heritage Centre (Ian Wilson), Real Aeroplane Company, RAF Scampton (Squadron Leader Tony Cunnane), Selby District Council (P. Johnson), Shepherd Homes Limited (Jolyon L. Harrison), Skypark (UK) Limited (S.A. Williams), South Cambridgeshire District Council (D.J. Rush), C. Walton Limited (David Walton), West Oxfordshire District Council (I.R. Morrow), Wrekin Council (Mrs J.M. Booth).

Brian Bonnard, Mick Davis, Harold J. Dixon, Mark Evans, Ross Ferguson, Roger A. Freeman, John Goodwin, Peter B. Gunn, J. Harris, Karl E. Hayes, Malcolm Holmes, Bill Hutchison, Bryan Jones, V.W.J. Lea, Mrs M. Monk, John V. Nickolls, Milan Petrovic, Les Povey, Neill Rush, Harold Sewell, Ken Sherwood, Pete Stevens, Ray Sturtivant, Roy Templeman, Wing Commander Eric J. Viles, Don Vincent, Eleanor Wadsworth, Chris Walker.

Also the vast number of others asked either in person or by letter who, if nothing else, confirmed how no official records relating to airfields exist in many parts of Britain.

And special thanks to my mother for her voluntary proof-reading assistance, at an exceptionally difficult time for both of us.

Can you provide any of the following:
Information? Photographs? Up to the minute news?
Send them to: K.P. Bannerman
               c/o IS Enterprises
               PO Box 379
               Clarkston
               Glasgow G76 8AD
Photographs will be returned if requested.

Terminology

Term	Meaning(s)
AA	Anti-Aircraft; or Automobile Association (civil)
AAC	Army Air Corps
AACU	Anti-Aircraft Co-operation Unit
A&AEE	Aeroplane and Armament Experimental Establishment
AAP	Aircraft Acceptance Park
AASF	Advanced Air Striking Force
ACHU	Aircrew Holding Unit
ADDL	Aerodrome Dummy Deck Landing (FAA)
ADGB	Air Defence of Great Britain
AEW	Airborne Early Warning (radar)
AFS	Advanced Flying School
AGS	Air Gunnery School
AI	Airborne Interception (radar)
ALG	Advanced Landing Ground
ANS	Air Navigation School
AONS	Air Observer Navigation School
AOP	Air Observation Post (relating to Auster aircraft)
AOS	Air Observer School
APC	Armament Practice Camp
ASR	Air-Sea Rescue
ATA	Air Transport Auxiliary
ATC	Air Traffic Control; or Air Training Corps
AuxAF	Auxiliary Air Force (RAuxAF from 1947)
BAT Flight	Blind (or Beam) Approach Training Flight
BDTF	Bomber Defence Training Flight
BEA	British European Airways
BG	Bomb Group (USAAF)
B&GS	Bombing and Gunnery School
BOAC	British Overseas Airways Corporation
CAG	Civil Air Guard
CCRC	Combat Crew Replacement Center (USAAF)

14

TERMINOLOGY

CFS	Central Flying School
Circus	Heavily escorted daylight bomber mission, meant to attract enemy aircraft
C&M	Care and Maintenance
CND	Campaign for Nuclear Disarmament
Con Flight	Conversion Flight
CPF	Coastal Patrol Flight
CU	Conversion Unit
D/F	Direction Finding; ground-based radio aid for aircraft navigation
DZ	Dropping Zone
E/A	Enemy Aircraft
EFTS	Elementary Flying Training School
ELG	Emergency Landing Ground
E&RFTS	Elementary and Reserve Flying Training School
Exercise *Spartan*	Combined RAF/Army exercise held during February/March 1943
FAA	Fleet Air Arm
FG	Fighter Group (USAAF)
FIDO	Fog Investigation Dispersal Operation; device for clearing fog around airfields
FIS	Flying Instructors' School
FRU	Fleet Requirements Unit (FAA)
FTS	Flying Training School
FTU	Ferry Training Unit
FU	Ferry Unit
GC	Gliding Club (civil)
GCI	Ground Controlled Interception; ground radar directing friendly night fighters towards enemy aircraft
Gp	Group
GS	Gliding School (ATC)
GTS	Glider Training School
HCU	Heavy Conversion Unit
HD	Home Defence
HE	High Explosive (type of bomb)
HGCU	Heavy Glider Conversion Unit
Highball	Weapon designed for use by Mosquitoes
HTCU	Heavy Transport Conversion Unit
H2S	Navigational and target identification radar aid carried aboard RAF bombers during World War Two
IRBM	Intermediate Range Ballistic Missile
K (or KQ) site	Type of decoy airfield
LFS	Lancaster Finishing School

THE AIRFIELDS OF BRITAIN: VOLUME I

MAEE	Marine Aircraft Experimental Establishment
MAP	Ministry of Aircraft Production
MCA	Ministry of Civil Aviation
Met	Meteorological
MoA	Ministry of Aviation
MoD	Ministry of Defence
MT	Mechanical Transport (vehicles)
MU	Maintenance Unit
Nickel	Propaganda leaflet dropped from aircraft or mission to do so (as in *Nickelling*)
NJG	Nachtjagdgeschwader; Luftwaffe night fighter wing
Noball	V-1 or V-2 missile site
(O) AFU	(Observers) Advanced Flying Unit
OCU	Operational Conversion Unit
Operations:	
Crossbow	Attacks against V-weapon targets 1943/44
Gisela	Enemy title for a large intruder raid upon airfields in eastern England during night of March 3/4 1945
Market	Airborne invasion of Arnhem and other Netherlands targets in September 1944
Starkey	Deliberately false invasion of Pas de Calais area during August/September 1943
Varsity	Airborne operation over River Rhine in March 1945
OPMAC	Operation Military Aid to the Community
ORB	Operations Record Book
OS	Ordnance Survey
OTU	Operational Training Unit
(P) AFU	(Pilots) Advanced Flying Unit
PFF	Pathfinder Force
PRO	Public Record Office
PSP	Pierced Steel Planking (type of runway)
Pundit	Either two letters placed in signals square beside control tower or lights flashing in Morse Code to provide the identity of an airfield.
Q site	Type of decoy airfield, less elaborate than K or KQ site and only for use at night
RAAF	Royal Australian Air Force
RAE	Royal Aircraft (later Aerospace) Establishment
RAFGSA	Royal Air Force Gliding and Soaring Association

TERMINOLOGY

RAFVR	Royal Air Force Volunteer Reserve
Ramrod	Escorted daylight bombing raid against a specified target
Ranger	Long-range offensive sortie against targets in a defined area
RAT Flight	Radio Aids Training Flight
RAuxAF	Royal Auxiliary Air Force (AuxAF until 1947)
RCAF	Royal Canadian Air Force
RFC	Royal Flying Corps
RFS	Reserve Flying School
Rhubarb	Fighter mission flown at low level and in cloudy weather against short-range targets
RLG	Relief Landing Ground
RNAS	Royal Naval Air Service; or Royal Naval Air Station
RNZAF	Royal New Zealand Air Force
Rodeo	Fighter sweep
Rover	Patrol hunting for enemy shipping
RS	Radio School (World War Two); or Reserve Squadron (World War One, RFC)
r/t	Radio telephony
SAM	Surface-to-Air Missile
SAR	Search and Rescue
Scarecrow	Coastal patrol of 1918 flown against U-boats
Scatter Scheme	RAF tactic of early World War Two period to send bomber units to more inland airfields for brief periods and lessen chances of enemy attacks
SFTS	Service Flying Training School
SLG	Satellite Landing Ground
SMT	Square Mesh Track (type of runway)
SOC	Struck Off Charge (relating to condition of aircraft)
TAF	Tactical Air Force
TCG	Troop Carrier Group (USAAF)
TDS	Training Depot Station
TS	Training Squadron (RFC/RAF)
TT	Target Towing
Turbinlite	Type of airborne searchlight fitted to Douglas Havocs and Bostons for night fighter use
USAAF	United States Army Air Force (US Air Force from 1946)

The Airfields of Britain

THE AIRFIELDS OF BRITAIN: VOLUME 1

Abbots Bromley, Staffordshire

Alternative Name: Stone

Most of you will have heard of some airfields in this book and subsequent volumes. Sadly, the great majority of our historical and social revolutionists remain virtually unknown to the general public. Just one of the latter is the alphabetical opener to Britain's glorious catalogue of airfields.

Abbots Bromley was born in a hurry. By the beginning of June 1940, Germany had rolled westwards so quickly that France seemed in imminent danger of collapse. The increasing possibility of a major Luftwaffe assault on Britain put inoffensive training airfields in southern England under extreme threat as well, so many instructional units were forced to rapidly move away from the front line. Among them was No 5 Elementary Flying Training School at Feltham on the western edges of London, which had transferred to Stoke-on-Trent's pre-war municipal airport at Meir by mid-June. Abbots Bromley itself soon started up business as one of the fairly new Relief Landing Grounds to help out Miles Magister monoplanes belonging to the EFTS.

One of the most recurrent factors with our airfields is their air of mystery. And it is with the first eighteen months or so of Abbots Bromley's life that this factor becomes apparent. Wartime records relating to various types of training units such as EFTSs are often notoriously vague, as shown by the lack of any mention of this forced landing field – as RLGs were then still generally known – until November 15 1940. It is at this time surprisingly called Stone, even though this market town lies twelve miles away to the north-west, quite a distance for an airfield's nominal inspiration. A separate map dating from December however lists the airfield as Abbots Bromley.

Initial details about Abbots Bromley are limited to aircraft accidents. Crashes occurred on June 1 and 16 1941, then two more in two days during November, with two fatalities happening on the 6th. Only on this last occasion is the name Abbots Bromley now quoted after months of 'Forced landing field' or 'F.L. field': airfield research is not for those of an impatient character. Perhaps the reason for this sudden mention was a village situated half-way between Stone and Abbots Bromley named Stowe, alongside which the new bomber Operational Training Unit station of Hixon neared completion by the autumn of 1941, and planners wanted to

THE AIRFIELDS OF BRITAIN

avoid any possible confusion.

No 5 EFTS closed in December 1941 but more Magisters and de Havilland Tiger Moth biplanes continued to appear when No 16 EFTS at Burnaston in Derbyshire gained control of the RLG. Apart from this unit change and gradual dominance of the Tiger Moths, basic pilot training carried on and Abbots Bromley kept active until the end of World War Two.

While peacetime meant relative longevity for both Burnaston and Meir, their former aide suffered one of the fastest run-downs of any British airfield used in the second world conflict. Only one week had passed since VE Day when the RAF's Flying Training Command handed Abbots Bromley to Maintenance Command on May 15 1945. Surrounded by a minor road and generally unsuitable for further development, this site closed to flying but did not undergo the rapid path towards military derequisition like many other grassy RLGs around Britain. No 21 Maintenance Unit stayed for bomb storage duties, even after labour shortages in July 1946 forced Abbots Bromley to lose its independence and come under the control of the officer in charge at No 21 MU's main sub-site Tatenhill, another Staffordshire airfield unavailable to aircraft at that period.

By February 1949 work was in hand to clear Abbots Bromley and pass it to the Air Ministry Works Department. Once 28 tons of mortars had gone to No 53 MU at the famous old East Anglian airship station of Pulham in March, closure resulted on the 31st and this place given to AMWD in August for use by an Airfield Construction Works Flight.

Its personnel have since vanished as well to leave a mixture of farming and poultry rearing; Abbots Bromley's last service to aviation was as a turning point for civil aircraft competing in the 1950 King's Cup Air Race. Another feature now shared with so many other disused airfields in Britain is how hidden Abbots Bromley has become. Find a derelict guardhouse by the B5014 road and you will then see a Robin hangar standing on a hill. Again the mystery element of our airfields is evident, for Abbots Bromley possessed nine Blisters during World War Two, and one can only suggest that the Robin was brought over from a nearby Satellite Landing Ground for aircraft storage – maybe Hoar Cross or Teddesley Park to the south – to help out No 21 MU. Whatever the answer, nobody can doubt the small but significant part Abbots Bromley has played in Britain's military and social history.

128/SK074255. Immediately NW of village on right side of B5014, 8½ miles S of Uttoxeter.

Abbotsinch, Strathclyde

Alternative Name: Glasgow

If few people have heard of Abbots Bromley, it is safe to say that fewer still have not heard of Britain's number two site on the A to Z airfield roll of honour. Abbotsinch: Glasgow Airport. This fact alone helps, yet Abbotsinch has not had the sort of settled career one would expect an airport should have when looking back at its past. Even today, Glasgow's aerial gateway faces more changes. There have been allegations that the main runway is sinking, while people living around and about object to extremely high noise levels. And then there is The Big P ...

The most durable airports have turned out to be those ones named after obscure localities sited way out into the countryside without suburbia troubling them. Heathrow owed its title to a hall and a hamlet, Gatwick a racecourse of all things, while the place some Glaswegians regard as the arch-enemy – Turnhouse or Edinburgh Airport – was partly inspired by a farm. In Abbotsinch's case, another farm donated its name along with some land, and still stands in empty semi-derelict condition after years of military and civil aviation service amid modern office buildings marginally inside the eastern airport boundary. So typically unknown was this area that a lot of people persisted in calling the new airfield Abbots or even Abbotts Inch for several years after it opened.

Abbotsinch first welcomed No 602 (City of Glasgow) Squadron on January 20 1933. This day bomber unit had previously resided at nearby Renfrew, Glasgow's original airport which hindered Abbotsinch's surrounding airspace and vice versa in what became a major example of circuit overlap and the increased chances of mid-air collisions between aircraft. By the 1930s the mud and murk that represented Renfrew already almost bordered on the legendary, and forced its new next door neighbour to act in an unofficial diversionary capacity should airliners be unable to land at their rightful destination. Other early but more authorised civil use followed in the middle of World War Two when Renfrew at last received hard runways.

Allowing for these distractions, it was nevertheless military aviation which kept Abbotsinch busy for three decades. No 602 Squadron replaced its Westland Wapiti biplanes with Hawker Harts in early 1934, succeeded in turn by Hinds in June 1936. Nos 21 and 34 Squadrons were two more Hind units present in 1936 before coastal patrol Avro Ansons of No 269 Squadron arrived at the year's end. By then the Hinds had left for far-off Lympne in Kent on November 3 in somewhat controversial fashion as fierce gales during the night of October 26 which caused bad damage to Glasgow as a whole mauled twelve aircraft in their six Bessoneaux. Five of these World War One vintage canvas hangars were wrecked but opinions varied enormously on overall damage, ranging from the RAF's 'surprisingly small' to estimates of £50,000. The subsequent hasty departure of regular RAF personnel somehow did not tally entirely with the policy thinking supposedly behind this joint unit movement.

As the war clouds gathered, so Abbotsinch gradually became more prominent. The Auxiliaries of No 602 Squadron went through a brief phase of operating Hawker Hector army co-operation aircraft prior to receiving Gloster Gauntlet fighters in January 1939 and Supermarine Spitfires in May. No 269 Squadron had meanwhile been given a greater taste of things to come by flying to Thornaby in north-east England during the Munich Crisis of 1938. Both Abbotsinch squadrons would be eventually posted to Scotland's east coast, with the Ansons going to Montrose just days before fighting started. No 602 Squadron and its Spitfires followed in the same general direction, this time to Grangemouth, on October 7 1939.

Abbotsinch emphasised its air of being unsettled in the opening years of World War Two by having an odd job role. Hugely different aircraft could be spotted, none more unusual than the Tiger Moths of No 2 Coastal Patrol Flight which flew unarmed anti-submarine patrols until the spring of 1940. The Torpedo Training Unit stayed around for some time too, mainly operating twin-engined Bristol Beaufort monoplanes, while No 309 (Polish) Squadron arose in October 1940 as a Westland Lysander army co-operation force but soon left for Renfrew. No 88 Squadron's Douglas Boston light bombers passed through in May 1942, and neither did Nos 225 nor 239 Squadrons stay long that month as well: they were only converting to fighter-reconnaissance North American Mustangs before going south again.

Considering all this activity, the wonder is that it continued in the face of an often waterlogged landing area, poor weather and a certain amount of industrial haze. At least Abbotsinch did not get caught up in the Clydeside Blitz, apart from one harmless occasion late at night on April 7 1941 when four bombs exploded on the landing area and a fifth hit the main Abbotsinch-Inchinnan road. But most of all Abbotsinch had no real sense of direction — until 1943.

Some Royal Navy aircraft had already stayed here since earlier wartime days, hundreds more being repaired, but it took until August of that year for the station to be officially transferred from RAF to Fleet Air Arm hands. Abbotsinch was now known as HMS *Sanderling* and primarily served as an Aircraft Maintenance Yard or naval answer to an RAF MU. The usual transitory FAA squadrons kept appearing from their anchored aircraft carriers in addition. Two notable exceptions present during the last year and a half of World War Two were Nos 730 and 768 Squadrons, the first employed for communications duties and the other for deck landing training on carriers in the Firth of Clyde. Both units eventually moved to Ayr II.

Navy aircraft remained at Abbotsinch after 1945 to retain its recently acquired air of stability: this base's close proximity to the River Clyde had great beneficial effects. No 1830 Squadron reformed in 1947 as part of the new Royal Naval Volunteer Reserve, the FAA equivalent of the Royal Auxiliary Air Force, to fly mainly Fairey Firefly fighters and Grumman Avenger anti-submarine types. It was joined in 1953 by No 1843 Squadron, which subsequently shared aircraft with its sister unit until both disbanded on March 10 1957. Many FAA aircraft in general met their ends at Abbotsinch in peacetime when this scrapping task was given to the Aircraft Holding Unit, though it also made ready various types for further military use. Abbotsinch was no stranger to aircraft storage, having held many RAF machines in readiness since early on in World War Two.

But for all this ostensible consistency, the airfield had really lapsed back into old ways. One familiar non-naval face became No 602 Squadron when it proudly reformed on May 10 1946. Times had barely changed as Spitfires still remained available for their part-time pilots; it is claimed with some justification that No 602 operated more variants than any other RAF unit during eleven years of adventures at home and abroad. Jets in the instantly recognisable twin tailboom shapes of de Havilland Vampires replaced the Spitfires in 1951 before No 602 Squadron shut down on March 10 1957 along with all other RAuxAF and RNVR units. A Flight of RAuxAF Auster Air Observation Post monoplanes belonging to No 666 Squadron did likewise to signal the steady military departure from Abbotsinch.

The airfield finally closed as a service base on October 31 1963. Major reconstruction work had occurred in the early 1950s to force Abbotsinch to operate on at least a reduced

THE AIRFIELDS OF BRITAIN

footing for a while, with No 602 Squadron having to fly from Renfrew or Leuchars during 1949-54 and No 1830 Squadron from Donibristle between December 1950 and November 1952 as their usual home completely closed to let hard paving supersede metal runways. Now a decade had gone by as the builders moved back in. Planners viewed this ready-made, superior and less cramped site as an ideal replacement for Renfrew. The old and new Glasgow Airports closed and opened on May 2 1966, just 30 minutes separating these two events, and Abbotsinch has since never looked back. Internal and foreign airlines, the popular shuttle service to Heathrow, charter firms and flying clubs all ensure healthy daily aircraft movement totals.

Life has however turned out to be far from plain sailing in more recent years. Everyone agreed that almost anywhere was better than Renfrew for use as an airport but even Abbotsinch has proved rather difficult to enlarge. The Black Cart Water exists at one end and a motorway at the other; extension work to lengthen the main runway resulted in considerable re-routing of the A726 road. The secondary runway is also short, a north-south stretch has long vanished, the aforementioned sinking problems are said to persist and fog often does its best to hinder operations. Even airfield and aircraft buffs have not been pleased by the closure of an open air viewing walkway at the terminal, although views from surrounding roads are not too bad by normal British airport standards. In the past a number of good areas gave spotters many interesting spectacles of Aircraft Holding Unit activities until it left for Brawdy in south-west Wales during the 1960s.

Despite these faults, Abbotsinch's shortcomings have not prevented it from threatening the sheer existence of Scotland's greatest ever airfield, the universally revered Prestwick. This is something of a bad joke when one compares their weather records alone. But still the place affectionately known to millions as The Big P receives almost daily dog's abuse as the Glaswegian business community, or the 'merchant princes' as they have become derisively known, try frantically to make a silk purse out of a sow's ear by promoting Abbotsinch.

This prolonged slanging match has reached quite bizarre levels at times. There was the occasion when Prestwick allowed in a huge Russian Antonov transport to take away specialised engineering equipment, Abbotsinch then conveniently inviting along an equally big United States Air Force Lockheed Galaxy next day. Another pro-Abbotsinch and anti-Prestwick lobby has been the airline Air 2000, so vociferous that it fought

25

through the Scottish courts to start a transatlantic passenger service from Abbotsinch instead of Prestwick on September 17 1989. Yet both this airline and the 'merchant princes' stayed strangely silent later on in the autumn as stubbornly thick fog sent dozens of Glasgow-bound aircraft scurrying to the safety of Prestwick.

One far less trumpeted argument involving Abbotsinch concerns airfield supporters more interested in architecture. What amount of hangarage has this place exactly possessed? Records for 1943 state how one A, one C, four Bellmans, three Callenders and a Callender-Hamilton were available. But a year or two later sees other official files quoting the score as two Cs, six Bellmans, three Callender-Hamiltons and a Mainhill. What happened as well to the rare 100 feet span Hinaidi hangar clearly depicted in a local newspaper during mid-1932 while in the process of being built? And as if all this is confusing, remaining vintage hangars on Abbotsinch's west side consist of two Cls, a Callender-Hamilton — and three Blisters. Two more Blisters, one C, one Bellman and other small hangars stood too but some and possibly all of the survivors will go to make way for airport development, as might resident flying clubs.

These buildings demonstrate how Abbotsinch has not enjoyed the simplest of lives. By 1930, long before the airfield had even opened, doubts were being aired about the land; test borings in 1939 revealed that Abbotsinch sat on a lot of peat. The airport meets the needs of Glasgow as best it can — development of the terminal emphasises how many people still hold their faith in the place — but remains considerably flawed. No doubt the arguments will go on.
64/NS479670. W of Glasgow, leave M8 at Junction 28.

Aberporth, Dyfed

Alternative Name: Blaenannerch
Military flying continues at this tiny airfield which first came into being during the late 1930s. The major difference between then and today was that AA co-operation served as Aberporth's original task.

No 1 Anti-Aircraft Co-operation Unit was one of these RAF elements which seemed to pop up everywhere as it helped provide ground batteries around many parts of Britain with essential firing practice. One area was Wales, and some of the AACU's aircraft may just have visited Aberporth before 1939,

THE AIRFIELDS OF BRITAIN

although official denials and a temporary landing ground near Pembroke named Flimston Down which saw use during parts of 1937 and 1938 make this idea extremely unlikely.

Why such uncertainty? Again we must return to questioning the huge gaps in official records. While the early career of Abbots Bromley might be sparsely noted, at least there is some reference to its activities. But try to discover what 'B' or 'X' Flights of No 1 AACU did in 1938 and you will find a complete blank. Yet aircraft certainly operated from Aberporth during 1939 until training on the various ranges abruptly ceased on August 24 as partial mobilisation was declared in Britain.

World War Two duly began within a fortnight but the little grass field quickly resumed duties as an essentially temporary place aiding AA gun crews. 'B' Flight is significantly stated as having *re*opened the radio-telephony station at Aberporth on September 23, so this indubitably proves how the detachment or another portion of No 1 AACU had come earlier in 1939. A further complication however arises for, assuming such an event had happened in 1938, the Flight would not have operated Hawker Henley monoplanes to tow target drogues but Westland Wallace biplanes. This miniature detective story only goes to prove the shocking historical neglect of our airfields: there are literally thousands of other examples, from the exceedingly important to relatively trivial.

Aberporth was found suitable enough for use as a permanent airfield soon into wartime and managed to get rid of its stop-start past when aircraft called on request for army practice firing camps. Reopening came again in September 1940 to allow in 'X' Flight and radio-controlled de Havilland Queen Bee pilotless target drones for gunnery practice from Watchet in Somerset, a road convoy arriving at Aberporth on the 3rd and the unit movement being completed two days later. Still greater solidity resulted in December as the airfield achieved independent status.

Other Flights of No 1 AACU travelled to this fairly detached station as it established ever firmer roots, being given numbers instead of letters during October 1942 as planners finally gave up trying to monitor the nightmarishly involved meanders of No 1 AACU's Flights. Another change of name on December 1 1943 saw Nos 1607, 1608 and 1609 Flights join forces as No 595 Squadron, No 1621 Flight's Queen Bees leaving the scene, though the AA co-operation role remained throughout World War Two. The towering control our airfields finally achieved beyond all doubt at this time inevitably made its mark at Aberporth, which emerged from humble beginnings to control other AA co-operation bases at Manorbier and Towyn in the early war years.

A number of ageing aircraft types worked out of Aberporth as one might have expected with such a task. Examples of a second Hawker product in the ubiquitous Hurricane joined the much rarer Henleys earlier on during hostilities but Spitfires, Miles Martinets and Airspeed Oxfords latterly predominated. Some No 595 Squadron machines were detached to airfields as near as Brawdy or as far as Hawarden's satellite at Poulton in Cheshire to keep up with AA co-operation training schedules. Aberporth performed its duties well, though it had one major drawback in not being suitable for night flying because of the surrounding hilly geography. Several British airfields suffered from this problem during World War Two, one being Carew Cheriton, another haunt for wandering No 595 Squadron aircraft.

Daily routine was not entirely devoted to AA co-operation. Anson detachments of No 6 Air Observers School appeared from Staverton in Gloucestershire during 1942/43. But No 595 Squadron easily outlasted them, only moving to another former detachment airfield at Fairwood Common near Swansea on April 27 1946, the air party having left a day earlier. Aberporth slumped into inactivity from May 15 after the unit had departed and looked doomed.

Events thereafter only tended to confirm this notion. Lingering on a caretaker basis, best described as a terminal form of Care and Maintenance, the War Office took charge of Aberporth from Fairwood Common when the former closed on September 1. Fairwood Common did not have long to go either but there is a happy ending to its story, and the same applies here.

This airfield's unlikely saviours in 1957 became not civil aircraft but missiles. Testing of these weapons had been evident at the Aberporth ranges close by since 1940; the rocket batteries used for urban AA defence were developed there. Present too was the Royal Aircraft Establishment to supervise the Projectile Development Establishment, which has since gradually evolved into its present arrangement as the Defence Research Establishment.

It is often said how Duncan Sandys acquired his maniacal ideas about missiles while based in this area. But as the demonic Sandys set in motion post-war his plans to annihilate every airfield and aircraft in sight, the RAE sub-unit near Aberporth village finally needed a communications site for visiting aircraft. Such was the ultra-tight security needed to enable the missile firing ranges to work in peace that

Aberporth as a whole remained almost entirely unpublicised until the mid-1950s. The Bristol Bloodhound defensive weapon eventually enabled the airfield to reopen.

Several generations of guided missiles have passed through since the Fairey Stooge appeared in 1947. This type was originally intended to take on Japanese kamikaze aircraft in the Pacific, being successful if too late for active use, but Aberporth became involved in some real fighting when Sidewinder air-to-air missiles were hurriedly tested to fit on RAF British Aerospace Harrier fighters during the Falklands conflict of 1982. Officials coming by air to the local airfield to assess trials have also arrived in a variety of aircraft; helicopters are more common than fixed-wing designs these days. Aberporth may have a one-dimensional duty if likened to Abbotsinch but is frequently busy.

A control tower and two Bellmans are still around today to cope with aerial incomers. One inhabitant no longer flyable is an old Hawker Hunter jet fighter belonging to No 1429 Squadron of the Air Training Corps. Two Blisters have suffered a worse fate in total removal but Aberporth has been more than recompensed by being given a hard runway. This useful asset compares with the grass landing surface of World War Two. A small clutch of wartime support buildings have survived and continue in everyday use. Photography is still not particularly recommended but a reasonable view can be obtained from the adjacent main road.

Aberporth is still known locally as Blaenannerch after a small nearby settlement, a name the RAF mostly never touched with a barge-pole, as has been the case with certain other airfields in Wales. Situated in an area of Britain not renowned for airfields, there is no doubt that this little place has enjoyed a lot of luck, unlike many other British sites in more recent years.

145/SN250494. 4 miles NE of Cardigan by A487.

Abingdon, Oxfordshire

Abingdon's history can be split into four distinct sections: use by Bomber Command, initially for operational squadrons and later for training, then employment by Transport and Support Commands. A history of more steady service is hard to find — and now everything is being thrown away. Time to give some financial freaks a severe lesson in real history.

Opened prior to the Expansion Period, so revolutionary in

THE AIRFIELDS OF BRITAIN: VOLUME 1

airfield development, Abingdon accommodated several bomber squadrons in the 1930s after September 1 1932. No 40 was first to arrive in October with Fairey Gordons, common sights in Africa but rare at home. Light bomber squadrons such as the famous No XV – here the unit unusually started using Roman numerals – which reformed in 1934 with Harts soon subsequently appeared in numbers. The speedy Hawker bomber's improved offspring the Hind also proved a common sight at Abingdon pre-war as a procession of squadrons reformed with the type. Nos 98 and 104 did so in 1936, with Nos 52 and 62 doing the same in 1937 plus Nos 106 and 185 in 1938. The Hind was an interim design and the RAF's last biplane light bomber but filled a critical void until monoplanes could enter service, and inhabited many a British airfield as we have seen with Abbotsinch.

Despite this activity, Abingdon had seemed to be the starting point for units as most of them moved elsewhere not long after creation. The airfield's two oldest residents, Nos XV and 40 Squadrons, stayed a bit longer but their replacement Fairey Battle monoplanes for the Gordons and Harts then flew to France as part of the Advanced Air Striking Force on September 2 1939. Not many returned.

Although two more Battle squadrons arrived at Abingdon on the 9th, they marked the station's first role change as both units were only intended for training purposes. World War Two had made the inter-war RAF Wessex Bombing Area theory of placing bombers in central England obsolete overnight to force operational aircraft out to eastern England or France. Airfields in these areas however could not function indefinitely at full power without replacement aircrews, so Armstrong Whitworth Whitley medium bombers of Nos 97 and 166 Squadrons replaced Abingdon's latest residents later on in September and became collectively known as No 4 Group Pool.

The first winter and early spring of World War Two showed how the Group Pool instructional system at Abingdon and elsewhere was a basically awkward idea with none too clear aims. More reorganisation had to be carried out in April 1940 to retitle Nos 97 and 166 Squadrons as No 10 Operational Training Unit: the confusion was solved. Abingdon's Whitleys were already not exactly in their bloom of youth but served up to 1944 until replaced by Vickers Wellingtons. Neither were the Whitleys restricted to basic training and propaganda leaflet dropping or *Nickelling*, for Abingdon proved prominent in all three spectacular Thousand Bomber

Raids against Cologne, Essen and Bremen during the late spring of 1942. A special detachment of No 10 OTU stayed at St Eval in Cornwall from then into the following year for maritime patrol training and also encountered some action, this time against U-boats.

Wartime activities at Abingdon were not confined to No 10 OTU's Whitleys and Wellingtons. Fighter affiliation aircraft helped trainee bomber crews in giving them an idea of what it was like being attacked by Luftwaffe machines. Present too was No 1 (later 1501) Blind Approach Training Flight, formed in January 1941 to make personnel become accustomed to using Standard Beam Approach or SBA radio landing aid equipment while approaching an airfield in poor visibility. Its Oxfords transferred to Abingdon's satellite at Stanton Harcourt on April 18 1943.

This austerity period airfield became most invaluable later on in World War Two by keeping No 10 OTU in business from March 20 1944 until November 16. Abingdon, still equipped with a grassy landing area, needed hard runways. Construction workers laid two stretches at virtual right angles to each other — a third runway was an impossibility because of surrounding obstructions — not before time but forced Abingdon to miss D-Day. The airfield lay largely closed but not entirely, aircraft still coming in for maintenance, the main effect being upon training by day. A total of 1,200-1,400 yards of the new north-south runway opened for use on August 26 but Stanton Harcourt performed well on its own, No 10 OTU being hardly disrupted until the all-important day flying capability at Abingdon could resume in mid-November.

Having emerged from World War Two with fine credentials and firsthand experience of what that epic period in history had been all about by suffering nuisance raids in 1940 and more serious Luftwaffe attacks in 1941, one person dying that year on March 21, Abingdon was retained in peacetime thanks to its permanent Expansion Period looks. Poor old Stanton Harcourt, on the other hand, experienced the most diabolical eventual fate of gravel excavation. No 10 OTU disbanded in September 1946, No 525 Squadron from Membury on the Berkshire-Wiltshire border heralding another new era at Abingdon when this transport unit arrived in October. It was renumbered as No 238 Squadron on December 1, though Avro Yorks instead of Douglas Dakotas would make their presences felt here. Nos 40 and 59 Squadrons reformed at the end of 1947; joined by Nos 51 and 242, all four York squadrons operated to good effect in the Berlin Airlift of 1948/49. They stayed on until June 1949 and then moved to

Bassingbourn, with the exception of No 242 Squadron which left for Lyneham.

Abingdon transport occupants during the 1950s included three Handley Page Hastings squadrons, Nos 24, 47 and 53. One Hastings brought back to Britain in 1953 after imprisonment in Korea the airfield's most notorious visitor: traitor George Blake, who described on camera while addressing journalists assembled on the apron his time in detention as '... very monotonous' (a likely story).

The last two units mentioned above flew Blackburn Beverleys later on, No 53 Squadron disbanding in 1963. These heavy high-tailed four-engined machines able to make short take-offs and landings were the tallest aircraft in RAF service when No 47 Squadron started acquiring them in March 1956 but particularly notable for being the first original British aircraft designed to drop unwieldy Army equipment while in flight. Beverleys could bear the equivalent payload weight of two wartime 22,000 pound *Grand Slam* bombs or conversely carry nearly 100 troops and became a most useful asset to RAF Transport Command. Engine problems initially dogging these aircraft culminated in a bad crash on March 5 1957 when a Beverley forced to turn back to Abingdon after take-off demolished a house at Drayton, killing three aircrew, twelve passengers and two civilians, but such difficulties were soon overcome. Aberporth still managed to outwit the type's special airfield performance in 1959 as a plan for Beverleys to fly in Bristol Bloodhound SAMs from North Coates in Lincolnshire for testing was not thought wise.

Aviation historians would have meanwhile noticed a deliberate coincidence the Beverleys created at Abingdon. The RAF has always loved tradition – unlike those airfield killers called politicians – by using methods such as reviving distinguished old squadron numbers. In this case reasoning was not so obvious but the RAF chose No 47 Squadron to first fly Beverleys as this unit arose in the beginning at Beverley in Yorkshire during 1916.

Not all that long before No 47 disbanded on October 31 1967, Nos 46 and 52 Squadrons reformed in late 1966 with Hawker Siddeley Andovers for lighter tactical transport duties as opposed to the heavy-lift strategic jobs carried out by the Beverleys. No 52 almost immediately moved to Singapore but No 46 remained at Abingdon until shifting south to Thorney Island in September 1970.

Now the stage was set clear for Support Command to take over as part of the major reorganisation in RAF Command administration at this time. Several assorted elements resided

THE AIRFIELDS OF BRITAIN

at Abingdon in the early 1970s as a result. One was still No 1 Parachute Training School, which had stayed since 1950 and only left for the great Brize Norton in 1976. An otherwise happy period of instruction at the base had been marred by a terrible accident on July 6 1965 when a Hastings of No 36 Squadron from Colerne in Wiltshire crashed east of Abingdon at Little Baldon. All six crew and 35 parachutists on board died in what remains the RAF's worst ever accident. Abingdon naturally stood entirely absolved from blame; another unit touched by disaster was the Chilterns Gliding Club of the RAF Gliding and Soaring Association which had come by 1971 after a major fire the previous year at Benson, though it soon left again for Halton.

The airfield afterwards held down a vital job as a maintenance/repair/salvage/storage base for all kinds of RAF aircraft from jet trainers to operational types and transports. Abingdon had a first taste of this role in the early 1950s when RAF pilots ferried aircraft to and from the site. Best known types undoubtedly became Canadian-built North American Sabre jet fighters which epitomised the woeful lack of British fighter development and gross embarrassment among the politicians and military alike when they first entered RAF circles in January 1953. A more minor task was basic flying instruction on light aircraft.

This utterly reliable and eminent airfield little changed in appearance over the years, if one excluded a large hangar of the post-war period. A C and four older pre-Expansion Period As hinted at Abingdon's origins. Views of the airfield were far from good as is usual with RAF stations, probably the best spot being a minor road on the north side across which aircraft used to disperse. From there you could acquire a clear but distant view of the technical area; much nearer by the perimeter track's north-west side stood a typically highly isolated control tower dating from after World War Two.

More changes will surely happen in the future – but not because Abingdon has any life left in it. The idea which many of us would fiercely dispute that the Cold War is allegedly over has instilled into our politicians more than ever before rabid 'let's get at the airfields' feelings. We know for sure that the Conservatives have brazenly admitted how they do not give a damn about history – except, no doubt, when castles and stately homes are involved. This disgraceful impudence reached new heights in July 1991 with a brief statement that Abingdon was to close by May 1993. Closure fears had persisted for a few years, and worse news followed as the authorities pushed forward the RAF pulling out date to July

33

THE AIRFIELDS OF BRITAIN: VOLUME 1

1992. The last British Aerospace Jaguar ground attack aircraft left after routine maintenance in April, remaining resident flying units later going to Benson.

The author visited Abingdon during the last two days of its great life while on operations to see a piece of real history slowly die. Airfield supporters would not have been encouraged had they witnessed the general scene on the evening of July 30. A handful of people lolled around the landing area, where a couple of Hawker Siddeley Buccaneer strike bombers without wings or tails stood. A boy manned the station entrance, and a policeman in the guardroom summed up the situation by saying: 'Nobody knows what the hell's going to happen.' Next evening, once Abingdon had officially closed at noon, the entire area had further quietened down with domestic accommodation even more vacant and the landing area only disturbed by a red civilian car racing down the main runway for no obvious reason.

And how did the mass media respond to all this? No mention in national newspapers, nothing in national television news bulletins, and a passing mention at the end of the regional television news long after being told about a weight-lifter failing a drugs test at the Olympics. Fifteen minutes at national level about him and two others, a minute mentioning the sad death that same day of Lord Cheshire: that shows you the mentality of far too many people in Britain today.

Now the worst has happened, everything relating to a marvellous life may go, right down to the numerous road signs which Aberporth cannot boast of due to its more secretive role. You have to ask when stars of this magnitude are in trouble, where next? Although the Army has moved in and tends to keep airfield buildings in excellent condition, it would not be at all surprising if yuppie housing overwhelms Abingdon in the long run. While desperate stuff, the end is not quite nigh, so how about an en masse anti-defence cuts protest to support our airfields as the Army has proposed? Try and get out of that one, all you politicians.
164/SU473994. Take A34 S of Oxford, airfield to W of town.

Aboyne, Grampian

Few airfields are more comparatively detached from others of their kind on the British mainland than Aboyne in north-east Scotland. Land to the west is an effective desert, and you have to travel a lot closer to the Scottish east coast to meet such familiar airfields as Dyce and Edzell. Recreational gliding is the unlikely activity at this inland site and takes place all year round.

A Welsh Deeside GC existed during the 1950s at Sealand but the definitive club of this name started using Aboyne in 1965. Members decided to replace the previously grassy landing area with a tarmac runway in the mid-1970s, though livestock still tend to graze at quieter periods. Installation of a second tarmac stretch in only eleven days by Army engineers during August/September 1991 shows how this is one successful airfield not having to worry about possible closure. Hangarage plus other support facilities have also been built to ensure Aboyne is self-sufficient. Visitors are welcome to watch light aircraft tow sailplanes into the air from this airfield during the day.

44/NO495983. By A93 between Banchory and Ballater, 2 miles W of village.

Abridge, Essex

Alternative Names: Essex, Loughton (Air Park)
Controversial Stansted is not Essex's first airport. A claimant to that title — a very dubious one, as Maylands should really receive the honour — was now unknown Abridge, a site near airfield survivor Stapleford Tawney and not one of our better places for flying.

First mention of an airfield here came in October 1930 when the South Essex Aero Club said it had obtained a new ground in this area; its last home had been a private airstrip south of Stapleford Tawney at Havering since certainly July 1930. What use (if any) the club made of Abridge is far from clear but by March 1931 it had secured yet another new airstrip at Langdon Hills, Laindon, a small settlement south of Billericay which is now built up. Gliding is known to have occurred there from May.

Hopes for sustained flying remained as Sir Alan Cobham staged one of his famous displays at Abridge on July 16 1932. A while later on November 29 the site was given a licence to be a private airfield under the ownership of a haulage contractor named Wilfred J. Lewington, and what became known as Essex Airport officially opened on June 17 1933. In practice the alternative title Loughton was preferred, sometimes extended to Loughton Air Park to fit in with the carefree civil airfield expansionist philosophy of that age as most evident at Feltham or Hanworth Air Park.

One early user became Commercial Airways (Essex) Limited. This company which Lewington developed interestingly operated a World War One vintage Bristol Fighter at Abridge from 1933 and had purchased other machines in hoping to start a flying school. However, these biplanes never saw use and were eventually scrapped, the sole flyable example going the same way. Commercial Airways also intended mounting regular air services to many parts of Britain but this idea similarly proved over-ambitious. About its only real achievement was operating the East Anglian Aero Club, which ran for a while and gave limited pilot instruction to anyone who wanted to learn.

Wilf Lewington tried hard to make his airfield a success. He extended the landing area northwards to make it stepped in appearance rather than L-shaped, and wanted to enlarge Abridge away to the east towards the distinctive Piggotts Farm. Nobody could blame him for lack of trying but Abridge never managed to attain the targets once planned because of a suspect grass surface. This shortcoming prevented Lewington from getting required official acknowledgement for 'all types' aircraft use and unfettered activities. A restricted position beside a railway line did not help either, nor did facilities amount to much, hangarage only consisting of one main building and three small lock-ups on the east side.

Vacant by April 1 1936, once Lewington gave up after a gallant fight, Abridge was declared unfit for use on June 17 and necessary levelling operations made it unsafe for aircraft use in the summer. This forced the airfield to be temporarily unlicensed, being given special brief allowance on June 28 for a flying circus event which a respectable 5,000 people attended. Display organiser was Tom Campbell Black, one half of the duo who won the great 1934 England-Australia air race, a man who would die in horrifying circumstances during September in a freak ground accident at Liverpool's airport Speke.

By then Abridge had just returned to flying duties. In place of Wilf Lewington came Atlas Air Services, registered as a private company only two days before the airfield first became empty. This firm which also used Croydon Airport again had big plans for a flying and engineering school. An Abridge Flying Club did appear and helped give the place what someone described as '... a new lease of life' but all the old problems would not go away, and Abridge lost its licence altogether on August 7 1937 before the expiry of this yearly grant on September 4. Air Ministry requirements had not been met for suspension and immediate closure to come into effect.

People surprisingly still remained interested in the possibilities of this sub-standard airfield. Father of British gliding Robert Kronfeld considered using Abridge for glider training. The Romford Flying Club at Maylands was keen too but officially prohibited to fly from here, the Air Ministry digging its heels in by declaring Abridge dangerous and too near Stapleford Tawney, by 1938 used for RAF Volunteer Reserve flying training. That peculiarity called circuit overlap had made another unwelcome early appearance as at Abbotsinch and Renfrew, which incidentally lay even closer together.

A visit to Abridge on January 7 1938 revealed a deserted clubhouse in the south-east corner with smashed windows and a hangar in service as a cow shed: the airfield was really dying on its feet. But it seems that like every good British site Abridge refused to give in as privately operated light aircraft continued to use it in a minor unlicensed capacity from the spring of 1938 or thereabouts until the outbreak of World War Two in September 1939 finally stopped all activity. Global conflict made this unsuccessful airfield pass into oblivion, and the M11 motorway has since scythed through these open fields.

Stop north of Abridge village at Piggotts Farm before walking along a public footpath to reach the site. Local memories of a bygone age must surely have faded completely. Not so, for the author encountered a man strolling down that path who still remembered Abridge – and he lived in Canada! Now that is what you call a towering control, exceptional influence for a fundamental flop. And if you think this was a bad airfield . . .

177/TQ456975. E of Loughton, turn left off A113 at Abridge village on to B172, footpath on left immediately past bridge.

Acaster Malbis, North Yorkshire

We can only describe the situation as typically quirky that in this alphabetically ordered story of the world's greatest ever airfields a few less than perfect sites should feature so early. Abbotsinch, technically not a good airfield; Abridge, again defiant but essentially poor; and even such successes as

THE AIRFIELDS OF BRITAIN: VOLUME 1

Aberporth have had limitations in one way or another. Only an absolutely minute percentage of British airfields since 1909 can still be classed as downright failures: alas, this Yorkshire base is one of them.

About our worst airfield of World War Two, succeeded solely by its catastrophic county cousin Cottam, two main problems made life hell for the oddly-named Acaster Malbis. The River Ouse flowed past not far away; bad enough, but it in turn frequently created misty conditions impossible for aircraft to operate in at length. Now you may be wondering why Abbotsinch has lasted so long with similar difficulties, yet it is fairly close to the Firth of Clyde, where a good stiff breeze can in time blow away any fog. Acaster Malbis however was positioned over 40 miles inland from the open sea, and the Vale of York in general is a notorious fog zone without major rivers further choking up the atmosphere. This place should have been called Acaster Malice instead.

Acaster still had grass runways when opened on January 1 1942. It may well have caused trouble even before starting up as to which suitable name planners should have allocated. The nearest village was not Acaster Malbis to the north but Appleton Roebuck to the west. But as a former World War One Home Defence landing ground further north in Yorkshire at Appleton Wiske was being actively considered for use once more as an airfield – a plan eventually dropped – Acaster Malbis won the contest.

No sooner did this unusual airfield first breathe life than it received an equally odd visitor. No 601 Squadron arrived on January 6 to test the unconventional Bell Airacobra, a fighter known back in its native America as the P-39 with a single piston engine sited behind the pilot. The Airacobra achieved considerable success in USAAF hands but No 601 Squadron had a most unhappy time right from August 1941. Air and groundcrews found the type baffling, No 601's operational sortie tally out of Manston in Kent during October reached a grand total of four, while pilots had to master what was to them still a relatively alien design feature in a tricycle undercarriage. At Acaster Malbis several crashes occurred, one being fatal, and it was a relief moving to firmly established Lincolnshire airfield star Digby on March 25 1942. By this time the unit was flying everyone's favourite, the Spitfire.

Oxford Flights of No 15 (Pilots) Advanced Flying Unit were later present until January 25 1943 after the Airacobras had gone. Acaster Malbis still proved to be a meteorological jinx as various trainers crashed in the vicinity. No 15 (P) AFU had a tough time that year in every way as its main base Leconfield

THE AIRFIELDS OF BRITAIN

was officially closed for rebuilding work, while the school's other RLG at Kirmington (the future Humberside Airport) was only meant as a stopgap aide.

Little did student pilots or anyone else know what airfield designers had planned as far back as September 1942, four months before No 15 (P) AFU left for Andover. Incredibly, Acaster Malbis was obstructed on February 15 1943 and closed on the 27th so that it could switch from Army Co-operation to Bomber Command on March 4 and be converted into a heavy bomber station. Although fully reopened the same year on November 1, no squadrons of this nature would be held here, which was most fortunate for them. Constant fog or heavy mist would have destroyed vital take-off timing at the start of bombing raids, with all the dire consequences that situation entailed, as the Americans discovered to their terrible cost during the epic Schweinfurt raids of 1943. Similar weather could additionally have forced returning aircraft to unnecessarily divert to other airfields.

The nearest Acaster ever came to seeing 'heavies' was when Heavy Conversion Unit Handley Page Halifaxes from Marston Moor to the north-west started using it as an RLG. No 4 Aircrew School also stayed in the later stages of World War Two, as did No 91 MU for bomb storage purposes, but hardly any other flying occurred apart from a Station Flight for local communications duties. Storing paint in a hangar as happened here for a time should never have happened to an airfield. Having already reverted to C&M for a short while in early 1944 to allow the completion of further building work, Acaster Malbis fell away to this state again in December 1945.

As with Abridge, though, this infinitely worse airfield whose weather record would have made Prestwick shudder was unwilling to accept defeat. Acaster Malbis indeed became something of a success and started doing a worthwhile job – but not as an airfield in the basic dictionary sense of being a place where aircraft reside. For this change of direction it had to thank Maintenance Command, which took over from Bomber Command on February 28 1946.

Next month No 80 MU began using Acaster Malbis as a bomb storage sub-site, receiving its first deliveries in May. German PoWs provided assistance and gave no trouble, unlike indigenous squatters, who caused a lot of trouble at airfields all over Britain during 1946 and to a lesser extent for some years to come. Acaster Malbis escaped the worst by being restricted to one or two scares but on one occasion prospective homeless people had to be asked to leave. Such harsh measures were totally justified as squatters not only destroyed

THE AIRFIELDS OF BRITAIN: VOLUME 1

security considerations but were unruly and showed worrying signs of Communist insurgency.

Between January 17 1947 and the 21st No 80 MU moved its headquarters across the River Ouse from Escrick, a non-airfield where the unit had resided since March 1942. The MU lost its self-accounting powers on October 15 prior to disbanding but No 91 MU then returned a month later to more than ever store all kinds of weapons that formed part of the huge stockpile of surplus munitions filling Britain after World War Two. Tremendous amounts of ammunition, bombs, shells, missiles and apparently even a few nuclear devices arrived at Acaster Malbis to be held in readiness for eventual disposal or transfer elsewhere. Former HCU station Riccall proved a notable aide; Cottam helped out No 91 MU too, the HQ changing to Acaster from there on February 11 1949.

A certain amount of farce still continued to dog Acaster Malbis during this otherwise estimable period of its history. A civil Auster decided to land at the airfield on March 14 1948, doing so dangerously but safely. However, on preparing to take off, the monoplane hit a fire tender, both aircraft and lorry being badly damaged. Someone in No 91 MU actually proposed forming an aircraft recognition club in January 1953 but a year later on January 26 1954 saw one aircraft which should never have appeared when a Gloster Meteor jet fighter based at Linton-on-Ouse crashed here, the crew being uninjured.

No 91 MU averted this potential disaster and lasted until closing on March 1 1957. A local newspaper marked this event by emphasising how Acaster Malbis used to be an important explosives storage base not after but during World War Two, conveniently failing to mention its failure as an airfield. No 93 MU at Newton in Nottinghamshire immediately took over the site, including an oxygen production plant now based there in a hangar, and began disposing of 2,000 high explosive bombs. Acaster's military days were fast ending as the HEs had gone by July 19, the airfield closing on August 1 and coming under the control of Linton-on-Ouse's RLG Rufforth and then fighter airfield star Church Fenton until the land was finally relinquished.

Today, this disastrous site for flying is fairly easy to view as a minor road crosses it. All three runways and the perimeter track are in fair condition, and were considered suitable in 1984 for storing coal during the protracted miners' strike. The black gold has featured before in this airfield's life as 38 tons of the material mysteriously vanished in December

THE AIRFIELDS OF BRITAIN

1946! East of the road can be seen the control tower employed as offices after years as a ruin and, behind it, the remaining T2 of two originals now used for haulage purposes. Acaster Malbis was equipped with only four Blisters in its early days until these hangars made way for the T2s and a B1. Many support buildings abound in the surrounding fields: some are disused, others acting as a farm for pigs – turkeys would be more apt.

The worst joke of all is that Acaster Malbis still serves in an unlicensed role for light aircraft use and has done so since the early 1970s: much is made of the fact the airfield is close to York racecourse. Look at the glorious line of superstars to come – such as the next airfield in this book – where aircraft can no longer visit. It may seem incomprehensible but this strange situation is all part and parcel of the British airfield story. Taking everything into consideration, a lot remains of Acaster Malbis, one airfield which should never have existed. Whether a 'new town' which may occupy half of this area in the near future will leave any traces at all remains uncertain.

105/SE579430. Take A1036 S of York, turn left on to minor road before A64. Go south via Bishopthorpe and follow directions to Acaster Selby.

Acklington, Northumberland

Alternative Name: Southfields

If our disused airfields were human, their medical conditions would range from slightly injured to plain dead. Acklington, a true superstar and arguably the greatest airfield of all time in north-east England, can be best described as mortally wounded. A few buildings have formed parts of two prisons but mining has eaten away the landing area. What a tragedy.

A Home Defence landing ground called Southfields existed here in World War One. While sometimes also known as Acklington during this period, military planners preferred to use the former name after a residence which has since disappeared. Biplane fighters belonging to No 36 Squadron had use of the site from October 1916 to the Armistice.

The place most people came to know as Acklington did not begin its illustrious career until April 1 1938. By then it did not contain fighters but trainers of No 2 Air Observers School, at first known up to November 21 1938 as No 7 Armament Training Station. Flying activities had restarted very shakily as

THE AIRFIELDS OF BRITAIN: VOLUME 1

Acklington originally should have let No 7 Armament Training Camp materialise on December 1 1937. This formation was postponed at the last minute until April 1938, when No 7 ATS arose instead, so throwing into some disorder numerical synchronisation as Nos 6 and 8 ATCs already functioned either end of Britain at Warmwell and Evanton respectively. Although the situation stabilised to allow realistic training over ranges at nearby Druridge Bay, uncertainty lingered thereafter as No 2 AOS was proposed to move to the new south Wales airfield of Pembrey during the summer of 1939, leaving Acklington to again hold No 7 ATS. These changes never happened; nor did a similar plan scheduled for mid-1940 occur, by which time Acklington was otherwise engaged.

Only when World War Two broke out was Acklington designated a fighter station. No 10 AOS at Warmwell had absorbed its sister unit in Northumberland once its aircraft reached the south on September 4 1939. A Care and Maintenance party remained further north but Fighter Command then took charge of Acklington on the 9th, No 152 Squadron becoming the first of many more aggressive units to come when it reformed at the beginning of October. The squadron flew Gloster Gladiator biplanes before receiving Spitfires and eventually moved like No 2 AOS to Warmwell on July 12 1940. Other elements had visited by the time No 152 Squadron left, No 607 Squadron going to France via Croydon with Gladiators on November 14 1939 after a month's stay.

Four days had passed when the Hurricanes of No 43 Squadron appeared at Acklington for coastal patrol duties. Luftwaffe bombers had started making their presences felt with anti-shipping raids off Britain's north-eastern coastline, and it was while trying to counter them that Acklington made its first major mark upon history when three No 43 Squadron pilots between them shot down a Heinkel He111 near Whitby on February 3 1940. This machine of Kampfgeschwader 26 became the first enemy aircraft to crash on English soil during World War Two at a place still marked by a plaque. Able to credit himself with a third of a kill was famous RAF fighter pilot Peter Townsend.

Another fairly early Fighter Command visitor was No 72 Squadron, which had been posted to Acklington on March 2 1940. Despite being a Spitfire unit, it strangely had to revert to Gladiators for a brief period during that month as the airfield's landing area was too soft. No 72 Squadron spent a few days east of London at Gravesend in June to help cover the Dunkirk evacuation but returned as that mercy mission

THE AIRFIELDS OF BRITAIN

finished, a second unit to rest up north being No 79 Squadron, whose Hurricanes arrived on July 13. Further excitement had arisen the day before with what became Acklington's most notable forced landing, the cumbersome Handley Page HP 42 biplane transport *Hadrian* suffering from engine failure.

The relatively quiet time here of convoy patrols, rest and re-equipment was shattered on August 15 when a large force of He 111s escorted by Messerschmitt Bf 110 heavy fighters attempted to wreak havoc in the general area. Enemy thinking was basically sound: a classic two-front strategy in conjunction with the heavy Luftwaffe raids upon southern England to severely stretch RAF Fighter Command. But not so correct by any means were these Scandinavian-based crews' hopes of a quiet day out. Acklington's fighters plus aircraft from other airfields on the east coast met them head-on over the North Sea; further hampered by fierce friendly flak once overland, the Luftwaffe lost fifteen aircraft without shooting down any RAF machines in return.

The chief airfield defender rightfully basked in glory as a result of its greatest ever achievement. This raid which turned into one of the Battle of Britain's most significant individual encounters had been sheer madness on the Germans' part, who never again attempted to bomb north-east England in full daylight view. Luftwaffe bombers stumbled about in the dark a few times trying to find Acklington but failed miserably to hit it. Only one actual attack occurred much later on during the summer of 1941.

After Nos 72 and 79 Squadrons went to Biggin Hill at the end of August 1940, Nos 32 and 610 Squadrons' fighters held the fort at Acklington until the close of 1940. Their home possessed an excellent record of victories over enemy aircraft for a supposedly quiet area of Britain, thanks in no small way to the events of August 15. Nos 315 and 317 Squadrons soon moved away early in 1941 after both Polish Hurricane units had formed but there was still plenty of work to do. Night fighters appeared from May to defend Newcastle as German bombers learned how night offered far better protection than some Bf 110s. No 406 (RCAF) Squadron arose in May to start patrols with Bristol Beaufighters, going to Ayr II in January 1942, followed by No 141 Squadron which stayed until June. A detachment of this unit had already flown Boulton Paul Defiants from Acklington in the summer of 1941.

Future squadrons at this airfield in World War Two were kept fully occupied with convoy patrols, night fighting duties or aircraft conversion. No 539 Squadron became just another

43

of the luckless *Turbinlite* searchlight-equipped Douglas Havoc night fighter establishments after initially forming as No 1460 Flight on December 15 1941. No 1 Squadron was at Acklington between July 1942 and February 1943 for conversion to Hawker Typhoon fighter-bombers, while No 316 Squadron proved one of the more settled visitors later on, operating Spitfires during September 1943 – February 1944.

Last operational fighters to stay any length of time here for a while were obsolescent Hurricanes belonging to 'B' Flight of No 309 Squadron. This Polish unit had changed quite a bit since its formation with army co-operation Lysanders at Abbotsinch in October 1940. Mustangs were later received but their Allison engines gave extreme trouble in service. Now the squadron placed its HQ back in Scotland at Drem, that other highly influential rearward fighter station of 1940 like Acklington, though 'B' Flight operated at first instead from Hutton Cranswick in Yorkshire. The detachment later shifted up to Northumberland after D-Day but left again on August 29 1944 for Peterhead, where No 309 Squadron linked up as one once more in mid-November.

By now the days of a steady tally of kills were long gone. But Acklington had more than achieved its intended objective – and still had a lot of work lined up for the future. A quiet few months passed by to enable the airfield to be generally refurbished. Many different types of aircraft still visited, and the station's Operations Record Book intriguingly states how the Q site of Widdrington to the south-east closed on October 6 1944, so proving beyond doubt that decoy airfields did last at least a little longer than September when these sites deliberately created for enemy aircraft to attack became non-operational.

No 59 OTU reformed on February 26 1945 to end this period of enforced rest. World War Two was slowly but surely coming to an end in Europe, and this was why the Typhoon training force only operated at reduced strength as a ½OTU, flying half the number of aircraft normally available. Once No 59 OTU shut down on June 6, front line fighters returned to Acklington, No 219 Squadron arriving with de Havilland Mosquitoes on August 14. No 263 Squadron came as a Meteor unit in September but the jets moved to Church Fenton in April 1946.

The activities of No 219 Squadron during these past few months turned out to be far more noteworthy in the long run. Having already made a couple of quick trips to Germany for air-to-air firing practice, its night fighters then flew down England's east coast to Spilsby on March 25 1946 for more

THE AIRFIELDS OF BRITAIN

training, coming back on April 17. Spilsby figured even more greatly on May 1 for, as No 219 Squadron moved to Wittering, so the Armament Training Station formed at Acklington and soon absorbed its counterpart No 2 APS at the Lincolnshire base plus a diversity of aircraft types. Unit movements at Britain's airfields have always been remarkable: few exceeded those of No 2 APS, which in recent months had relentlessly moved northwards from Kent via Essex to Lincolnshire and now Northumberland. Second-line piston and (from 1950) jet-engined aircraft towing drogues or more effective miniature target gliders however served at Acklington until well into the 1950s to counter such previously transient ways.

Along with other APSs, the many Armament Practice Camps of World War Two had virtually disappeared in peacetime to leave Acklington competing with Lubeck and Sylt in Germany to welcome in RAF squadrons. Sylt proved to be an especially durable place but as Acklington was British, nearer at hand and conveniently stood by the sea for safe armament training, it made more sense to keep units at home.

Fighter squadrons frequently passed through the airfield to brush up on their air-to-air firing accuracy. The first seven months of 1947 served as a typical example of many unit movements. After having started on an unusual note with No 92 Squadron reforming at Acklington as a Meteor unit and almost at once going to Duxford, No 1 Squadron brought things back to normal on February 24 by arriving from its peacetime station of Tangmere for a month's stay. No 29 Squadron at West Malling did the same, more Mosquito night fighter squadrons visiting as Nos 23, 141 (already here during January/February) and 264 at Coltishall and Wittering resided instead at Acklington from April 28 to June 5/6, followed by No 29 returning from West Malling with No 85 on June 16. This second squadron departed after a fortnight but No 29 held on until July 24.

Acklington prospered with Fighter Command for the first dozen years or so after World War Two. Suddenly Duncan Sandys loomed large to signal the end for the APS on May 27 1956. Fighters had nearly always been a part of Acklington's life but it did not give in to this political impostor and from July 27 became a mixed jet fighter/Search and Rescue helicopter station.

Britain's airfields at this time were taking a heavy pounding from a soft population equipped with over-critical minds and too loose tongues. Never mind the Cold War and many people in a job: so long as Jack and Jill in the adjacent neighbourhood were all right, nothing else mattered. Abingdon had recently encountered this hard fact of life when a call came in the House of Lords for all flying to be banned there from Lord Lucas (of Chilworth, about ten miles away, surprise, surprise, and who indeed lived yards from Abingdon's north-western boundary at Cothill). Now a year and a half later brought hassle to Acklington as the local council protested to the Air Ministry during the autumn of 1958 after low flying was supposed to have interrupted church services.

Changes were nevertheless in the air as No 6 Flying Training School replaced the Gloster Javelins and Hawker Hunters of Nos 29 and 66 Squadrons in August 1961. Acklington possessed longer runways than the school's former home of Tern Hill, and it was just as well No 6 FTS had left Shropshire for soon the unit exchanged Hunting Provost piston-engined trainers for British Aircraft Corporation Jet Provosts. When the FTS disbanded on June 30 1968, No 18 Squadron flew Westland Wessex Army support helicopters until August 1969. Cuts made another proposed flying training scheme fall through, despite £1.2 million being spent upon Acklington's looks in the mid to late 1960s.

Closure rumours involving Acklington had by then been extant for some months. Similar speculation had abounded as early as October 1947, when the APS was proposed to move to West Raynham or its neighbour Great Massingham: where the Central Fighter Establishment at these two Norfolk airfields would have gone was anyone's guess. This newer hearsay almost 22 years on was officially denied as No 18 Squadron left for Odiham: helicopters would remain. But, as ever, the Government was saying one thing and really meaning something else as a prison opened later in 1969.

This truly great yet now severely emasculated airfield's last unit became an SAR Flight of No 202 Squadron. Westland Whirlwinds carried on giving the superb social service provided for a long number of years since the 1950s but calamity struck in 1974 when Acklington's three runways were ripped up. The base had not even fully closed to add to its distress. Eventually closure did happen once the helicopters went a few miles north to Boulmer at the start of October 1975. A legend passed into history without any comment whatsoever by the mass media.

So ended a gloriously eventful life after several years of lingering death. The subsequent decline of Acklington has proved rapid. Such was the initial disorganisation in this switch from recognised airfield superstar to unknown place of incarceration that three separate escapes happened in three years, culminating in a double break-out during October 1972. These statistics made even more depressing reading when remembering how this particular prison was a low category installation for inmates thought unlikely to escape under any circumstances. The prison has since tightened up security; now there are two of them, the newer one standing north-east of the original site and called Castington to deal with young offenders. This facility opened in January 1983.

Driving south-west along a diverted minor road towards the airfield is now not the most pleasant of experiences. Massive excavation work has massacred Acklington's landing area layout so much that only the western perimeter track is left. Quickly you encounter the technical site on the south-east side. It is all naturally fenced in but a building with a curved roof still remains prominent, local sources confirming this is the post-war Gaydon hangar installed. One could investigate more deeply, but can you imagine going up to the prison gates and asking how the hangar is generally faring? Acklington always had an unusual hangarage arrangement as two pre-war vintage Fs – standard fittings for Armament Training Stations – were later joined by an example of the common Bellman and sixteen Blisters as fighters piled up in wartime days.

As you look about, it is difficult to understand why those people who tore the heart out of this magnificent old warrior are not in these prisons too. How many other countries in the world would have attacked such a national hero which kept the peace so brilliantly? That's a tragedy.

81/NU230007. SE of Alnwick, 4½ miles SW of Amble-by-the-Sea.

Acton, Greater London

Alternative Name: North Ealing
Acaster Malbis, Acklington and Acton: the bad, the good and the diabolical. A big star sandwiched between two rogues – with the bread of extremely poor quality. Even so, Acton has along with Acaster Malbis tended to survive better architecturally than the tragic Acklington.

To be fair, aviation was still very much in its infancy when Acton opened in 1910. A lot of what happened afterwards could be put down to unavoidable outside circumstances. Excuses aside, this was a poor place for an airfield as railway lines existed on all three sides. Bad luck followed bad planning as disaster hit the self-styled London Aviation Ground on May 15 1911 when a fire destroyed four hangars and five monoplanes. Acton residents managed to save two other aircraft but this catastrophe only made aerial activities more disorganised. Desultory flying however continued until the start of World War One, one visitor being the pioneer of inverted flying in Britain, G.L. Temple.

Nothing much of note happened at Acton for the next two and a half years until the Ruffy, Arnell and Baumann Aviation Company was registered as a commercial concern in January 1917. The gradual winkling out of civil flying schools from overcrowded Hendon forced the company to find another airfield, though the real reason for its fairly fast move to Acton in March lay with another airfield some distance away. Ruffy, Arnell and Baumann wanted to open a second school at Hardwick in Cambridgeshire but was firmly told at high official level that financial help would only be given if Acton came into being. Nothing could be done to counter this effective blackmail, and Acton's privately operated flying school struggled on up to mid-1918. Flying conditions must have been absolutely terrible pre-war; workmen preparing the airfield for use once more were noted as clearing away not only hedges but oak trees.

The cessation of training here saw the Alliance Aeroplane Company take over Ruffy, Arnell and Baumann. Now the plan was to manufacture aircraft but misfortune continued to dog Acton as World War One ended and killed off any hopes for large-scale military production.

Alliance persevered and optimistically turned towards the civil market. Only one example of its P.1 biplane design was built, while a 'massive' increase in production resulted with the P.2 Seabird – all two of them. One of these machines later crashed on November 13 1919, worse still killing both crewmen in the process, and this almighty run of misery proved enough to finish off the Alliance Aeroplane Company as 1920 began. At this point the old flying school's Caudron biplanes and their canvas hangars remained on view but all were very much the worse for wear. The single P.1 was scrapped in November 1920.

Even then the agony refused to end. A court case started next month concerning the crashed P.2's insurance, involving extremely precise queries over time and identity of the machine. An insurance company complained that its policy only covered the P.2 flying around Acton – not an attempted flight to Australia! Perhaps not surprisingly given this startling fact, Alliance lost the case. Ruffy, Arnell and Baumann tried its luck in the courts too during 1921 by claiming alleged Government breach of contract over control of the training programme in 1918. Again the company lost out and received a paltry £250 in compensation instead of many thousands of pounds as hoped for. Swiss-born co-founder Aimé Baumann was grateful just to be alive, for he had wanted to pilot the P.2 but only Australian citizens were allowed to take part in the contest to reach their homeland finally won by Ross and Keith Smith.

No more mention of Acton as an airfield transpired – at least of any certainty. Scant evidence suggests the site may still have been active in 1924: hard to believe, and a second report of activity *circa* 1931 is surely spurious. No aircraft of any description could have possibly landed safely without harming either itself or anyone on board.

Housing and industry gradually appeared but a big hangar dating from World War One has survived by the adjacent dual carriageway known as Western Avenue. Various companies have employed this building, which produced Mosquito components in World War Two, though the best known owner was Waring and Gillow. This noted local furniture firm of decades past created the Alliance Aeroplane Company: as we have seen it achieved little, yet Lord Samuel Waring received his title for services to aviation. While Waring was admittedly also owner of the useful British Aerial Transport Co Ltd and the Nieuport and General Aviation Company, who knows what honour would have been bestowed upon him had Alliance become successful – declared as God?

The Acton story is one now best forgotten. Airfield designers learned from their mistakes such as this one and turned out immensely better sites which enjoyed more good fortune as well. This early example might not have displayed staying power but its old hangar has proved mightily durable, a beacon of success amid a sea of failure.

176/TQ195820. On W side of London, 2 miles directly S of Wembley Stadium beside A40 (Western Avenue), hangar close to pedestrian bridge crossing main road. Alternatively turn first left off A4000 N of bridge over Acton railway station, then third right and over bridge into industrial area.

Aintree, Merseyside

Think of Aintree and you immediately think of the Grand National. Few people have associated this world famous race-

THE AIRFIELDS OF BRITAIN: VOLUME 1

course with airfields or aviation, despite one colossal hint in the vicinity which lasted for generations.

Many of Britain's racecourses have airfield-related pasts. Famous flying pioneer Sam Cody made demonstration flights at this one during November 1909. Problems meanwhile plagued Reverend Sidney Swann, the rector of Crosby, as from that month his Santos Dumont type monoplane refused to fly before the wind flipped over and all but wrecked the machine. Conversion into a biplane brought no improvement and Swann had given up by July 1910 after his aircraft charged into some sheep, one flock not pleased to see the clergy. Britain's original aerobatic pilot B.C. Hucks later performed with his customary excellence on December 26 1913.

Although Aintree was not a tremendously great place for flying like Acton, it bore a certain similarity by becoming involved with military aircraft production in the final stages of World War One. The Coalition Government belatedly ordered construction of three large factories to markedly boost manufacturing capacity. A site sprang up west of the racecourse and became known as National Aircraft Factory No 3, numerically following other hastily devised factories at Croydon in London and Heaton Chapel near Manchester. Placed in charge of this third industrial area was the Cunard Steamship Co Ltd.

Any comparisons with Acton end here as Aintree played a valuable part in helping to win World War One. Cunard received a contract in November 1917 and a total of 126 Bristol F.2b fighters took off from the turf after March 1918 once churned out of the nearby factory. However late the National Aircraft Factory system had come into operation, it could be counted as a success.

Aircraft production in Britain abruptly ceased following the Armistice of November 1918. This event ought to have finished off flying at Aintree but failed to as machines could still be intermittently seen for years afterwards mingling with horse-racing. Most prominent post-war occupant was the Aircraft Disposal Company (later called ADC Aircraft Ltd) which established a supportive depot previously in RAF hands since March 1919 in the former National Aircraft Factory No 3 to complement its main base at Croydon's old NAF No 1. Despite many protests by Cunard workers back in January 1919 about such an idea in the first place, money could be made out of old rope as the general public snapped up at greatly reduced prices war-surplus aircraft or their

THE AIRFIELDS OF BRITAIN

components, often for purposes totally removed from aviation.

Apart from use by one or two privately-owned aircraft, Aintree witnessed another new activity in 1924 when Northern Air Lines employed it as a base for newspaper carrying flights to Belfast. Unfortunately, this experimental exercise which started on April 30 proved both unsuccessful and short-lived by ending during June as poor weather and the airfield's restricted nature conspired to badly hinder operations. Aintree was too small for a de Havilland DH 50 transport: this resulted in an unrealistic situation, whereby the aircraft had to fly unloaded to the sands at Southport and only then pick up its precious cargo.

The sands of time were fast running out for Aintree. By October 1925 negotiations had taken place between the Treasury Surplus Stores (Liquidation Department) and the British Enka Artificial Silk Company for the acquisition of ADC Aircraft's depot. Once this property was transferred as the year came to an end, closure of the airfield looked not far away, and in April 1926 Aintree was declared as sold and no longer available to aircraft because of extensive surrounding building areas. But someone must have at least tried to land as warning notifications had to be given again in March 1927 to forbid pilots landing on the by now dangerous touchdown area.

All this time the local authorities in Liverpool stood by and did nothing to help the air-minded. It appears that officialdom in this part of the world was none too keen to possess an airfield for the city, which explains Speke's constantly uncertain life as an airport. Liverpudlian city fathers 'felt more comfortable' with ships than aircraft. And, of course, who ran Aintree during World War One . . .

The Grand National still ensured that aircraft appeared around Aintree into the 1930s and beyond. Visitors came to the 1930 and 1931 events to a field east of Aintree Hall Farm until electricity pylons carrying 50,000 volt cables eliminated this site in 1932. Next year the Automobile Association provided a temporary new site, close to the racecourse and a quarter of a mile from the old one, which proved extremely popular as over 50 aircraft stopped there. As late as 1964 Aintree made the headlines in an aviation context when a Piper Apache air taxi crashed in a nearby field on March 21 while trying to land and killed five people on board.

What was that one big reminder of Aintree's days as an airfield? Yes, none other than the National Aircraft Factory

No 3. Another superb survivor like the old Alliance hangar at Acton and thousands upon thousands of other airfield buildings in Britain managed to beat off all kinds of opposition for years as Courtaulds succeeded Enka Silk after World War Two to run a textile mill until the late 1970s.

Britain's service industry has thrived at the expense of our manufacturing equivalent since those troubled days. People do remember Courtaulds, Enka Silk and even NAF No 3 but the factory has gone now, replaced by the Racecourse Retail Park. It is a sign of the times that for biplane fighters and cloth, today read Asda and Halfords. A turn for the better or worse? Local residents must have mixed feelings. 108/SJ373984. By A59, 8 miles N of Liverpool city centre, 1 mile S of Junction 7 of M57.

Akeman Street, Oxfordshire

Alternative Name: Crawley

One or two airfields in Britain have been built over Roman roads: Scampton is the most obvious example. A lesser light was Akeman Street, actually named after the road which crossed it.

Part of the fascination in our airfields lies with nothing more than their names. To choose the correct title for a site became a practised art as potential names stood like a minefield before the planners. When the military requisitioned this place as an intended RLG for Little Rissington in January 1940, the preferred name was Crawley. Certain settlements keep appearing near airfields without any airfield connection themselves – villages called Monkton exist close to airfield superstars Manston and Prestwick – and Crawley's name comes into the same category, though there was an abortive Home Defence landing ground during 1917 known as such.

So how did Crawley create problems? The complete lack of any official records means that we shall never know for sure but the following explanation may provide some clues as to why this name was rejected. A village called Crawley is near famous RAF/FAA Hampshire station Worthy Down, and North Crawley not far from noted Bedfordshire base Cranfield. But the name Crawley is still best associated with the Sussex town: Gatwick lies close by, and even by 1940 the future second London Airport of today had already become a fairly well-known airfield. A different name therefore had to be selected but further problems existed as airfield veteran

THE AIRFIELDS OF BRITAIN

Witney had come back into RAF use. A village to the north-west called Leafield possibly sounded too bland, nowhere else looked feasible and, as this part of Oxfordshire proved deceptively remote, airfield planners had no choice but to use the name Akeman Street.

The first five and a half years of Akeman Street's career seemed sheer simplicity compared to what must have gone on beforehand. Aircraft definitely first used it on August 18 1940, although this fairly primitive site had lain in unrecognised readiness for some time previously, and a separate file suggests that night flying instruction may have gone on from the 7th. Nobody ignored Akeman Street after a sensational Luftwaffe bombing raid upon Brize Norton on August 16 left 46 aircraft destroyed. Many training machines fled this famous base as a direct result of the worst small-scale assault ever seen on a British airfield, some of them starting flying training here for sure on the 18th.

Airspeed Oxfords of No 2 Service Flying Training School (later known as No 2 (Pilots) Advanced Flying Unit) at Brize Norton lasted at Akeman Street until the school disbanded on July 14 1942. Little Rissington then finally came along to supervise it for No 6 (P) AFU but Oxfords remained on view as equipment.

Akeman Street has mysterious beginnings: its final days remain as equally obscure. The question marks started on December 17 1945 as No 6 SFTS reformed out of No 6 (P) AFU and gained the airfield as a satellite. What happened before the SFTS moved to Tern Hill in April 1946? We do not know as the school's records for this period are mostly missing. Official documentation for No 3 MU is conversely intact but Akeman Street does not feature by name. When did this unit cease employing it for storage during 1946? About all we can confidently state without fear of correction is that Akeman Street was in use for farming by mid-summer, cleared of equipment on September 26, totally emptied in January 1947 and closed on February 1.

This historically evasive grassy area is today open farmland once again. Leave your car by a minor road, walk up a short hill path which forms part of the ancient road and you have reached Akeman Street. There is little to see apart from a ruinous support building and the perimeter track; OS maps only show the southern half but in fact all of the perimeter track has survived, though its northern section in particular is overgrown. A Bellman and ten Blisters which formed Akeman Street's hangarage – only the Bellman seems to have been around by mid-war after being constructed in the autumn of

1940 – have disappeared. Akeman Street, the airfield, may have lasted only a handful of years and its novel inspiration a couple of thousand, yet both still create a unique effect upon the landscape in their own ways.

164/SP333137. 4 miles NW of Witney; pass through Crawley and head 1½ miles towards Leafield. Stop at fork in minor road where path is marked on right.

Alconbury, Cambridgeshire

Alternative Name: Abbots Ripton

The Alconbury of today is completely different from that of yesteryear, especially in acreage. Although later a United States Air Force base, it will always retain a place in RAF history as Britain's original satellite airfield. Here started a trend towards far more functional airfields which initially, if not always entirely, heavily relied upon their parent stations for support in both men and materials.

Thoughts first turned to the idea of satellites in 1936. New RAF stations were coming on stream as the Expansion Period brought good times to military airfields in Britain again after fifteen years of absolute misery, but many planners feared the dire effects enemy bombing might cause. Much simpler airfields without fancy support facilities were needed where aircraft could safely disperse. Attention was mostly directed pre-war towards RAF bases around Greater London and civil airfields which looked like possible future satellites. These included some rather odd or quite unsuitable places and, as events unfolded, only Abridge's tormentor Stapleford Tawney finished up being a satellite in World War Two when it came under the control of North Weald.

A wholly different development occurred in East Anglia in May 1938 when Fairey Battles of No 63 Squadron at Upwood travelled to an open area of land at Alconbury for an exercise to assess the viability of whether military aircraft could transfer to a site equipped with next to no back-up. This new idea of aircraft dispersal worked, and on June 1 Alconbury was officially provisionally selected for development as an airfield.

Time passed until well over a year later when Upwood sent to this grass expanse more Battles, this time of No 52 Squadron. Everything had radically changed as the light bombers arrived at Alconbury on September 1 1939 – the day Germany attacked Poland. No 52 Squadron's detachment left after a week but World War Two soon brought this

THE AIRFIELDS OF BRITAIN

previously obscure satellite more into play. Wyton became its new parent as Bristol Blenheims, Short Stirlings and Vickers Wellingtons from Nos XV and 40 Squadrons dispersed at Alconbury until 1942. This second unit came as a whole on February 2 1941, a detachment being sent to the Middle East in October. What was left of No 40 Squadron became No 156 Squadron on February 14 1942, whose Wellingtons left for Wyton's other satellite at Warboys in August. Inevitably Luftwaffe intruders appeared during this period while on their rounds but attacked to no real effect, so illustrating the true worth of satellites.

The USAAF arrived next month to bring even more activity to rapidly expanding, increasingly aggressive and now independent Alconbury. Consolidated B-24s of the 93rd Bomb Group started operations in October 1942 before moving overseas as the year ended, their former base being occupied by the 92nd BG for another mix of training and active service. One of its squadrons – the 327th – received twelve Boeing YB-40s, pre-production examples of a gunship version of the B-17 heavy bomber. These aircraft were packed with machine-guns but dropped after operational evaluation as they proved incapable of keeping up with their bomber brethren, especially when their bombs had been released while the YB-40s still carried their enormous ammunition loads and extra armour plating.

A more terrible event occurred on May 27 1943 when several bombs accidentally exploded at Alconbury. Such a calamity of this nature always lurked in the backs of peoples' minds at all wartime bomber bases as a very small but significant enough possibility. Few premature detonations ever happened but those that did usually brought considerable death and destruction. This particular incident became one of the worst by leaving in its wake nineteen personnel dead, four B-17s destroyed plus many other men and aircraft wounded and damaged to varying degrees.

Just prior to the 92nd BG's departure to Podington in Bedfordshire in September 1943, the 482nd BG appeared, operating B-17s and a squadron of B-24s as pathfinding aircraft to guide USAAF bombers in poor weather. Some Mosquitoes were also used to carry out experimental work testing *H2X*, the American version of Britain's *H2S* navigational and target finding radar as carried aboard Avro Lancasters. Later in addition a pathfinding instructional unit, the 482nd BG had gone home by late June 1945 after its air echelon left during May 27-30, having won a Distinguished Unit Citation award despite a preference for training duties.

This altogether unusual unit was different in another way for being the only 8th Air Force Group to form in Britain rather than America.

A geographical position more on the edge of East Anglia, therefore offering slightly more safety as further inland, ensured that Alconbury was better suited to less run of the mill jobs. Radio countermeasures aircraft also briefly stayed but more important was this airfield's role as a USAAF bomber maintenance depot. Again tactical reasons dictated the siting of this and other facilities on the fringe of such a vital operational flying area. These depots were regarded more as separate installations in their own right, with Alconbury's example existing more towards the small village of Abbots Ripton to the north-east. This is probably why older local residents still tend to call their nearby airfield Abbots Ripton instead of Alconbury, a dubious legacy largely born out of wartime ignorance.

Erroneous or not, Abbots Ripton nevertheless ruled over Alconbury for a long period after World War Two. No 264 MU inhabited the first place from August 15 1945 as an Equipment Disposal Depot and received items cleared out from a frighteningly big list of British airfields in the process of closing: Alton Barnes, Bodorgan, Gransden Lodge and Mount Farm to name but a tiny handful. Stocks grew and grew, so it was a good move allowing the MU to acquire Alconbury for extra space. The official date in Maintenance Command records is given as November 26 1945 but the ceremonial USAAF to RAF transfer took place on December 3. PoWs were later also accommodated at Alconbury during 1946.

In time equipment began to dwindle as auction sales were held in 1947 and 1948. The general public forked out tens of thousands of pounds for frequently surprising purchases, everything from bicycles to generators, radio equipment to workshop benches, fire tenders to ladders and landing lights. All were reduced to dirt cheap prices, although exactly what buyers intended doing with these surplus articles often defied explanation, as was the case at Aintree after World War One.

Its holdings exhausted, No 264 MU disbanded on September 30 1948. A C&M party remained at Alconbury until the airfield was abandoned on November 11 and parented by Headquarters (Unit) Technical Training Command. The Abbots Ripton facility was simultaneously reduced to inactive status and shifted to Bomber Command on March 28 1949.

Alconbury need not have worried about the future as it was not considered surplus to requirements like most other inactive stations. The Americans came back in 1953, subsequently heavily enlarging and refurbishing the airfield. This once typical wartime USAAF heavy bomber station with two T2s now held characteristically fairly unsophisticated but still effective 1950s style North American B-45 Tornado jet bombers from 1955 to 1959, after which the 10th Tactical Reconnaissance Wing operated Douglas RB-66 Destroyers on its arrival. More elderly Boeing WB-50s of the 53rd Weather Reconnaissance Squadron were at Alconbury in 1959 too but only because these descendants of the B-29 atomic bomber had been forced to evacuate the gigantic USAF logistics support airfield at Burtonwood in Cheshire. Their stay in Cambridgeshire as a result proved brief.

McDonnell Douglas RF-4C Phantom IIs replaced the twin-jet Destroyers in the mid-1960s. These excellent new machines ended a period of uncertainty earlier that decade when Alconbury was lined up for closure. The American military authorities had stated in October 1961 that the airfield's run-down for total closure in 1964 was continuing: the Phantoms stopped this madness from happening, and one of the 10th TRW's two squadrons remained in this part of East Anglia for over two decades until becoming known as the 10th Tactical Fighter Wing with Fairchild A-10A close support types.

Most important aircraft in recent years at Alconbury were Northrop F-5E Tiger IIs of the 527th Tactical Fighter Training Aggressor Squadron. These jets involved themselves since the mid-1970s with US fighters plus those of other air forces by pretending to be the 'opposition' and displaying their colour schemes and tactics, notably dogfighting techniques. The 527th – by now possessing the title Aggressor Squadron and more advanced General Dynamics F-16 fighters – moved to Bentwaters in Suffolk during the late 1980s.

As you have seen, there have been phenomenal changes over the years. Alconbury became quite huge, used since February 1983 by Lockheed TR-1A specialised reconnaissance aircraft which were essentially updated versions of the U-2 spying type so immortalised ever since the 1960 incident involving Francis Gary Powers. This is no doubt why viewing areas around the airfield became exceptionally poor by normal standards for USAF stations in Britain.

The early 1990s saw many alterations, starting on some high notes before gloom set in. More aircraft came in from other bases at home and abroad: again they were off-beat to fit in with Alconbury's traditions. Lockheed HC-130s and Sikorsky helicopters of the 67th and 21st Special Operations Squadrons arrived from Bentwaters' neighbour Woodbridge, with

THE AIRFIELDS OF BRITAIN: VOLUME 1

Germany formerly being home to more C-130 variants of the 7th SOS, armed to the teeth with large cannon and Gatling-type machine-guns. These aircraft looked as awkward as the YB-40s of World War Two but could rip any enemy ground target to shreds with devastating ferocity.

Alconbury made a considerable contribution once a little country which everyone only knew as a major oil producer and was called Kuwait suddenly suffered invasion and capture by Iraq. The TR-1As of the 17th Reconnaissance Wing's 95th Reconnaissance Squadron immediately flew out to Taif in the western half of Saudi Arabia in August 1990 as the Gulf crisis started, while the 10th TFW's 511th Tactical Fighter Squadron also resided in that country from December. Crisis turned into conflict, a speedy victory, and these units victoriously returned home in March 1991.

Their British base continued to struggle to resemble wartime conditions of the World War Two type – not that anyone complained. Many modern supportive buildings arose on the south side. Three runways were laid in 1941 but the old NE/SW main one proved impossible to extend post-war, so a new primary stretch ran in a NW/SE direction. Abbots Ripton has gone, and changed too were the days from when Alconbury lay in an isolated area of Cambridgeshire, with the extensive surrounding domestic housing for personnel and their families. More than ever you could feel the huge power our airfields radiated upon everyday social life.

Until, that is, in this case 1992. Alconbury probably little feared the A-10A squadron leaving by May as the military knew how the 10th TFW was similarly in the process of saying its goodbyes from Bentwaters and Woodbridge. But alarm bells started ringing in August as the American authorities announced that the lease on the airfield's housing estate would not be renewed. An extremely ominous development, and in May 1993 came still worse news with remaining resident aircraft to withdraw and Alconbury to partly close. The reconnaissance jets soon quietly moved out after staying more than a decade, the special operations squadrons being scheduled to go to Mildenhall by March 1995. Six months later the Ministry of Defence is intended to regain most of the site: a small portion will keep alive to carry out ground duties and let communications aircraft land but such is the general political horror at the levels of defence spending these days that all the facilities may well be finally given up. Suicidal short-term thinking in an unstable world with far too many people out of work.

The British airfield story is packed with success, luck and

unpredictability. Alconbury used to enjoy all of these factors but might not for many more years to come. As in the beginning, this place no longer controls its own destiny. Me and money, politics and pacifism now call the shots. All wrong.
142/TL206765. 4 miles NW of Huntingdon.

Aldeburgh, Suffolk

Maybe Alconbury was Britain's original satellite airfield, but in some ways the great World War One Royal Naval Air Station of Great Yarmouth can be credited with sowing the seeds of this idea as several smaller airfields under its control provided support. One was a grass site at Aldeburgh, commissioned in October 1915 as an 'extra arm' for Great Yarmouth-based RNAS landplanes and mainly used as a night landing ground into 1918. Fighters occasionally took off to tackle Zeppelins but met with no success because of their general inferiority.

Aldeburgh showed enough potential during the conflict to develop on its own. A gap was noticed in the RAF's training syllabus for the instruction of marine observers in the increasingly successful fight against U-boats. Plans to open a new school for this purpose came into action during June 1918 and the Anti-Submarine Inshore Patrol Observers School formed at Aldeburgh in August after this airfield had lain closed for a while to enable redevelopment work to take place. Several biplane types equipped the new long-winded inhabitant but most suitable was the Blackburn Kangaroo, notable as few military examples of the world's first truly effective anti-submarine patrol aircraft flew elsewhere other than at Seaton Carew in north-east England.

Although the unit became No 1 Marine Observers School on January 1 1919, Aldeburgh closed after the establishment departed, probably in September. Due to its late start as a permanent airfield as opposed to being a sub-station for Great Yarmouth, this site was scheduled to have four Belfasts and a smaller Aircraft Repair Shed but these hangars were rated as only ten per cent complete towards the Armistice. Estimated date for their completion was January 31 1919, though it is doubtful if every building – whether a hangar or less conspicuous support facility – reached totality with the savagely abrupt cancellations of all things aeronautical.

Now only a solitary ruinous building continues to stand fast in the surrounding farmland. Once Aldeburgh's hangars stood in its south-west corner near the trees north of Grange Farm, while support buildings existed to the south-west again by the A1094. An airfield which rose to prominence from effectively nothing has seen the wheel of fortune turn virtually full circle. Will Alconbury go the same way?

156/TM443592. 2½ miles NW of town between A1094 and B1122.

Aldergrove, Antrim

Alternative Names: Belfast, Crumlin

Northern Ireland's greatest airfield by a veritable mile. Aldergrove has hardly ever stopped, especially since becoming Belfast Airport on September 26 1963. It has achieved many feats both in war and peace but little appreciated is how the first transatlantic ferry flight reached here on November 11 1940, thus paving the way for easy operations into and out of Prestwick.

Aldergrove was originally proposed to see service as a training airfield like all other early examples in Ireland. In then stepped famous Belfast industrial firm Harland and Wolff for the site to open as No 16 Aircraft Acceptance Park during 1918. The company was tasked with designing and building the huge Handley Page V/1500, a development of the O/400 heavy bomber but much larger overall and equipped with four piston engines in tandem pairs instead of two. This was a lot to ask of an industrial concern more accustomed to building ships – and almost became too tall an order.

Aldergrove emerged because Handley Page's design offices at Cricklewood in Greater London could not cope with the complexities of drawing up the largest British military aircraft of its day. Greater than usual secrecy surrounded this project as well, and a remote piece of land was needed for flight testing. A site east of Lough Neagh was secured on February 28 1918 and called Crumlin but this name was soon dropped in favour of Aldergrove. Cricklewood still stole the new airfield's thunder by having the V/1500 prototype fly from its grass after the machine had been shipped over to England in component form from Belfast. Development and production problems with the aircraft, building delays and disputes at Aldergrove and ultimately cancelled manufacturing contracts after the Armistice meant that few V/1500s emanated from Ireland or anywhere else.

Construction workers eventually began progressing nicely at Aldergrove to catch up on lost time once their quibbles had been settled. Unlike Aldeburgh, work was well in hand by September 1 1918 and expected to be finished on October 31. Among new buildings could be included a large hangar measuring 565 by 85 feet but the airfield needed to wait until December 20 before the first entirely complete Harland and Wolff V/1500 made its opening test flight.

At the end of 1919, the massive RAF airfield closure programme hit Aldergrove and all seemed lost. Not really, for only general flying ceased for a few years. This period still remains the only time Aldergrove has not kept wholly active. Even then either detachments or the full complements of Nos 2 and 4 Squadrons intermittently arrived with their army co-operation biplanes in case the delicate political situation suddenly deteriorated. All civil aircraft except large types could also use the site from March 1920 when the Air Ministry classed it as a List D1 airfield. Whether somebody gave special dispensation or the rules were simply accidentally or deliberately broken is unclear but the last two V/1500s did not leave Aldergrove until June.

Major flying resumed in 1925 when No 502 (Ulster) Squadron formed on May 15 as the first Special Reserve force. A hardcore of regular RAF personnel equipped each of these units to enable them to reach first-line status more quickly if an emergency arose. Only a handful of Special Reserve squadrons however appeared, were always heavily outnumbered by those of the Auxiliary Air Force and finally merged into this element in the mid-1930s. No 502 did so during 1937, by which time the squadron had operated various types of biplane bombers and changed from using heavy night machines to lighter ones for daylight purposes.

The year 1936 turned out to be highly significant in Aldergrove's career as it started to diversify. No 9 Squadron flew Vickers Virginia and then Handley Page Heyford heavy bomber biplanes here for several months, but far more noteworthy was the introduction of meteorological reporting. Aldergrove became recognised along with other places such as Bircham Newton, Duxford and eventually Tiree as one of the mainstay bases for weather analysis. A number of lives quite impossible to calculate were surely saved in years to come as aircraft flew far out over the sea for met duties, aircrews frequently risking losing their own lives – and often doing so – while struggling through atrocious weather conditions. Armament instruction began at Aldergrove in 1936 too, the training unit present being at last known as No 3 Bombing and Gunnery School from November 1939 after having absorbed No 1 ATS at Catfoss in Yorkshire the previous September. The transfer in addition during October of No 502 Squadron's quarters from Bessoneaux to an F hangar completed in December 1931 made 1936 a real year to remember.

Some Auxiliary Air Force squadrons were allocated to Coastal Command as World War Two edged nearer. These included No 502, which received Avro Ansons in January 1939 to patrol coastal waters. Aldergrove's circuit had all but filled up completely by 1940, what with its Coastal Command, training and met inhabitants. Other aircraft now came for storage as No 23 MU had formed on December 1 1939. Such intense activity was probably why No 3 B&GS closed in July 1940. Fighters were also needed to defend Belfast, so No 245 Squadron brought along Hurricanes on July 20. These aircraft stayed at the airfield for nearly a year before crossing to Ballyhalbert, not far away, and had scored a couple of victories against enemy raiders despite the all-round lack of support which virtually every RAF night fighter unit had to cope with during 1940/41.

The miracle amid all this activity was how Aldergrove coped with so many duties. It endured a punishing schedule but the place that deserved the nickname Alamogrove shouldered a heavy burden as Northern Ireland could not initially call upon many other airfields to assist its greatest servant. While those two other Irish veterans Newtownards and Sydenham gave their all, their smaller overall acreages restricted what each site could achieve, and it took until 1941 before such noted airfields as Ballykelly, Castle Archdale, Limavady and Nutt's Corner arrived to provide relief.

Before this cavalry came to the rescue, even Aldergrove occasionally needed to say no at times in 1940 to more work. The HQ of No 61 Group moved to an hotel in Belfast in August, only a month after forming, although this administrative element returned in 1947 as RAF Northern Ireland or RAFNI for short. Arduous non-stop ferry flights across the Atlantic soon stopped too once planners devised a longer but easier route to enable aircraft to travel via Canada, Iceland and eventually Greenland as well before touching down at Prestwick.

Taking into account all these jobs, further added to when No 1 APC started helping aircraft with weaponry practice at Lough Neagh, anti-submarine patrols increasingly took up a lot of time at Aldergrove. Lockheed Hudsons of No 233 Squadron assisted No 502 Squadron's offensively weak

Ansons until the Avros were replaced by the first Armstrong Whitworth Whitleys to enter Coastal Command service. No 272 Squadron came into being about the same time in late 1940 as a Blenheim unit.

Although the ever-present No 502 Squadron finally left on January 27 1941 after a stay of nearly sixteen years, going to Limavady, and the others went away later on as well, more Coastal Command squadrons kept up a guard on the Atlantic approaches. One was No 206, flying Hudsons between August 1941 and June 1942. Mid-1942 saw a brief break in operations to allow No 9 OTU to form with Bristol Beauforts and Beaufighters but they quickly departed and normality returned.

Construction workers turned Aldergrove from being an unusual four runway RAF station to a two runway one between 1941 and 1943. In another odd move, the airfield did not close to allow such massive rebuilding: it was far too important to lose temporarily. These completely new and realigned stretches each measured 6,000 feet, giving Aldergrove double the number of runways allocated to a standard Class A heavy bomber base, and were mainly made ready in time to bring along the biggest aircraft seen here since the V/1500.

Very long range Consolidated Liberators appeared in 1943 to cover the sector of water known as the 'Atlantic Gap' where U-boats had previously scored many kills in their incessant hunt for Allied shipping. Aldergrove's latest aircraft type found enemy submarines hard to find for long enough but the station hit a tremendous purple patch with five sinkings in the first five months of 1943. Three of these strikes were attributed to No 86 Squadron's Liberators, two U-boats being destroyed in the space of ten days. Occasional successes against patrolling He 111s and four-engined Focke-Wulf Fw 200 Condors furthermore ensured that for once Coastal Command victory tallies exceeded those of Fighter Command at an RAF airfield.

Aldergrove took more of a back seat from the autumn of 1943 and left the thrills and spills of operational flying to other airfields. Logic prevailed as maritime patrol base Ballykelly was coping perfectly well, coastal neighbour Limavady would soon resume front line service too, while more inland Aldergrove offered much better support facilities because of its Expansion Period looks. New RAF anti-submarine crews still had to be trained, though, so No 1674 HCU formed on October 10 1943. Only nine days had passed when the unit was sent to Longtown but it came back from this lacking Cumbrian airfield on February 1 1944, having that same year to work around builders increasing the depth of Aldergrove's runways and perimeter track and making new hardstandings. Airmen continued to train on four-engined types such as the excellent Liberator, still probably not appreciating at that stage how they could go a whole tour of operations without seeing a U-boat. Aldergrove could have easily told these advanced trainees about three and a half barren years of non-stop maritime patrol work before at last enjoying some success.

Once No 1674 HCU moved to Milltown in northern Scotland during August 1945, meteorological Handley Page Halifaxes of No 518 Squadron arrived on September 18. Met aircraft had already served in Flight form almost continuously at Aldergrove for nearly a decade, even some ancient Gladiator biplanes years after this fighter type had gone out of front line service. No 518 Squadron became known as No 202 on October 1 1946, more Halifaxes belonging to No 224 Squadron being present during 1948-51.

Specially converted Hastings appeared in 1950 and carried on flying vital if mundane sorties from Aldergrove way out into the Atlantic, only disturbed by passing birds and ships, until these aircraft were retired and No 202 disbanded in August 1964 as the RAF's last peacetime met squadron. A mixture of the anachronistic and futuristic — balloons and satellites — were subsequently relied upon to tell everyone what weather Britain could expect. Both of these devices were officially considered more efficient than aircraft: the real reason inevitably proved money but nobody disputed that neither balloons nor satellites would ever use airfields such as Aldergrove again. Airliners fitted with meteorological reporting equipment could — but that was another story...

Among other squadrons which stayed post-war was No 120 with Avro Shackletons. Maritime patrol once more returned to the agenda at Aldergrove as had happened during the first four years of World War Two, though the Shackletons also helped to transport troops out to Cyprus during trouble there in 1956. The old No 502 Squadron came back as well to operate piston and jet-engined fighters but Aldergrove lost its most famous unit in 1957 as the RAuxAF broke up.

One other event during the 1950s amounting to about the equivalent of a millisecond in this airfield's life still became extremely noteworthy and briefly revived memories of earlier days. On February 21 1951 an English Electric Canberra jet bomber left Northern Ireland for Gander in Newfoundland, from where seven Hudsons had taken off in November 1940

In alphabetical terms Britain's first airfield, so where better to start than with the first building anyone would encounter on reaching an airfield? The guardhouse at Abbots Bromley.

A mixture of hangars at Abbotsinch: *(above)* a Callender-Hamilton and a C1 and *(below)* two Blisters.

Real history in the making. The technical site *(above)* and main runway *(below)* at Abingdon on July 31 1992, the same day as this famous RAF station officially closed. An eerie and sad scene for those who attended.

Two of the runways at Acaster Malbis, with *(below)* a public road running through the site. In excellent condition – but then few aircraft ever landed at this unsuccessful airfield.

In nowhere near as good a state is the great Acklington. A Gaydon hangar *(above)* holds on inside prison grounds but the former landing area *(below)* is shattered.

(above) The Alliance Aeroplane Company's hangar at Acton.
(below) A perimeter track still disturbs the open field that World War Two training RLG Akeman Street has become.

Two Great War airfields with enormously contrasting fortunes. This derelict building *(above)* is the sole survivor at Aldeburgh but Aldergrove, now Belfast Airport, just keeps on going *(below)*.

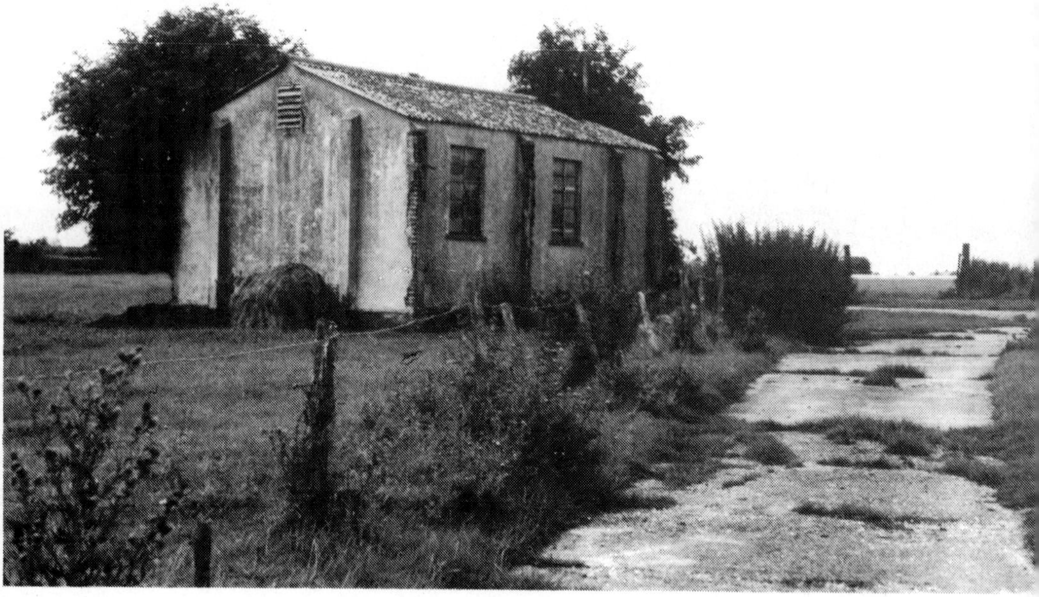

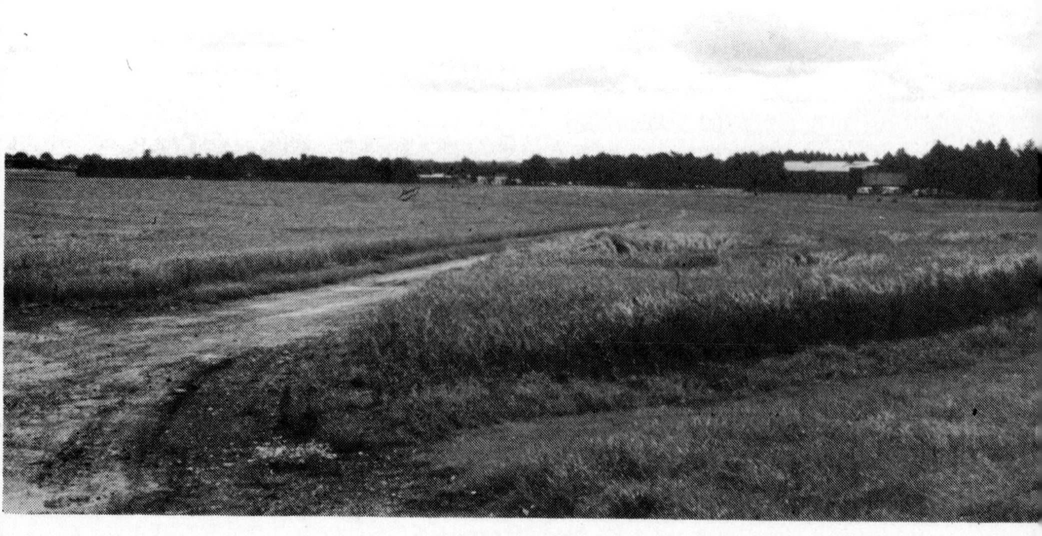

(above left) Little else marks Alton Barnes except for this minor support facility standing alongside the hamlet.
(below left) With only one Belfast hangar left, Andover is in severe trouble.
(above) Happier times as a Sikorsky Hoverfly of Andover's Helicopter Training Flight carries out another exercise. Climbing up a rope-ladder from the roof of a control tower might seem mundane now but was daring for 1945. *(RAF Museum)*

(above) Once used by the Americans, these two structures today assist a flying club at Andrews Field.
(below) The same airfield's most unlikely occupant, a French Dassault Mystère IVA.

(above) Angle on July 7 1946, four days before the War Office gained full control *(RAF Museum)*. What a change since then as the runways and about everything else have gone, and to find any traces such as this track on the east side *(below)* is a real feat indeed.

Naval airfields often produce unusual sights. Cattle use this firing butt structure at Anthorn as a shelter *(above)*, while on the extreme east side of Arbroath stands a special ¹/₂ Bellman hangar *(below)*.

THE AIRFIELDS OF BRITAIN

on the first ferry flight to Britain, before travelling to Baltimore where American aircraft company Martin subsequently built the type under licence. The B-57 in time proved as durable in USAF colours as the Canberra has in RAF markings.

Destined to survive longest of all was Aldergrove's most unsung inhabitant. No 23 MU had stored large numbers of aircraft throughout World War Two, especially Wellingtons. It worked on amid all the hustle and bustle into peacetime, joined by No 278 MU from 1948 until swallowing up this unit in 1957, and after Aldergrove was designated an airport in preference to nearby Nutt's Corner. No 23 MU at last shut down in April 1978 after excellent service but No 72 Squadron's Wessex helicopters have supported Army forces since 1981. A few Army Air Corps de Havilland Canada Beaver single piston-engined monoplanes also operated for some years on security duties until 1990/91, when AAC helicopters of Nos 655 and 665 Squadrons and Pilatus Britten-Norman Islander monoplanes of No 1 Flight concentrated at Aldergrove. As long as Northern Ireland continues to be beset by terrorist problems, at least a small number of military aircraft will always be seen mingling with civil airliners.

This is not the first time Aldergrove has existed as an airport. Away back into the 1920s it acted as Northern Ireland's unofficial civil port of call but the situation in those days was always tenuous, aircraft diverting from the disastrous Belfast/Malone airfield in 1924/25. While proper airport use started in 1933, not until 1934 did the Province receive a true airport with all the trimmings when Newtownards opened. Sydenham in turn replaced this site only four years later.

The reasoning behind this original switch was that local officialdom viewed Aldergrove as being too distant from Belfast for suitable airport employment. But it has come on by leaps and bounds since today's Belfast Airport officially opened on October 28 1963 with a new £500,000 terminal and also a replacement control tower. A final question to be resolved remained where airliners could go to if Aldergrove was unavailable. Aircraft at first needed to inconveniently divert to Dublin, Abbotsinch or even Manchester's airport Ringway until BEA considered Sydenham a reasonable alternative landing place in the 1970s. Early on in that decade the NE/SW runway increased in length to 9,000 feet to help with direct transatlantic flights.

Visitors today will surely notice the heavy levels of security before anything else on reaching Aldergrove. Walk into the terminal's entrance and armed guards almost immediately search you and any equipment you may be carrying. The airport authorities have considerately provided an enclosed viewing area for airfield/aircraft spotters but it is otherwise exceptionally difficult to see what is happening at Aldergrove with surrounding Army check-points, blocked roads and no allowed viewing areas alongside other roads. These measures seem to work as terrorism has hardly bothered the area; one of two IRA bombs planted on May 17 1973 exploded on a taxiway but caused little damage.

Architecturally, Aldergrove has been as consistent as its life as a whole. In World War Two the airfield owned six Cs, six Lamellas for aircraft storage, three Bellmans, an F and two miscellaneous hangars, and these buildings have survived pretty well intact to this day. Despite all the problems encountered from overwork to some vexatious nearby hills to make flying difficult, we can say that Northern Ireland's biggest ever airfield star has similarly battled on and done its country proud.

14/J150802. 4 miles S of Antrim, off A26. Terminal and car park on N side.

Aldermaston, Berkshire

Aldermaston — everyone has heard of the place and current position as the Atomic Weapons (formerly Atomic Weapons Research) Establishment. Far less known is its original purpose, because along with certain other airfields such as Long Kesh in Northern Ireland — now The Maze prison — Aldermaston was a 1939-45 vintage airfield that some areas of society have today no great taste for. This site lags miles behind Aldergrove in the popularity stakes. The Campaign for Nuclear Disarmament has certainly not liked it since the pacifist organisation mounted its first protest march here during April 1958. Parts of the mass media have since viewed protestors as heroes and Aldermaston as the villain. Yet the opposite should really be the case as this airfield has a great history and achieved much in its time. Let us now show these posing pseudo-political ninnies amid our midst what counts as a real hero.

Requisitioned in April 1941, plans for an RAF bomber OTU were dropped, and Aldermaston came alive in July 1942 for USAAF use. The 60th Troop Carrier Group passed through on its way to North Africa soon after, while part of the 315th TCG did the same during 1943. What was left completed nearly a year's stay by going to fellow Berkshire site Welford in November. A relative tranquility through the winter was shattered by the 434th TCG coming from a third highly controversial airfield of future years at Fulbeck in Lincolnshire in early March 1944. Aircraft at Aldermaston remained much the same as before: Douglas C-47 transports and Waco gliders.

Along with other similar units, the 434th TCG kept up a continual training schedule in preparation for D-Day on June 6. Aldermaston began experiencing secretive conditions for the first time in its career as the days prior to invasion grew ever shorter. Sorties to keep Allied ground troops supplied with everything they needed followed a Distinguished Unit Citation award for success in action, then in went the Americans to their second and much less successful airborne invasion, this time of the Netherlands. No blame whatsoever could be attached to the performances of USAAF and RAF stations such as Aldermaston: top-level military planners however had a lot to explain, especially Montgomery and his fanciful idea of ending World War Two in Europe before Christmas 1944. Once that all too nightmarish experience was over, the 434th's sole worry became the increasing distance between Aldermaston and Allied forces on the Continent. The Group therefore moved to France in February 1945 to be nearer at hand.

Little flying occurred at Aldermaston for over a year. No 25 (RCAF) Aircrew Holding Unit stayed in the second half of 1945 to process Canadian personnel but that was about all. The airfield even lay inactive from the year's end until civil aircraft unexpectedly arrived in May 1946. In came four-engined transports from Ossington in Nottinghamshire, twin-engined ones from Bristol's airport Whitchurch and an engineering unit previously based not far away at White Waltham to form a centralised training school for BOAC. Airlines around the world were starting up again, and Aldermaston achieved much at British level to help convert former military personnel to civil flying duties. A school known as Airways Training Ltd formed in June 1947 to carry on creating these new jobs out of old, also providing refresher courses in instrument flying and checks on general flying ability.

By the early months of 1948 this scheme showed itself to be a tremendous success. Around eighteen months of constant activity had resulted in over 1,000 ex-RAF pilots qualifying to fly civil transports; many others passed as navigators, radio operators and other roles associated with airline flying.

THE AIRFIELDS OF BRITAIN: VOLUME 1

Despite some difficulties with the sheer amount of aerial activity and – surprisingly for an airfield once home to an ACHU – a certain lack of accommodation, Aldermaston had by then allowed almost 30,000 take-offs and landings to safely take place. Only one slight accident to an aircraft's undercarriage happened during this entire period.

From May 1946 for nearly the next four years many civilianised bombers, as the early post-war British transport scene seemed typified by, used Aldermaston to good effect. Just as Aldergrove acted for a long while as an airport with uncertain credentials, so too did this place. But Labour nationalisation of Britain's airline companies left them with appalling monetary resources and huge operating losses in peacetime. Reductions in both civil and military front line flying spheres always tend to affect training organisations first, and cut-backs necessitated that Airways Training Ltd cease operations towards the end of 1948.

The prototype Fairey Gannet anti-submarine/airborne early warning patrol aircraft made its maiden flight on September 19 1949 but this event, important as it was, meant relatively little to Aldermaston and the airfield's future well-being. Other civil commercial ventures did not last any great length of time, and flying was told to stop altogether when revolutionary new plans for nuclear use were announced during the first week of April 1950. Charter operator Eagle Aviation reached Luton and quickly completed its move there.

The rest of Aldermaston's career, to use that increasingly excrutiating cliché, is history. Following the initial pacifist march here came illegal intrusions of the site. Cinema and television audiences soon became used to seeing hordes of pickets standing close to the old southern airfield entrance with hangars clearly visible in the background. A pilot even flew low over the now long disused airfield in August 1958 and was lucky to have all charges against him dismissed. Since then occasional unconfirmed reports of fires, explosions and other accidents have given Aldermaston an undeserved spooky aura.

AWRE briefly came under threat from aviation in the 1960s when a plan was formulated to build a third London Airport in the adjacent Padworth area. This idea never stood a realistic chance of moving off the drawing board as not only would it have forced the facility to close but also have knocked out Farnborough and given Heathrow airspace problems. Whither nukes or noise: if one almighty decision to take, no doubt local residents preferred an odd fright to perpetually high decibel levels.

THE AIRFIELDS OF BRITAIN

Such is the secrecy in this area of Berkshire that what now remains of Aldermaston is questionable. Two runways and a small part of the NW/SE stretch apparently survive among the buildings built around them. Hangarage used to consist of four T2s on the south side plus a B1 further south again across the A340 road. This detached building was specially employed by the Vickers company during World War Two to assemble Spitfires for test flying, Aldermaston having taken over this role from Henley-on-Thames near Reading. Housing rules today in this particular area of the former airfield but an occasional support building has stubbornly survived here and there to provide excellent public service. Other instantly recognisable items such as dispersals alongside a roundabout on the west side help give more clues as to past events.

Partly hidden by woodland, Aldermaston has handed out innumerable jobs to a grateful population but is an unwelcoming place to outsiders, so under no account go near it. This book and future volumes are designed to encourage you, the general public, to visit our airfields. By all means do so but give Aldermaston a wide berth if you do not want to be arrested for security reasons at Britain's 'bomb' factory. Should a place which has won a war, saved the lives of many wounded servicemen, revolutionised communications and social life, created thousands of jobs plus still helps to defend Britain however be regarded as a villain? There is surely only one answer to that question. Pacifists, take note.

174/SU597635. 9 miles NW of Basingstoke, S of village.

Alderney, Channel Islands

Channel Islands Airways built an airfield on Alderney, first of the three island airports, in 1935. Various civil airlines had spasmodically served Guernsey and Jersey since 1923, and French military seaplanes used the former place in World War One, but aviation was a new experience for Alderney. Islanders were still not blissfully ignorant of developments elsewhere as they thought an airfield could have given a good account of itself against U-boats during the Great War. For whatever reason, nobody in the military took up this suggestion.

The land on Alderney tends to slope away from the west and south. No other option therefore remained but to use the south-west side for aerial purposes. Intentions to get the airport ready for either June or July 1935 suddenly hit trouble with obstinate rock outcrops and delayed fulfilment of these plans. Although an aircraft landed in August, not until October did Alderney receive a commercial licence, and it was only the spring of 1936 before the airfield could become wholly operational.

The following few years saw Alderney settle into a fairly constant routine. A de Havilland Dragon Rapide belonging to Channel Islands Airways' subsidiary Jersey Airways called here from Southampton's airport at Eastleigh, connecting with a Saunders-Roe Windhover amphibian of Guernsey Airways. Flights normally intensified in summer months during the 1930s as tourists came via Alderney to a large new hotel, built with the airport in mind, which enjoyed good trade. Other aircraft could land by request, though bookings had to be made by telegram as neither radio nor telephones existed on the island.

Inter-island and other flights continued until the outbreak of World War Two. Reduced services resumed on October 24 1939 after the enforced temporary cessation of all British civil aviation activities but by June 1940 France looked doomed, and during June 19-21 many civilian inhabitants were evacuated by air or ship from the various islands. Next day, the airfield was put out of action when a tractor ploughed furrows across the landing area; its driver then promptly scarpered for safety in a waiting boat. This drastic action created an unenviable record as many disused British civil airfields were obstructed in wartime with the help of stakes, old cars and other impediments but Alderney remains the only one to have been completely and deliberately spiked.

The Germans discovered an almost deserted island when they arrived at the beginning of July. Between this fact, an immobilised landing area and the airport's inability to cater for big or fast aircraft, one hardly needs say that the Luftwaffe did not use Alderney in any major way during World War Two, unlike Guernsey and Jersey: only three machines are thought to have ever landed. Still, the enemy did install telephones, so at least airport staff were happy after liberation in May 1945!

Civil passenger services took longer to restart at Alderney than at Guernsey and Jersey for two reasons. The island's unconventional wartime use as a concentration camp — faint traces can still be seen close to the airport — had not exactly helped. Who says Aldermaston tops the airfield league for notoriety? Another hindrance proved the local inhabitants' return only in December 1945. What a nasty surprise awaited

THE AIRFIELDS OF BRITAIN

them as their island, never mind the airport, was in an absolutely shocking state. It was hence only natural how their overgrown and generally severely neglected primary asset did not find its feet again until reopening for inter-island services on February 1 1946.

Problems of different kinds soon arose. Alderney's cramped geographical position and limited support facilities meant it struggled from the early 1950s. One particular shortcoming was how the original terminal stood precariously near the landing area. The airport simply looked increasingly out of date, as antiquated as the reliable Rapide airliners which maintained air links. BEA withdrew these biplanes in March/April 1956 as part of an operating agreement with Jersey Airlines covering certain Channel Islands routes to let modern de Havilland Herons take over flying commitments but these four-engined monoplanes only fended off far worse difficulties for a while.

The inevitable crunch came in 1966. While never a particularly economic route, past airlines realised how much their schedules meant to Alderney in social terms. British United Airways acknowledged this fact but showed far greater concern about running costs, claiming heavy losses and arguing with islanders over fare increases. The locals themselves confused matters by not wanting concrete runways for their airport, worrying about building costs and lost agricultural land. Most curious was the general notion that this proposed development would vastly increase noise levels with more aircraft landing and make Alderney less attractive to tourists as a result. Changes were nevertheless urgently needed, and in 1966/67 the airport received a more detached terminal, a new control building, some supportive facilities and detailed attention to its landing area at a cost of £43,000. Drainage work countered bouts of flooding, while a taxiway and hardstandings gave the worn grass a bit of a breather.

These improvements ought to have solved Alderney's problems: they did not. The situation became so uncertain people feared that air activity on Alderney might cease completely. But Aurigny Air Services started operations in March 1968 to save the day, adding routes to the mainland from 1970, and this real 'bus stop' airline with a rapid turnover of flights carries on inter-island services. Aurigny uses distinctive Pilatus Britten-Norman Trislanders, a three-engined variant of the highly successful Islander transport.

A first impression of Alderney to many visitors for decades was always a rough grassy landing area. No defined runways existed as such prior to World War Two until three stretches

appeared. Yet the main runway has more recently been aided by bituminous macadam to harden the surface, while a Visual Control Room perched on stilts provides Air Traffic Control, so even this primitive little airfield with its perennial limited hangarage and few buildings has managed to keep up with the times.
No OS coverage. SW side of island.

All Hallows, Kent

Alternative Name: Sheerness
Authorisation was given on November 11 1916 for the development of a landing ground at All Hallows in one of Kent's more obscure areas. This T-shaped site had come into use by the end of 1916 but approval was soon given on February 17 1917 for the southern stretch to be ploughed up to leave a narrow east-west strip. Home Defence fighters of No 50 Squadron had All Hallows available to them if necessary, as did No 143 Squadron later on in World War One, aircraft potentially able to visit including types such as Royal Aircraft Factory BE2 variants and Sopwith Camels.

All Hallows remained active at the Armistice but eventually reverted to being nothing more than an area of farmland beside its village namesake. The gentle passing of time has strangely seen the spelling of this place change to Allhallows. Flying had not quite ceased as years later during the 1930s an airfield again arose in these parts, just west of a new railway station and by all accounts the same old Great War landing ground, when the Southern Railway system opened All Hallows as a pleasure resort in 1932. A private individual named John Stark then announced the opening of his airfield, complete with a hangar, during September 10/11. Stark had an eye to the holiday trade and gave joy-riding flights in his Spartan Three Seater I biplane.

This brief resurgence in activity at All Hallows ended when the machine was sold off in the early months of 1933. Although the surrounding scenery is now dominated by caravans, and the railway line has gone as well, flying days finished in some style as Southend-on-Sea Flying Services Ltd decided to make All Hallows an optional intermediate stop for its two Short Scion monoplanes working on the company's Southend-Rochester service during the summer of 1935. A refreshingly unusual end for a landing ground in wartime deemed restricted enough to be put into the lowest possible category as regards suitability.

178/TQ830774. Take A228 NE of Rochester towards Isle of Grain, turn left at Lower Stoke. Site immediately W of Allhallows village.

Alloa, Central

Alternative Name: Forthbank
Landing grounds massively multiplied in strength during World War One. Another big increase that became evident was the rise of factory airfields. Aircraft companies moved into or alongside many major British towns and cities, and their histories have usually been reasonably recorded for posterity. But some firms failed to become household names, further clobbering their chances of future recognition by being based in smaller towns and not places such as Coventry, London or Manchester.

The British Caudron Company was an offshoot of the famous French concern and sited at Cricklewood on the edge of London. Soon into World War One its owners decided to expand and opened in 1916 a second plant at central Scotland town and seaport Alloa, best known in those days as now for producing beer. An eccentric choice to say the least, though alcohol could not be blamed for company logic, unlike what happened at another altogether more celebrated airfield near Hull featured towards the end of this book.

It is a struggle to say a great deal about Alloa's life as historical records are so sparse. World War One is bad enough alone: virtually nothing is known about British Caudron's activities, and even how many aircraft left the factory is a mystery. Fifty BE2s were certainly built but whether examples of the conspicuous Caudron G.3 trainer or any other design constructed under licence appeared is unknown. National advertisements of the day are puzzling too by seeing fit to restrict publicising Alloa solely to the year 1917, while readers are made to feel aware of Cricklewood's presence until the Armistice in November 1918 and beyond.

If peacetime sheds a little more light upon this enigmatic airfield positioned alongside the River Forth, all it does is to give snapshots of a very broad outline for researchers and writers to work on. British Caudron stayed on for a period and tried to keep flying going, stating in August 1920 it intended to begin pleasure trips in the near future. Alloa had become a listed Avro 504K airfield by the previous May; joyriding undoubtedly occurred in 1920, as in 1922 from around about June when the Kingwill and Jones Flying Company bought the site. Three years later this small-scale commercial aviation firm moved out to finally call to a halt Alloa's severely strained claim to be a proper airfield. The land here turned into a crude residential area for shipyard workers based next door to the old aircraft factory but this industry soon dramatically crashed, leaving the purpose-built houses to be cleared away during 1932/33.

These last two years saw Alloa make a last stand as an 'airfield' with a brief return to aerial exhibition activity. Sir Alan Cobham and his troops visited 'The Old Aerodrome', as he described it, on September 13 1932 and also in July 1933 during his immensely popular display tours around Britain. Of that there is no doubt but we cannot say if Scottish Motor Traction Co Ltd used Alloa in the early 1930s; if so, did aircraft land at the Forthbank area? This pioneering airline is a real nightmare for airfield historians because SMT licensed over 60 named fields in Scotland and northern England without mentioning their precise positions.

Thus the Alloa story ends as it began in a mire of vagueness. Farmland has left nothing of this 20th Century riddle whose history is fearsomely difficult to decipher. Have a quick look at the end of this book, though, and you might as well call Alloa Biggin Hill compared to the airfields listed there!
58/NS890915. ¾ mile SE of town.

Alness, Highland

Alternative Name: Invergordon
Alness, the former Invergordon until renamed on February 10 1943 for reasons best explained later, was an operational flying boat station in the early part of its career which gradually shifted to training duties. It owed much to Invergordon's position as a major naval base during World War One.

Royal Naval Air Service flying boats and floatplanes are said to have at least passed through, and perhaps permanently inhabited, the Cromarty Firth area in that conflict. Official records have still to be discovered if this was the case; aircraft do not seem to have stayed in 1918 anyhow. RAF machines certainly occasionally visited while on their travels from the 1920s to stop ships hogging the scenery. Three Felixstowe F.5s from their airfield soundalike stayed for four weeks in 1924 during a cruise and patrolled fishing grounds in an unsuccessful but worthwhile experiment to try and locate herring shoals from the air to aid fishermen.

A combined exercise involving flying boats was held at Invergordon in July 1938. Fairly mundane stuff as usual, but the moment which markedly assisted aviation aspirations soon arrived as summer ended when large numbers of RAF units were posted to their war stations during the Munich Crisis. Among elements leaving their normal comfy abodes were Nos 201, 209 and 228 Squadrons, at Invergordon with various biplane flying boat types in September and October. The emergency passed as Prime Minister Neville Chamberlain saved Britain from a fate worse than death and the three units quickly moved back to their southerly primary haunts.

Invergordon in the meantime returned to being a basic alighting place without special back-up equipment that recognised marine bases needed. Viewed as temporary for an exercise in August 1939, the volatile political situation and threatening German aggression made the site permanent, forcing No 209 Squadron and its Supermarine Stranraers to come north again for more North Sea patrols on the 12th along with No 240 Squadron. Chaos ensued amid the tension as No 209's HQ abruptly shifted back to Felixstowe and then once more to Invergordon as August came to a close, so enabling aircraft to receive overhauls at their pre-war haunt before rushing to northern Scotland as fast as humanly possible. Now everybody could only wait and hope.

Sure enough, fighting started on September 3. While both resident units left in the autumn of 1939, the Saro Londons of No 240 Squadron flew back to Invergordon in early 1940 for another short stay. No 210 Squadron became one more short-term returnee at this time and went through a period of uneventful maritime patrol duties like its sister forces. About the sole excitement — if that was the word for it — came from a few special transportation trips to Norway by the Short Sunderlands of No 228 Squadron's detachment from Pembroke Dock in the spring of 1940 as these flying boats were given a hard time while Germany invaded this part of Scandinavia.

Again next to nothing happened at Invergordon as in the days before World War Two for another year. This rambling site with little in the way of support facilities had effectively been pressed into service as a stopgap base to cover a vulnerable sector of British water. Planners had not forgotten the airfield, construction workers steadily expanding Invergordon to improve upon the canvas camp and requisitioned buildings taken over in the town as offices and

THE AIRFIELDS OF BRITAIN: VOLUME 1

stores which sufficed at first. Airmen kept quietly busy too holding the fort, flying ostensibly at a low ebb in 1940/41 but single Sunderlands often visited on transit flights, night flying training sorties or diversions, notably from Sullom Voe in Shetland.

Activity perked up from 1941 once No 4 (Coastal) OTU arrived from Stranraer in June. This establishment trained crews with a vast array of flying boats initially, the number of types decreasing as older machines were Struck Off Charge (SOC) or retired. Sunderlands and Consolidated Catalinas eventually became standard mounts for trainee aircrews. Of note was a detachment of No 422 (RCAF) Squadron at Invergordon in 1942, flying Hurricane fighter spares to Russia, but instructional duties mostly remained to the fore until No 4 (C) OTU left for Pembroke Dock on August 15 1946. An unusual but highly useful event was the occasion one aircraft sank a U-boat on May 24 1944.

Daily life proved complicated here in the war years. Flying boats originally moored in and around Invergordon harbour. Yet maintenance became a severe problem, coupled with the positioning of domestic and most other supportive sites close to Dalmore, just south-east of Alness town. As a slipway had been built there two years earlier, the sensible solution was to shift general activity to this westerly site, which accounted for a change of airfield name during 1943. Greatly increased numbers of water-borne advanced training aircraft taxying up and down the Cromarty Firth showed how Alness had won its long battle to achieve permanency – albeit briefly.

The base was reduced to holding a closing down establishment on the same day as No 4 (C) OTU moved to Wales. Closure on January 5 1947 demonstrated the nationwide decline of marine airfields after World War Two but the RAF rated Alness desirable enough to order the slipway to be retained indefinitely. The clock turned back time as flying boats visited now and again, such as the handful of No 230 Squadron Sunderlands which appeared in mid-1947 for exercises.

Into the 1950s aircraft diverted to Alness. A typical year was 1952, with a Sunderland landing on February 18 for communications purposes and another on September 3 with engine trouble. Although flying boats totally vanished once the last two British-based squadrons disbanded at Pembroke Dock in February 1957, their disappearance allowed RAF marine craft to fully dominate for rescue and training duties. Formation of the Marine Branch on December 11 1947 will always rank as one of the service's stranger actions as, before creation, less control existed over this varied fleet of vessels which assisted aircraft to function properly; previously, each station manned its own Marine Section. Why therefore co-ordinate all these boats if hardly any aircraft now used marine bases?

Despite being deprived of flying boats, Alness stayed active for many years as personnel of No 1100 Marine Craft Base Unit (the word 'Base' was dropped on July 1 1946) worked around a cluster of residential buildings and a Bellman hangar. The MCU's boats might no longer have been able to rearm, refuel, service and generally communicate with aircraft but performed useful work in non-flying roles. Exercises with landplanes from Kinloss involved target towing, dinghy dropping, radar homing and sonobuoys for detecting underwater noise from submarines.

Somehow, Alness managed to beat off several politically engineered crises affecting the entire RAF. Duncan Sandys in the late 1950s, Labour forcing Commands to merge during the 1960s and that party implementing a Conservative-inspired plan to eradicate more military bases a decade later: all made not the slightest difference. But the Conservatives' return to power in 1979 revived financial fears in RAF circles, and the entire RAF Marine Branch disbanded in 1986 as MCU commitments were civilianised. This action has left Alness with a most uncertain future, more doubtful than ever before in the airfield's history. The re-routed A9 road which runs much closer to the site could be argued to have not helped its cause either. Little else other than the Bellman and the Flying Control building on Alness pier survive.
(Invergordon area) 21/NH710683. Harbour area, S side of town (Alness area) 21/NH652679. S of town, take minor road on W side of River Averon down towards Alness Point.

Alton Barnes, Wiltshire

Alternative Name: Brown's Farm
Not all airfields in Britain can claim to be readily evident once disused like Alness: far from it. Just one support building and a few air raid shelters remain at this long closed grass field which became a more embodied airfield. Alton Barnes was also known as Brown's Farm, and a road in this sleepy hamlet almost totally cut off from the outside world is still called Brown's Lane.

The Central Flying School, one of Britain's most famous individual military aviation elements, had despatched aircraft

77

to Alton Barnes for regular forced landing practice since at least 1936. No machine could have landed at this place or three other ones in similar use prior to the last third of 1935 for the simple reason that CFS transferred to Upavon in September from Wittering in eastern England, to where the training unit had gone in 1926.

Into World War Two, and for some time during the conflict, Alton Barnes continued as a humble ELG but aircraft activity made this classification increasingly absurd. CFS eventually realised how its aide deserved better recognition and subtly changed the airfield's status in 1941 as records show. On June 18 three personnel died in an accident involving a Master and an Oxford at the ELG: two more deaths happened at the RLG on September 4.

Alton Barnes soon came under the control of No 29 EFTS at Clyffe Pypard, being actively managed by this newly-opened base nine miles to the north up to July 1945. Tiger Moths and Magisters now actually stayed full-time and instructed not only trainee RAF pilots but Army and FAA ones as well at different periods. This airfield soldiered on reasonably well, provided everyone took notice of several not inconsiderable shortcomings. The centre of Alton Barnes' landing area suffered badly after rainfall, while general undulation and nearby hills prohibited night flying; needless to say that the RLG was not recommended for front line aircraft types except in any emergencies. Nevertheless, the place did its job and lasted until July 9 1945, that extremely significant and gloomy day for so many RLGs all over Britain when they shut down and passed to a C&M state. All military links ended after a couple of years, though Alton Barnes remained aligned with Clyffe Pypard for a sizeable chunk of 1947.

It would be fair to say that many RLGs stood little or no chance of surviving long into peacetime. This operationally and geographically restricted example lost out even more than usual: grass runways rendered it obsolete but Alton Barnes did not have a hard perimeter track either, only one made of metal Sommerfeld Track. Ten Blisters, through which one of them a disgruntled instructor once astonishingly flew a Tiger Moth in 1944 without touching the hangar's sides, cannot be seen too amid farmland. Most of the air raid shelters are on the north side but only an expert eye can sadly really make out Alton Barnes at all today.
173/SU100620. SW of Marlborough and 5½ miles NW of Pewsey. On W side of village.

Andover, Hampshire

Alternative Name: Weyhill

The highly historic airfield of Andover stayed open for military use virtually non-stop ever since World War One – no mean feat. Andover survived lean periods, bombing raids and economic hardship; its motto could have been 'know your enemy'. However, as is tragically evident these days, is friend worse than foe?

Purchased for airfield use from two individuals, in the beginning Andover saw differentiated instruction mix with the usual World War One era RFC/RAF squadrons working up to operational readiness before theoretically flying to France. First occupied in 1916, No 104 Squadron later came from Wyton on September 16 1917 with Airco DH9 day bombers. No 106 Squadron formed on the 30th, and No 105 Squadron was not terribly long in following the road down to Hampshire by travelling from Lincolnshire on October 3. At that time there remained one big difference as Andover was not known by its well-noted name, then being called Weyhill instead after a small village to the north-west. Not for another fortnight after No 105 Squadron arrived did a change of title take place.

The traditional style of Great War British airfield operation carried on for a while as Andover's initial occupants steadily trained, and No 104 Squadron moved as planned to France in May 1918. But No 105 Squadron meanwhile went against the trend by changing to Royal Aircraft Factory RE8 reconnaissance biplanes like No 106, accompanying it not to the Western Front but Ireland via Ayr I. Five other squadrons which either formed or regrouped with bombers in this period also soon left.

When these units had all gone, No 2 School of Navigation and Bomb Dropping arose to give Andover a greater taste of the more specialised training which became noticeable at some airfields in the dying months of World War One. Known post-war from December 1919 as the Air Pilotage School, instructional duties rapidly dwindled and the unit closed at the end of 1922.

Much noteworthy activity still happened at this airfield in the short term post-Armistice period. Andover did hit the headlines – if not always in manners it would have wanted. The RAF showed considerable interest in long distance flying during 1919, and one such trip saw two Handley Page O/400s

THE AIRFIELDS OF BRITAIN: VOLUME 1

take off on April 19 for a tour around Britain. In stages the bombers travelled via East Anglia, the east coast of England and Scotland to Inverness, Aldergrove, Tenby in south-west Wales, Cornwall, Devon and the English south coast before returning on the 22nd. Triumphant feelings at their base had already evaporated earlier the same day as another O/400 belonging to No 2 School of Navigation and Bomb Dropping taking off at night on a similar training flight hit the roof of a building, failed to clear it and crashed, killing five airmen aboard. For those days this accident involved a high number of fatalities.

A different kind of unwelcome publicity received airing the following November as heaps of wood consisting of surplus hangars from other surrounding airfields were noted lying about, brought to Andover as it was the most convenient place where to put them. Whether such a system became national practice has yet to be proven but this particular 'dump' gave rise to further complaints about its positioning on agricultural land. Here stood no farming territory, though no doubt many people would have liked to see that situation become reality.

As Andover owned permanent facilities, the RAF decided to retain the station. Former APS personnel were brought together as No 11 Squadron in January 1923 but still had to cope without available aircraft of their own on moving to Bircham Newton in September. Having to use types from another service source for mundane communications purposes showed how desperate the early 1920s were for Britain's airfields as a whole.

Luck began to side with Andover and elsewhere as the 1920s wore on. Yeovil-based aircraft manufacturer Westland sent over a number of prototype designs for their maiden flights in this decade and the next one, including the company's fascinating tailless Pterodactyl machines. At RAF level, No 13 Squadron helped increase overall aircraft movements and not depend upon communications sorties as seen in the last four years by staying during 1924-29 for army co-operation, arriving about the same time as No 12 Squadron. This was the RAF's only unit to fly the Fairey Fox light bomber, a revolutionary type as this single-engined biplane was the fastest bomber of its age at over 150 miles per hour, so swift contemporary fighters could not catch it.

No 101 Squadron, present between October 1929 and December 1934, possessed other rarities to become the only twin-engined day bomber squadron in RAF service for several years. The Boulton Paul Sidestrand had broken new ground as the first RAF medium bomber to end a long stranglehold

THE AIRFIELDS OF BRITAIN

on official policy since World War One by so-called light and heavy bombers. After No 142 Squadron's much more numerous Harts arrived in January 1935, both it and No 12 Squadron stayed away from Britain during the Abyssinian crisis until 1936. Still bombers came along to Andover, four Hind units forming in 1936 and 1937, while Nos 12 and 142 Squadrons later received Battles.

This professed advance in bomber design marked the end of a major stage in Andover's life, one that is quite detailed by normal standards for a pre-World War Two military airfield. Germany now looked to be the enemy should any future war occur, not France, and that meant bombers ought to be sited in eastern England rather than more centralised parts. The Battles moved to Bicester on May 9 1939 for Andover to gradually slip back into its old 1920s army co-operation role as No 59 Squadron appeared to slowly accept Blenheims in place of Hector biplanes. No 11 (Fighter) Group Pool also formed on January 14 but left for St Athan in Wales on July 1.

Many more changes resulted as soon as World War Two started. No 59 Squadron altered from a night to strategic reconnaissance role and stayed only another month before going to France. The bombers which had swamped Andover for so long had well and truly left, and the airfield switched to a training function. No 2 School of Army Co-operation opened in October 1939 but found home airspace increasingly dangerous.

Station old boy No 59 Squadron returned briefly in May 1940 along with No 53 Squadron, though both units were fortunate to leave when they did. While not a fighter airfield, Andover was subjected to occasional Luftwaffe raids throughout the Battle of Britain and into 1941. August 13 1940 saw it become one of the tragic triumvirate of airfields – Kent's Detling and Eastchurch being the others – to be mistakenly attacked. The Station Flight came off badly as three rare Miles Mentors and a Magister were damaged but their master did not suffer quite as badly overall; deaths here alone proved a tiny fraction of the 80 plus lost at Detling and Eastchurch combined. Two more personnel died in a raid on the 14th which severely damaged the D/F radio station for aerial navigation.

The Luftwaffe dished out far heavier blows in 1941 as lone intruders, or 'singletons' as they were dubbed, illustrated how effective individual roaming aircraft could be. Alternatively, these unwelcome visitors provided minor nuisance value, such as a luckless Junkers Ju 88 which spent thirteen minutes trying to punish Andover on March 26 1941. The raider's

81

bombs were dropped at too low an altitude and failed to explode, one device crazily bouncing along the ground into a Blenheim and a petrol tanker, and strafing achieved little either before the airfield's anti-aircraft section shot down the machine. Less than an hour later a second Ju 88 also fluffed an attack to mainly limit Andover's worries to eight Blenheims and four Ansons damaged but a nocturnal strike on April 7 destroyed two Belfast hangars and killed two. Staff needed to attend to more blasted support facilities after a second stick of bombs landed on the 16th.

Considering these raids, it is surprising how No 2 School of Army Co-operation, renamed No 42 OTU in July 1941, and its frequently holed aircraft only moved to Ashbourne in Derbyshire on October 26 1942. The Blenheims and Ansons should have flown north out of harm's way over two years earlier, though Army Co-operation needs and the relatively close proximity of Salisbury Plain tended to override this theory.

The OTU had certainly given Andover a settled time but 1943 proved an unsettled year. Notable visitors were fighter-reconnaissance Mustangs of No 16 Squadron, FAA fighters and Oxford trainers. No 15 (P) AFU had been pushed out of Leconfield and aides, including the dreaded Acaster Malbis, the HQ leaving for Babdown Farm in Gloucestershire on October 28 but its Servicing Wing remaining until January 15 1944 to let builders complete Babdown. Totally unfamiliar aircraft then came in February to already venerable Andover: USAAF Lockheed P-38 fighter-bombers of the 370th Fighter Group, present until July when they crossed the English Channel.

This airfield gradually quietened down afterwards, although No 43 OTU quickly arrived to carry on its Army support involvement. AA co-operation aircraft of No 285 Squadron also stayed between November 1944 and January 1945 as second-line flying became safer once again in southern England, and three Canadian-manned Auster AOP squadrons formed in the final months of World War Two. The Auster OTU remained to become No 227 Operational Conversion Unit in April 1947, going to Middle Wallop the following January with RAuxAF Austers of No 657 Squadron.

Andover's more recent occupants were of special note as they helped bring into military service new flying machines which we all now take for granted: helicopters. No 529 Squadron at Henley-on-Thames had stolen the glory slightly by operationally using a Sikorsky Hoverfly from May 1945 but the Helicopter Training Flight made real strides in terms of

THE AIRFIELDS OF BRITAIN

development work after accepting its first craft on February 8. Originally part of No 43 OTU, it separated from the unit on April 9 and disbanded on January 16 1946. A Flight of No 657 Squadron later spent six months at Beaulieu III during 1946/47 for further helicopter training. Early types such as the Hoverfly were unsatisfactory in many respects but from these unsteady beginnings arose vastly superior designs able to tackle numerous military and civil-orientated tasks in the future.

Little else other than communications aircraft subsequently disturbed the peace as Andover served primarily as an administrative ground headquarters. The RAF Staff College came back in February 1948 as the base passed to Maintenance Command after having already stayed almost twenty years here before World War Two, and eventually clocked up four decades in residence. Maintenance Command's HQ lasted almost as long, forming on April 1 1938 and hanging on until merging into Support Command on September 1 1973. Sporting RAFGSA gliders also kept flying in evidence for many years after World War Two before the Wessex GC ceased operations in 1963. Helicopters were never far away from Andover either, and three years earlier No 225 Squadron had formed out of the Joint Experimental Helicopter Unit, though it left for Odiham after only a few months.

No 21 Squadron later reformed in February 1969 to carry on communications duties but disbanded on March 31 1976 when the previous year's notorious Defence Review, announced in December 1974, gunned for a dozen big name RAF bases. At first these airfields were not named to leave everyone in the dark but Andover's days undoubtedly looked numbered: *Intentionally Blank*, the name given to the station magazine, took on a worrying new meaning. No 21 Squadron's departure killed off flying bar an odd helicopter, the airfield's fate being sealed in November 1976 with the RAF deciding to combine Support and Training Commands on June 13 1977. The new Support Command would be based at the RAF ground station of Brampton in Cambridgeshire, burnt down in a fire during October 1985.

As one door closed, another opened for the great survivor. More administrative use started at Andover as the Army gained control. The site also acted as a supportive airfield to Middle Wallop, one or two Army Air Corps helicopters being based here and other aircraft occasionally landing until flying finally ended in the first half of the 1980s. Middle Wallop's Museum of Army Flying stored a few more 'choppers' and

THE AIRFIELDS OF BRITAIN: VOLUME 1

fixed-wing types away from the Battle of Britain superstar, one airfield the Luftwaffe bombed with justification as then being a fighter station unlike Andover. Back in the 1950s a preserved ex-Luftwaffe Messerschmitt Bf 110 night fighter had interestingly resided in storage too but its advanced wartime position and lack of enough hangarage could never have enabled Andover to hold aircraft in large quantities. These reasons might be argued to have made the presence of Maintenance Command a touch weird.

Time stood still for years at this airfield which latterly almost looked like a superbly equipped 1930s era Automobile Association civil landing ground with hay bales perched on the grassy landing area. The only real concession to more modern developments was a perimeter track. And that in time became the problem, for never did Andover receive highly useful new items like Hardened Aircraft Shelters, such as the larger than usual structures now at Alconbury. Nor did the always wavy landing area ever progress to having anything harder than a metal surface. All metal runway types gave excellent service but were considered at best semi-permanent and could badly puncture aircraft tyres if not constantly inspected, the reason why No 602 Squadron left Abbotsinch in 1949.

One battle Andover recently lost out on became an intrusion through its northern half by the A303 road and Weyhill Service Station but this action seemed minor compared to what happened in 1990 and 1991. Unthinkably, most of the surviving four Belfasts and a similarly sized Aircraft Repair Shed were demolished to leave only one hangar still standing; twelve Blisters disappeared long ago. This diabolical decision to let go of these extraordinarily important older buildings because the owners would not pay for their upkeep must however put the continued dogged architectural resilience of the entire airfield into some doubt. The last Belfast could go at any moment, and support buildings on the landing area side of a public road which passes through are said to be intended for sale in the future for other unspecified uses.

Many people might say that Andover in the past ought to have been regarded more as a disused or at least redundant airfield rather than an active one. Certainly times have changed from the days of heavy aircraft movements and widespread ground activities. No more do piston-engined bombers exist in profusion or personnel watch with amazement as a man climbs up a rope-ladder from the control tower's roof to a Helicopter Training Flight Hoverfly hanging in the air directly above, considered quite a feat in 1945. A

hardstanding now waits in vain for helicopters. But so long as the Army remains on Salisbury Plain, the ageless airfield star of Andover will never wholly disappear either.
185/SU330458. W of town by A303. Reasonable general views of airfield at medium range from nearby roads.

Andreas, Isle of Man

The least known of the three World War Two Manx airfields opened on September 1 1941, just under a year after being requisitioned. A detachment of No 457 (RAAF) Squadron quickly occupied Andreas by flying from nearby Jurby and came in full on October 3. Its Spitfires stayed until March 1942, with more of No 452 (RAAF) Squadron appearing for further convoy patrol duties until leaving for their Australian homeland in June. No 93 Squadron immediately reformed on the 1st with more fighters as a British-manned element for a change but departed in September.

Still at Andreas was an ASR detachment which had come around the same time as the station's first Australian fighter unit. No 275 Squadron's Westland Lysanders and Supermarine Walruses duly helped to save many lives until it moved as a whole from Valley in Anglesey down to Warmwell on the English south coast in April 1944.

This airfield only had a settled major establishment from May 1 1943 when No 11 Air Gunnery School formed with Ansons and Martinets. Andreas might have seemed oddly placed for a wartime base but in reality its position was an asset. Fighters found this a fine airfield from where to guard Allied shipping and also rest; Andreas was centrally sited for ASR work; and even a number of aircraft being ferried across the Atlantic diverted to this place. Now gunnery trainers could operate over the Irish Sea with relative safety and without annoying anyone else.

For the next three years, Andreas went about business in its usual quiet but effective manner. A Wellington conversion Flight for No 11 AGS formed at Jurby in October 1944 and necessitated more hardstandings to be built at the airfield they were intended for. Being Mark IIIs and veterans of Bomber Command's mid-war offensive against Germany, these tired aircraft did not have good serviceability, so Mark Xs taken from Nos 2 and 12 AGSs at Dalcross in northern Scotland and Bishops Court in Northern Ireland eventually replaced them. No 11 AGS also received some Spitfires in March 1945.

THE AIRFIELDS OF BRITAIN: VOLUME 1

More pronounced variation in normal activity occurred during 1945 when part of No 772 Squadron operated from here with various aircraft types as an FAA Fleet Requirements Unit over the spring and summer months, coming back again for a shorter stay in the the spring of 1946. No 772 had not been the first Navy squadron at Andreas, for Nos 808 and 825 had briefly passed through with their Fairey Fulmar fighters and Swordfish torpedo bombers at different periods in 1942.

Most AGSs finished operations shortly after World War Two ended. No 11 even outlasted its few peacetime contemporaries and survived up to October 1947 but spent the unit's last year at Jurby. Andreas was always the 'poor man' of the Isle of Man's wartime airfield trio in relation to Ronaldsway and Jurby on account of lesser support facilities; their particularly dispersed nature, while good for safety, made administering the station that shade more difficult. The airfield always seemed to lose out too as far more people attended the 1945 Battle of Britain display at Jurby, and terrible weather saw only 500 visitors at the 1946 event. But much more significant was the difference in pre-war aviation experience and/or policy. Ronaldsway had invited in civil airliners for many years, Jurby was a purpose-built Armament Training Station with suitable buildings, but Andreas could not lay claim to any peacetime links. Being fairly close to Jurby – yes, circuit overlap makes yet another appearance in the British airfield story – and sited in a comparatively remote spot by Isle of Man standards ensured that here was one airfield with a grim future.

What transpired after No 11 AGS moved to Jurby on September 19 1946 did so with frighteningly clinical speed. Andreas rapidly emptied during the rest of September, all domestic sites being vacant by the 30th, as the intention was to either hand the place to another Government department or simply abandon it. The unit movement was fully completed on October 21 and left the AGS's former home on C&M, final clearing up duties occurring by January 1947. Minor motor sport activities today owe their origins to a request by amateur motor cycle racers to use the airfield for training in April. After acting as an aircraft turning point for the Isle of Man Air Races on May 24 and 26, the Manx Government made arrangements to purchase Andreas in October.

Few buildings have since remained to mark this unpretentious hero, except for a derelict control tower and some support facilities now used by a farm. Everything is not lost as all three runways are happily complete and the NE/SW stretch has even returned to flying use as a landing strip for

THE AIRFIELDS OF BRITAIN

gliders and microlights. Just as many people might have previously questioned the validity of still classing Andover as an active airfield, so the opposite applies with Andreas as it is supposedly a disused site – or maybe not. Alas, the current hangarage position cannot get any worse as all three Bellmans and eight Blisters have disappeared. Such a lack of these distinctive buildings on the landscape makes virtually certain that potential tourists who appreciate what history is really all about will not readily spot this deceptively important old airfield. A few Australians could show them the way.
95/SC427999. 4½ miles NW of Ramsey by A9, ¾ mile E of village.

Andrews Field, Essex

Alternative Name: Great Saling
If Andreas was not the Isle of Man's most famous airfield, where does that place its neighbour Hall Caine? This 1930s civil airfield, named after local novelist Sir Hall Caine and also known as Ramsey, was positively obscure in comparison but notable for being one of only two British sites named after people instead of towns, villages or whatever. The other airfield lay far away in East Anglia – and still survives.

Andrews Field is indebted to Lieutenant-General Frank M. Andrews, original head of the US 8th Air Force until killed in Iceland as the result of an air accident on May 3 1943. Even so, when the airfield opened less than a fortnight earlier, it was initially known until May 21 as Great Saling after a village to the north-east. Possibly a more cynically realistic reason for this titular change was that several British airfields bearing a 'Great' name already existed and planners did not want too many of them. And, by sheer incredible chance, immediately south lay Boxted Wood, even though *the* Boxted of considerable USAAF fighter fame stood a fair distance away to the east. Those woodland-inspired airfields Shepherd's Grove and Spanhoe perhaps received their names from this added complication. Who knows?

The 96th BG came to Andrews Field in May 1943, going to Snetterton Heath in June. Its B-17s were replaced by Martin B-26 medium bombers of the 322nd BG from Rougham, Bury St Edmunds as it was alternatively known. The Marauders soon proved their worth attacking tactical targets and succeeded in losing their early general reputation as dangerous aircraft to fly. Many American aircrews in those days ominously referred to the B-26 as the 'Widow Maker'

87

because of its high accident rate. Problems revolved around a high wing loading ratio which affected flying characteristics but, once this and one or two other quirks were accepted, the Marauder became recognised as an efficient bombing type.

Range limitations after D-Day eventually forced the Distinguished Unit Citation winning 322nd BG to move to France in September 1944, Andrews Field then being taken over by the RAF. From mid-October a remarkably high number of Mustang fighter squadrons began using this base for daylight bomber escort missions. Some units were present for only brief periods but all played their part in protecting RAF heavy bombers as they ventured into enemy airspace. Germany had lost much of its radar coverage and night fighter force, so 'heavies' could now do what once seemed inconceivable by flying without the cover of darkness, further assisted by places such as Andrews Field.

Several Polish squadrons stayed at Andrews Field during the belated Mustang period. Nos 315 and 316 became two examples which both arrived in October 1944 and resided until August and November 1945. Mustangs did not have Andrews Field completely to themselves, though, as a few early Meteor jet fighters of No 616 Squadron made a flying visit in February and March. Far less dynamic users were No 276 Squadron's ASR Walruses which spent most of the summer of 1945 at Andrews Field before travelling to Norway in August.

Two Mustang squadrons inevitably had to have the final say in the active career of this airfield. No 303 had appeared in April 1945, gone to Coltishall a month later and returned in August. Again the unit left on November 28 for Turnhouse, No 316 Squadron also flying north that same day to Wick, where it would be rejoined by No 303 in January 1946.

The station ORB only continues for another 48 hours after Nos 303 and 316 Squadrons moved out until November 30 1945 and then abruptly stops. No reason is given but look up Fighter Command records and you will see that Duxford parented Andrews Field on a C&M basis from December 1. While an identically named American airfield in Maryland enjoyed major post-war military service, its British rival stagnated, passing to Technical Training Command on May 4 1946 as satellite to Great Sampford. This former satellite to Debden did nothing apart from make bi-weekly inspections, and was eventually abandoned along with Andrews Field on April 12 1948.

Temporary housing use occurred in the short run but this airfield gradually withered into agricultural land in the main.

Andrews Field might well have faded away completely had it not been for the efforts of flying club enthusiasts during the 1970s. In 1972 they managed to create on the west side a grass landing strip as most of the three runways and other tracks had disappeared; part of the perimeter track in this area had become a minor road. The Andrews Field Flying Club and airfield were in full flow a year later, a clubhouse sprang up in 1975, and the reborn site received a licence in 1976. A good number of light aircraft now fly from here, the small Rebel Air Museum being another occupant until leaving in 1986. The organisers decided not to take a Dassault Mystère IVA with them and this French jet-engined fighter-bomber now gently rusts away near the clubhouse.

Although the Americans are still remembered by way of a memorial inexplicably placed in Great Saling village, about the only really major reminders from those days are two T2s in storage use and two smaller buildings moved from elsewhere to settle in among today's facilities. But not a single Mustang is to be seen. Personalised airfields abound in America but Andrews Field is now unique in Britain and that is its real trademark.

167/TL694248. 7 miles W of Braintree, turn right off A120 for Stebbing Green, then right again.

Angle, Dyfed

From one curious airfield to another ... A Short Sunderland of No 461 (RAAF) Squadron took off from Pembroke Dock on May 29 1943 to pick up the crew of another Sunderland which had crashed the previous day. The duty was successfully carried out but heavy seas punched a huge hole in the aircraft's hull. As flying directly back to Pembroke Dock was out of the question, pilot Flying Officer G. Singleton landed his Sunderland at the 'dry' airfield of Angle. There followed a strenuous attempt to move the machine to a beach two miles away where it was repaired, though as events transpired the flying boat never again became airborne. This was the first Sunderland land airfield arrival in Britain, and another unusual touchdown of this kind would occur at Andreas' neighbour Jurby during 1945.

Memories of Angle are always enlivened by this famous incident. A rather unwelcoming place due to a detached geographical position, the base opened under Fairwood Common's control on June 1 1941. Andrews Field and Angle totally opposed each other as regards construction

THE AIRFIELDS OF BRITAIN: VOLUME 1

development: whereas the first American-built airfield in Britain came not only on stream as scheduled but three months ahead of expectations, Angle lay incomplete for months afterwards. The first winter of its career proved a most dire affair.

Such personal deprivations mattered relatively little to the planners. Angle's all-important landing area was ready for fighter squadrons to mount convoy patrols despite sundry difficulties, the first being No 32, whose Hurricanes stayed between June and November. More Hurricanes plus Spitfires of other fighter units used Angle for brief periods up to early 1943, these aircraft belonging to Nos 152, 312, 412, 421 and 615 Squadrons. Easily the most glamorous fighter squadron was No 263, which flew the twin-engined Westland Whirlwind. Examples of this good-looking design with a troubled life stayed at Angle from April 18 to August 15 1942, being particularly useful for convoy escort duties to which Angle seemed permanently in use for. The destruction or damaging of several Luftwaffe bombers showed how worthwhile this routine could be.

Policy changes brought No 794 Squadron in July 1943 with assorted FAA target towing types after Angle had been commissioned as HMS *Goldcrest* in May. A detachment of No 759 Squadron from Yeovilton in Somerset joined the Naval Air Firing Unit, as No 794 Squadron was alternatively titled, but the Royal Navy soon swapped places with Coastal Command Development Unit at nearby Dale in September for the convenience of Flying Control. Angle became satellite to famous flying boat base Pembroke Dock: so arose the unusual situation of a marine airfield controlling a landlubber, though this was not an entirely unprecedented idea as we have seen with Great Yarmouth and Aldeburgh.

Another wide variety of aircraft types moved in as CCDU proceeded with testing in order to successfully combat U-boats. Vital service and tactical trials evaluated Coastal Command illumination, photographic and especially ASV radar equipment, results finishing up in top secret dossiers. For all its social disadvantages, Angle was a perfect area for this work by lying right out of the way on a peninsula.

To create a new establishment which allowed research to greatly expand, CCDU became known as the Air-Sea Warfare Development Unit on January 1 1945 and concurrently started afresh at a bigger airfield. An advance party moved to Thorney Island on January 5, the main element going to Sussex nine days later.

ASWDU's departure heralded the end for Angle. The

THE AIRFIELDS OF BRITAIN

airfield carried on as satellite to Pembroke Dock but was gradually running down on a C&M basis, not assisted by either Coastal Command envisaging any further use or the Air Ministry authorising the transfer of Angle to Maintenance Command in June for explosive storage. Allegations that a prototype Vickers Windsor heavy bomber conducted firing trials here and at Pembrey along the south Wales coast in the spring of 1945, as well as a year earlier, are true despite reports to the contrary.

Aircraft rarities however could not stop any decline and the War Office accepted Angle on September 21 1945 for Army purposes. The gift remained subject to conditions as the site went to this new owner on Loan II terms, meaning pending final disposal, whereby the Air Ministry retained a title to the land. 'Retention stations', as the Ministry liked to describe inactive airfields such as Angle after World War Two, could be offered to other Government departments under Loan I (five years) or II stipulations but a parenting base still had to attend to certain duties at the closed airfield. All removable equipment was to be cleared, others given notice about equipment which could be damaged or stolen, inspections of the whole airfield made every two weeks as Great Sampford did with Andrews Field, ensure that buildings were securely locked and any damage or unauthorised occupation reported. More intricate jobs involved keeping down grass and weeds and arranging for rat disinfestation if necessary. No doubt Pembroke Dock made all the required provisions but did not mention Angle in its records: few active stations ever did say what was happening at their disused charges, and unfortunately bi-weekly inspections often turned into sloppy affairs leading to the neglect so painfully obvious today.

In March 1946 civil commercial aircraft were tentatively granted facilities at this and certain other Coastal Command airfields of mixed suitability. This idea proved unrealistic, and the War Office gained Loan I or unlimited control on July 11 as Angle was required for the Polish Resettlement Corps. Further aviation links did occur during the early 1950s when a Loran radio transmitter station to aid aircraft navigation was built nearby.

Bleak in World War Two, Angle is now a sad and unrecognised site. Its perimeter track is mostly complete but all three tarmac runways have been virtually torn up. A 'bathandle' once comprised the main runway's eastern stretch where the perimeter track was extended to accommodate this narrowed section largely caused by wartime economies. Nearly every building has also gone, as has the airfield's entire hangarage of a single T2 and four Blisters. These structures developed so slowly as this base did as a whole that only the Blisters existed by 1943. Farming helps to further conceal Angle, the airfield which saw one of World War Two's most bizarre incidents.

157/SM859018. 7 miles W of Pembroke by B4320, 1 mile S of village.

Annan, Dumfries and Galloway

The towers of Chapelcross nuclear power station loom large over what used to be a home to many Hurricanes. Like Angle, Annan was an effective but ungenial place situated in deceptively isolated countryside. This is what the staff of No 55 OTU came to realise after moving from Usworth in April 1942.

Aircraft had already landed at Annan beforehand as Battles and Blenheims of No 18 MU at Dumfries dispersed there from December 3 1940 into 1941. Precisely when this practice ceased is unknown but it may well have been March as planners selected this unofficial Satellite Landing Ground for more extensive development. Far more mysterious is whether 1930s airline Scottish Motor Traction Co Ltd held a licence for what became the future military site, somewhere else, or if its aircraft ever landed. Undoubtedly Annan's tale is Alloa in reverse as aviation connections grew stronger in years to come.

No 55 OTU arrived in the same piecemeal style as CCDU/ASWDU went from Angle to Thorney Island, an advance force coming on April 14 1942 and the bulk a fortnight later. The unit provided training in all spheres of fighter and fighter-bomber techniques once installed at Annan. A glut of fighter-reconnaissance pilots plus the needs to keep them busy while waiting for operational postings and give more simulated front line experience saw the OTU being renamed No 4 Tactical Exercise Unit in January 1944. Another change of name two months later made No 4 TEU become No 3, immediately replacing a unit bearing the same title which had disbanded at Hawarden in north-east Wales.

By this time Hawker Typhoon fighter-bombers were being brought more and more into play to replace the ageing Hurricanes. But even before D-Day Annan looked set to lose

No 3 TEU at any time. That time finally turned out to be July 17 1944 when the establishment moved south to Aston Down in Gloucestershire to join up with a detachment which had made a much more meandering trip through England over two months earlier.

Flying days were at an end but Annan still ensured that the RAF would keep the airfield in business for a long while. On August 17 No 14 MU moved in for ground storage duties. No 249 MU later formed to store explosives at Maintenance Command's new sub-site on May 16 1945, unusually before the unit did so at parent base Great Orton on June 5, and also became a durable resident. Annan closely co-operated with this airfield over the border, 70 tons of incendiaries having to be sent there in January 1947 because local civil authorities wanted to reopen a public road which crossed a runway. In the same year squatters put an additional slight strain on safety considerations but Nos 14 and 249 MUs carried on until the latter disbanded in August 1952.

On July 1 1955 Annan ceased being an inactive station. No 14 MU nevertheless assumed parenting responsibilities again from September 1 1956, although this time only in a liaison capacity, a procedure as worth mentioning as the Loan I and II scheme which affected Angle. By the 1950s disused airfields had become more worthy of that description, still inactive but also viewed as surplus and frequently used by other elements such as the Ministry of Agriculture, Fisheries and Food. Parenting stations now looked after (or neglected) their silenced friends even less, yet still had an albeit slight say in developments affecting any site: world tension and the chances of another global conflict demanded that right. This was the case with Annan until No 14 MU was relieved of parenting duties on April 1 1958. Hopes of a return to flying duties had gone but just as spectacular a future beckoned as a consolation prize.

Only a transient Boston light bomber squadron from Great Massingham in Norfolk disturbed the fighter-trainers at Annan during 1942-44: now no fixed-wing aircraft can possibly hope to land. Plans revealed for nuclear use in the second half of 1955 forced much of this airfield to be cleared from November by a Peterborough-based construction company before the power station opened on May 2 1959. Annan was equipped with two runways at right angles to one another but only a few stretches remain with some perimeter track. One curious feature was a total of 74 hardstandings, peculiarly high for an RAF site and even half as much again as the average USAAF heavy bomber station. A handful of support buildings and one T1 have also kept going: two more of these hangars existed in Annan's heyday, as did eight Blisters.

You are not recommended to view Annan too closely, for the atomic authorities operate their own police force. These people might get the wrong impression if they see someone equipped with binoculars and a camera. But one airfield's ultimate sacrifice to help keep Britain running from day to day has proved a totally worthwhile exercise. Our airfields have completely revolutionised society for the benefit of all. They might not be pretty but, the same as atomic facilities, they are awesomely effective. The authorities should at the very least reciprocate by officially acknowledging Annan. 85/NY215698. 3 miles NE of town.

Ansty, Warwickshire

Alternative Name: Coventry
Another disused British airfield to have created tremendous socially benevolent impact is Ansty near Coventry. Where it differs from Annan is in sheer durability during flying days.

A large field directly south of Ansty village was developed in the mid-1930s for use as a training airfield. Operator would be Air Service Training Limited, the Armstrong Whitworth (later Hawker Siddeley) subsidiary based at Hamble on the south coast of England. Good business sense prevailed as Armstrong Whitworth possessed aircraft construction works not far away at Whitley, soon to be superseded by a larger factory airfield at Baginton. Flying instruction also offered great potential for making money in this age of militarisation, though, hence why Ansty appeared.

From January 6 1936 No 9 Elementary and Reserve Flying Training School fulfilled the intentions of AST Limited. World War Two resulted in the E&RFTS becoming an EFTS, Avro Cadet biplanes surviving in service until Tiger Moths ousted them during 1941/42. A second visitor at Ansty had been No 4 Air Observers Navigation School but its Ansons moved to Watchfield in Oxfordshire in July 1940. This training unit had still stayed around long enough to experience an early taste of air attack when enemy raiders dropped several bombs in Ansty's direction on June 25. Most of these devices fortunately missed and caused no damage bar blowing out a few windows, this being the one and only time Luftwaffe aircraft seriously bothered the airfield.

THE AIRFIELDS OF BRITAIN

Eight Blisters dotted around the perimeter assisted both main hangars installed at Ansty as World War Two progressed. As the conflict lengthened, AST Limited became increasingly aware of a new rival for space, car producer Standard Motors which ran a Ministry of Aircraft Production shadow factory in Coventry to boost output. To this convenient airfield came 750 Airspeed Oxford trainers for final assembly and flight testing before Standard undertook work on Mosquitoes from 1943. Suddenly No 9 EFTS disbanded on March 31 1944 and its base passed to MAP control as manufacture of the advanced de Havilland type became more important than pilot instruction. Ansty received a hard runway to replace grass ones which could not have coped for long with the strain.

Standard Motors had built 1,066 Mosquitoes by Christmas 1945. An excellent effort, but as early as the previous February the shadow factory proposed to switch back to making cars. Although Ansty was relegated to being an interim Ministry of Supply equipment store, and motor cycle racing occurred for the first two years after World War Two, promisingly fresh aviation-related jobs were in the offing. While most of these future duties would not involve aircraft taking off or landing as such, they established a solid foundation that has continued right up until the present.

The Bristol company's Aero-Engine Department led the way in 1946 by founding a rocket engine division at Ansty. A special test house was created to allow the first firing to take place in November 1947. In this year Armstrong Whitworth's engine arm Armstrong Siddeley Motors Ltd began thinking of constructing a separate jet engine compressor testing plant on seeing its great rival at work and started building facilities too during 1948 as the concern's Parkside works did not have enough room. Ansty was coming back into popularity without doubt when AST Limited then returned in 1949 to open a civil aeronautical engineering school.

Bigger than ever events than of late happened at the site in 1951. Armstrong Siddeley's jet area came into operation, the school moved to Hamble, but best news of all was that Ansty held aircraft once more. As Armstrong Siddeley did not require the whole airfield, AST Limited opened No 2 Basic Flying Training School on March 17, instruction beginning on the 27th. After a slightly shaky start when the revived wartime runway became unserviceable in April, the unit and its 31 de Havilland Canada Chipmunk monoplanes took full advantage of the initial post-war flying training boom in Britain. Government penny-pinching soon however threatened and

95

THE AIRFIELDS OF BRITAIN: VOLUME 1

No 2 Basic FTS stopped recording daily activities on February 23 1953 shortly before disbandment. No 9 MU at Cosford in Shropshire was left to deal with the Chipmunks.

AST Limited had been forced to quit unwillingly for a second time within ten years. Perhaps aircraft production needs could be accepted: questionable economic measures could not. A Coventry weekly newspaper recalled torrid earlier aviation history by describing the 1950s military reserve school closures as '... a 1953 Geddes axe.' Aircraft departed again but Ansty survived as Armstrong Siddeley Motors Ltd, also known for building cars, sent over part of its works from constantly overtaxed Parkside in June 1953, vehicles being tested at and conveyed from the abruptly silenced airfield. The establishing of both a rocket division in 1954, which brought engine noise complaints in June 1955, and a new engineering centre during 1957/58 showed how the company was determined not to leave Ansty underemployed as before.

Today's situation stems from when Armstrong Siddeley Motors and Bristol Aero-Engines Limiteds formed into Bristol Siddeley Engines Limited in 1958. Having merged with Hawker Siddeley the following year, this new firm became a subsidiary of Rolls-Royce from October 1966, which consolidated all rocket activities at Ansty in 1967 and opened a major engine noise research facility. Design, development and production duties have since continued not only on jet engines for aircraft but gas turbines for ships and industry at what has become Rolls-Royce's Industrial and Marine Division.

Of the original Ansty, there is comparatively little left. Many major buildings were demolished after World War Two to make way for testing equipment but the runway is still there beside the M6 motorway. If not an active airfield any more, Ansty's influence lives on, and countless military personnel who served aboard RAF aircraft such as the Tornado or Royal Navy ships powered by exceptionally reliable Rolls-Royce engines owe it a round of thanks for the Gulf War being so phenomenally successful. So give three cheers for this unknown winner, in other words a typical British airfield.

140/SP403814. 8 miles E of Coventry. Turn first left off A427 past Coombe Countryside Park, site 1½ miles further on alongside minor road.

Anthorn, Cumbria

Alternative Names: Cardurnock, Solway House

THE AIRFIELDS OF BRITAIN

Annan and Ansty might still make their marks upon the landscape, but one disused airfield not all that far away from the former place hammers them into insignificance in this respect. Even in death, Anthorn is still extremely prominent as thirteen large aerials used for secretive military communications work today dominate this windswept site and can be seen from many miles around: one can hardly call them obscure.

Anthorn has vague beginnings. Within the later airfield's boundary lay Cardurnock or Solway House, a little known World War One Day Landing Ground acting as a link point for RFC aircraft travelling between north-west England and southern Scotland. It is not impossible that planners remembered this long-forgotten airfield in use by February 1918 and then decided to construct Anthorn. Stranger things have happened to our airfields.

Put into service on September 7 1944 as HMS *Nuthatch,* Anthorn's main role was to prepare FAA aircraft for operational needs. Navy types needed various structural additions or modifications for whatever policy required at their eventual operating bases. The first and main resident here became No 1 Aircraft Receipt and Dispatch Unit, which carried out the above tasks plus also tested and ferried aircraft; a Ferry Pool which post-war became a Flight and then a Pool again remained on hand for this last job. Hangarage had to be fairly considerable to allow No 1 ARDU to function efficiently and consisted of thirteen Pentads and 21 smaller Mainhills, these buildings being used for aircraft storage, servicing, equipping and erecting.

FAA airfields generally endured a rough deal during World War Two because of building preference towards the RAF. Its late entrance into the conflict and important nationwide duty ensured that Anthorn met better luck than most, and the ARDU soldiered on for years afterwards, easily outlasting No 2 ARDU at Culham in Oxfordshire. By then aircraft coming and going for essential naval adjustment had steadily graduated in technological advancement from piston-engined American-built Grumman Hellcat fighters among others; although Hawker Sea Fury final generation propeller driven fighters and early jet types such as the company's Sea Hawk design often visited, the airfield mainly dealt with anti-submarine machines later on. Turboprop-engined Fairey Gannets became common sights once Aldermaston's most famous one-off user entered FAA service during the mid-1950s.

A few squadrons stayed post-war at Anthorn. The only

THE AIRFIELDS OF BRITAIN: VOLUME 1

sustainable one was No 772, an FRU present from May 1946 with detachments at Andreas and subsequently Jurby after Andreas closed until going to Arbroath in June 1947. None of them dislodged the airfield's ARDU but those nasty 1950s defence cuts helped kill off about as many FAA bases as RAF ones. The 1958/59 Navy Estimates announced on February 18 1958 devastated our airfields and led to such greats as Donibristle, Ford and Worthy Down among others shutting down. This Government action was irrelevant to Anthorn, for it had fallen victim to cuts in the summer of 1956, and only ten days of activity now remained before being 'paid off' on February 28 1958. Put on to a C&M level on March 31, final abandonment came in November 1959.

The aerials of today date from the early 1960s when construction of a specialised radio transmission station started in 1961. It opened three years later and is especially useful for communicating with nuclear submarines – the naval link lives on.

Little can be seen of Anthorn from the days when this place served as an airfield. Traces are limited to sections of three runways – apparently the RAF was originally meant to be here during initial planning phases – and perimeter track, together with a number of firing butts for armament testing. In February 1958 the married quarters were made available for civilian use but the local council rejected this generous offer. The dwelling which gave the old Cardurnock's alternative title and stood in the south-west corner of Anthorn has gone, though one permanent memento will always be the redirected minor road between Anthorn and Cardurnock hamlets. To reach either place you have to travel close to the sea: the previous public right of way was more direct and cut through the centre of Anthorn's landing area-to-be.

These poor remains and colossal aerials tend to overpower the onlooker, making most passers-by oblivious of how important Anthorn once used to be when it accommodated aircraft. Peacetime Navy-organised open days attracted remarkably good crowds despite this airfield being in the middle of nowhere. Visitors probably first had to consult an atlas to see where Anthorn stood: now all a hack navigator has to do is go west of Carlisle and follow the skyline. Perhaps flying no longer occurs but, if anything, this place's importance has increased even more.

85/NY180580. 4 miles NW of Kirkbride, W of hamlet.

Anwick, Lincolnshire

Alternative Name: Sleaford
No 38 Squadron gained a landing ground at Anwick in October 1916, shortly after it had been approved for requisition on September 5. A month or so between a site's securement and readiness was about normal for Home Defence landing grounds to allow military engineers to carry out what usually proved fairly minor clearance and preparatory work.

This L-shaped stretch of agriculture with roughly north-south and east-west runs was later employed by No 90 Squadron, another HD unit, and in use by November 1918. Nothing has lasted to mark this area once available to fighters such as Royal Aircraft Factory BE2 and FE2 variants or Avro 504Ks as is usual with Great War landing grounds.
121/TF110515. 5 miles NE of Sleaford, NW of village.

Appledram, West Sussex

Many landing grounds dating from World War Two have disappeared as much into history as their earlier counterparts like Anwick. Prime examples are the Advanced Landing Grounds which became far more offensive and versatile than the improvised World War One fields created to aid airmen in trouble. Not surprisingly, there is no trace of Appledram, an ALG in 1943 and 1944. This farmland converted into a temporary airfield was eventually given two Sommerfeld Track metal runways and four Blisters – tents otherwise sufficed.

Typhoons of Nos 175, 181 and 182 Squadrons arrived at Appledram from Lasham in Hampshire on June 2 1943 and left at the beginning of July for either Lydd II or New Romney II. Both of these Kentish ALGs ironically failed to see operational use during 1944 but Appledram had easily passed its short intensive course of front line service and airfield suitability.

The winter of 1943/44 dragged past while this site lay quiet as in line with every other ALG, only disturbed by airfield construction parties making general improvements. From the spring of 1944 Appledram saw several Spitfire squadrons present for fighter-bomber duties. Nos 310, 312 and 313 all appeared on April 3/4 and kept busy right past D-Day. When they left for Tangmere in late June, another Wing made use of Appledram between June 28 and July 16; Nos 302, 308 and 317 Squadrons had come from Chailey in east Sussex. Some fighter-bomber operations continued to be successfully flown but, after this Spitfire Wing moved to Ford, Appledram fell silent. Authority for derequision was given in November.

While Appledram may be no more, here is a word of warning should you decide to visit. The locals prefer to call their village Apuldram these days. At least this is entirely intentional unlike Ansty, frequently misspelt as Anstey in various publications, but do not be confused all the same!

No-one still ought to be ever in any doubt as to the stunning short-term effectiveness of this particular airfield. Nor are they allowed to as a museum by the village opened well over 40 years after Appledram closed to relate its story and that of the D-Day period in general. Even more amazingly for an airfield with a blink-and-miss lifetime, a memorial garden has been installed to remember the ALG and everyone who served there: a superb move. Only four and a half months of activity – but one can safely wager that the airfield achieved a damn sight more in that time than its village namesake did in centuries. All right, so Appledram used to be a major salt producing centre. So what?

197/SU840018. SW of Chichester, on W side of A286 before Chichester Canal.

Appleton Wiske, North Yorkshire

Appleton Wiske was a Home Defence landing ground used during the second half of World War One which has since been given back to agriculture in conjunction with Anwick and Appledram. Fighters of No 76 Squadron became able to employ the site shortly after approval for requisition on January 16 1917. The western boundary formed the road connecting Appleton Wiske and Picton villages, while the landing area tapered off in a stepped fashion towards the east.

Still active at the Armistice of November 1918, the RAF later relinquished Appleton Wiske in August 1919. Airfield associations had not quite ended, for requisition orders unexpectedly once again occurred on December 10 1942 – the same date, incidentally, as those for Appledram and most other ALGs – when this Yorkshire spot became earmarked as a heavy bomber station. No building or aircraft use however resulted: no doubt the War Agricultural Executive Committee opposed the idea of taking away more alleged vital farmland for another of these absolutely disgraceful airfields.

In a bizarre millions-to-one coincidence that could only happen in Britain, a proposed SLG in Wales named Picton was also dropped during World War Two. Appleton Wiske may have lost out too but thankfully hundreds of its friends did not.

93/NZ402062. E of Scotch Corner and 10 miles E of Croft Autodrome. Turn left off A167 going S at Great Smeaton, 1½ miles NE of Appleton Wiske village, to right of minor road before fork.

Arbroath, Tayside

A Scottish east coast town famous for fish and a surely unbeatable football world record could — and should — also be noted for a nearby airfield. Arbroath or HMS *Condor*, commissioned by the Royal Navy on June 19 1940, was an important FAA base that has survived extremely well for Royal Marines use.

Nos 751, 753 and 754 Squadrons arrived at Arbroath from bomb-shattered Ford and Lee-on-Solent on the south coast of England in late summer 1940 to form up as No 2 Observers School. Two of these units lasted into 1944, by which time other squadrons had joined this combined force, while No 753 Squadron resided here up to the autumn of 1945. Another survivor was No 783 Squadron, not employed for observational training but ASV radar instruction and flying a diversity of aircraft like Arbroath's other main occupants during a six year stay at this airfield from 1941 to 1947.

Additional squadrons present in World War Two meant Arbroath was never idle. Naval airfields are first and foremost static aircraft carriers, and operationally subservient to these ships in that respect, but pilots have always discovered there is a lot more to serving aboard a 'flat-top' than touching down or taking off. Aerodrome Dummy Deck Landing (ADDL) instruction at airfields therefore simulated the layouts and restricted conditions of aircraft carriers before pupils progressed to deck landing training on real vessels. Arbroath added this duty to its other ones but by mid-war looked strained to breaking-point and required somewhere else to take away some dwelling aircraft. Help was literally close at hand when new FAA station East Haven opened in 1943, the deck landing units mainly moving down the coast to this airfield near Carnoustie.

THE AIRFIELDS OF BRITAIN: VOLUME 1

Just because a Navy base only acted in a training capacity did not prohibit front line aircraft from using it. Arbroath proved no different as operational squadrons in the 800-class category often passed by as well, not knowing where on earth they would stop at next. No 1771 Squadron's Firefly fighters spent a couple of days in Angus during March 1945 — and then immediately proceeded to Australia aboard an aircraft carrier for active service in the Pacific. Most unusual visitors for this or any other FAA station had to be the RAF Spitfires of No 65 Squadron, staying from December 29 1942 to January 3 1943 as preparation for special aircraft carrier deck landing training conducted from Machrihanish in Kintyre.

Although Swordfish tended to predominate at Arbroath in wartime, aircraft spotters would have been glued to their binoculars with the great assortment of designs on view had they been allowed such an opportunity. Everything from elderly Blackburn Shark biplanes of pre-war vintage to even the odd Wellington, a big aircraft for a reasonably small site, made good use of this airfield. The most invaluable type seen surely had to be the Hawker Sea Hurricane, which first entered FAA circles with No 880 Squadron in March 1941 and became a vast improvement upon previous shipborne fighter equipment.

For sheer flamboyant variety, no unit could hope to match No 778 Squadron. This element evaluated a small army of new aircraft and variants for possible future FAA service. Most of them succeeded but inevitably there were failures or mediocre types only thought worthwhile for lesser duties, such as the American Vought-Sikorsky Chesapeake dive bomber which suffered from having too long a take-off run for smaller British aircraft carriers. Undistinguished use ashore with FRUs and training squadrons had to do until this single-engined monoplane's FAA career petered out in 1943/44. No 778 Squadron spent two periods at Arbroath, from July 1940 to March 1943 and again from August 1944 for another twelve months, between times staying at Crail in Fife as Arbroath became too busy.

Squadrons continued to appear in the years following World War Two but from 1945 Arbroath possessed a new primary role as an air engineering school. Officially closed to flying once the radar testing Fireflies of No 703A Flight left on June 30 1954, the airfield increasingly turned into a navalised Andover, acting as headquarters for FAA aircraft supply administration and harmonising the work of Aircraft Repair Yards, Holding Stations and Sections. Mechanical training became another ground role after Bramcote in

THE AIRFIELDS OF BRITAIN

Warwickshire closed during 1958. A Supermarine Walrus now installed in the FAA Museum at Yeovilton also underwent years of painstaking restoration at Arbroath in the 1960s once reclaimed from dereliction at Thame in Buckinghamshire.

A proposal made in 1960 that Arbroath become an airport for Dundee not entirely surprisingly remained one scheme never taken up with any enthusiasm. The base was technically shut in an aerial capacity, about twenty miles from the city, and civil aviation does not as a general rule fit in comfortably at a service airfield. Dan-Air's Douglas DC-3 airliner service therefore only lasted during 1961/62 but allowed Arbroath to become a recognised joint military/civil active airfield from then until 1970. Although occasional flying displays took place, gliders mainly caught the eye, and have not budged since the Royal Naval Gliding and Soaring Association Condor GC first formed in 1947. No 662 Volunteer GS has been around for many years, having moved from Edzell in 1957, while more gliders of a civilian rather than Air Training Corps nature belonged to the Angus GC. This club formed in 1970 but decided in 1993 to go to a more inland site.

Our airfields have an uncanny knack of producing cyclical unit movements. So it was with Arbroath when the Air Engineering School totally moved out to Lee-on-Solent in September 1970, exactly 30 years after Nos 753 and 754 Squadrons had hurried north to further avoid the Luftwaffe. Arbroath ran down on all fronts in that year and finally closed as an FAA base in March 1971 but instantly accommodated No 45 Royal Marine Commando, supported by helicopters of the Montforterbeek Flight which assist the Marines on exercises in Norway. The town has enjoyed the accompanying economic and employment benefits to this day.

As with most of Britain's other military airfields, either active or closed to flying, Arbroath (now fittingly known as Condor Barracks) is not too easy to view. You can see from a distance a large control tower and considerable assortment of hangars. There existed in World War Two nine Bellmans, a hangar of no recognised design with a strongly gabled roof measuring 250 by 110 feet, 82 small Dutch Barn storage buildings to mix in with major dispersals on Arbroath's north side and two ½ Bellmans with dimensions of 66x78x27 feet each. Hangars known as ½T2s became relatively common on Hebridean airfields but this last design was a real rarity. Most of these larger structures survive, as do three T2s and also a Blister for glider use. The complete tracks are somewhat odd in themselves as five runways can be counted instead of the usual four for a naval airfield; this fifth stretch was specially

103

created for ADDL purposes.

Despite seeing few aircraft these days, Arbroath carries on with its busy life and thoroughly deserves this excellent state of preservation. Tawdry travel books naturally disregard such meritoriousness and stick to 'smokies' and freak sporting results. Pap rules, OK.

54/NO623435. NW of town by A933.

Ashbourne, Derbyshire

This idea of airfield disassociation as personified by·Arbroath can be found all over Britain. Most people link Derbyshire market town Ashbourne with mineral water or a wild free-for-all football match held every Shrove Tuesday. Few remember an airfield to the east of the same name which helped in the buildup to D-Day.

There was a World War One Home Defence landing ground south-west of Ashbourne at Roston but the average local probably only saw his or her first aircraft when an Avro 504K belonging to the Berkshire Aviation Company appeared in the area during November 1921. Two thousand people watching on the Sunday of the week in which this biplane gave joy-rides certainly bore out that assumption. Bad weather – a significant factor in future activities – still could not stop 86 individuals from taking a pleasure flight.

The first unit to be based here after Ashbourne opened as planned on June 12 1942 as a military airfield was No 81 OTU, formed on July 10 of that year. When this Wellington establishment moved to Whitchurch Heath (later renamed Tilstock) in Shropshire on September 1, all was quiet for a month until No 42 OTU came from Andover on October 26. This became Ashbourne's major unit and remained at the airfield up to disbandment on March 20 1945.

A policy change during 1943 from army co-operation to airborne forces instruction resulted in tricycle undercarriage Armstrong Whitworth Albemarles taking over from Blenheims and Whitleys as the main aircraft types on view. Facilities were also available to trainees at Darley Moor, Ashbourne's satellite two and a half miles south-west which has since faded even more into history. Constant training at the parent eventually took its toll as the overworked main runway had to be resurfaced in 1944 between September 25 and October 9 by burning off wood chippings used for camouflage and replacing them with asphalt.

THE AIRFIELDS OF BRITAIN

D-Day and Arnhem became the collective peak of airborne forces diligence as paratroopers were rapidly ferried across into occupied Europe. All the unsung preparatory groundwork Ashbourne and fellow aides had carried out could not be faulted. But RAF squadrons employed on these tasks at operational airfields in the Midlands, then East Anglia after Arnhem for range reasons, soon discovered with equal speed how their specialised services were little further needed. Using front line transports as temporary bombers to raid German targets virtually blind as Bomber Command did in earlier wartime days hinted at desperation and forced the end for airborne forces training elements such as No 42 OTU. Already by September 1944 a move south had looked a realistic possibility.

Its non-operational home fared no better afterwards. Military flying ceased when the OTU closed and Ashbourne passed next day on March 21 1945 to the control of Flying Training Command in the hope of installing a pilot training school here. This idea quickly proved abortive, though, and another administrative change occurred on May 28 as Maintenance Command took charge. By July No 28 MU, based at an RAF ground station south of Buxton named Harpur Hill, looked after 5,600 tons of bombs at the site.

The MU used Ashbourne into the 1950s. A removal policy became evident as munitions were taken to Cairnryan near Stranraer in south-west Scotland and dumped from ships out at sea. Once cleared of bombs, Ashbourne closed on August 23 1954, although the land was not given up until after No 21 MU – Abbots Bromley's old guardian – had gained parenting control once No 28 MU disbanded in 1960. At one point the site was apparently briefly considered as the possible future East Midlands Airport but weather patterns soon put an end to that idea. A savage downhill drop into Ashbourne town and faint chance of a distressed airliner disintegrating over houses below Lockerbie-style may have contributed to planners saying no as well.

Years crept by as the usual gratuitous destruction left this airfield with few support facilities. After the normal clearance work came the equally widespread lack of appreciation as local objections stopped parachuting activities in the 1970s. Considerable publicity was given to a farcical incident in October 1975 when a member of the Peak Sky Diving Club slipped on the wheel strut of a Cessna 182 while attempting his first jump and became stuck. His reserve parachute deployed, dragged him from his position and spun the light aircraft upside down, putting it into a spiralling stall from

2,000 feet until landing inverted on Ashbourne. It was thanks only to that opened parachute which slowed the aircraft's descent and a fortunately near-empty fuel supply both the young would-be jumper and three others aboard miraculously escaped with their lives.

The flying fraternity did not give up easily. In moved the Burton and Derby GC as an emergency measure in 1977 after being thrown out of Derbyshire airfield compatriot Church Broughton. But again little flying was achieved, forcing the club away to Marchington in 1979.

However, changing times and attitudes towards the merits of our disused airfields have seen an industrial estate appear from the early 1970s. Ashbourne's control tower is employed as offices, the walk-round balcony being removed in August 1991 during renovation and extension of the building, and three out of four T2s survive. The three runways are virtually complete and perimeter track too to a lesser extent. Items such as Blenheim Road help to relate past events; indeed, to call this area the Ashbourne Airfield Industrial Estate is about as good an honour as one can get.

This was one airfield which did not stand a great chance of returning to major flying. Ashbourne lay in a fairly remote area often shrouded in fog. Its poor weather record must have played a big part in the absence of 'lodger' units as at most other RAF training airfields, but the nearby town's healthy and sporty folk now recognise Ashbourne's true value. 128/SK198455. 1 mile SE of town by A52. Minor road crosses S edge of airfield.

Ashford, Kent

Alternative Name: Great Chart
Both the RAF and USAAF used an ALG at Ashford, which accounted for two Sommerfeld Track, then PSP runways and virtually nothing more. Approval for requisition came on December 10 1942 as at Appledram further along the English south coast.

A Canadian ordnance depot existed at Ashford in World War One: Magazine Road in the town acknowledges this historical fact. It was therefore fitting that RCAF fighter-reconnaissance Mustangs of Nos 414 and 430 Squadrons first stayed at the ALG between August and October 1943, No 414 tending to suffer at the hands of Luftwaffe fighters. Once these units had gone, Spitfires of Nos 65 and 122 Squadrons resided during October 5-15.

Winter had passed by when Republic P-47s of the 406th FG arrived in early April 1944. The south of England ALGs lost little time in gearing up for action again after their enforced climatic break and Ashford's Thunderbolts soon became busy over enemy territory in a fighter-bomber role for which the 'Jug' was well suited.

Close support sorties from the ALG continued at a hectic pace up to July 27. On that day, the Americans moved to France and Ashford gradually became farmland again, a good job done. The town whose name it bore resumed a feeble link with aviation when British airfield superstar Lympne was renamed Ashford Airport in the late 1960s but hardly anything now marks this short-lived World War Two site. Look hard, extremely hard, and you might just spot an odd piece of fencing made out of old metal runway sections. A camping area sometimes occupies the north side.

The alternative title of Great Chart mainly stems from yet another case of civilians mistakenly using a different name for their local airfield, though No 653 Squadron bewildered everybody in the late summer of 1943. During August and September this AOP Auster unit operated from a separate Great Chart while on exercises away from Penshurst. Northwest of the ALG on the other side of a railway line, this competitor lasted even less time than Ashford.

189/TQ971405. SW of town by A28. Turn left for Stubb's Cross, road junction being N side of airfield.

Ashingdon I and II, Essex

Alternative Names: Canute Air Park (for II), Rochford (for I)

Ashingdon is an historical paradox. Known in ancient times as Assandun, here a battle of great future importance was fought in 1016 when Canute beat Edmund Ironside. Yet no-one knows where the contest occurred, unlike the sites of two much more recent airfields which conversely have comparatively little to their pasts.

Before Rochford's revival as an airfield, the Southend Flying Club had stayed in the nearby Ashingdon area since December 1931. This restricted field was also referred to as Rochford, which must have led to some confusion similar to Ashford and Great Chart, but more north and already a landmark as once being a racecourse in the 1920s. Southend-on-Sea Flying Services Ltd later mounted a ferry service to

THE AIRFIELDS OF BRITAIN: VOLUME 1

Rochester in Kent during the summer of 1934, as well as air taxi flights.

When the original Rochford prepared to officially open as a municipal airport in 1935, everyone made ready to evacuate Ashingdon. The Southend Flying Club took charge of its new facilities on March 25 and sold the old clubhouse to the Bata Shoe Company of Tilbury for use as a sports pavilion. Housing threatened the new recreation field but in October the Aero-8 Flying Club formed to operate the Pou-du-Ciel or 'Flying Flea' homebuilt aircraft designed by Frenchman Henri Mignet at a different site. The exact location of Ashingdon mark two is a mystery, although we can narrow down the search as this second airfield is known to have stood by the more southerly of two minor roads running towards the village of Canewdon, making an area near Ashingdon village look the most likely target. V.N. Dickinson became the organisation's instructor after variable levels of previous success in civil aviation, ranging from his days as chief pilot of the Manchester Aviation Company to more recent failure in trying to establish an airfield at St Albans in Hertfordshire.

Fleamania soon caught on in this country as abroad because of the tiny aircraft's low cost, simple construction and seemingly easy flying capabilities. Britain's first rally of this nature was held at the by now aptly-named Canute Air Park on April 6 1936. Five thousand Bank Holiday visitors watched with growing impatience as seven Poux stood on show but only two flew. This event, not helped by an autogiro going over on its nose, finished with spectators invading the landing area and sounding off their car horns as a mark of protest.

While the Aero-8 Flying Club recovered from this set-back to enjoy better days, reports came in from all over Britain of fatal accidents involving Fleas, mostly attributable to unwise small modifications to individual machines. A joke that the club ought to appoint the local undertaker as vice-president now looked in extremely bad taste. Tests at Farnborough exposed certain defects and led in late September 1936 to an effective ban upon Flea flying in Britain, with no more aircraft being allowed to receive civil registrations. Like other fads, the craze had ended as swiftly as it had started, and forced both the Aero-8 and Ashingdon II to close down not long afterwards.

As said before, these otherwise insignificant little airfields would not have held out for much longer due to their sizes – not forgetting World War Two. Now only housing is evident at the first site, and farmland at what we presume to be the second one. But at least Ashingdon I can be credited with

getting today's Southend Airport back on its feet after post-Great War annihilation.
(I) 178/TQ874912. 4 miles N of Southend, on N side of Rochford.
(II) 178/TQ873929 (probable position). 1½ miles N of Rochford, immediately to E of Ashingdon village.

Ashington, Northumberland

Similarly empty farmland marks this World War One Home Defence Flight Station in north-east England. Given the go-ahead on July 21 1916 for development as an airfield, Ashington opened in the autumn for 'C' and then 'B' Flights of No 36 Squadron to fly patrols with various biplane fighter types.

No enemy bombing raids towards the end of World War One allowed the squadron to adopt alternative tasks. One became training as more distant HD airfields from the front line turned into unofficial OTU bases in all but name long before World War Two. FE2bs from Ashington and fellow Flight Station Seaton Carew near Hartlepool also looked out for U-boats from early 1918, Airco DH6s belonging to No 256 Squadron being present as well during that year for *Scarecrow* anti-submarine patrols. Maybe wartime activity here was not the most exciting of any home airfield with no action seen, though Ashington's dogged passive deterrent value remained incalculable. No 36 Squadron later disbanded in unison with several others of its kind in Britain on June 13 1919.

A railway line lay on the west side of this square-shaped field. Support buildings stood in the south-east corner, as did the hangarage of two aeroplane sheds measuring 140 by 65 feet each and a temporary Bessoneau. Yards off from a minor road in this area is a small curious foundation that may well date from the World War One period. Ashington had gone out of RAF service by September 1919 and then quickly disappeared but even by the 1930s local inhabitants still liked to refer to 'their' airfield. Yes, the airfields of Britain have always been a class apart, simply something else.
81/NZ240885. 3 miles NW of town, turn right off A197 on to minor road ¼ mile W of A1068.

Askernish, Western Isles

Alternative Name: South Uist
While the good people of Ashington fondly remembered their

defunct old airfield, other active ones were busy aiding everyday social life and spreading Britain's airfield net into the bargain. One area which greatly benefitted became the Outer Hebrides.

Airliners of Northern and Scottish Airways helped South Uist by flying to a site placed at the island's southern end. First tested in mid-1934 by the ill-fated Midland and Scottish Air Ferries company, flights to Askernish became more frequent during 1935 and a regular route established on January 21 1936. Aircraft came until the outbreak of World War Two but had resumed charter trips because of low demand and their inability to operate little more than at half-load due to the airfield's poor condition. Askernish continued as an RAF landing ground for distressed aircraft in the conflict, according to official maps.

The war brought huge changes to life in these islands. A new road now connected South Uist with its northern equivalent and Benbecula. This last island's small civil airfield had also developed into a recognised RAF base with all the trimmings, so 'Askernish Airport' was really no longer needed, despite being considered for extension with great difficulty because of extremely rough ground and rabbit holes on the sandy landing area shortly before World War Two started. It lay on what is now a golf course, quite close to Askernish House. Again the vastly underestimated power of our airfields can be illustrated in that Loganair apparently considered re-creating an airstrip as recently as the mid-1970s. 22/NF728240. 5½ miles NW of Lochboisdale.

Aston Down, Gloucestershire

Alternative Name: Minchinhampton
Many storage hangars still stand to mark this noted airfield which first opened in World War One not only for a different purpose but with a different name as well.

Minchinhampton served as a home from home for Nos 5 and 6 (Training) Squadrons of the Australian Flying Corps. Both units employed assorted aircraft types of that era to instruct prospective fighter pilots from the first months of 1918. The Australians left Minchinhampton after a year, another year or so passing before the Ministry of Munitions' Disposal Board seized the airfield in 1920.

Every Great War period building had soon been mercilessly removed. Minchinhampton was not the only World War One airfield to suffer such endless eradication, an inexplicable move which showed how politicians and landowners had given no thought at all what to do with our disused airfields. Have times really changed?

Their actions became even more contemptible when Minchinhampton was reselected as an airfield, albeit being known by the better-sounding name of Aston Down. Although reopened during October 1938 as the Munich Crisis receded and intended for aircraft storage duties with No 20 MU in charge, this 'new' site soon found itself additionally acting as a fighter training station once more. No 12 Group Pool formed in August 1939, changing title to No 5 OTU on March 15 1940 and No 55 OTU in November as these units massively multiplied. Fighter, bomber and other OTUs might have arguably arisen over twenty years behind schedule, if recalling Ashington's history, but now were making up for lost time.

Flying activities mirrored events of 1918 to an extent as several aircraft designs remained available for a while until No 55 OTU eventually concentrated upon using Hurricanes. Minchinhampton did not control a satellite either but late on in 1940 Aston Down wanted assistance from a second Gloucestershire airfield. The resulting search reached out north-east towards the county's outer limits and Moreton-in-Marsh was taken on in November. Standing 27 miles away and still under construction, No 55 OTU could not stay long for two more practical reasons as No 21 OTU formed at Moreton with Wellingtons in January 1941, and soon Aston Down would be vacated too. Usworth, a place with which Ashington had extremely strong connections during World War One as the third Flight Station for No 36 Squadron along with Seaton Carew, became No 55 OTU's new home in March 1941.

Another fighter OTU appeared at Aston Down in August. No 52 had been sensibly removed from Magnificent Seven Battle of Britain member Debden and flew so many Spitfires that Chedworth to the north of Cirencester was a necessary and more accessible satellite. The OTU disbanded on August 10 1943, replaced by the Fighter Leaders School from Charmy Down near Bath, but this unit travelled north to Milfield in Northumberland during January 1944. For once Aston Down now saw a front line unit inhabit its airspace: No 4 Squadron's visit was nevertheless deceptive by specifically staying away from main Hertfordshire base Sawbridgeworth from January to March to re-equip with photographic reconnaissance Spitfires and Mosquitoes. Typhoons of No 3 TEU later flew down from Annan on July 17 and kept up training commitments until No 55 OTU, as the unit was by then titled, disbanded on June 14 1945. Chedworth resumed its bridesmaid role in 1944/45 after breaking off to aid other airfields for a year and a half.

All the while No 20 MU had quietly worked away at Aston Down by preparing many aircraft for operational use elsewhere. Not surprisingly with all the fighter training schools present, the unit's speciality became single-engined fighters such as Spitfires. The numbers of aircraft coming to No 20 MU and generally heavy amount of flying packed this airfield with machines, so the introduction of SLGs for MUs enabled a lot of pressure to be lifted from storage bases and their occupants. No 20 MU operated two SLGs in World War Two, of which another site near Cirencester like Chedworth at Overley transpired to be the far more durable.

Maybe Aston Down needed every piece of land available at this time, but clearly still enough existed for the station to claim one top honour in a more unusual area of airfield operation. Unit gardens, those sadly unrecognised areas of territory voluntarily tended by RAF personnel to grow much-needed food, steadily increased as World War Two lengthened. Planning had altered since World War One took the idea to extremes, from limited agricultural duties at active airfields to drastically closing entire Home Defence landing grounds; peacetime between the wars brought abeyance. Now prices per acre rose from £37 in 1941 to £39 in 1942 and £48 both in 1943 and 1944. The year 1945 created another new record as 339 unit gardens on RAF airfields grew £188,700 of food at a price of £51 per acre. And Aston Down could proudly claim to have the RAF's biggest unit garden that year, an impressive 298 acres yielding £6,263 of produce – not that anyone particularly bothered to focus upon this fine achievement.

Surely all those much more prominent aircraft which had spectacularly won World War Two would be infinitely better acknowledged? Tragically, peace meant the breaker's yard instead for thousands of machines; 1,465 aircraft lay in storage at Aston Down by June 1946 alone. This desperate task became No 20 MU's main job until ceasing to exist on September 30 1960 as storage airfields in Britain ran down in strength. Civilianisation of duties here in 1955 had given notice that the MU might not be around for ever.

Other post-war RAF involvement was minimal except for aircraft ferrying. Maintenance Command performed this work from February 1946 since replacing the wartime Air Transport Auxiliary organisation, Transport Command assuming responsibility in June 1952. No 187 Squadron

THE AIRFIELDS OF BRITAIN

formed in February 1953 out of an earlier unit and continued to take aircraft about Britain and abroad up to disbandment in September 1957. Movement levels had still been high enough for the Air Ministry to agree in June 1956 to include traffic lights at the end of Aston Down's main runway to assist both aircraft and general public vehicles.

The marvellous facilities here have enabled Aston Down to never fall out of favour with the authorities or anyone else. During the 1960s the airfield was officially inactive but helped out the Central Flying School as an RLG after being marked down for this purpose as soon as No 20 MU disbanded until shortly before its famous base at Little Rissington closed in 1976. Still aircraft refused to clear out, for recreational civil gliders of the Cotswold GC had settled in at Aston Down by the end of 1967 after transferring from Long Newnton. The club users had to leave their new home in November 1980 when the airfield came up for auction on December 4 but returned in early 1981 as owners in an excellent piece of business. As Aston Down had hosted the National Gliding Championships both in 1961 and 1962, members knew a promising soaring site when they saw one.

This airfield is now mostly used for other forms of storage rather than aircraft as the Ministry of Defence (Procurement Executive) Central Stores Depot. Vehicles and equipment for aviation support duties have been held in prepared states since the mid-1960s. Strange jobs such as noise reduction experiments have also gone on but flying still continues. A lay-by on the north side gives a reasonable view of a small control tower which is now the clubhouse for sailplanes placed alongside in dismantled open storage.

The old Minchinhampton's four Belfasts, two storage sheds and many Bessoneaux have long gone but hordes of hangars remain. Six Bellmans, one C, four Ds, six Es, two Ls, seven Blisters, seventeen Robins and three Super Robins were present in World War Two; three Robin types are evident for farm storage use by a minor road to the south near the village of Cherington. Such enormous separation of these buildings from the main airfield area had to be done to counter any vulnerability from possible Luftwaffe attacks.

So magnificently has about everything survived that it is now impossible to imagine this area of Gloucestershire without the airfield. Aston Down may look as if waiting for another crack at the big time – but successive Governments wisely prefer to keep this place on their books. And no wonder: they would be mad not to.

163/SO912010. 6½ miles W of Cirencester by A419.

Atcham, Shropshire

Most people remembering World War Two think that the Americans entirely encamped in East Anglia. Do they remember this airfield, far removed but surely one of the busiest in its area?

Atcham was solely an RAF station at the beginning and end of a worthy career. Requisitioned in October 1940, construction started almost immediately and the airfield declared more or less complete on opening on August 20 1941. At least that was the opinion stated in the station ORB: a different story revealed itself away from the landing area. Even this part of Atcham needed further attention as rubber chippings still had to be laid on top of all three tarmac runways. Rubber served as a highly useful camouflage aid to tone down the reflection runways created, and only went out of fashion because countries producing this material in the Far East succumbed to Japanese invasion and stopped supplies coming to Britain. Atcham must have been one of the last recipients of rubber.

No 131 Squadron transferred from Tern Hill on September 27 as the first of a few fighter elements under RAF control to fly from Atcham. Its Spitfires moved to Llanbedr in west Wales on February 8 1942, the squadron's ground echelon following on a day later, Nos 74 and 350 Squadrons later using the airfield for short periods on more uneventful defensive duties. Last RAF fighter squadron at Atcham became No 232, which reformed with Spitfires on April 10 and stayed until May, going to Llanbedr as did No 131 Squadron.

The 8th Air Force unexpectedly arrived at Atcham just one month further on. USAAF Fighter Groups were based here at first in order to become battle-ready and familiarise themselves with Britain. Shropshire surely seemed to many a silly area where to train Americans but perhaps there was some psychology involved in employing this part of western England. While this county's northern section is fairly level, it is hilly as a whole. So if Americans could cope with such relatively hazardous geographical conditions, infinitely flatter East Anglia would therefore be a piece of cake to operate from.

America supplied thousands of aircraft to Britain under Lend-Lease terms in World War Two but this bartering did not go all one way as the USAAF greatly admired home-made designs. The Mosquito not surprisingly proved popular, and several hundred Spitfires 'changed sides' after the three American volunteer RAF *Eagle* squadrons present in Britain before America entered fighting in December 1941 had no doubt put in a good word for the type. US pilots initially trained on Spitfires at Atcham, having discarded the P-39s they had brought in following RAF advice about Airacobras and the fighter's unhappy days at Acaster Malbis and Duxford. Eventually a Combat Crew Replacement Center was created, evolving into the 495th Fighter Training Group in December 1943. P-47s now dominated and became common sights, though many accidents occurred, sometimes due to the sheer ages of aircraft involved.

Amid all this hustle and bustle few noticed that the RAF continued to maintain a detachment at Atcham. Visiting aircraft belonged to No 61 OTU from Rednal's satellite Montford Bridge on the other side of Shrewsbury, appearing in a semi-spurious squadron capacity under the *Saracen Scheme* which allowed OTUs to despatch aircraft if any emergency arose. An occasional Spitfire flew across to this slightly more advanced operating base to hunt without success an odd enemy raider until the RAF entirely gave up Atcham in late 1943 before the 495th FTG formed.

When the FTG moved to Cheddington in central England during February 1945, RAF Flying Training Command regained Atcham in mid-March. Instructional units had used the airfield briefly in the past: No 5 SFTS during February 9-28 1942, and its descendant No 5 (P) AFU for night flying in June/July 1944 to allow runway repairs at Condover. This satellite featured again as the AFU had proposed to switch from there to Atcham on April 30 1945 and put Condover on to C&M. The plan was soon officially cancelled, although in reality delayed, for No 5 (P) AFU – still at Tern Hill but a different force as having disbanded and reformed in June – in due course decided to send over aircraft.

Apart from the trainers, there was comparatively limited flying post-war, only part of No 577 Squadron from July 1 1945. The airfield cyclical process came largely true once more as Tern Hill aircraft became about the last as well as first types to fly from Atcham when both No 5 (P) AFU and the AA co-operation detachment left in the spring of 1946; No 577 Squadron's machines flew off on a sortie on April 8 and landed at Hawarden, a supportive ground party leaving by road next day. Their site instantly started life on C&M, closed on October 22, vehicles later standing in storage for some time. In 1952 the War Office returned this inactive airfield to the Air Ministry for Shawbury to parent but was got rid of in January 1958.

One of the airfield's three runways, all incomplete with the perimeter track, is now the B4394 road. The control tower and eight Blisters may have gone but support buildings and three Callender-Hamilton hangars are used as a trading estate. A tragic and yet farcical accident occurred on February 15 1963 when a wall suddenly fell on top of an electricity worker operating in a building and killed him. It could only have happened at an airfield – or was Atcham getting its own back at the anti-disused airfield brigade?

Many years have passed since then but this forgotten American base which quietly helped win World War Two still makes a big mark upon the landscape. By no means is Atcham dead and buried.

126/SJ570102. Turn left for B4394 off A5 7 miles SE of Shrewsbury.

Attlebridge, Norfolk

Numerous turkey houses sit on foundations of the three runways and perimeter track at Attlebridge, an airfield in more accepted American-manned territory and similar to Atcham in once being used by both the RAF and USAAF. These runways had not yet been laid when this East Anglian airfield first opened in 1941, and would not be until the start of 1943.

Transformation of this fairly remote area from farmland to airfield after requisition in July 1940 proved relatively straightforward. Selecting a suitable name must still have given planners cause for concern as two small nearby villages possessed the name Weston as part of their double-barrelled titles. With other sites such as Weston Zoyland in Somerset already active, this posed too much of a risk, so another tiny village called Attlebridge some distance away to the north-east had to do instead. An Army guard arrived on May 31 1941.

Attlebridge's parent was initially Swanton Morley, No 88 Squadron coming from there on August 1. Its Blenheims saw use for anti-shipping attacks but became outclassed and replaced by Bostons. These American bombers were faster and all in all far better aircraft for bombing targets at low level. If anything, No 88 Squadron gained notability for the number of detachments made. Exercises meant trips to

THE AIRFIELDS OF BRITAIN

airfields as far apart as Ford on the English south coast, Long Kesh in Northern Ireland and Winfield in the Scottish borders, these three places alone not exactly renowned as bomber bases.

After the Bostons moved to Oulton on September 29 1942, the USAAF acquired Attlebridge on October 1 and B-26 medium bombers momentarily trained here and at Horsham St Faith, each airfield holding two squadrons. The 319th BG maintained a scanty presence after the Group largely flew off to North Africa in November but the runways were being built and rendered Attlebridge mostly incapable up to the end of March 1943.

No 320 Squadron subsequently positioned Dutch personnel to train on the North American Mitchell, a famous but difficult medium bomber always noted for heavy controls. As with No 88 Squadron's Bostons previously, flying would be at low altitude but this practice had to stop to allow available airspace for the USAAF. No 320 Squadron hence moved to Lasham of current gliding fame on August 30 after a stay of exactly five months. Much shorter residents turned out to be Typhoon fighters of No 247 Squadron, present during August 7-13 for an exercise while temporarily away from their ALG at New Romney II in Kent.

Attlebridge receded to a C&M state on September 7 while going from Fighter to Bomber Commands and effectively closed altogether for rebuilding from October 31, active again in February/March 1944 when the 466th BG moved in. B-24 heavy bombers duly proceeded to maul a large variety of targets to almost the end of World War Two and happily settled at this part of Norfolk. But relations with the local civilian community soured a bit as the result of an incident on December 3 1944. Two drunken American servicemen had stolen rifles from the armoury at Attlebridge to go poaching in the grounds of Honingham Hall, two miles south of the airfield. There they encountered the owner who had heard shooting – and shot him dead. Execution after a court martial in January 1945 of a trouble-making private named Smith showed how life with the Americans was not always a bed of roses.

Public relations soon returned to normal following this unsavoury episode. And it was thankfully only for strategic operational reasons that the 466th BG left in typically fast American style during July 1945, the Group's air echelon having departed even more quickly in mid-June. Attlebridge made an equally swift transition to RAF Maintenance Command and No 231 MU on July 12 to signal the end of its flying life, though a Mustang from Horsham St Faith crash-landed on January 10 1946.

The Army accepted buildings on November 21 1945, more support facilities being offered to the War Office for accommodation purposes in 1946 but MUs mainly prevailed at the site instead. No 94 superseded No 231 from January 27 1948, weaponry storage going on until Attlebridge – now increasingly derelict, weeded and wildlife infested – closed and was made inactive on August 5 1956. Soon afterwards on October 2 No 94 MU let Swanton Morley mind the airfield once again but Duncan Sandys wasted no time putting the boot in by declaring Attlebridge and too many other redundant heroes surplus to RAF needs during the infamous lists published in May 1957. Flying Training Command parenting finished on March 15 1959.

This place is now one of six former airfields owned by a nationally known food producer who appreciates, shall we say, 'booty'. His stated dislike of our disused airfields – they have only created over 2,500 direct jobs for grateful company employees, that's all – has not stopped him from using Attlebridge's now removed control tower as offices in the past. Runway and perimeter track sections straddling minor roads help show how progression up the bomber weight scale resulted in a complex layout with sizeable extensions and winding access roads. A standard Braithwaite water tower also remains but few other structures relate to this period of history. Early wartime hangarage here is a small mystery: by 1943 a single Blister was mentioned as available and nothing else, although two T2s appeared for the USAAF B-24s.

One saving grace is how Attlebridge can be easily inspected unlike many other disused airfields. A pity your first sight is of those profanities alternatively known as broiler houses.
133/TG105151. Between A47 and A1067 roads, NW of Norwich. Depending upon road used, turn right/left shortly after Honingham/Attlebridge villages and head towards Weston Longville. Parts of perimeter track converted into minor roads surround airfield.

Atwick, Humberside

If only the trials and tribulations of World War Two airfields such as Attlebridge had been as well recorded in World War One. British airfield research into these older times is all too often frustrated by a dearth of historical records. Uncertainty,

THE AIRFIELDS OF BRITAIN

poor notetaking, official mismanagement and the blatant destruction of thousands of priceless files leave many questions still to be properly answered about Great War sites. One example is Atwick.

Only spasmodic informational bursts can be found about this landing ground later changed into a full airfield. Active since the summer of 1915 for Royal Naval Air Service aircraft defending Yorkshire, No 33 Squadron at Beverley I controlled Atwick during April-October 1916 when the task of aerially guarding Britain passed to the Royal Flying Corps. No 76 Squadron also used it for Home Defence purposes until 1918. Nobody ever mixed up Atwick with Lincolnshire's Anwick, though a different story could have ensued had fighters been able to carry r/t sets.

Temporary Bessoneau hangars erected in mid-1918 enabled Atwick to take on a more permanent and separate role as DH6s of No 251 Squadron's No 504 Flight started anti-submarine patrols. But along then came the Armistice to close down the airfield, probably in December, and it cannot be easily traced today. The Stream Dyke formed the western boundary of this vague old airfield where only agriculture is apparent.

107/TA180510. 2½ miles N of Hornsea, W of village.

Auldbar, Tayside

Every World War One RNAS/RAF airship station came equipped with at least one sub-station during 1918. Longside was no different, this major site in north-east Scotland having a much more southerly mooring-out base at Auldbar ready by the spring. Here non-rigid airships dispersed for either operational or climatic reasons until the Armistice. Auldbar subsequently quickly disappeared from service circles, still recorded as being active on November 19 but having faded away by January 1919.

Atwick can be described as enigmatic, and Auldbar is the same – for a wholly distinct reason. Where did it exist? A large-scale map held in the Public Record Office which shows every British airfield active during 1918 pinpoints this site as lying north-west of Montrose and about 1¾ miles south of Marykirk, close to the A937 road. This marking however appears to be erroneous, not least as no locality named Auldbar has existed in the vicinity, and the real position seems to be an open field surrounded by woodland south-west of

119

Brechin. Trees were always a common and necessary feature of mooring-out bases to counter the wind and aid camouflage.

Another strange trait is how nearby farms and a castle are spelt Aldbar, while the long defunct railway station a few miles south-west by Balgavies Loch was known as Auldbar Road. Trying to find much information about airship activities in this area is bad enough, but why on earth do people keep changing the spellings of place-names?

54/NO57?56? (not absolutely confirmed but probable position). SW of Brechin, turn second left off B9134 past River South Esk, to left 2 miles down minor road.

Ayr I, Strathclyde

Many early British airfields arose from racecourses. Ayr's first airfield was one, where No 1 School of Aerial Fighting opened for business in September 1917 after one final unofficial horsy event. Planners looking for new sites in south-west Scotland — one of which became Loch Doon, the worst British airfield of all time — had maybe stumbled upon Ayr and thought that if areas such as Yorkshire could provide them with good ready-made places for flying, then why not this one as well?

A policy change to incorporate gunnery training meant that Ayr lost its resident in May 1918. RE8s of Nos 105 and 106 Squadrons flitted through in this month while making their long flight between Andover and Ireland but the racecourse kept quiet until a new establishment formed in July. This was the North Western Area Flying Instructors School, whose biplanes continued to employ Ayr's single Belfast and fifteen Bessoneau hangars to good effect.

Military flying ceased when this second school departed for Redcar near Middlesbrough in January 1919. Racing restarted in April, the airfield having long gone down to List E Disposal Board status by September in time for the course's major Western meeting, but Ayr I never quite lost the flying bug. The Berkshire Aviation Company gave joy-rides in July and August 1921 with spectacular success. Hundreds of passengers were honoured to have as their pilot until he left for Stafford on September 1 the legendary Oscar P. Jones, soon to be co-founder of the Kingwill and Jones Flying Company at Alloa but best remembered (apart from his prominent beard) as a veteran airline captain with Imperial Airways and British Overseas Airways Corporation.

In 1939 British-American Air Services applied for an

airfield operating licence. Officialdom considered the landing area too restricted and prevented this Heston-based taxi/charter transport operator which already made trips to various home courses from touching down at Ayr as well but some flying did occur on racedays for a number of years after World War Two. Aeronautical history remained even more evident as the Great War Belfast could be seen nestling among other buildings. The venerable hangar served as a most useful facility and was a pleasant sight to behold – until October 1989...

On October 5, the author drove into Ayr and passed the Belfast as many times before: all was well. But another sortie on the 21st brought a shock as this priceless historical artefact was nowhere to be seen; even every piece of rubble had disappeared. A letter was hurriedly posted to the racecourse secretary to ask what had happened, and eventually a curt one-line reply came back to say that the Belfast had been demolished. Was there any regret, any explanation or any apology for its passing? Not a bit of it. Further emergency research in Ayr's main library showed how not one newspaper published in the town bothered to feature any mention of one of the worst anti-airfield atrocities seen in recent years.

A quite horrendous supermarket has since sprung up to complete this highly depressing chain of events. Mass media reports suggest that bad business deals have lost all advantages in selling land for vast financial gain. Still the eradication of our premier historical sites goes on. The idea of wood and fabric biplanes taking off from Ayr I is now harder than ever to imagine.

70/NS353220. On E side of town.

Ayr II, Strathclyde

Alternative Name: Heathfield
Similar treatment has been dished out to the second Ayr airfield, if not in such lightning fashion as to its predecessor. Since the mid-1980s in particular a gradual withering has become noticeable. Hardly any buildings survive and the former technical site has modern light industry sitting there instead. Little perimeter track is left, except on the eastern and southern sides, while Ayr II's west side and three runways have suffered badly from steadily encroaching housing. Only the old NW/SE stretch can claim to be intact to any great extent but, the way things are going, for how much longer?

THE AIRFIELDS OF BRITAIN: VOLUME 1

The reason for Ayr II's slow decline into possibly complete oblivion lies extremely close by: Prestwick Airport. Over four years on from when that celebrated airfield officially opened in February 1936 another area of land not far south was requisitioned for development in July 1940. Occasionally called Heathfield after a local suburb, Ayr II opened on April 7 1941. Some personnel provided assistance in capturing Hitler's deputy Rudolf Hess when he parachuted into Scotland near Glasgow during May.

Spitfires of No 602 Squadron may have stayed from April to July 1941 but night fighter units were destined to see action as the Luftwaffe attempted northerly raids. No 141 Squadron proved a long resident at Ayr from April 29 to January 29 1942, going to Acklington, where detachments had already been placed. Boulton Paul Defiants scored several aerial victories, unlike the more advanced Bristol Beaufighters No 141 re-equipped with in mid-1941. Other night fighter squadrons here were No 406 in 1942 with Beaufighters and another Canadian force, No 410, which formed on June 30 1941 to operate Defiants.

Although day and night fighters continued mounting defensive patrols from Ayr II, much quieter skies over Scotland caused by the general withdrawal of Luftwaffe bombers towards Russia meant that this place evolved into an area where future fighter elements could form, rest or train. Being situated alongside a seaside resort with plenty of distractions for off-duty personnel made Ayr a popular posting. Flying Control staff probably did not display such enthusiasm as circuit overlap difficulties with Prestwick always kept them occupied, though incessant vigilance prevented catastrophic mid-air collisions from ever happening. In this way both airfields managed to happily co-exist alongside each other during World War Two, far better than Scampton and Dunholme Lodge in Lincolnshire, another case of a huge star and its little known neighbour which ended in tears for the latter airfield.

Ayr II became a meeting-place for various Spitfire squadrons, notably No 165 which reformed on April 6 1942, but lots of different units appeared to disprove that the airfield only showed a penchant for single-engined day fighters. Army Co-operation Mustangs of No 241 Squadron arrived in May, converting to Hurricanes and moving to North Africa in November. A mixture of visitors followed, including No 652 (AOP) Squadron in the second half of 1943, No 488 Squadron's night fighters and No 169 Squadron,

THE AIRFIELDS OF BRITAIN

reformed on October 1 1943 for eventual intruder duties in East Anglia.

This month became highly significant in Ayr II's life by bringing about the creation of No 14 Armament Practice Camp. More fighter units than ever came along for intensive training as D-Day approached but enough room still existed to allow in a detachment of No 278 Squadron for ASR work during early 1944. January and February saw fresh fighter squadrons form as French airmen transferred from North Africa started flying Spitfires as Nos 329 and 345 Squadrons, while No 440 (RCAF) Squadron arose to use Hurricanes before quickly switching to Typhoons. And all this time No 516 Squadron's varied types gave constant reminders of what was to come by co-operating with naval landing-craft in training for D-Day, having to fly from Ayr late on in 1943 and well into 1944 as construction personnel carried out major runway alterations at their permanent base Dundonald.

No 14 APC was later withdrawn in order for the Royal Navy to commission Ayr II in a totally new role as HMS *Wagtail* during October 1944. Assorted FAA squadrons came to their shore base from aircraft carriers anchored in the Firth of Clyde in usual frenetic fashion. Grumman Hellcats of No 889 Squadron flew up from Woodvale in Lancashire to a carrier on September 10 1945 for proposed Pacific operations: a change of mind then followed, and the fighters transferred again next day to Ayr where they were summarily disbanded on the spot. Second-line squadrons which never used aircraft carriers meanwhile tended to stay a good deal longer at FAA airfields, as the FRU types of No 772 Squadron indicated by lasting from July 1944 to January 1946, going to another Lancashire FAA station at Burscough.

Such marked activity still failed to disguise the fact that Ayr II's future looked increasingly perilous. Not because this was a poor airfield — far from it — or even that peace had returned. But illustrious neighbour Prestwick still remained larger than life as ever, tremendously busy and now designated Britain's second international airport after embryonic Heathrow. Add to this the circuit overlap problem and there would only be one winner. So Ayr had to go, this fact confirmed in Parliament during December 1945, shutting its doors to aircraft after Dutch-manned Fireflies of No 860 Squadron left for Fearn in northern Scotland in mid-April.

Doubt ruled over the next five years as interested parties tried to either help or hinder the airfield. Opinions clashed in July 1946 as the Royal Navy said it wanted to keep Ayr, while a Labour MP claimed the site should be used for housing and development purposes. Periodic statements made in 1947 and 1948 seemed hopeful as Prestwick required runway strengthening and the Ministry of Civil Aviation wanted Ayr as a diversionary airfield; aircraft still diverted from Prestwick by June 1947. Reconstruction started on April 12 1948 but Ayr Town Council bitterly opposed not only Admiralty retention but all flying needs. This limbo situation remained, despite desperate council appeals for land derequisition in November 1949.

Prestwick did not forget its close ally. As the Navy gave up Ayr in the summer of 1951, the USAF decided at the same time to bring back transatlantic aircraft ferrying next door and employed Ayr as a non-flying storage area up to 1957. Just about everyone else let their memories slip, though, and all hopes of a last chance return to holding aircraft were ironically extinguished by Prestwick's 1950s era runway which ran into the northern half of Ayr.

Until not so long ago, you could walk along litter and rubble strewn runways before property developers moved in, people who could have easily erected houses on other surrounding parts of this town. The Ayrshire Transport Training Association is based on the last runway but attempts to start motor sport failed in March 1952 when the Royal Scottish Automobile Club tried ultimately in vain to convert Ayr into a racing circuit. Motor and motor cycle engine testing later caused local residents to protest at noise levels in September 1953.

Few buildings now remain to mark the vandalic eradication of this historic site but notable exceptions hang on around the periphery if you know where to look. Although the total hangarage of four Bellmans and seventeen Blisters have mainly gone from view, one Bellman survives alongside the A77 dual carriageway as a fertiliser holding depot. A second example shifted a short distance away from its original position for other civilian use, became derelict but has partly turned into a wine warehouse. Travel south into the Whitletts housing estate and you encountered the most surprising survivor of all: a dispersed site which served until 1991 as a maternity hospital. Replaced by a brand new establishment built elsewhere, this facility was boarded up and later demolished.

If virtually unnoticed these days, certainly nobody appreciates how this unrecognised star is thought to have revolutionised British airfield construction by dispersing support facilities in more pronounced style than previously

seen on any site. Hundreds of houses stand around but there is a sad emptiness about Ayr II. Yet, as the maternity hospital demonstrated, this airfield which died to feed council and yuppie whims continued to create life too. Where are the visual thanks, if only even two or three roads bearing inappropriate airfield names? Answer? Nothing.
70/NS359243. On NE edge of town, take road past racecourse to roundabout at A77, then turn left for Heathfield and industrial area.

Babdown Farm, Gloucestershire

Alternative Name: Leighterton
Another frenzied burst of disused airfield demolition during the 1980s resulted in Babdown Farm's control tower and support buildings falling for no valid reason whatsoever. Other relics nevertheless carry on and show what can be done with a little imagination.

Babdown Farm was founded thanks to an airfield only a mile south-west. Leighterton had worked with Minchinhampton (Aston Down) in 1918/19 to provide training for Australian airmen, and later accommodated civil light aircraft on a limited scale between both World Wars. It is said that No 9 SFTS at Hullavington operated a forced landing field called Leighterton during 1939/40 but apparently this was the site which became Babdown Farm. One might have expected this new airfield to be named Beverston after a village to the east: a nearby farm on the north-west side donated its title instead. The Ashford and Ashingdon conundrum factors strike home again, and the research minefield becomes even trickier in that the real Leighterton assisted Hullavington during World War Two, briefly as an RLG but mostly as a decoy airfield to draw attacking aircraft away from genuine airfields.

Opened as a true RLG on July 30 1940, Babdown Farm lasted under No 9 SFTS (later No 9 (P) AFU) to March 21 1942. Nocturnal activity had partly saved Hullavington from more Luftwaffe punishment, though it was really Leighterton's job to lead enemy bombs astray. Reopened in August after having improvements made, No 3 FIS became the new unit at Babdown Farm, again based at the parent airfield and staying until September 1943 when replaced from

October 28 by No 15 (P) AFU from Andover. No 1532 Blind Approach Training Flight was also present with distinctive triangular marked Oxfords as standard for these elements. The Airspeed type generally dominated at now self-accounting Babdown Farm throughout the second half of the airfield's life, as single-engined Miles Masters did in the first half. Hurricanes and Hart family biplanes could have been spotted in lesser numbers at this time as well.

Runway difficulties hampered the latter part of Babdown Farm's active career. Heavy rainfall created abnormal soil alteration and restricted flying activities, testing all those advances in soil and sub-soil stabilisation seen during World War Two. The conflict's last winter brought matters to a head, made far worse by landing area problems at the satellites of Castle Combe and Long Newnton. No 15 (P) AFU had experienced a wearisome war after being shunted around such unlikely airfields as Goxhill, Greenham Common and Grove, not to mention Acaster Malbis. Training schedules still had to be met despite this latest crisis, so the AFU took the unusual (though not unprecedented) step of temporarily using an SLG two miles south of Babdown Farm. Down Farm, often rated as Britain's best airfield in its class, became a great short-term help until the spring of 1945.

No sooner had the parent airfield's landing area dried out and normality returned than World War Two ended in Europe. Both No 15 (P) AFU and No 1532 BAT Flight hurriedly disbanded during June, the dreaded shadow of C&M descending over Babdown Farm on the 19th. Administrative control switched to Maintenance Command on July 31 for No 7 MU to make use of the airfield as a vehicle storage site.

The Command agreed with its Flying Training opposite number in February 1946 that No 3 FTS should employ the Standard Beam Approach landing aid facilities at Babdown Farm. SBA ground equipment installations were retained at several airfields for a while after flying had ceased at them, being too valuable to immediately throw away. But the South Cerney school soon left in April for Feltwell in Norfolk to let Nos 7 and 251 MUs have Babdown all to themselves. No 251 only stayed in 1946 until the year ended when No 7 took over the former's duties and vehicles. This MU remained until all equipment had been cleared on September 13 1950, Babdown Farm closing on the 30th.

Turn off from the A4135 today and you have instantly encountered Babdown Farm's perimeter track. Northern and eastern sections act as an access road down to three T1 hangars which give excellent service as a small trading estate. There were also four Blisters here in wartime: one of these buildings has survived too but all three Sommerfeld Track metal runways have not surprisingly vanished.

For all the relative anonymity, runway problems and more recent partial demolition, this is still one disused airfield which has lasted fairly well. Babdown Farm is streets ahead of the two Ayrs and many other sites in that department. But if the author of a book about Gloucestershire had his way, things would be very much different: 'Others (airfields) which were used during the last war — one at Babdown, near Beverston, for instance — are closed and their crumbling buildings and runways form eyesores as do the relics of other wartime sites used for anti-aircraft guns and searchlights.' How dare Babdown Farm and its many friends have won World War Two virtually single-handed...
173/ST847939. W of Tetbury by A4135, 1 mile past Beverston.

Bacton, Norfolk

We have already talked frequently in this book about satellites. Babdown Farm used to be one mid-war before becoming self-accounting and employing others. Alconbury is thought to be our original satellite airfield — but maybe this accolade should be accorded to another East Anglian airfield of much earlier vintage.

RNAS aircraft at Great Yarmouth had a night landing ground available to them at Bacton from the spring of 1915. This site became the famous parent's first sub-site or 'satellite' in all but name, displaying all the quirks of these less handsomely equipped airfields later so common in World War Two. Diligent attempts to attack Zeppelins enjoyed no luck as at many other World War One airfields initially, Bacton airmen actually coming in for criticism during the spring of 1916 for their tactics. An attempted bombing raid by one airship on their home rubbed salt into the wound later that year on September 2/3, the same night as William Leefe Robinson at Sutton's Farm close to London shot down the SL.11.

Another Zeppelin raid on the night of November 27/28 managed to give Bacton the last laugh. Flight Sub-Lieutenant E.L. Pulling took off in a BE2c to engage the LZ.21 over the North Sea and received credit for destroying the airship. Both he and a second pilot had in truth only fired off a few rounds each, the real glory belonging to Flight Lieutenant Egbert Cadbury from fellow Great Yarmouth sub-site Burgh Castle, but this victory totally shut up the faultfinders.

Bacton carried on as a subordinate to Great Yarmouth throughout the remainder of World War One until closing in 1919; the site was under cultivation by September. Not much marked the airfield, apart from a small hangar measuring 66 by 42 feet, and it has since reverted to farmland. In the 1920s and 1930s Bacton was maintained as a private airstrip for two Avro Avian IV biplanes owned during 1929-34 by farmer W. Pat Cubitt. On July 5 1931 a dozen or so aircraft of the Norfolk and Norwich Aero Club at Mousehold landed at this small field, other club members coming by car, and held a beach party in those delightfully eccentric days before rules and regulations swamped aviation altogether.

Today the name of Bacton is associated with a gas terminal which stands less than two miles north-west of the old airfield. Visiting civil helicopters keep a certain link with flying and the North Sea, two causes perhaps our premier satellite tried so hard to defend.

133/TG342325. 4½ miles E of North Walsham by B1150, ¾ mile S of village.

Baginton, Warwickshire

Alternative Name: Coventry

Mainstay of RAF Bomber Command in September 1939 along with the Vickers Wellington was the Armstrong Whitworth Whitley. All 1,814 examples of the latter design emanated from the company, centred at Baginton, Coventry's municipal airport.

Popular legend would have us believe that Baginton opened in the beginning for Armstrong Whitworth's needs during 1936. Not so, for many years before a small air transport firm bearing the odd name of By Air Limited operated a war-surplus Royal Aircraft Factory BE2e, two Airco DH6s and an Armstrong Whitworth FK8 from mid-1919 as one of the numerous commercial concerns which arose after World War One.

Trouble comes in threes, goes the old saying. That homespun maxim undoubtedly applied to By Air Ltd as it lurched from one calamity to the next. The most serious reverse occurred on April 1 1920 when the company received a massive collective fine for contravening the new Air

Three views of Ashbourne. The main runway's south-eastern end *(above)* does not look remarkable but the control tower *(below left)* has a new lease of life now an extension on its right side has been added. Signs at the main entrance meanwhile nicely recognise history *(below right)*.

Pilots of No 122 Squadron pose in front of a Spitfire IX during their short stay at Ashford in October 1943 *(above)* *(RAF Museum)*. The ALG has long become empty again *(below)*.

Old World War One airfield Ashington can still pass for an airfield *(above)*.
Much less certain is this strange foundation alongside the landing area *(below)*.

A Robin hangar trying to hide at Aston Down *(above)*.
(below) For one of Atcham's three runways, now read the B4394 road.

The immensely historic World War One Belfast hangar at Ayr I *(above)*, pictured shortly before its disgraceful demolition in 1989. Ayr's second airfield has fared slightly better. This Bellman *(below)* stores fertiliser.

The scene elsewhere at Ayr II is not so good. A converted maternity hospital *(above)* has also gone, while *(below)* only the NW/SE runway holds out against modern housing. At the far end is installed a driver training school.

Part of the perimeter track at Babdown Farm *(above)*, sadly going nowhere.
(below) Two of Baginton's several Bellmans.

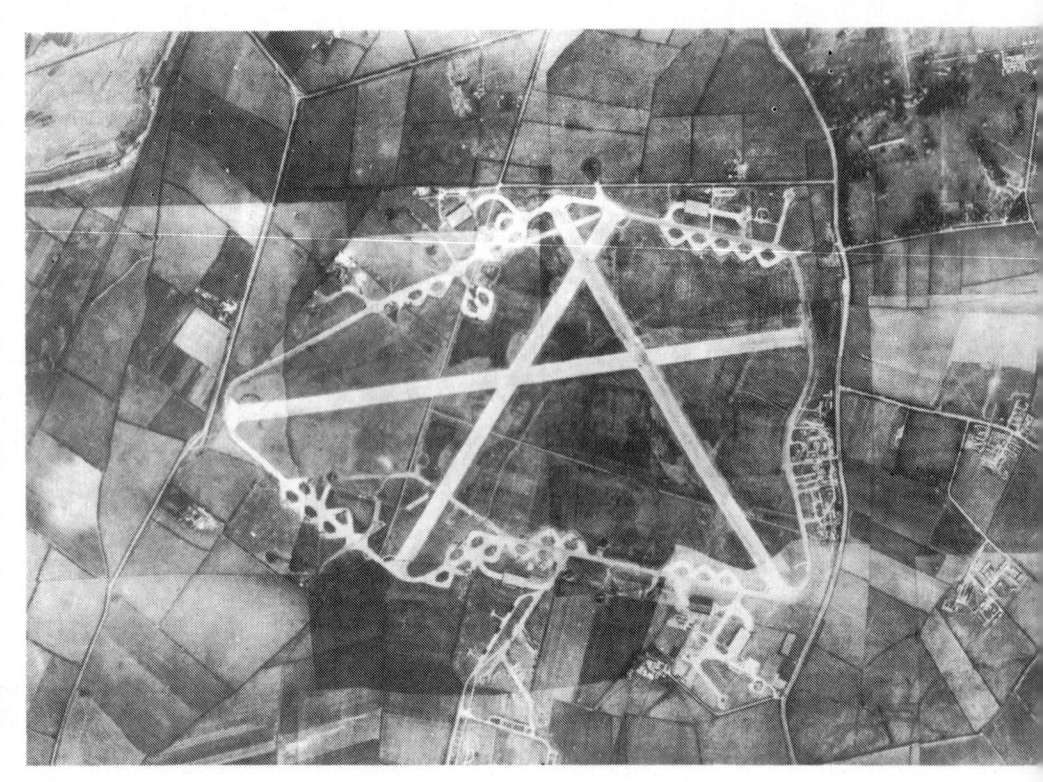

If anyone ever wonders why so many of us feel aggrieved about the abuse dished out to Britain's airfields, Balderton provides a devastating case for the prosecution.
(above) Balderton at its peak. *(RAF Museum)*
(above right) The same aerial view, taken at lower altitude, in mid-1991 – and appalling slaughter *(Milan Petrovic)*.
(below right) At ground level the sense of desolation becomes still greater. This track is all that marks what used to be the southern half of the NW/SE runway.

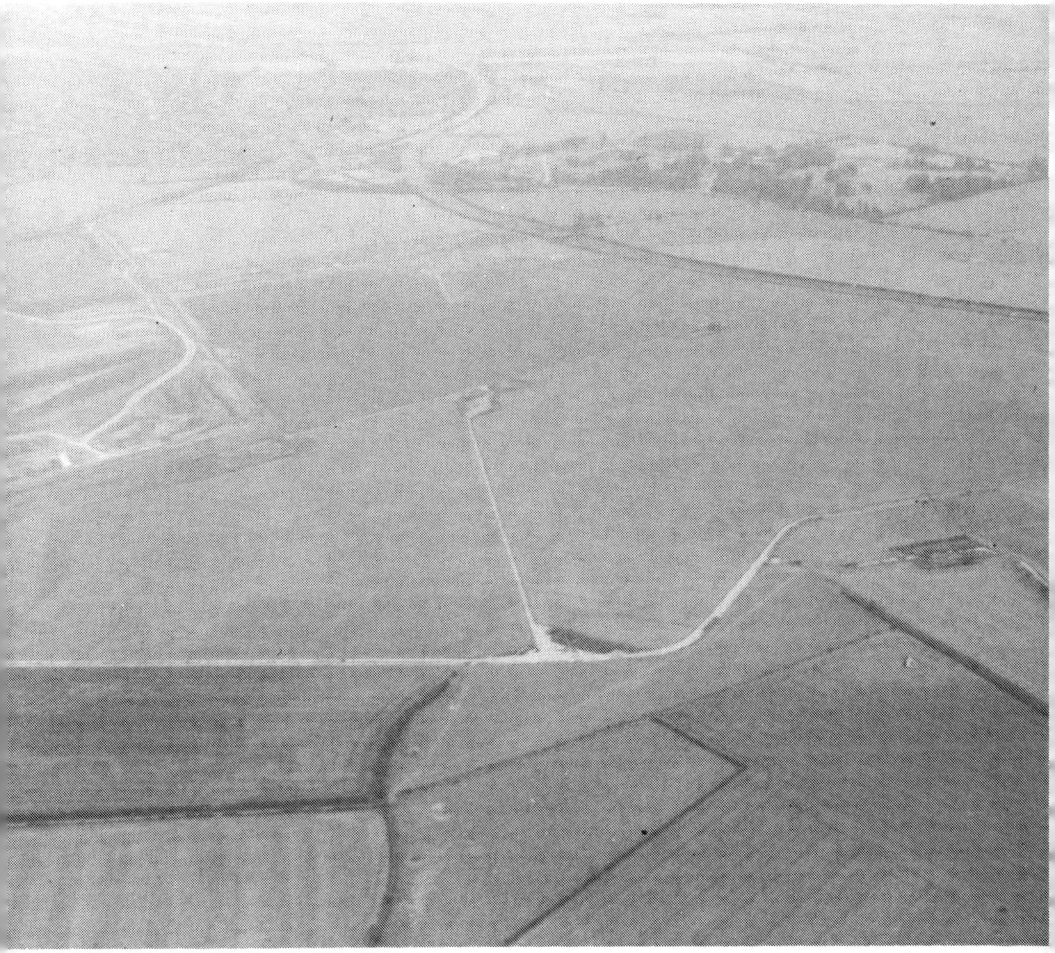

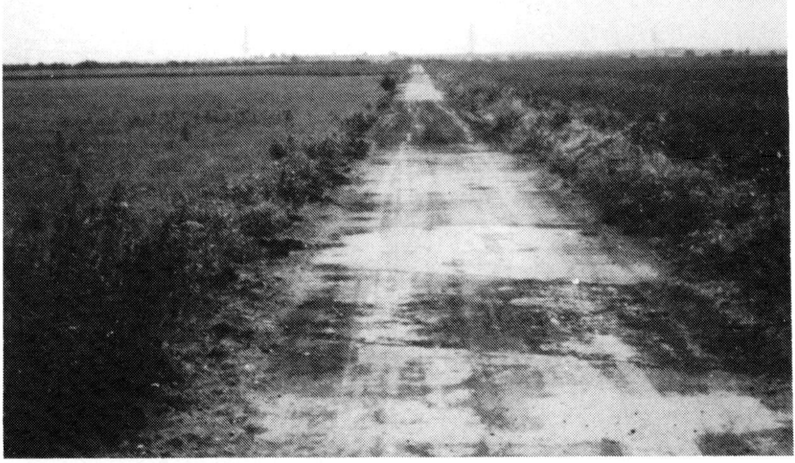

Ballyhalbert's 518/40 control tower: not exactly in a great state *(above)*.
(below) Bad outside, terrible inside.

(above) In complete contrast is the main runway at Ballyhalbert, in phenomenally good condition for a disused airfield.
(below) A train crosses a runway in front of a Consolidated Liberator during March 1944. Where else but Ballykelly? *(IWM)*

A still reasonable main runway *(above)* at Banff leads to a control tower *(below)* which, if also not in use, is in not quite as bad a state as its opposite number at Ballyhalbert.

THE AIRFIELDS OF BRITAIN

Navigation Act, being the first offender to be prosecuted. A pilot had stopped at Bletchley in Buckinghamshire with engine trouble and given some flights once his aircraft had been fixed as he could not pay a hotel bill. These trips broke the law and By Air was found guilty on various counts involving licensing and aircraft certification matters.

After the FK8 crashed near Bedford on August 16, disaster number three became complete collapse. Most joy-riding and charter companies had folded, hurried on their way by the severe financial downturn of 1921, and By Air Ltd succumbed to the inevitable late on in 1920. Its operating base meanwhile returned to being nothing more than an open field for another sixteen years.

Baginton's rise to prominence after this initial false start happened through sheer necessity. Armstrong Whitworth badly required a new airfield where to flight-test aircraft as Whitley, although reasonable enough for 1920s types, visibly struggled a decade further on. Wing flaps and slots, despite being remarkably effective in aiding machines to take off and land, could only achieve so much on their own. The company therefore spotted a bigger site across the River Sowe which the local council had purchased in 1933 and built a large factory on what became the east side of Baginton's landing area. This installation was ready by May 1936, the same month as a Scimitar – an unsuccessful biplane fighter and one of Armstrong Whitworth's least known products – became the first company type to fly from Baginton on the 26th. Not until December could this airfield still be described as fully operational as a whole.

Whitley production at Baginton proved so slow initially that the type was already obsolescent on entering RAF service in 1937 at Dishforth in Yorkshire, such being the tremendous progress in aircraft design. Not much better was available, though, and hence Baginton churned out example after example of this angular bomber up to mid-1943. The Whitley gradually improved in performance once given Rolls-Royce Merlin inline engines instead of Armstrong Siddeley Tiger radials, an increased bomb load and power-operated gun turrets, crucial factors in making the design a success with both Bomber and Coastal Commands in the early war years.

Fighter squadrons arrived at then grassy Baginton just after the Battle of Britain reached its peak in September 1940 in order to defend heavily industrialised Coventry and Armstrong Whitworth's assorted works. Hurricanes transferred from Speke on the 25th but No 308 Squadron was unable to counter the disastrous night raid during November which claimed so many lives.

Soon the Luftwaffe began taking notice of Coventry's main nearby airfield as a single enemy raider attacked on April 11 1941 to leave three Whitleys damaged. Baginton was a stopgap fighter base: this shortcoming showed, though in fairness the combined effects of aircraft production priority, little preparation for fighter use and the dearth of night flying aids aboard RAF fighters made failure a virtual certainty. Fighter Command hopes that the airfield would be useful as having good approaches, ample acreage and an all-weather landing surface had not met expectations. Salvation came when Honiley succeeded Baginton in the defensive role and used the airfield as a satellite for a while afterwards. No 308 Squadron moved south at the end of May 1941, several other Hurricane and Spitfire units either forming or preparing for overseas service well into 1942.

A different problem hit Baginton a year later when Armstrong Whitworth was tasked to build Lancasters instead of Whitleys. A second airfield at Leamington already assisted with aircraft dispersal but heavy bombers would quickly maul any grass landing area, forcing the company to acquire bomber OTU satellite Bitteswell, situated twelve miles north-east of Baginton. Sharing this airfield at first with RAF units became slightly awkward but eventually the military disappeared to allow a useful partnership to develop.

After having constructed over 1,000 Lancasters, post-war times saw the factory at Baginton again largely build aircraft designed by other companies. Bitteswell's all-important hard runways mostly took care of the test flying side of production – and, as events proved, would ultimately outlast its master in the British manufacturing scene. Avro Lincoln heavy bombers, Gloster Meteors, then Hawker Sea Hawk and Hunter jet fighters for the FAA and RAF respectively all appeared in their hundreds after World War Two. Armstrong Whitworth's own aircraft did not enjoy much success, typified by the disappointing Argosy transport: only moderately successful in RAF spheres and hardly wanted for civilian use, it lost the company a considerable amount of money.

The numbers of people working in Britain on aircraft manufacture and repair fell alarmingly in the early 1960s as famous firms merged or were nationalised. In February 1963 the total stood at 270,500 but had fallen to 262,000 a year later. Coventry winced as the work-force halved rapidly following a merger within the Hawker Siddeley Group during 1961, and Armstrong Whitworth severed its long links with Baginton when the factory shut down in July 1965. Around

5,000 aircraft had emerged from there since the late 1930s.

This closure, coming on top of the various other difficulties throughout these years, ought to have sunk the airfield without trace as much as long forgotten By Air Ltd. (A charter company of the same name which started operations at Horsham St Faith in 1969 only lasted until 1970). But the distant past was Baginton's answer to assured future activity, and Coventry Airport now has a steady stream of light and executive aircraft passing through. A single stretch built over several months in 1960 at last solved the hard runway weak spot, surviving the attentions of a freak whirlwind not long after in July 1961. New hangars also arose but a proposed second runway did not until as late as 1993 as hopes to create a true airport have never really materialised. There has been competition with Birmingham (Elmdon) Airport, a hopelessly unequal contest, though considerable business and recreational flying is a good consolation award. Gliding used to be noticeable too from January 1953 until increasingly heavy use meant that the Coventry GC had to go to Husbands Bosworth in Leicestershire in the mid-1960s. One later arrival became the Midland Air Museum in 1976.

Some scenes have not changed. The old Armstrong Whitworth works still remains, albeit under alternative ownership, while a cluster of seven Bellmans on the opposite side of Baginton's landing area continue in existence near a small control tower. As ever, the past and present mingle happily at a British airfield: only a few brand new Whitleys are missing. The last surviving machine was broken up at Baginton in the spring of 1949.

140/SP354746. On S side of city, S of A45.

Balado Bridge, Tayside

Alternative Name: Kinross
Giving an airfield a suitable name was far more difficult than anyone imagined in World War Two. The planners had to think long and hard about the eventual title for this diminutive Scottish airfield. In no way could it be called Kinross, despite local persistence and being fairly near the town, with famous north of Scotland base Kinloss already around. A bridge on the site's south side crossed the South Queich stream; several nearby dwellings and a railway station bore the name Balado too, so this airfield became known as Balado Bridge.

Balado Bridge's career proved nowhere near as complicated. First acknowledged on June 30 1941 as being prepared for future use, the airfield opened on March 20 1942 — marginally over a year after official land requisition — as satellite to Grangemouth. No 58 OTU, known as No 2 TEU from October 1943, performed advanced instruction with Spitfires providing main aircraft equipment. Coastal Command communications machines also used Balado Bridge in World War Two to link with No 18 Group headquarters at Pitreavie.

After going on to C&M on June 12 1944, Balado seemed to have become one of the many second-line British airfields to suffer a premature run-down before World War Two had even ended. No 9 (P) AFU at Errol toyed in July with the idea of moving the unit's satellite to the site from Findo Gask but decided not to, Balado Bridge being a satellite to Turnhouse from September 1 until officially passing to War Department control in November.

Post-war Leuchars parented the now surplus station. While the future looked ominous, the Scottish Gliding Union found use for the airfield in this organisation's pre-Portmoak days during 1946-57. Its residence marked one of the first instances where a recreational gliding club flew from a redundant military base.

The Loch Leven Aero and Country Club appeared as well in 1946 to operate half a dozen British Aircraft Swallow 2 1930s vintage monoplanes plus some other types. For a while this was the only flying club of any real note in Scotland after World War Two but the Swallows left when sold to Eire later on in the 1940s. FAA aircraft being scrapped into the 1950s by a small firm which operated the airfield brought still more activity to Balado Bridge.

In 1952 the RAF nicely surprised everyone by returning. News reports contrived to describe Balado Bridge as a wartime OTU headquarters, which goes to show never believe what you read in newspapers. Out went the Loch Leven Aero and Country Club but a glider training school moved in, the RAFGSA Coastal Command Gliding and Soaring Club for more leisurely pursuits.

Civilian and military flyers alike had to move out in 1957 as the Americans acquired their home for secretive use as a satellite tracking station, the SGU gliders going across Loch Leven in June. Balado Bridge's two runways and perimeter track are still complete, though poultry buildings lie at either end of the main east-west stretch. Crossed by the B918 road, this airfield has lost most of its original buildings apart from the old control tower and would be a bare landscape these days but for a curious spherical object in position. This casing protects monitoring equipment and is a tiny version of the gigantic radomes that became an unusual tourist attraction at Fylingdales in Yorkshire until pulled down.

Hangarage at Balado Bridge comprised of an exceptionally mixed bag. Blisters such as the four once possessed here were normal for a lesser training airfield but heavy bomber stations better suited a B1, and storage bases a Super Robin. One hangar and some land were later sold for the astonishingly low sum of £4,350 on April 25 1962. Oh, and the locals stubbornly refuse to call Balado Bridge by any other name than Kinross. Will people ever learn?

58/NO095032. 2 miles NW of Kinross.

Balderton, Nottinghamshire

Initially used by the RAF, then the USAAF and finally back in British hands, Balderton became just one of many quiet airfield heroes to meet a desperate end. A distinctly turbid air caused by ever-changing policy decisions represented its other prominent feature.

Poland was making final death throes as a free country when Balderton received the nod for development once approved for requisition. Syerston would be parent, though over another year had to pass before even this airfield opened in December 1940. Balderton followed suit in June 1941 – only to become satellite to not Syerston but Finningley. No 25 OTU sent over an advance party on the 14th, six Handley Page Hampdens and six Wellingtons of the unit's 'B' Flight arriving two days later. This situation of a parent lying over 30 miles away was completely illogical on any long-term basis and No 25 OTU only remained until a site much nearer to Finningley at Bawtry (later called Bircotes) became available during November. By then the Luftwaffe had bombed Balderton twice but caused no damage.

Next month Syerston finally came along to do its originally intended job as Balderton held Hampden medium bombers of No 408 Squadron up to September 14 1942 instead of the parent. A major detachment was placed at North Luffenham from late January, returning in mid-March, but the Canadians departed as one for Leeming to allow Balderton to accommodate heavy bombers. Such massive conversion work naturally took time and the airfield became officially rated as

133

on C&M from December 1.

This gap of two and a half months between when No 408 Squadron left and now allowed Oxfords of No 14 (P) AFU at Ossington some breathing space before that station's permanent satellite at Gamston opened. However, Balderton continued to see aircraft despite an inactive tag as No 2 Heavy Glider MU used the airfield for glider storage. Even a few experimental jet aircraft appeared because Rolls-Royce's main base at Hucknall did not have hard runways, in an indirect way giving Baginton a warning of future events to come. Military commitments forced these precious machines to move again to Church Broughton, where they found a more settled home.

Once Balderton reopened in August 1943, No 1668 HCU formed with Halifaxes and Lancasters on the 15th. But these types soon left for Syerston on November 17 and threw Balderton back into a sea of uncertainty. Someone could always find it useful as No 12 (P) AFU proved in December when this Lincolnshire-based unit brought over a few Blenheims because Grantham and Harlaxton both suffered from suspect landing areas. Their difficulties lasted so long that the Blenheims had to adopt even more extreme emergency measures during 1944 by going to Woodvale in Lancashire, down to Poulton in Cheshire and then back to Woodvale.

Not until January 1944 did the Americans appear at Balderton – and quickly left again. The 437th and 439th TCGs were both around fairly briefly, and only in September did the latter Group return. Balderton had surprisingly played little or no part in the D-Day extravaganza but countless C-47 transports and Waco gliders partly made up for this loss by making their way to the Netherlands where heavy fighting raged.

When the Americans moved on later in September, RAF Lancasters of No 227 Squadron came from Bardney to mount heavy bomber operations. Yet the jinx which always seemed to hang over their new home struck again when No 227 knew as early as March 30 1945 that it would be moving further east to Strubby. An advance party duly went there on April 4 and the squadron next day to leave Balderton on C&M once more from the 25th. Selected as World War Two started but slowly constructed, and now out of action before the end of fighting, here was one airfield which enjoyed no luck at all.

June 1945 saw Maintenance Command take control as Balderton became a Bomber Command Equipment Disposal Centre. No 254 MU received military apparatus from 22

THE AIRFIELDS OF BRITAIN

doomed airfields during that month alone as Britain's huge winners were given astonishingly shabby treatment. The MU lasted until July 8 1946, turning into No 267 MU which changed base to Croughton in Northamptonshire on the 17th. Fulbeck, another former heavy bomber station employed for equipment storage, began looking after Balderton from then prior to No 255 MU's disbandment on November 30 1948. In stepped No 93 MU to hold munitions but little used the sub-site and brought to a close RAF involvement with the airfield when relieved of parenting duties on November 1 1958.

The picture today is of a desolate wilderness, far worse than Balado Bridge, agriculture containing little else other than tiny scraps of all three runways and perimeter track. Hangarage used to consist of four T2s and a B1; two of the T2s were designed more for glider use and came in handy when these engineless craft inhabited Balderton in some numbers. For what real constructive purpose has so much money been spent since then on their removal and eradication of just about everything else?

A second question you might ask is why Balderton had such an uneasy life. Maybe the answer lay in its geographical position: a bit too much on the edge of 'bomber country' but a bit too advanced as a training station, this airfield stood in a kind of no man's land. Certain comparisons can be made with Bottesford later on in this book, although that site a few miles south felt military planning vagaries a lot less. That said, Balderton could always be described as a success by never failing to welcome any aircraft or unit, no matter how unusual the circumstances. Officialdom anything but versatile in mind decided upon demolition post-war, Balderton's reward for good work.

130/SK815496. 4 miles SE of Newark-on-Trent by A1. Enter by SE side which immediately leads on to former landing area.

Balhall, Tayside

Training aircraft of No 2 FIS at Montrose used several minor airfields sited more inland for forced landing practice in World War Two on an occasional basis between 1942 and 1945. The most isolated of these crude places was a stretch of farmland at Balhall, which merits greater mention than the rest as the site has a longer aviation history. A supportive landing ground for No 8 SFTS from certainly 1940 (and undoubtedly earlier) until the FIS replaced this school, it is thought to have served in the same capacity under Montrose in World War One. ELG status reigned by 1944.

Balhall's title related to a couple of farms incorporating the name. These localities had to suffice, for the nearest place of any note was a small village called Fern but confusion would have easily resulted with FAA station Fearn in northern Scotland. Nobody could fault the planners in this case for doing their homework.

44/NO520625. NW of Brechin, to S of minor road between Fern and Tigerton.

Ballard Farm, Strathclyde

Alternative Name: Coll
Various small airstrips have existed at one time or another on the Inner Hebridean island of Coll since the mid-1930s. Fourth and latest place to have provided tremendous social benefits for inhabitants has been Ballard Farm. This single grass runway site opened in 1975 for irregular Loganair flights and succeeded nearby Totronald.

A Piper Cherokee Warrior light aircraft crashed on take-off here on June 10 1990. Happily none on board was hurt but Ballard Farm closed the same year. While returned to action in 1991, the airstrip is now only unlicensed and so has joined the unlucky list of Breachacha, Ben Feall and Totronald, also positioned on the island's west side.

46/NM165552. W side of island, W of Arinagour.

Ballyhalbert, Down

Ballyhalbert was the most important airfield on Northern Ireland's distinctive Ards Peninsula, a base for day and night fighters in RAF and FAA colours. It typified those airfields in Britain during World War Two which kept steadily busy and maintained a solid front, while at the same time staying largely in the background.

Final approval for requisition of the land which turned into Ballyhalbert was given in July 1940. At first military planners had hoped to open their latest airfield in April 1941 but constructional difficulties delayed this event for some weeks. When at last opened on June 28, Hurricanes of No 245 Squadron came from Aldergrove for a period as Ballyhalbert

THE AIRFIELDS OF BRITAIN

replaced Northern Ireland's greatest airfield as a fighter Sector station. Yet problems continued as summer ended with parts of this site still to be finished; other complaints by personnel started about support facilities being too dispersed. And no airfield in Northern Ireland came complete without moans about the weather, one factor that affected Ballyhalbert more than most as time progressed.

Other RAF fighter squadrons after No 245 arrived on defensive stays until 1944. No 504 Squadron was both at Ballyhalbert and its satellite Kirkistown with Hurricanes and Spitfires between August 26 1941 and October 19 1942, Spitfires of No 501 Squadron immediately following the unit until going to Westhampnett in Sussex on April 30 1943. As Northern Ireland needed night fighter protection, No 153 Squadron reformed on October 24 1941 to operate Defiants and then Beaufighters which were declared operational in May 1942. These machines were posted to North Africa during December to take part in the renewed Allied onslaught there but retained a detachment at home into January 1943.

Ballyhalbert became a welcome retreat for tired pilots, who usually transferred from deep in England to perform less exacting jobs such as guarding the shipping routes. Typical was No 303 Squadron, a Spitfire unit which arrived from Northolt on November 12 1943 and moved far away to Horne ALG in Surrey at the end of April 1944. Flying activities proved pretty uneventful, though the airfield provided plenty of talking points among personnel – if not always for the right reasons. Incessant rainfall during the winter of 1942/43 left Ballyhalbert's support buildings little short of a shambles; water was described as literally cascading down the stairs of the sodden control tower. Cloudy or misty conditions often frustrated Flying Control staff too, as shown by the occasion on January 24 1944 when eight USAAF B-17s encountered such poor visibility while diverting that some of them had to make several attempts at landing despite the airfield's Drem lighting being switched on at full power.

All this rain made it somewhat appropriate that FAA fighters became increasingly common at Ballyhalbert from the middle of World War Two. Slowly but surely entire squadrons or detachments pushed out the RAF before the Royal Navy acquired this airfield as HMS *Corncrake* in July 1945, making Kirkistown satellite again after a break of over a year. But no sooner had the FAA officially moved in instead of being a 'lodger' than the service perversely used Ballyhalbert far less for flying in comparison with 1944, and got rid of it on November 13 1945.

C&M reigned into 1946 as RAF Coastal Command gained the airfield in January. The authority held on to the base whose great history directly follows for over twenty more years but could find no use for Ballyhalbert and handed this place to the Northern Ireland Government on February 14 for storage purposes, items such as furniture being held for a while.

Obscurity rather than inactivity dominated for a long time before Ballyhalbert was publicly listed for execution in May 1957 with Attlebridge, Balderton and too many other airfields. Slightly over a year later world-famous aircraft ejector seat maker Martin-Baker talked with the Air Ministry about buying the site to establish a second production line. However, the company decided in 1959 to purchase ex-USAAF station Langford Lodge alongside Lough Neagh.

Turn right off the A2 coastal road going south and you now find the Ballyhalbert Caravan Park. People had holidayed in the area before, for Belfast schoolboys camped at the airfield during the summer months shortly after World War Two. An administrative building at the entrance contains a good aerial colour photograph of Ballyhalbert as it is today but field investigation shows few structures remain apart from a derelict control tower and air raid shelters; hangarage used to be two Bellmans and twelve Blisters. While the perimeter track has also largely vanished, all three runways are in great form to let caravans stand on them.

For the last word on Ballyhalbert, we must return to the subject of weather. A minor era perhaps fittingly ended at this less glamorous airfield when No 1402 Met Flight – present from November 1944 to August 1945 – made the last meteorological reporting sortie in a Gladiator biplane on January 7 1945. Public awareness has increased with the weather in mind, and an airfield memorial would be a fine further gesture.

21/J639639. SE of Newtownards, 4½ miles S of Ballywalter by A2, on N side of village.

Ballykelly, Londonderry

Ballykelly: scourge of the U-boat. A tremendous way to be remembered, yet many airmen recalled this major Irish base which saw a great deal more action than Ballyhalbert in a different operational duty for an entirely separate reason. True to form, quite a number of British airfields have had

THE AIRFIELDS OF BRITAIN

(and often still do have) weird arrangements in one way or another. Ballykelly's case was wholly unnerving as one runway crossed a railway line! All went well, Flying Control keeping in touch with the nearest signalling building, but the system must have been awkward for air and ground staff alike. Not even a Liberator or Fortress would dare argue with a train.

This airfield came alive on June 1 1941 after a period of less than six months since being formally lined up for requisition. A remarkably short time for such an important site, considering how the average British airfield took about a year to build, and indeed Ballykelly had opened prematurely. Little activity therefore resulted for another six months to let construction work continue. Experimental aircraft belonging to CCDU then arrived from Wales in December before going to Scotland in June 1942.

At last Ballykelly finally now geared up for the role which best suited the airfield. Fortresses of No 220 Squadron quickly replaced CCDU on June 20, followed by No 120 Squadron's Liberators on July 21. Anti-submarine patrols gradually brought dividends as a No 120 machine flying from Iceland on detachment claimed the scalp of a U-boat during mid-October to open the account, No 220 sinking two more in the space of four days in February 1943.

But just as Ballykelly was leading the way in Britain's fightback against enemy submarines as war in the Atlantic Ocean reached an all-time crescendo, the Forts and Libs cleared out that month on the 14th to Aldergrove. Once the airfield temporarily closed for runway repairs between March 10 and the 26th, FAA units used Ballykelly as a shore base from next day, notably some squadrons equipped with Swordfish biplanes. This was a strange and tactically bad move taking away four-engined maritime patrol types until Nos 59 and 86 Squadrons came during September as certain areas of the Atlantic lacked a heavy RAF presence. Close neighbour Limavady could not be relied upon either as that airfield held a non-operational Wellington OTU, leaving only Aldergrove and Lough Erne marine base Castle Archdale to deal with any possible U-boat.

The appearance of Nos 59 and 86 Squadrons from Aldergrove almost immediately showed what aircraft could have achieved had Ballykelly been allowed to conduct maritime patrol operations non-stop. Germany's U-boat fleet had voluntarily withdrawn for a while from hunting Allied shipping after extremely heavy fighting and considerable losses in the late spring of 1943. Ballykelly missed out at that time but spectacularly caught up for its enforced absence by blasting submarines out of the water in October. No 86 Squadron sank one U-boat and shared in the destruction of a second on the 8th; this unit chalked up another victory and No 59 Squadron two 'half-kills' on the 16th; No 59 then shared the task again in despatching a third U-boat a day later. Yet another craft going beneath the waves involuntarily with help from No 86 Squadron just under a month on made Ballykelly the envy of most other similar stations.

No 120 Squadron came back from Reykjavik as No 86 Squadron left for there in March 1944 to join No 59 in the continued search for U-boats. Despite becoming gradually harder to find, still Ballykelly's Liberators managed to winkle them out. Results varied as ever because of assorted climatic and human factors but several more absolutely confirmed victories were notched up. May 1944 became quite fruitful for No 59 Squadron with two U-boats sunk in only two days. Another submarine fell to No 120 Squadron in June before a fallow period ensued up to the spring of 1945, when this same unit ran up two more 'kills' in March and April, the second happening only days prior to the close of fighting.

Ballykelly had performed superb work in World War Two as this marvellous operational record showed. Immediate peacetime during that summer of 1945 however sadly ensured that no airfield, no matter how great, would be richly rewarded. No 120 Squadron's hurried disbandment on June 4 was ample proof, and transfer to Transport Command and East Anglia in September became the dubious thanks for No 59 Squadron. No 281 Squadron came from Limavady on August 13 but this ASR unit also disbanded on October 24. Ballykelly was reduced to holding an FAA detachment of No 744 Squadron from Eglinton for anti-submarine training with Fairey Barracudas from November 29 1945 to May 1 1946.

By then closure plans had already reached an advanced stage. A meeting held on March 6 1946 between RAF officers and the London Midland and Scottish railway company regarding Ballykelly's unusual runway looked worrying; in time 500 yards would be lopped off the main stretch to assist trains. Soon instructions arrived on April 1 for the airfield to be reduced to holding a closing down party, while facilities granted to civil aircraft do not appear to have been taken up at that period. The authorities seemed to be wasting yet another airfield.

Station records ostensibly tend to unceremoniously mark the grim finality on June 28 with a Vickers Warwick crashing on the main runway and being totally burnt out. Thankfully, the real state of affairs was different, due to the Joint Anti-

Submarine School which operated from the Royal Naval Barracks at Londonderry and previously mainly used Eglinton as a flying base. But this former RAF and now FAA airfield could not safely accommodate the latest four-engined maritime patrol types such as Lancasters, being primarily a place for single-engined fighters and strike aircraft. Although Ballykelly held a closing establishment, a small party remained to handle JASS commitments as further trial courses were held in 1946 with Warwicks, the first Lancaster arriving by September.

Post-war necessities for still more co-ordinated anti-submarine duties between aircraft and ships after their success in World War Two and the Cold War now under way could only benefit Ballykelly. On November 15 the equipment clearance element was suspended for JASS to continue indefinitely, and the school officially opened on January 30 1947 after having experimentally existed since November 1945. Destroyers and frigates thereafter helped develop tactics, aircraft of foreign air forces sometimes visiting.

A second welcome incomer arrived in May 1948 when the Air-Sea Warfare Development Unit – successor to the old World War Two CCDU – came from Thorney Island. This force left for St Mawgan in Cornwall in May 1951 but Ballykelly became best associated with Avro Shackletons. These aircraft were much better for ocean-going patrol work than the Lancaster, from which the Shackleton was indirectly descended via the Lincoln heavy bomber. Many examples stayed to form a famous Wing and made such an impact upon the local community that the Army renamed Ballykelly Shackleton Barracks on gaining the site in 1971. Twenty years before the airfield had required to close on July 1 1951 as the runways, perimeter track and hardstandings were redeveloped and new quarters built. The railway line eccentricity remained but JASS aircraft flew from Aldergrove meantime.

Nos 204, 240 and 269 Squadrons appeared in the early 1950s to begin the Shackleton era, No 269 finding runway and lighting alterations still going on when first arriving in March 1952. These last two units were renumbered in turn as Nos 203 and 210 Squadrons in 1958, residing with No 204 at Ballykelly for over ten more years before moving elsewhere. No more were U-boats to be seen but the 'Shacks' kept busy on tasks ranging from exercises to SAR. Often these aircraft temporarily transferred to other parts of the world, notably to Christmas Island in the Pacific Ocean during 1957/58 for the controversial nuclear weapon tests held there. Ballykelly took the chance to have its control tower rebuilt with an angled window Visual Control Room put on top.

The RAFGSA–controlled Red Hand GC provided a minor diversion when formed in 1958, lasting into the 1960s, but that decade became far more prominent for a massive hangar constructed at Ballykelly for the Shackletons. This cantilever design was 725 feet long, 158 feet wide, and cost a considerable amount of money in the process. Cash also had to be spent on rebuilding the Shackletons in the mid-1960s as this type aged faster than expected in Coastal Command service, with no obvious successor available for the maritime patrol role.

Especially considering the new hangar, the Government displayed a usual pathetic lack of economic sense not tremendously long afterwards by making deep cuts in both RAF administration and spending. No 203 Squadron flew to Malta early on in 1969 prior to Coastal Command losing autonomy on November 28; No 210 then disbanded on October 31 1970 and No 204 officially doing the same on April 1 1971, standing down a day earlier. These two squadrons immediately reformed at other airfields but left Ballykelly stranded. As for the JASS, anti-submarine warfare training had dwindled by the 1960s to a low extent, and finished when FAA Wessex helicopters of No 819 Squadron left in 1971.

A suggested plan revealed in December 1970, approved by Londonderry County Council, to turn the airfield into Northern Ireland's second airport with an industrial estate added never came off. The authorities viewed Aldergrove as being more than adequate on its own, making the old excuse that Ballykelly lay too far away while pondering whether or not to close Belfast Airport for extensions. As Eglinton has now become established as Londonderry Airport, that notion is even bigger rot.

At least the Army has not squandered Ballykelly, or the Londonderry-based JASS HQ which became a barracks. AAC helicopters of No 655 Squadron lately reinstated flying in the 1980s until going to Aldergrove. While one or two minor roads skirt the site, current security considerations with our Army friends in mind mean that public viewing is inadvisable; surveillance cameras scan the main Limavady-Londonderry road. Detailed architectural description is not wise either but Ballykelly is doing well in general terms. In World War Two the airfield had three runways, plus five T2s and eight Blisters as main hangarage, though other types can also be seen.

The not so good old days live on as a blank space marks

Ballykelly on maps, harking back to the time when the Ordnance Survey ignored all British airfields. Terrorist sensitivities have led to several active and disused sites in Northern Ireland being entirely or partly blotted out, from Long Kesh to even Aldergrove. These circumstances must remain but this is an unfortunate way to treat a star of Ballykelly's calibre.
7/C630240. By A2, 3 miles W of Limavady.

Ballywalter II, Down

Although opened during World War Two on the same day as Ballykelly, June 1 1941, Ballywalter served a quite different purpose as an SLG. There was another big dissimilarity too as a nearby airfield had tried to appear in World War One for RAF use. The almighty Aldergrove got through the Armistice and beyond but Ballywalter I was never completed and only acted as a landing ground.

Renewed fighting over twenty years later brought airfields back in strength to what was now Northern Ireland and the Ards Peninsula in particular. Five sites became earmarked as SLGs but the chronic dearth of airfields in the country forced three of them to change into more substantial places for flying. The other two lay close to the Irish Sea and were the least strategically positioned of this quintet, so Ballywalter and another County Down SLG south-west of Downpatrick at Murlough did not face wavering military thinking. Ballywalter fitted in about half-way between Ballyhalbert and Millisle, Britain's only unfinished airfield of World War Two, without any fuss and settled down to storing aircraft under the supervision of No 23 MU at Aldergrove.

Whether events in 1918 influenced planners in selecting this SLG to any level will always be unknown. Certainly comparatively little more has been left for posterity by way of notes about Ballywalter's second successful stab at being an airfield, apart from the usual comings and goings of personnel and aircraft. Various types arrived for storage but Wellingtons tended to catch the eagle eye more than most.

Ballywalter II closed shortly before World War Two ended on March 14 1945. Fields which straddle the A2 road blend in with trees, always useful for hiding aircraft from the enemy, and two small structures survive. Light aircraft are said to have landed in the Ballywalter area during 1990 but this claim has yet to be authenticated.

THE AIRFIELDS OF BRITAIN: VOLUME 1

(For Ballywalter I see Other British Airfields)
21/J630675. 3½ miles N of Ballyhalbert and 1 mile S of village by A2, on SE side of Ballywalter Park.

Banff, Grampian

Alternative Name: Boyndie
When the Banff Strike Wing formed in the autumn of 1944, unit commander became Group Captain Max Aitken, son of Press magnate and wartime Minister of Aircraft Production Lord Beaverbrook. Equipped with Mosquitoes, the Wing revelled in as much success as other Coastal Command airfields late on in World War Two.

There is naturally more to the Banff story than this glorious episode. The Scottish Motor Traction airline licensed a field somewhere in the area in the 1930s but military planners had a rough idea of an eventual operational role when requisitioning an open piece of countryside west of Banff town in September 1941. Here lay an unremarkable part of Britain, where the nearest settlement was a place called Boyndie, consisting of a church, a lunatic asylum and not much else. As ever the die-hard locals dubbed their budding airfield Boyndie but this name probably sounded too obscure. Another locality not terribly far away known as Upper Dallachy only compounded difficulties as would soon become clear. Nowhere else looked obvious either and made everyone settle upon calling this airfield Banff, despite being considerably west of its town namesake.

Negotiations for the airfield in 1942 included closing three small public roads and the disposal of manure from a nearby farm for the sum of £80. Construction work had more or less finished than initial intentions were almost predictably aborted. Operational flying hopes never came to immediate fruition as Oxfords of No 14 (P) AFU reached Banff from Ossington on May 25 1943 after the airfield opened on April 21. Dallachy and Fraserburgh acted as satellites instead of places such as Balderton until the unit disbanded on August 31 1944, while Edzell surprisingly became involved too in spite of the relatively long distance between that airfield and the parent station. BAT Flights equipped with more Oxfords worked closely with the AFU trainers, No 1512 being positioned at Banff.

Coastal rather than Flying Training Command at last gained control of this airfield due to U-boats suddenly

THE AIRFIELDS OF BRITAIN

operating in strength in the North Sea. Mosquitoes of Nos 235, 248 and 333 Squadrons plus Beaufighters of Nos 144 and 404 Squadrons were duly sent to Banff in September 1944 to smoke them out. But enemy military and merchant shipping proved more readily available targets in the closing months of World War Two, as No 404 Squadron soon showed on October 9 when its aircraft sank three vessels.

A fortnight or so later both Beaufighter squadrons were posted to now self-accounting Dallachy as a separate Strike Wing formed there. No 143 Squadron instantly replaced them while converting to Mosquitoes to make Banff packed with well over 100 of these machines at any one time.

The Mosquitoes became extremely busy by harassing German shipping either in the North Sea or at their Norwegian harbours, then progressively concentrated upon the Kattegat and Skagerrak waterways about Denmark as the Allied noose tightened around Germany. Many ships of all shapes and sizes were sunk, set on fire or damaged at the hands of Banff's Wing. No 248 Squadron possessed a number of Mosquitoes equipped with a 57 millimetre Molins gun in the nose of each aircraft until they were phased out in January 1945 but more favoured weapons became three-inch rocket projectiles, not always accurate but devastating against shipping. Often marked losses during fierce operations emphasised how World War Two was far from over. Although the Mosquitoes could take care of themselves, RAF Mustang squadrons gave extra cover, No 65 briefly staying at Banff as opposed to its normal base of Peterhead at the end of January 1945.

April and early May of that year resulted in Banff-inspired attacks reaching their climax. U-boats finally came into view – but not for long as the *U-804*, *U-843* and *U-1065* all succumbed to Wing Mosquitoes on April 9, as did the *U-251* ten days later. Gallant Luftwaffe attempts to fight back, regarding the fearful pummelling their airfields were receiving at this time, only met with disaster when eighteen Junkers bombers ran into the Mosquitoes on April 21 and lost half their number. Banff virtually rounded up the airfield's superb wartime career on May 2 when Nos 143, 235, 248, 333 and 404 Squadrons – this last unit not long back from Dallachy – destroyed both a minesweeper and the *U-2359*.

Within a week came peace: within a month started an exodus as Banff's units left as quickly as they had appeared. The newly-returned No 404 Squadron became first to go when it disbanded on May 25. No 143 Squadron became known as No 14 on the same day, while the split No 333

145

Squadron's Mosquito element transferred home to Norway in June as No 334 Squadron. After No 489 Squadron, at Banff since June 16, disbanded on August 1 before becoming operational on Mosquitoes, it was left to No 14 Squadron to fly the flag until departing for Gatwick on August 29. As this frenzied activity showed, many unit movements kept Britain's airfields fully occupied right up to the end of World War Two – and their lives.

No more military flying subsequently occurred as Banff closed to aircraft on September 7 and was reduced to C&M on October 15. RAF personnel slowly cleared away equipment but there would be no last minute Coastal Command reprieve as happened at Ballykelly when this airfield was given on Loan I or full terms to the Ministry of Works on April 30 1946; this Government department took the technical site and shared domestic ones with the War Office. Just under a year later FAA squadrons at Lossiemouth II began using Banff as a bombing range for 'pretend' simulated attacks, a duty Dallachy also performed post-war.

Another unexpected turn of events came in the 1970s on this land owned by Lord Seafield. Enthusiasts worked away for four years to let Sir Max Aitken gladly officially open the Banff Flying Club and airfield on June 2 1976: a far cry from complaints made in September 1946 about overgrown thistles spraying seeds on to adjacent arable land. The control tower was lovingly restored as a clubhouse and part of the main runway revived for light aircraft use. Ambitions grew to bring back all three runways and develop the site to bring in executive and oil-related aviation but these plans stalled after a bright start. Banff abruptly closed again in early 1982 to leave its future once more in doubt. Farming and occasional go-kart racing have to thrive at a place where the main runway is intact, both subsidiaries mostly so and the airfield's perimeter track also mainly complete. The old operations block survives as well.

Sadly, as all three T2s and thirteen Blisters have been removed and the control tower is a shell again beside the parachute store. we can only consider what lies ahead with trepidation. Surely this war hero with a fabulous history deserves better. Pleas for a memorial here – now there are two of them, the second dedicated to No 14 (P) AFU – were belatedly granted on September 28 1989, a stone being unveiled as a lone Mosquito made a low fly-past, though this event had come far too late for Sir Max Aitken and many of his friends who were similarly no more.

There is a disturbing story lurking behind this apparently

THE AIRFIELDS OF BRITAIN

honourable ceremony. Is it not frightening to think that among the major powerful stimulators with any influence of that commemoration could not be counted Britons but Norwegians? What on earth did the local council do? What a potentially magnificent tourist attraction Banff is, infinitely more important than the town's primary preferred site of alleged value, an utterly irrelevant stately home called Duff House. Yet those in power are still either wilfully against this disused airfield or sit on their backsides doing nothing. These are the sort of people Banff fought and ultimately died for: you wonder at times whether it and all our other supersites should have ever bothered.

29/NJ619642. 4½ miles W of town, follow go-kart racing signpost off A98.

Bangor, Gwynedd

U-boat hunting during World War One was a frustrating task which produced much less spectacular results than those Ballykelly and Banff scored. A variety of factors from the limited operating radii of aircraft to their not wholly suitable offensive armament meant that home airfields could only claim to have sunk a dozen enemy submarines solely or with Royal Navy assistance. But what these places lacked in tremendous concrete achievement they made up for in deterrent value, and helped themselves by introducing airfields to many previously barren parts of Britain. A typical example is now one of Wales' least remembered airfields.

Bangor opened in July 1918 to allow coastal patrol DH6s to operate around this area. No 244 Squadron formed in August from a nucleus provided by No 255 Squadron at Pembroke in south-west Wales. The new unit came via the airship station on Anglesey at Llangefni, the sole other airfield at this time in north-west Wales, and sent aircraft as far afield as Ireland and even south-west Scotland. After a quiet time for the *Scarecrows,* their squadron disbanded on January 22 1919. Relinquishment of Bangor followed in May.

This very much forgotten piece of history has long since disappeared from view. Situated north of a railway line, only a few canvas Bessoneau hangars for resident aircraft disrupted the outlines of these fields. Bangor's most unusual feature was an extremely jagged boundary which tapered off towards the west in a diagonally tangential stepped fashion. Such a weird shape must have made flying more difficult, though it failed to deter civil light aircraft as they appear to have used the same site as a landing ground during the 1920s.

On September 1 1932 Sir Alan Cobham staged a display at an alternative place near the town. Official pride soon wanted a municipal airport but this was always an unreal plan. Land between the railway and sea, probably the old Great War DH6 airfield, had been vaguely suggested in 1933 for potential development. Effectively nothing else is known about activities in this period as before to further deepen the air of mystery that surrounds Bangor.

115/SH620723. 4 miles NE of town.

Bardney, Lincolnshire

Some memorials connected with Britain's airfields have lasted longer than the ones at Banff — though in most inappropriate places. The Andrews Field stone in Great Saling village is a classic example but far from alone. Drive through the Lincolnshire village of Bardney and you will see a Lancaster propeller acting as a unit (not airfield) memorial. Erected in 1980, it commemorates No 9 Squadron, an RAF heavy bomber unit which operated from an airfield to the north-east. Why was the memorial not placed there instead?

Bardney had as good a career as any airfield, only troubled by a slow evolution from farmland to largely unappreciated star. At first proposed to open on November 21 1942, this event was postponed until January 18 1943. But No 9 Squadron could only arrive from Waddington on April 14, almost two years after Bardney had been approved for requisition, because slow planning and construction work dictated affairs.

The second greatest British bomber airfield after Scampton and former home to No 9 Squadron considerably influenced Bardney during World War Two. Introduction of the Base system to Bomber Command in 1943 resulted in both this airfield and Skellingthorpe becoming sub-stations or satellites of sorts in No 53 Base in mid-November. This scheme greatly helped out with day to day administration duties; major aircraft servicing was better co-ordinated too as groundcrews carried out inspections at the Base station or 'parent', in No 53 Base's case Waddington.

These organisational refinements arose at a time when Bardney needed as little hassle as possible. By February 1944 construction workers still had to complete a hangar, the

THE AIRFIELDS OF BRITAIN

station required to be generally cleaned and tidied up, while the runways and perimeter track wanted final improvements in addition. These final two items plus their supportive lighting became serviceable on March 1 to ease any pressure Bardney may have felt, although the most spectacular accident seen here still had to occur when a Lancaster swerved on the main runway, then crashed and blew up as No 9 Squadron set off to raid Brunswick on April 22. The crew survived but a fire tender coming to their aid ran into an obstruction on the perimeter track to create more confusion.

No 9 Squadron's Lancasters stayed at Bardney until moving back to Waddington on July 6 1945. They participated in many raids; among personnel was Flight Sergeant George Thompson, awarded a posthumous Victoria Cross for saving his colleagues despite terrible injuries. Most famous of all attacks became those made against the mighty German battleship *Tirpitz* while docked in a Norwegian fjord. No 9 Squadron, along with No 617 Squadron at Woodhall Spa, found it necessary to detach from their Lincolnshire bases to take on this monster. First stop was Yagodnik in Russia during September 1944; two trips soon followed to Lossiemouth II, Kinloss and Milltown in northern Scotland, this second visit on November 12 resulting in the *Tirpitz* being sunk. Nos 9 and 617 Squadrons co-operated again on an anti-shipping duty in January 1945 when they destroyed an 800 ton minesweeper for good measure.

A few other units also arose at Bardney to ensure that No 9 Squadron did not grab all the headlines. No 227 Squadron began reforming on October 7 1944 but moved to Balderton after only a number of days. Another Lancaster heavy bomber squadron, No 189, was born here on October 15. Although it went to Fulbeck on November 2, this unit made a second appearance at Bardney during 1945 between April 8 and October 15. As No 189 once more arrived, so Lancasters of the Bomber Command Film Unit travelled in the opposite direction after having formed at Bardney in March.

Activities at this station gradually dwindled after World War Two ended. The comment 'Nothing to report' in Bardney's ORB became increasingly ominous in regularity. No 53 Base disbanded in November 1945, yet every day bar one in that month featured this same depressing typed message. The end was nigh, and sure enough Bardney fell to a C&M state on December 10. Army vehicles were later stored on the site.

Officialdom never completely let go of hundreds of Britain's airfields for many years into peacetime. And just as well, for Bardney became home to No 106 Squadron from

July 22 1959 to May 24 1963. However, this unit had not arrived to fly piston-engined 'heavies' or even jet-engined V-bombers but supervise three of the 60 Douglas Thor intermediate range ballistic missiles (IRBMs) held in Britain. These controversial nuclear weapons bore considerable shortcomings in certain areas and lasted shorter in their concrete launch pads than anyone expected.

Still more surprising was the defiant refusal of civil aircraft to quit Bardney altogether. Flying stuttered along since the 1950s in the face of everything from inflexible authority to the Thor IRBMs. The Lincoln Aero Club had fought tenaciously to use the site from 1956 but the forthcoming RAF missiles forced out the organisation in 1958. Gliders became particularly noteworthy on-off occupants between 1964 and 1978, landowners hindering the Lincolnshire GC so much initially that its first flights had to be made at Derby's airport Burnaston in December 1964.

Trying to take off from Bardney's three runways is now just not on. Broiler houses stand on two of them, although all three stretches and the perimeter track are complete in length. Woodland growing right up to the perimeter track's eastern edges does not help either. Farmland mixes with light industry, a B1 and a surviving T2 out of two originals in use as warehouses, but the control tower nearby (in more recent times a clubhouse for the gliders and then a ruin) is now wonderfully restored as offices for a haulage firm. The inevitable support buildings around too consist of a few huts.

For all the changes at this less hailed disused airfield, flying did continue. Hardy cropspraying aircraft kept alive the old traditions – but an airfield memorial at the airfield itself would be far better. After all, how will we attract more people towards supporting our disused airfields if they do not visit them in the first place?

121/TF140713. Turn right off A158 NE of Lincoln at Wragby on to B1202 towards Bardney village. Turn left for B1190 at village and then immediately left for broiler area. Airfield best viewed from S side.

Barford St John, Oxfordshire

'Climb out of valley and try to ignore monster aerial array to right (after all, it is for our protection).' This passing comment

THE AIRFIELDS OF BRITAIN

in a travel guide to Shakespeare Country and the North Cotswolds slags off yet another airfield. But where is the airfield? Those somewhat cryptic words between the brackets help give a clue. Aesthetes, so beloved of castles and stately homes, will no doubt have their own warped interpretation but in fact the aerials stand on the disused airfield of Barford St John and act as a transmitter annexe for a secretive military radio communications station several miles east at another former airfield named Croughton.

All these masts tend to obscure past activities of early British jet aircraft. Barford St John was one of various interim airfields the Gloster company employed for test flying, in this case during the better months of 1943. The original E.28/39 prototype – Britain's first ever jet-engined machine – came here, as did F.9/40s, forerunners of the Meteor fighter. Gloster eventually moved to its permanent test base at Moreton Valence in Gloucestershire in October and remained there for almost another two decades.

Jets could never have used Barford St John in earlier days. Grass runways prevailed when the airfield first opened on June 30 1941, after being specifically requisitioned back in March 1940 as an RLG for Kidlington. Aircraft might not have come at all as the £45,000 thought needed for building the following August would only produce a few landing strips, and that if Weston-on-the-Green was available Barford could be dropped. A small collection of huts and tents allowed No 15 SFTS to carry on training with Oxfords until 'R' and 'S' Flights returned to the parent on January 5 1942 as the school prepared to run down. No 101 OTU tested Barford St John that year for possible glider pilot instruction but found the site unsuitable for this purpose.

The RLG expanded from April 1942 into a bomber OTU satellite, reopening as such in an 'unbuilt' or unfinished state on December 15 with three hard runways added, of which only the east-west stretch remains along with the airfield's perimeter track. Full use in this new role began on February 4 1943 as Wellingtons of No 16 OTU at Upper Heyford steadily flew from Barford up to December 1944, being replaced by Mosquitoes in January 1945. The OTU gave this airfield a reliable stream of bread and butter work: apart from the Gloster jets, only Army Co-operation Command Mustangs of Nos 4 and 169 Squadrons provided some variation during World War Two. These fighter-reconnaissance types briefly stayed from March 1 1943 until the 5th to participate in Exercise *Spartan*, the combined RAF/Army dummy run for D-Day in all but name, and left for other airfields not exactly accustomed to fighters.

Barford St John closed on November 26 1945 but still served as satellite to Upper Heyford – if simply in a nominal sense – for a few more years. Current radio monitoring links date back to when Croughton began operating in a similar non-flying role during the early 1950s, and Barford faithfully tagged along. These two airfields are well matched, for Croughton also used to be a satellite of Upper Heyford at one time and stands on a plateau like its present day aide.

A minor road running along the west side of Barford St John would today provide a good view if only those spooky aerials were removed. Official records fail to state exactly how much hangarage existed here in World War Two, though standard bomber OTU satellite equipment of one T2 and one B1 stood to daily service No 16 OTU's aircraft. A Blister visible and now used for storage is clearly evident: perhaps others used to be around, and would have come in handy for the transient Mustang squadrons present in 1943.

Guesswork unfortunately has for once to suffice as, taking into account Barford St John's delicate military role, prying eyes are otherwise discouraged. As that tourist guidebook says, you are best advised to dismiss what goes on in this area. Of course, that still does not mean you forget about its historical and social importance. None of our airfields deserves to be ever forgotten.

151/SP442340. 5½ miles S of Banbury and 1½ miles SE of Bloxham.

Barking Creek, Greater London

Unmarked and even more unrecognised than Barford St John, Barking Creek is now totally obliterated but just as significant in British airfield history. For on this marshland Handley Page – makers of the famous 0/400, Halifax and Victor heavy bombers – began its illustrious life.

The company's initial and unsuccessful machines were built on this site named after a river which flows into the River Thames near Creekmouth. What formed the landing area was literally made of rubbish, and colloquially the same in terms of smoothness, flying rights being granted to the Dagenham Dock railway station area about one and a half miles to the north-east. Barking Creek nevertheless still has one major claim to fame as Britain's first works created solely for aircraft production over the summer of 1909. Frederick Handley Page bought three aeroplane sheds which stood further down the Thames at Dagenham for £40 to replace buildings wrecked by high winds in January 1910 but his company eventually transferred to Cricklewood in early September 1912.

Little flying had occurred at Barking Creek during this time, maybe not entirely surprising as one unusual feature here was an artificial hill for glider experimentation. What activity mainly took place did so at two World Wars veteran and one-time would-be London Airport Fairlop to the north. Although claimed to possess many advantages when put up for sale, Barking Creek has since been built on, so there is not a lot to see. General home to No 1 Balloon Squadron of the RFC in World War One, the area later became associated with a notorious fake air battle in the opening hours of World War Two as false alarms made the RAF and other armed services extremely jumpy about enemy intentions.

The borough of Barking returned the compliment to Dagenham in 1925 when a power station which lasted for many years opened on the old Handley Page site to assist the massive new Ford motor factory placed on only Britain's third airfield. A replacement facility to be built on this Central Electricity Generating Board land was dropped in late 1990 in favour of a new power station to be constructed much nearer Dagenham. However, plans changed again and Thames Power will operate a gas fired generation building from 1993 at Barking.

177/TQ465818. SW of Dagenham, S of A13 alongside River Thames.

Barkston Heath, Lincolnshire

In far more pristine condition is Barkston Heath. This particular airfield is much quieter than it used to be, especially around the D-Day period, but has served as Cranwell's RLG with hardly a break since reopening to aircraft in the late 1940s. A modernised control tower plus six T2s and a B1 still remain, though the hangars are now mainly used for storage. Many wartime support buildings have not met so kind a fate and been removed.

Before three runways and a perimeter track were installed, Barkston Heath started off as a simple grass airfield, like today an RLG for Cranwell. Active from the mid-1930s, the

RAF College SFTS continued flying from here well into World War Two despite problems with Luftwaffe intruders belonging to our airfields' bogey unit, I Gruppe of Nachtjagdgeschwader 2 during 1941. Bombing killed one person on April 9, enemy aircraft damaging trainers both in the air and on the ground in May.

Barkston Heath later accepted a permanent night flying Flight on August 10 1942. Oxfords remained in force by 1943 but big plans had been scheduled for the airfield. Authority decreed that this humble RLG with few facilities would instead become an operational bomber station; Caistor replaced Barkston as a training RLG on April 1. Official approval for land redevelopment had come in September 1942, as similarly happened with Acaster Malbis. Both Barkston Heath and this nightmarishly bad Yorkshire site strangely shared other common characteristics too: both accommodated Oxfords before closing for rebuilding work, both had by late 1942 the same amount of hangarage (four Blisters) and both never held RAF heavy bomber elements. Barkston transferred from Technical Training to Bomber Commands during December in preparation but there the comparisons ended as Acaster Malbis soon proved to be a flop, unlike this airfield.

Massive revamping followed in 1943 as the Blisters and a minor road were swept aside to make way for everything and anything associated with a heavy bomber base, right down to a bomb dump on the north-west side which ultimately lay unneeded. The Americans made sure of that as transports of the 61st TCG came in force after Barkston Heath's reopening on January 1 1944. Hordes of C-47s later departed from the airfield shortly before midnight on June 6 as part of the successful D-Day operation. Paratroops did not disappear as Arnhem soon loomed in September, Waco gliders leaving for the Dutch killing ground with C-47s serving as their tugs. British rather than American paras flew out of Barkston Heath on this occasion: not many came back.

The 61st TCG finally left for abroad during March 1945 and was succeeded by a second TCG, the 349th, which remained until the middle of April. After the Americans had vacated the airfield, No 17 SFTS did a little night flying training at Barkston Heath in May as the school moved from Cranwell to Spitalgate before Bomber Command put the site on C&M on the 20th. Maintenance Command in turn gained control on June 1.

No 2 RAF Regiment Sub-Depot stayed from September 1945 until the summer of 1946 but of greater immediate consequence became storage duties as No 7 Equipment Disposal Depot formed on June 1 1945, being known as No 256 MU from the 15th. Stocks survived the infamous winter of 1946/47 when snow piled up to sixteen feet in height at Barkston Heath in February 1947; strong gales a month later helped clear the airfield but also blew many roofs off.

No 256 MU disbanded on December 31 1948 to leave Barkston Heath on C&M and with an uncertain future. More storage or MT holding use was envisaged but Flying Training Command and the RAF College officially chose the base as an RLG on February 11 1949 and have not deserted it since. Aircraft may indeed have landed before then as No 256 MU said on May 1 1947 that Cranwell could use this airfield for flying, though whether they did or not is unclear. Successive species of piston and jet-engined trainers have certainly come and gone, Barkston having had to close and be altered considerably from April 1959 to let the RAF College acquire Hunting Jet Provosts. Necessary runway reconstruction work ended in December 1960 but the taxiways needed attention until early 1961. Grassy Spitalgate covered for Barkston Heath in its absence.

Now that aircraft are back, the RAF should be around as long as Cranwell is active. Barkston Heath has had quite a noticeably subdued life for a British airfield with no real blood-and-thunder life-style but still copes admirably in an RLG role. This term differs in general meaning from World War Two days as military aircraft now only use such sites on a more non-committal basis as opposed to determined flying virtually every day. The relevant OS map reflects changing times and decreased activity by describing Barkston Heath as just 'Airfield' instead of quoting the full name.

A Flight of Bristol Bloodhound surface-to-air missiles belonging to No 25 Squadron at Wyton joined training aircraft during the 1980s for local airfield defence. The SAMs added a new dimension to daily operations for a time at what remains one of Britain's best preserved active austerity period airfields. Being situated in our top airfield county with one of the world's most famous airfields as master undoubtedly helps. But then as one over-effusive female television personality prattled while flying over Barkston Heath in a helicopter: 'Gosh, there seem to be a lot of airfields in Lincolnshire.' Surely understatement of the 20th Century!

130/SK969414. 7 miles SW of Sleaford and S of Ancaster. B6403 (old Ermine Street Roman Road) separates four T2s in row from airfield landing area.

THE AIRFIELDS OF BRITAIN: VOLUME 1

Barlow, North Yorkshire

Alternative Name: Selby

Well-known British aircraft company Armstrong Whitworth decided during 1913 to build an airship production factory in the Selby area of Yorkshire. The end result was Barlow, a place dating from an earlier age than Barkston Heath which until of late also lasted to an extent way beyond all architectural expectations.

Slow progress marred the intentions of this Newcastle-based firm. Still no definite word about Barlow had occurred by 1915 when Armstrong Whitworth decided to cut its teeth in the airship business and constructed several non-rigid SS types for anti-submarine patrol duties. An order then arose in October of that year for the R.25, a much larger rigid design, and this event enabled Armstrong Whitworth to give the green light for Barlow. Work on building a factory started in January 1916, construction being sufficiently advanced by the summer for company staff to begin their functions.

The Admiralty commissioned Barlow in early 1917 as a sub-station of Barrow-in-Furness to put the final finishing touches upon this new airfield. Exactly two years after being ordered, the R.25 first flew and proved a success. Two more rigid airships built at Barlow became even more noteworthy: the R.29 was the only one of its type to see action against enemy forces and helped sink a U-boat, while the R.33 logged more flying hours than any other British rigid.

Our airships and their stations had achieved everything asked of them during World War One. The authorities however typically thought differently, forcing Armstrong Whitworth to close its airship department in the autumn of 1919. Relinquishing the buildings and land became just as slow as Barlow's development, only happening on August 3 1921, but anti-airfield elements soon wasted not too much time in demolishing the main 700 feet long airship shed. A general purpose atlas amazingly stated Barlow as still being active in 1939, though there is no evidence whatsoever of any further flying use and a gentleman born in the year the station was given up has confirmed that this vague report is spurious.

This site later saw employment as a depot for the Royal Army Ordnance Corps. Where Barlow beat most contemporaries was that an airship shed still stood here: not the 700 feet example but a shorter one measuring 260 feet in length which lay alongside and supported its 'big brother' as a

combined frame/girder/fabric shop and offices. The smaller building could only be seen from a distance as the entire area was blocked off – land around the hangars in flying days stretched both north to a sharp bend of the River Ouse and some way south – but suddenly disappeared in the mid-1980s once the RAOC's Northern Command Ordnance Survey Depot closed. To leave Barlow as inconspicuous fields where to dump ash from Drax power station without this distinctive airship area is a terrible pity, considering how few of these remarkable structures survive in Britain today.
105/SE655285. 4 miles SE of Selby, E of village, 1 mile NW of Drax power station.

Barnsley Park, Gloucestershire

After a chequered start, this stretch of farmland served a useful purpose. It is now difficult to imagine that an airfield ever existed in these parts but one relic as significant as Barlow's lost airship shed still carries on regardless.

Barnsley Park should have entered service much earlier than it eventually did. The site opened on June 23 1941 as an SLG for aircraft storage but the value of this exercise was highly debatable. Various difficulties meant that very few aircraft appeared for long enough, not coming in strength until after November 8 1943 when the airfield reopened. No 5 MU at Kemble had already taken over control on September 26 1942 from Brize Norton's No 6 MU, who gave up out of sheer frustration after having to put the SLG on C&M in November 1941, but at last problems of earlier days had been solved and Barnsley Park could carry on normally at full power. Single-engined fighters such as Spitfires were among aircraft types which arrived for safe storage, being taken into the park after flying into the airfield's north side. A new runway built to add to the original one arose later on in World War Two.

As with most other SLGs, Barnsley Park possessed extremely few buildings. The only one remaining today is the most important: a bungalow which once used to be the combined watch office and guardroom is now a dwelling. So effective were camouflage techniques during World War Two in disguising SLGs that this building currently serves in the task for which the enemy thought it ostensibly performed.

By June 1945 the airfield knew that closure was imminent and shut down in September. The last event in Barnsley Park's aviation-related life left as much a lingering bad taste as the protracted run-up to total activity. A General Aircraft Limited Monospar monoplane ran into trouble while in flight one day in June 1947 and had to make a forced landing at Barnsley Wold, immediately west of the old airfield. Now trees were the bane of SLGs because their falling branches could easily damage aircraft: one tree caused infinitely worse trouble when the Monospar hit it and was destroyed in the resultant fire. What survived of this aircraft remained at its final resting-place for years and became something of a local landmark.

Passing sightseers did not notice the airfield this wrecked machine might have tried to land at. They almost certainly still ignore the former without knowing but Barnsley Park can count itself lucky in one respect, for at least aircraft did come to this green (and metal runway strengthened) sward. A short distance west lay Calmsden, intended as another SLG for Kemble but never used by that airfield or any other in the event.

163/SP075073. 6 miles NE of Cirencester, turn left off A433 at Barnsley. Go past park and turn right for Winson. Best vantage point is shortly after first bend on this minor road as you can look south down the former landing area.

Barra, Western Isles

Alternative Name: Northbay
A spectacular – and safe – landing with lashings of sea spray can always be assured when an aircraft touches down on the Traigh Mhor's foreshore at Barra in the Outer Hebrides. Passenger services to this island are highly unusual in being governed by the tides. Available on arrival or departure is a waiting room, as are supportive facilities, a vehicle having to occasionally chase straying sheep off the landing area.

Barra is a remarkable airfield in many respects. It has proved to be Britain's only really successful and durable sandy site of all time. Early flying pioneers in particular often tried to establish airfields on beaches but the effects of sand and salt water affecting aircraft components, too strong winds, frequently inclement weather and incoming tides restricting activities drove these people elsewhere and doomed their airfields to the history books – if any book of this kind bothered to mention them. Summertime joy-riding is the best option these exposed places can hope for, as the Southport duo of Birkdale Sands and Hesketh Park have affirmed.

Good as it is, even attempts have been made to drop Barra. Demands for a new site came in the 1950s after an air ambulance overturned on landing but the most determined assault happened in the early 1970s when a move was made to build an airstrip at nearby Eoligarry. This scheme eventually foundered as the proposed available land was too narrow and would be susceptible to soil erosion. Other problems cropped up as well to sink the plan without trace.

Airliners first landed at Barra in 1934. Licensing of the site for use by Northern and Scottish (later Scottish) Airways occurred as a natural progression on August 7 1936. BEA subsequently took over the Glasgow-Barra route in 1947 before the advent of Loganair in 1974. Several aircraft types have called in at this unique place over the years, from de Havilland Dragon Rapide biplanes and Heron monoplanes to Britten-Norman Islanders and Trislanders to short take-off and landing de Havilland Canada Twin Otter high-winged monoplanes.

General aviation circles knew Barra for being run by the local Macpherson family until Loganair took charge in the 1970s. The new terminal building opened in 1978 to replace a hut. There is one source of worry these days as some islanders claim that removing shells from the Traigh Mhor for facing the walls of houses may erode away their aerial lifeline's landing area but here is otherwise one airfield with a rock solid future.

31/NF705055. N side of island.

Barrhead, Strathclyde

The name of this town near Glasgow may not mean much to the average Briton – perhaps even many airfield fans. But Barrhead was only Scotland's second airfield after Lanark, opened on June 3 1911 for operation by the Scottish Aviation Company. A Farman biplane flew from there to give pilot instruction – a Bleriot monoplane never became airborne – and famous music hall comedian of the time Harry Tate received some flying lessons among others. His name became the rhyming slang nickname for the important Royal Aircraft Factory RE8 reconnaissance type used in World War One.

Barrhead did not live to see those days. Frequent high

winds affected activities at the airfield, which suffered its final blow when a fire destroyed two or three aircraft (accounts differ) on April 13 1912. Today no-one sadly recognises the considerable historical value of a field partly covered by houses lying alongside the town's main school.

64/NS511587. SE of Paisley, to E of minor road from roundabout on A736 towards Newton Mearns and Balgray Reservoir.

Barrow, Cumbria

Alternative Names: Walney, Walney Island

One of Britain's more unlikely active airfields continues to be Barrow. It may sit in an isolated position, have a less rip-roaring history and not be used all that much but this is one site still on the go while others have fallen into disuse. One might describe Barrow as a Cumbrian Barkston Heath.

If not quite as long as ships and submarines, aviation has long maintained a significant place in the history of Barrow-in-Furness, both around the town and neighbouring Walney Island. When airships appeared during World War One (see below), a loose twin airfield arrangement was devised so that lighter-than-air craft could use either the mainland or Walney Island sites. Civil light aircraft operated from this second area in the late 1920s, though Barrow-in-Furness' more officially and publicly acknowledged airfield was then a little-known landing ground situated north of the town near Furness Abbey. 1920s era airfields displayed poor staying power and aerial activity had ceased well before the time World War Two started. The shipyards meanwhile only further increased their huge operating capacities to cope with naval demands but airfielditis would soon strike again.

Just north of where the old Walney Island airship station once stood lay a piece of land which Barrow Corporation considered suitable in 1939 for conversion into a municipal airport. The owners caused delays by declaring the scheme uneconomic as they rated the territory a valuable source of sand and gravel. Fortunately officialdom persisted to good effect and was given permission in July to buy 634 acres of discouraging farmland, marshes and rabbit warrens.

World War Two stopped the airport from appearing but the site was again requisitioned – this time militarily – in September 1940. Originally intended to have installed RAF fighters, air gunnery training took place instead after an

THE AIRFIELDS OF BRITAIN

opening up party made the airfield self-accounting from October 20 1941 until June 1946. Avro Ansons proved common sights in the fullness of time as they trundled in and out of their well-placed home for air-to-air firing practice over the Irish Sea. No 10 AGS came from Castle Kennedy on December 14 1941 and soon dominated so much that hardly any other RAF element ever dared to appear. Barrow – as the station simply became known – performed with quiet efficiency, despite being hindered by an unsuitability for night flying because of its close proximity to Barrow-in-Furness.

Unit records for No 10 AGS are pretty dull but provide researchers with a testing puzzle. Flying is mentioned as having ceased at Barrow on June 15 1946; further comments are made up to the 30th before one discovers that records are missing for the period covering July to November. The problem can however be solved if you investigate Command files, as too many alleged experts seem to fail to do in general airfield research, Flying Training Command ones to be exact. We can now reveal that the AGS officially disbanded and Barrow went on to C&M on June 30, though an RAF party stayed on, ready to shift to Valley in north-west Wales. The school was later listed as being at C&M level on September 3 and moved to the great Anglesey airfield on October 5, where it reformed on December 1.

After No 10 AGS left, Barrow struggled for some while to hold on to flying status. Inclusion as one of the 40-odd proposed airport sites put forward by the Ministry of Civil Aviation in July 1947 damaged more than improved future prospects. Many places mentioned in this somewhat notorious Government plan never attained this dizzy height of international Customs capability – and, truth be told, never had an earthly of doing so either. Only ATC gliders were therefore mainly present from the late 1940s at this '... sorry, vacant site', as one commentator described Barrow. But the MCA partly made up for fanciful ways in 1951 by certifying this airfield for public use to end five years of extreme uncertainty. Soon the Furness Aero Club helped bring powered aviation back into consistent view, although Barrow could not be said to have really got going until the early 1960s.

Barrow has post-war primarily survived to hold light aircraft Vickers (now VSEL) uses for business trips; there are also some flying schools resident. The Lakes GC is another inhabitant and has stayed from when it began operations with Vickers' permission on December 1 1962. At this time based at Tebay, where officially formed on June 9 1957, the club gradually phased out this isolated hill site north-east of Kendal and stuck to solely using Barrow.

Commercial passenger air traffic used to mostly ignore the Barrow-in-Furness area, possibly thinking that any route to or from the town could not pay. A couple of small airlines did try after World War Two around the time when the MCA controlled the airfield's destiny but soon moved away. Air Furness tried to overcome such negative attitudes with various services to airports in northern England, the Isle of Man and Northern Ireland once formed in February 1984. Passenger levels however depended too much upon the Vickers connection, and this concern went out of business in July 1988 as the direct result of a long strike at the Trident nuclear submarine construction yard.

British airfield survivor Barrow now still contains an original control tower and three Callender-Hamilton hangars. Nineteen Blisters have succumbed to time, while the three runways go in and out of use. Vickers forever changed Walney Island as the 20th Century started by creating the village of Vickerstown for its work-force: the airfield here has turned out to be no nine day wonder as well.

96/SD175710. 3 miles NW of town, at N end of Walney Island.

Barrow-in-Furness (airship), Cumbria

Hardly had the R.1 or *Mayfly* emerged from its shed at Barrow-in-Furness on September 24 1911 than the rigid airship collapsed. Not exactly the best of starts for a place where the first British submarine was also built. One admiral became so disgusted by this fiasco that he described the *Mayfly* as '... the work of a lunatic.' Yet Barrow-in-Furness made up for such a disastrous beginning by being very evident during World War One, mixing airship construction with RNAS anti-submarine patrols over the Irish Sea.

Vickers continued to display such confidence in the future of airships that the firm decided to open a separate department in this field of aviation in April 1913. Among the design team was a young man destined to become one of Britain's greatest ever inventors, the legendary Barnes Wallis. Helped by the leasing of Cavendish Dock from the London Midland and Scottish railway company to enable airships to safely manoeuvre, orders for two craft came in the summer to justify Vickers' faith. The *Mayfly* affair still rankled in higher echelons of authority, though, and certain bigwigs doggedly wanted all naval airship construction to be abandoned.

This clash of interests meant that Vickers made negligible progress with building its first rigid up to August 1914; work then stopped entirely as the company was forced to devote energies to churning out ships. Diversification soon resumed but, as Barlow similarly found out, the whole business of trying to establish an airship station and build just one rigid design could be a terribly protracted process. Not until November 1916 did the R.9 first become airborne.

While Barrow-in-Furness gave rise to a number of rigid and smaller non-rigid airships during World War One, the station also helped mount maritime patrols. Virtually no action was seen but U-boats greatly threatened all around Britain's coastlines and every possible measure had to be taken to counter them.

One major difference seen in the conflict was how some airships found the shed in Cavendish Dock too small. This necessitated a second major building 539 feet long and 148 feet wide plus a portable airship shed measuring 300 by 45 feet standing alongside to appear on Walney Island and turn the base into a twin airfield, though by 1918 only the Walney end lasted as a recognised landing place. Vickers and the Admiralty had actually planned to use this other area and build four hangars there since 1913: maybe mindful of Barrow-in-Furness' later limitations, the company selected mid-war an entirely different replacement site further east at Flookburgh. Material shortages ensured that this proposed successor was never even completed but basic planning thinking did at least prove correct when Flookburgh opened in World War Two as training airfield Cark.

Barrow-in-Furness built another three big rigid airships after the R.9. Last to appear was the famous R.34, which made the first double aerial crossing of the Atlantic Ocean during 1919 by travelling from Scotland to America and then back to East Anglia. For whatever reason, hardly anyone recognised this marvellous achievement, and within a couple of years airships in Britain became little more than a memory. Empty of craft from the spring of 1921, the RAF relinquished Barrow-in-Furness in September.

Not much remains as the sheds have disappeared, the big Walney Island one under housing after being sold for scrap in February 1926, having previously survived being shelled by a maverick surfaced U-boat in January 1915. North-west of where airships moored following a sortie before ground

handlers walked them into this building later became the landing area for Barrow in World War Two. A few offices lasted at the Cavendish Dock spot but huge reconstruction work has recently occurred in order to accommodate the new Trident nuclear submarines being built. A multi-warhead atomic missile launched underwater is a long way from several hundred pounds of bombs dropped from an airship but the principle of deterrence still lives on.
(Cavendish Dock) 96/SD207683. S side of town.
(Walney Island) 96/SD181702. 2 miles W of town, ½ mile SE of Barrow airfield.

Barton, Greater Manchester

Alternative Name: Manchester
Manchester's first permanent airport opened on January 1 1930, with Customs facilities quickly arising. Barton was also Britain's first municipal airport, blazing a trail for that unfortunate breed of 1930s airfields upon which national and local government planners placed far too great hopes. We can however count Barton as a success, even though this airfield has had a rocky career at points and has faced its most fearsome threat of closure after past narrow shaves.

Barton stands on Chat Moss. For years this area of land used to be nothing more than a morass until largely reclaimed. Aircraft had operated from here before municipal airport days when Northern Air Lines transferred to Barton from Didsbury, after this airfield much closer to Manchester's city centre was forced to shut down in 1924 as part of a pre-arranged official agreement. Having tried with limited luck air services to Northern Ireland from Carlisle and Stranraer into 1925, the concern resorted to joy-riding for a while but Northern Air Lines soon had to pack bags again by 1929 as the airport grand plan took shape. Latest destination would be Wythenshawe, a stand-in 'airport' which sufficed in the intervening period while redevelopment work went on at Barton.

Every town of any note in Britain seemed to want a municipal airport between the wars. A national newspaper had correctly gauged future aspirations as early as March 1914 by stating that '. . . the time will come when, with the development of aviation, every town of any importance will need an air-port (*sic*) as it now needs a railway station.' From the late 1920s councils tried with highly varying skill or will to have an airport to call their own. Councillors showed slight interest as at Bangor, provisionally reserved land or made more definite approaches such as at Barrow-in-Furness. Blackpool and Stoke-on-Trent were other towns initially going the whole hog and putting plans into practice but Manchester beat the lot of them.

Domestic airlines such as Railway Air Services began obtaining good business once this revolutionary new type of airfield returned to activity. The opening three years required some fine tuning as Barton's grass landing area — said to be the first in Britain with defined runways — remained a bit skeletal before filling out, and the famous control tower which is still present today was only under construction by the summer of 1932. These local difficulties had ended when Fairey acquired the old Great War National Aircraft Factory No 2 at Heaton Chapel from the Willys-Overland Crossley motor company and started using Barton to test products, including early examples of the ill-fated Battle light bomber which suffered an extreme mauling in France during 1940.

Equipped with the first wireless station for any British municipal airport, this place looked to be doing well in every way by the mid-1930s — but the good times did not last long. Barton had one drawback: a small landing area. Many other pre-war municipal airports endured the same problem because of too short-sighted planning, and those airliners destined to operate from them stood less and less chance of appearing. The bigger and current Manchester Airport at Ringway therefore took away all resident airlines in 1938 after Fairey had already left for there a year earlier.

People still always wanted airfields for recreational and small business use: what we now call general aviation, that is all civil air activity excluding airlines. Organisations such as the Northern Aviation School and Club Ltd continued to provide their now vanquished airport with employment. This example flew single-engined Hillson Praga monoplanes, mediocre light aircraft of Czech origin built under licence in small numbers by F. Hills and Sons Ltd, based at Trafford Park to the east of Barton. Hills created the Northern School of Aviation, which adopted this longer title on September 24 1937.

No 17 E&RFTS became another 1930s resident but the school had to disband in September 1939 in tandem with the cessation of civil flying. Although the following brief suspension could have seriously harmed Barton, the civil scene was soon revived as Irish airline Aer Lingus began

THE AIRFIELDS OF BRITAIN: VOLUME 1

operating to and from neutral Dublin between August 1940 and November 1942.

World War Two also saw major aircraft construction and repair work here, the former task carried out by F. Hills and Sons which built Percival Proctors. The majority of these single-engined fixed undercarriage monoplanes capable of being either radio trainers or communications aircraft were assembled in this area, instead of in Percival's works at Luton, and became Barton's main contribution to the war effort. F. Hills could be accredited with supplying 25 Proctor Is, 437 IIIs and over 200 IVs, this last variant differing from earlier marks in being adaptable for both of the above roles. One of our more unsung World War Two aircraft types, the Proctor gave great service in RAF and FAA colours for many years and particularly made itself familiar with trainee radio operators.

Tiger Moths and Chipmunks belonging to No 2 RFS later stayed at Barton during 1948-53 but predominant peacetime user has been the Lancashire Aero Club. Trying to derequisition civil airfields back to their pre-war states proved a common difficulty all over Britain: Barton followed the trend as its greatest club only officially reopened on September 21 1946.

Grass runways have remained available to light aircraft since then and come safely through intermittent crises. Everyone had already accepted that airliners would not return for good; the small Airviews firm formed in 1948 but inevitably went to Ringway in 1951, a few other tiny charter companies not lasting long in the late 1940s. Barton survived past 1953 when No 2 RFS left and the airfield's closure looked certain for several months, moreover in 1967 as Manchester City Council granted another lease to the Lancashire Aero Club after more fears about the future. The club deserved this reward, having opened new premises in June 1964 to replace the previous clubhouse which had been destroyed in a fire. Air displays are held as usual too: one on May 15 1983 resulted in a replica Mustang fighter crashing and killing the pilot.

Despite standing in a most restricted area, especially now with the M62 motorway on the west side, Barton has kept active and conspicuously displays reminders of a worthy past. Apart from the control tower, two Blisters can be seen, as well as a Bellman positioned a short distance away from the main site. But the most noteworthy hangar is an old building which dates right back to early municipal airport days and still has the word 'Manchester' painted on each side of the roof. These large white markings sometimes featured on big airfield structures between both World Wars and helped pilots with their navigation.

As you look around from a nicely placed car park, comparatively little has changed at this success-cum-failure-cum-success. Whether the scenery lasts depends upon our efforts to stop Salford City Council, who plan to kill Barton and turn the land into a business park. The knives are out again for an airfield in the 1990s as aviation considerations and appreciation are posted absent. And where will flying club aircraft go to? To close such a valuable and historic airfield as Barton would be unforgivable local government vandalism.

109/SJ744973. W of Manchester, by A57 between Eccles and Irlam.

Barton Abbey, Oxfordshire

Barton is easily the best documented of five British airfields to bear this name, the others being Barton Abbey, Barton Bendish, Barton-in-the-Clay and Earls Barton. None of them was named after anywhere of geographical importance, Barton taking its title from various minor localities in the vicinity. Three of the rest are villages.

Least socially significant of this quintet in terms of origin was Barton Abbey, called after a 16th Century country house and deliberately so because all SLGs like this one never featured on Air Ministry maps and officially never existed to preserve their secrecy. Privacy at this airfield became no small feat, what with a major road running nearby and a clutch of airfields all around. Barton Abbey was locally known as Lower Heyford but just beyond this village stood Barford St John's parent, famous RAF and later USAF station Upper Heyford.

Parkland east of the abbey changed into a storage area where to hold machines sent from MUs, aircraft landing in an adjacent field. Barton Abbey was attached to No 8 MU at Little Rissington from February 8 1941 and opened on September 30 after test aircraft movements were made on the 26th. The SLG temporarily closed for the winter on November 17 but reopened on May 18 1942, builders having removed nearby electric power cables during January with flying safety in mind.

Frequent alterations in ownership of auxiliary storage airfields were not uncommon in World War Two. Colerne's No 39 MU planned to gain Barton Abbey in August 1942,

167

though it had to officially wait until October 10 to solve a delay over accommodation shortages. No 6 MU at Brize Norton followed from March 8 1943 and utilised the SLG for the rest of World War Two.

Trees proliferate at Barton Abbey as they do at Ballywalter II, both airfields sharing the same closing date of March 14 1945. Two huts survive here in Oxfordshire; airmens' quarters stood at a camp by Hopcroft's Holt, a well-known landmark which consists of a road junction with traffic lights and a large pub. Customers will not be aware of the history next door but the trained eye can still imagine types such as Wellingtons coming to visit.

164/SP463250. 11 miles S of Banbury, on SW side of crossroads of A423 and B4030 at Hopcroft's Holt.

Barton Bendish, Norfolk

Original satellite airfield to distinguished East Anglian bomber station Marham was obscure Barton Bendish. Normally records are weak for SLGs, if arguably discounting the 1941/42 period when one suspects that high-ranking RAF staff viewed them as novel and worth mentioning, but Marham's recorders deserve a slap on the wrist. Notes are so poor that they hardly refer to Barton Bendish, and not at all after the early part of World War Two. Squadron files are hardly an improvement.

Once purchase of land had been sanctioned on April 27 1938, aircraft first used the satellite on September 2 1939. Wellingtons of Nos 38 and 115 Squadrons often appeared from the parent and turned Barton Bendish into a useful bolt-hole, especially during 1940 and 1941 when Luftwaffe raiders repeatedly attacked Marham.

Army Co-operation Command aircraft types also passed through Barton Bendish while on exercises in the second half of 1941. No 268 Squadron from Snailwell in Cambridgeshire made three brief visits in June, September and October, and Gatwick's No 26 Squadron came along too in September. No 115 Squadron's Wellingtons meanwhile found operating from Barton Bendish still reasonable enough but Short Stirlings became a different matter altogether. Being a grassy site of limited acreage, it was not for these four-engined heavy bombers which replaced the Wellingtons of No 218 Squadron – at Marham since November 1940 – during the opening couple of months in 1942. A more expansive successor with hard runways had to be obtained: the answer existed further west at Downham Market, to where No 218 Squadron moved from Marham in July, although retaining a Flight at the fading satellite until October.

So abruptly ended Barton Bendish's life. For any relatively substantial airfield in Britain to close midway during World War Two was an unusual event indeed. The site had done its best but, whereas Barton ultimately lost out as a municipal airport due to a restricted landing area, this partial namesake lost out as an airfield full stop. While two pillboxes still stand on the north side by a private track, an open field now really tells the whole Barton Bendish story.

143/TF726043. 11½ miles E of Downham Market off A1122, 2 miles SE of village to W of minor road towards Oxborough.

Barton-in-the-Clay, Bedfordshire

What is it about the Bartons? All short on records, even the big gun by Manchester. And today we find that Barton-in-the-Clay does not technically exist. For some reason unknown to all except perhaps one or two gnomes in officialdom, everyone refers to this village or maybe burgeoning small town as Barton-le-Clay. A little-known airfield close by is no longer active either but remains readily evident at the end of a minor road as an industrial estate employs various buildings. Barton-in-the-Clay saw use both as a civil and military airfield, and strangely more information is available about peaceful than wartime days.

B.C. Hucks had to make a forced landing with engine trouble at Barton-in-the-Clay on July 23 1911 while flying his Blackburn Mercury monoplane in the major Circuit of Britain competition. His arrival was of course a fluke, true aviation links not starting until November 1935 when the brand new Luton Aircraft Ltd came to this area. Having recently formed under another name to construct gliders at Britain's top pre-World War Two gliding site Dunstable Downs, the company advanced to build and test small LA.2 high-wing monoplanes which became fairly popular as recreational machines.

Mention Barton-in-the-Clay and a much shorter word permeates the story: fire. A bad blaze at the airfield in 1936 meant that Luton Aircraft Ltd had to go to a bigger and new factory at Gerrards Cross in Buckinghamshire in the summer, still holding on to its Bedfordshire base but only for flight testing. Activity kept at a low level until another fire occurred in June 1937, though this one at the Cordwallis Works in Maidenhead brought International Aircraft and Engineering Ltd to Barton-in-the-Clay and so worked in the airfield's favour. This company was granted a provisional operating licence by the Air Ministry in August and enormously improved the site before being given a private use licence in December. Particular attention was directed towards the landing area with 300 trees and 1,500 yards of hedges removed, cables put underground, levelling, drainage and grass sowing. All the associated work had notably carried on without help from any other quarter.

Hangars and a clubhouse in the north-east corner assisted Barton-in-the-Clay in becoming a popular location, even more so when the Bedford School of Flying opened on January 1 1938. Yet another inhabitant late on in this decade was Marendaz Aircraft Ltd, a small company which produced only three examples of two attractive-looking monoplane designs that deserved better fortunes. O.M.K. Marendaz, general manager of International Aircraft and Engineering Ltd, did not have good fortune run in his favour since seeing the 1937 fire at Maidenhead destroy an aircraft. This mix of production and instruction, the second task increasing in importance as the Civil Air Guard quasi-militia pilot training scheme started in 1938, lasted up to September 1939.

World War Two immediately brought these activities to an end and forced Barton-in-the-Clay to shut down. Months of disuse followed until it was approved for military requisition and preparation on July 1 1940 as an RLG for No 24 EFTS at Luton. Aircraft returned to this grass airfield as RAF Magisters trained FAA pilots, though there is no mention of Barton-in-the-Clay in unit records before May 19 1941. Maps certainly show that flying had begun by December 1940.

Even less is documented about what happened in the period after No 24 EFTS transferred to Sealand in north-east Wales during February 1942. In the summer the Air Transport Auxiliary aircraft ferrying organisation established a school for elementary flying training. The unit instructed trainees who had no previous flying knowledge and stayed until 1945 but no individual records can be found to give a more detailed picture of what went on at Barton-in-the-Clay. Aircraft equipment consisted of Magisters and Tiger Moths.

Efforts to research what happened after World War Two descend into wild speculation and fading reminiscences. It is claimed that 'one or two' aircraft – whether even military or civil is unsure – flew from the airfield for 'a year or two' in peacetime. These loose statements and slight historical evidence suggest that Luton Aircraft Ltd may have spent at least 1946 at Barton-in-the-Clay to try and pick up from where it left off, though the fact that founder C.H. Latimer-Needham had no connection with the firm by then tends to throw a spanner in this argument. The company had suffered the catastrophic loss of its Phoenix Works at Gerrards Cross in a fire during 1943 in what amounted to a fatal blow but Luton monoplanes regained some popularity as homebuilt aircraft. This revival however took place long after World War Two and had nothing to do with the airfield.

To approach Barton-in-the-Clay, you used to have to turn on to a narrow lane marked by a cul-de-sac sign to reach the site. A new main road now bypasses the village and has cut this track in two but the industrial estate still has signs of past occupation. Heading the buildings is a hangar with a gabled roof, while painted inscriptions survive elsewhere.

This is the first time that the tale of Barton-in-the-Clay has ever been fully told. Admittedly there are gaps but your author has faced a huge struggle, not least in field research. Although workers in the industrial estate knew nothing, they gave directions to a village resident who promised to send on a letter – and never did, even with postage being supplied and the author making two wearing round trips totalling over 1,200 miles. The local library held no records but said that someone had made an unfinished attempt at compiling the airfield's history and lodged notes at a reference facility. Inquiries at other libraries and the Bedfordshire County Record Office to hunt them down proved fruitless, so one has to reluctantly wave a white flag unless you can help. This cautionary account shows how woefully both people and time have treated Britain's airfields, the greatest in the world, and we must be thankful for what exceptionally sorry scraps of information remain about Barton-in-the-Clay.

166/TL070316. By A6, 7 miles N of Luton, ¾ mile W of village.

Bassingbourn, Cambridgeshire

Many big name British airfields are linked with personalities, such as Scampton and Guy Gibson. Neither of the two most famous residents at this bomber base nearly as celebrated as the Lincolnshire station was human. One was an aircraft – the other a dog . . .

Bassingbourn, affectionately known to countless thousands of American airmen as the 'Country Club', was one of the magnificent Expansion Period airfields built before World War Two. Its first occupants after having officially opened on March 27 1938 became Nos 104 and 108 Squadrons which arrived on May 2 and received Blenheims. Early days at Bassingbourn proved largely uneventful, with these two units going to Bicester in mid-September 1939 and two more bomber squadrons staying. Thirteen Blenheims later left the airfield in November on a tremendously long trip to Romania in a barely concealed attempt at bribery in persuading that country to join forces with Britain and the other allies. This voluntary supply of aircraft turned out to be a mistake as Romania aligned with Germany in November 1940, then using the Blenheims against Russia from the summer of 1941.

Events back in Cambridgeshire gradually developed with far greater clarity. No 215 Squadron became No 11 OTU in April 1940 as Wellingtons continued to use the surrounding area for training RAF bomber crews. Bassingbourn stood in quite an advanced position for a non-operational airfield and suffered against Luftwaffe intruders as a result. A few bombs came its way in the autumn of 1940 but German aircraft discovered during 1941 how circuit attacks could bring greater profit as friendly aircrews tired after a hard night of flying exercises. A number of Wellingtons tragically fell victim in this fashion, though one 'Wimpey' also nailed a Ju 88 in unorthodox circumstances when both aircraft collided in Bassingbourn's circuit. Another bombing and strafing raid sadly killed ten people on August 13.

As if station personnel had not enough problems to be going on with, they began encountering further difficulties with the grass runways at Bassingbourn. Three hardened stretches were therefore laid: most of this paving has unfortunately since been lifted. What was generally regarded as the most demanding part of airfield construction always took up a lot of time but necessarily closed the site as the grass bomber base had no viable future with four-engined types now in service. As Steeple Morden was already a satellite, No 11 OTU's Wellingtons transferred there in December 1941. Others placed themselves at then unknown Tempsford, soon to be Britain's premier espionage support airfield, to keep up training schedules. By April 1942 construction work had reached a point where Bassingbourn could reopen but No 11

OTU was later sent away for good to Westcott in Buckinghamshire during September and October.

The unit had moved out because the 91st BG was due; formal conveyance from RAF to USAAF control had to wait until April 21 1943. B-17s took part in all the major USAAF raids up to April 1945, being awarded two Distinguished Unit Citations for efforts in the front line. The 91st BG became colloquially known as the 'Ragged Irregulars' for suffering the highest losses of any 8th Air Force Group: participation in the two Schweinfurt attacks during August and October 1943 helped bring about this unwelcome tag. But not every Fortress received a mauling as four of them flew well over 100 missions each, *Nine-o-Nine* beating all other 91st BG machines by mounting 140 bombing sorties.

Yet it was another B-17 which recorded a much smaller total that stole the show at Bassingbourn during World War Two. *Memphis Belle* became acknowledged as the greatest ever individual Fortress and the first to fly 25 raids over Europe. You may have seen the incredible wartime colour documentary/propaganda film of the same name in which this aircraft and Bassingbourn (anonymously) starred. The airfield atmosphere is captured perfectly, from the thunderous take-off to groundcrews waiting anxiously during the raid on submarine pens at Wilhelmshaven to aircraft returning with often heavy damage, and footage of aerial combat with Luftwaffe fighters sensational without going over the top. 'England' also receives a good plug as a '... super aircraft carrier'. Happily, *Memphis Belle* is now preserved in America.

And Bassingbourn's other familiar non-human face? That title went to a part-Labrador mongrel called Redline. Now its name may not be anywhere near as recognisable as Nigger, Guy Gibson's pet dog killed by a passing car outside the entrance to Scampton only hours before the Dams Raid. But everyone in the 91st BG's 401st Bomb Squadron knew Redline as the animal acted as unit mascot, flew on several combat missions while sitting in an ammunition box and even became a Sergeant. Whenever the B-17s waddled along Bassingbourn's perimeter track towards the main runway and make lumbering take-offs, their faithful friend always came out on parade to see them leave and hopefully return.

Peace finally resulted and the Fortresses left in June 1945. *Memphis Belle*, being an earlier B-17F variant and not a G with a distinctive 'chin' gun turret, had long gone home; what meanwhile happened to Redline is uncertain as the dog mysteriously disappeared amid all the hustle and bustle of the Americans' hasty departure. The animal was soon forgotten as the RAF took back its former station to place two Liberator transport squadrons. Both proved short-lived, disbanding on September 4, but more Liberators of No 102 Squadron came from Pocklington in Yorkshire on the 8th.

Although these aircraft switched bases again by going to Upwood on February 15 1946, they left Bassingbourn clear for No 24 Squadron. This famous unit had stayed at Hendon for many years and maintained this replacement airfield's recently acquired transportation role. As No 24 transferred to Waterbeach in Cambridgeshire in June 1949, so Avro Yorks of Nos 40, 51 and 59 Squadrons immediately appeared from Abingdon. The first element disbanded in March 1950, while the other two also ceased to exist in October.

It was just like old times when the Americans returned to Bassingbourn at this period, though they now operated Boeing B-29s and improved B-50s. These Strategic Air Command heavy bombers intended to tackle the Russians should the Cold War have unfrozen however only stayed for the next year or so as No 231 Operational Conversion Unit reformed in December 1951. Vital as No 11 OTU and the 91st BG were, this training unit would perhaps become the most important of Bassingbourn's users.

In that month Marshal of the RAF Sir John Slessor made an astonishing attack on the places upon which the service depended so much during a speech. 'If we are to operate 10,000 first line aircraft, that means a hell of a lot of airfields,' he stated, and went on to say that he considered the cost of airfields in terms of men and materials as appalling. What an absolutely disgraceful and baseless slur upon their good names and deeds, especially now that Bassingbourn was destined to hold English Electric Canberras. No 231 OCU lasted right up to the airfield's closure and saw a PR role being devised instead of bombing as this unsophisticated but highly effective type aged over the years.

So excellent was the Canberra that Bassingbourn remained constantly busy through the 1950s and 1960s. Sometimes airfields could get too occupied as Arbroath among others had found out, and part of the OCU moved to Somerset during 1955, first to Weston Zoyland in June and then south to Merryfield in October before returning in October 1956. These detachments were practical despite the distance from Cambridgeshire as Canberra squadrons prepared at Weston Zoyland during 1955-57 for nuclear tests in Australia and overseas use in Cyprus.

The loss of a Canberra Wing and four squadrons at the popular Cypriot RAF airfield of Akrotiri in January/February

1969 emphasised how the type would have to rely upon less aggressive tasks to a greater degree. Coupled with Command integration, this put airfields at risk. No 231 OCU moved to Cottesmore in Leicestershire in May to join more Canberras ousted from Norfolk star Watton and left Bassingbourn silent. The last military dregs had pulled out by the autumn.

Earlier exploits at the airfield had still not been forgotten as veteran members of the 91st BG began holding reunions; several have occurred and brought along hundreds of ex-USAAF air and groundcrews. A propeller memorial has arisen too to further dispel the laughable – not to mention grotesque – myth that our airfields are unpopular. The Anglo-American Air Festival in mid-1978 revived the glory days at Bassingbourn as past and present military aircraft gave overhead fly-pasts and displays. Over a dozen vintage North American Harvard monoplanes in civilian hands, as noisy as ever while taking off, briefly stationed themselves on the airfield as part of this large celebration but that meeting and a little gliding have been about the sum total of flying recently because of the increasingly perilous runway situation. 1990 hit film *Memphis Belle*, fictional but heavily influenced by its documentary predecessor, hence could not be shot at where the story really happened as was the case with Scampton and *The Dambusters* in 1954. Binbrook had to suffice, though this Lincolnshire base served as a convincing substitute.

The Army has at least retained Bassingbourn's buildings since acquiring the airfield as a barracks, yet one factor is immediately obvious to visitors. Poor views exist of four C hangars and support facilities; this situation is not helped by pretty restricted visiting allowances at a museum in a control tower. The perimeter track has survived too but there is not a B-17 or Canberra – and certainly no *Memphis Belle* or Redline – to be seen at Bassingbourn today. Unavoidably sad.
154/TL332461. 4 miles NW of Royston by A1198 (formerly A14).

Battlestead Hill, Staffordshire

Housing is beginning to encroach upon this open field and erstwhile training airfield, used from certainly the first half of 1941 (and probably the second half of 1940) to reduction to C&M on July 9 1945. Magisters and Tiger Moths flew from little Battlestead Hill, mainly under No 16 EFTS at Burnaston and with three Blisters for hangarage. Derby's municipal airport became a busy place during World War Two and needed some assistance: Battlestead Hill came to its aid, as did Abbots Bromley later on.

The Ministry of Works accepted Battlestead Hill on April 29 1946. Look at a map now and you would think that this RLG might have been called Tatenhill instead. But disunited from this village lay another airfield bearing the same name, still active these days and differing from Battlestead Hill by possessing hard runways. No airfield would ever want to be associated with a hill for obvious reasons but a rise very close to Tatenhill village provided inspiration and duly stuck. Still, Spittlegate/Spitalgate owed its name to a hill and had a great career — even if no-one could spell the airfield properly!
128/SK210230. 3 miles W of Burton-upon-Trent, to S of B5017 and just NE of Tatenhill.

Beacon Hill, Northumberland

Alternative Name: Morpeth
When is a hill not a hill? When it is Beacon Hill, a farm alongside which once stood a World War One Home Defence landing ground for biplane fighters of No 36 Squadron.

Approved for requisition on September 7 1916, the site entered service in October but was later given up in favour of another landing ground placed one mile north-east at Longhorsley. Typed confirmation for relinquishment on March 24 1917 gave no specific explanation as to why Beacon Hill had to go, though probably the ground here was too undulating for aircraft. A small wood immediately to the south-east which dictated this rudimentary airfield's boundary is still present.
81/NZ145918. 7½ miles NW of Morpeth, turn first left off A697 on to minor road and travel 3 miles to site.

Beaulieu I, Hampshire

Mention the name Beaulieu in an historical context and most people think of preserved cars. Far fewer remember two

THE AIRFIELDS OF BRITAIN

important airfields which shared the same name. Each gave great service in one World War but were rewarded with near-total annihilation by the usual cynically deceitful combined anti-airfield organisations.

The first Beaulieu found itself becoming one of Britain's early batch of airfields: this fact alone should have prompted preservation in subsequent years. Bleriots of the New Forest Flying School initially used the site from May 1910, seven monoplanes and a hangar then being available, run by Bournemouth garage owner W.F. McArdle and partly financed by American millionaire J. Armstrong 'Chips' Drexel. Even with a fine start and stunts such as McArdle causing quite a stir by arriving at the Bournemouth flying meeting in July with luggage aboard, for nobody dared to do that in those days, Beaulieu I discovered times hard like other trail-blazing brethren and closed in January 1912. Both McArdle and Drexel retired from the British aviation world and went their own ways.

Only in December 1915 did Beaulieu return to activity, now as a military training airfield for the RFC. Of second-line units present, No 16 Reserve (later Training) Squadron easily became the most prominent by lasting from the recommencement of flying until November 1917. Nos 84 and 103 Squadrons formed in the latter stages of World War One, while No 79 Squadron operated Sopwith Dolphin fighters for part of the unit's stay until moving to France on February 20 1918.

Sopwith's less familiar Great War product with the odd name remained at Beaulieu I as No 29 Training Depot Station required the services of this type as well as those of the Avro 504. On one occasion an Avro landed on top of East Boldre post office and stuck its tail-skid in the chimney. Some pilots treated the Dolphin more seriously, fearing being decapitated if their aircraft nosed over after a bad landing. Such worries stemmed from a combination of airmen dying by hitting their faces on an instrument panel and the aircraft's trade mark design feature of the top wing being in line with the upper cockpit area. Although the Dolphin could prove tricky to fly and many crashes happened at Beaulieu, it was not dangerous by any means and became another winner from the Sopwith stable.

Co-ordinated training procedures and better aircraft made Beaulieu I able to function better than ever. Life seemed too settled, though, and the airfield's world turned upside down when the RAF passed ownership of this pioneer site to the Disposal Board during July 1919.

THE AIRFIELDS OF BRITAIN: VOLUME 1

A mixed arrangement of hangarage, consisting of four Belfasts, three 1915 Pattern designs, Bessoneaux and civil hangars from pre-war days, equipped Beaulieu I at the airfield's peak. Just about every building had disappeared by the 1930s when an Automobile Association civil landing ground three-quarters of a mile to the north-east existed but the locals still set classic double standards by establishing a single support facility as their hall in the nearby village of East Boldre. Despite being scythed down in what amounted to an organised massacre, this veteran airfield still provides a public service. And so too does an adjacent disused airfield ...
(For Beaulieu II see Other British Airfields)
196/SU368008. 6 miles NE of Lymington, between B3054 and East Boldre.

Beaulieu III, Hampshire

The third Beaulieu stood across the B3054 from its military predecessor on Hatchet Moor. This area of land is sadly well named, for the Forestry Commission has carried out a huge hatchet job upon this former airfield.

Beaulieu III carved out a separate destiny in operational rather than training spheres. Requisitioned in June 1941, the airfield opened in an incomplete state on August 8 1942. No 224 Squadron came south from Tiree on September 9/10 and completed conversion from Hudsons to Liberators.

This job was about the only thing finished around here as construction workers still had much to do during the remaining months of 1942. Chaos ensued at Beaulieu III, so devoid of basic support facilities that on September 1 a temporary watch office had to be installed pending completion of a real 'tower' – and not just anywhere, but alongside the perimeter track on the pyrotechnic store's roof! Imagine the horrific problems Flying Control staff would have faced had a bomb hit this building, as happened in 1940 at St Eval, the legendary Cornish Coastal Command station which retained certain unit movement connections with Beaulieu. Even worse was the fact that no hangars remained available by October 1.

Urgent operational needs meant that the show had to go on in the face of such extreme difficulties. With U-boats wreaking havoc in the Bay of Biscay, No 224 Squadron began patrolling over this area and somehow succeeded in sinking two submarines on October 20 and 24 despite problems at home.

THE AIRFIELDS OF BRITAIN

Two Bomber Command Halifax units temporarily transferred to Coastal Command to assist the Liberators missed out on this second victory by only a day when No 405 (RCAF) Squadron and part of No 158 Squadron arrived from their Yorkshire airfields. Both however naturally lacked anti-submarine expertise and the detachment departed in December; the Canadians stayed a while longer until March 1943.

Daily life at Beaulieu III in the first six months of its career could never have been faulted for dullness as U-boats, immovable airfield builders and busy movements all vied for attention. Arduous maritime patrol sorties came not without loss as a No 224 Squadron Liberator crashed in a forest near the airfield on November 7 1942 and exploded, killing seven personnel. No survivors emerged from another bad crash on December 15 when a Halifax of No 405 Squadron ploughed into a wood south-east of Beaulieu, thus perversely further spiting the Forestry Commission at high cost by taking out a few more unimportant trees.

Five days earlier had occurred an event to top the lot for farce as rounds fired from a Bren machine-gun during RAF Regiment training accidentally killed an employee of builders John Mowlem & Company Ltd. All off-duty units later performed some DIY of sorts themselves by helping to build hardstandings at the ends of each runway for their airfield's control vehicle and floodlight. This job was estimated to have saved a sum of £1,000, which would otherwise have been paid to a contractor, though maybe it saved more embarrassment than money for all concerned after that wacky shooting incident.

When No 224 Squadron left Beaulieu III in April 1943, Wellingtons of No 311 Squadron appeared next month from Talbenny in south-west Wales. Liberators replaced the Wimpeys in the summer and had not been operational for long when No 53 Squadron transferred from Thorney Island in September. Both squadrons patrolled the waters until early 1944 with profit as No 311 shared in the destruction of a U-boat during November 1943, sinking a ship on its own a month later as No 53 Squadron did the same with another enemy submarine. Like Beaulieu I, this much more advanced airfield was then due to receive fighters, though future visitors would possess far greater fire-power than the frail biplanes of World War One.

Nos 53 and 311 Squadrons moved out in January/February 1944. Typhoons of Nos 257, 263 and 486 Squadrons attacked tactical targets until the USAAF displaced them in March. The 365th FG, which had moved its P-47s from Gosfield in Essex to be nearer the action, performed broadly the same aggressive fighter-bomber duties through the D-Day period and moved to France as June drew to a close. Another American unit formerly based in East Anglia was the 323rd BG, whose B-26s stayed at Beaulieu during July/August before similarly crossing the English Channel.

Regained by the RAF in September, Beaulieu III for once lay idle until the Airborne Forces Experimental Establishment came down from Yorkshire's Sherburn in Elmet as 1944 slipped into 1945. The airfield soon perked up again and made the days of successful anti-submarine operations seem distant as many types began undertaking numerous tests. Everything from 'heavies' such as Halifaxes and Stirlings to true transport aircraft to gliders and primitive helicopters could be seen. A few of these last machines, Sikorsky Hoverflies, equipped a Flight of No 657 Squadron at the turn of 1946/47.

Helicopters ultimately played their part along with several other factors in the decline of Beaulieu's fortunes. Military gliders had particularly fallen out of favour fairly rapidly post-war, primarily due to their essentially cumbersome nature; the heavy casualty rates these unpowered craft suffered during their wartime swan-song – Operation *Varsity* in March 1945 – hardly assisted their case for survival either. Even more worrying was how the RAF airborne forces role effectively disappeared after three Halifax squadrons ran down at Fairford in Gloucestershire in the autumn of 1948. AFEE therefore had to go sooner or later.

Already this special unit had laid plans to leave Beaulieu. A move looked likely to western England and Defford, flying base for the Telecommunications Research Establishment, but in October 1947 the Aeroplane and Armament Experimental Establishment's Boscombe Down was substituted instead. Queries about domestic accommodation as at Defford delayed matters and allowed Beaulieu to continue in business into 1950. Finally arrangements were agreed and heavy supportive equipment moved to Boscombe Down in August. A&AEE made AFEE lose independence by incorporating the concern in September as Beaulieu closed to flying on the 15th and went on to C&M a month later. 'D' Squadron replaced AFEE in the future.

Although retained by the RAF, and also a reserve USAF base for a while, there would be no more military aerial activity at this airfield. Maintenance Command passed Beaulieu to Fighter Command on January 15 1951, a 1952 plan for Meteor trainers of No 210 Advanced Flying School at

Tarrant Rushton to use it as an RLG being abandoned. Loose American control followed during 1953-55 before another spell under Fighter Command, and then back to Maintenance Command on February 1 1956. No 238 MU at flying boat station great Calshot was now in charge but in January 1958 the Air Ministry wanted to give up ownership of the inactive airfield. RAF parenting ended as a result on November 10 1959.

One minor but controversial and technically significant incident had earlier occurred on March 17 1956 when company director and well-known aviation enthusiast Norman Jones landed his Tiger Moth on Beaulieu and was fined £200 plus £30 costs in court for his trouble. The penalty was later reduced to £50 on appeal but he had clearly chanced his arm by arriving without permission and gave rise to questions about aircraft landing on redundant airfields marked with white crosses on their runway ends. Jones, in this instance frog-marched off Beaulieu by irate RAF personnel, gained a reputation for flagrantly disregarding air safety rules and appeared several times before the beaks.

Since then the Forestry Commission has shockingly torn apart the third Beaulieu, clearing everything except for an intact perimeter track which conveniently acts in places as car parking areas for tourists: what blatant hypocrisy. Two T2s and a Blister have disappeared with the rest, and only a small eastern section of the east-west runway remains of three standard stretches. You might spot the occasional model aircraft flying about but Beaulieu III is otherwise a desperately sad sight. Both this extremely historical place and its earlier service counterpart are noticeably separate from Beaulieu village, and you get the feeling that this almost suits everyone by not wanting to be associated with airfields as far as is humanly possible. Meaningless motors count more than achieving airfields: where did we go wrong?

196/SU350008. 5 miles NE of Lymington. Enter from SE side off B3054.

Beaumaris, Gwynedd

Flying boat development and Consolidated Catalina modifying plus servicing were carried out in Anglesey during World War Two. Beaumaris proved an excellent site, being virtually out of enemy reach and sight, something which could not be said of Saunders-Roe's main works at Cowes East on the Isle of Wight.

Civil-controlled airfields used by military aircraft during 1939-45 are traditionally difficult to historically decipher because of few available records. Beaumaris is typical, and only a faint general outline of its life can be formulated. The first marine type to come here seems to have been a Saro A.37 Shrimp, a small four-engined experimental flying boat later employed to try out the ill-fated Short Shetland's hull, which apparently transferred from Cowes East in late 1940. A slipway north of Beaumaris was built but the Shrimp made little test flying and moved to Helensburgh on the Clyde in early 1941.

Beaumaris expanded from this tiny start as a purpose-built factory cropped up on land beside the slipway. Other aircraft types visited from time to time, notably an experimental Auster floatplane, but Catalinas heavily outnumbered them as they continually flew in and out. This major period of flying lasted from mid-1941 to the autumn of 1945.

Although flying boats had gone from Beaumaris, Saro stayed on in Anglesey after World War Two to build 'grounded' boats until becoming part of the de Havilland company in July 1959. One nominal alteration after another followed as Hawker Siddeley swallowed up de Havilland in 1960, the Group's Gloster-Saro subsidiary factory then being sold to Cammell Laird and Co Ltd in August 1967 for around £200,000. Aircraft as well as marine components and airport support equipment have been produced since 1945, so aviation links do survive.

Industry remains and makes this airfield an exact opposite of the two main Beaulieus: tremendously preserved but impenetrable to closely view. The old slipway and two original hangars, a T2 and a B1, are still visible and constantly remind local folk of their town's real history. Pit an unknown airfield against a highly documented castle, purpose against pretension, and there should only ever be one moral winner. In reality, alas, morality is nowhere to be seen when it comes to history.
114/SH610776. N of town.

Beccles I, Suffolk

Abortive aviation plans are nothing new to the Suffolk town of Beccles. Oil industry workers know the name as a heliport but this World War Two base is not the first airfield to be called as such. That honour goes to a flying ground directly two miles north-west.

Beccles Common is a golf course today, bordered on its north side by the diverted A146 road which used to run through the town. Here private aviation experiments are said to have been conducted in 1909. More resolute testing happened from 1910 as Captain Haydn Sanders of the London Aeroplane and Aerial Navigation Company moved to Beccles in 1910 after making previous flights by the coast at Kessingland. He formed the Sanders Aeroplane Company and erected a large hangar on his airfield's west side to hold a biplane but bad luck plagued flying trials, one crash resulting before the aircraft had even lifted off the ground.

Sanders was one of these gallant but technically flawed British pioneers destined to gently fade into oblivion. Although he flew at Port Meadow near Oxford during 1911, little was heard of either him or Beccles afterwards, apart from popping up in north-east England in 1912 and 1913. The Sanders Aeroplane Company had vanished by World War One, and it may be the case that his East Anglian base had already been closed for a good while before August 1914. Thirty years would have to pass before aircraft returned. 134/TM435907. NE side of town.

Beccles II, Suffolk

Alternative Name: Ellough
Intended for the USAAF, transferred to RAF Bomber Command, then Coastal Command, occasionally used by the FAA and yet never a true Navy base, now a disused airfield but the scene of flying just the same. Such is the complicated history of the second Beccles, sometimes known as Ellough, the name borne by an industrial estate present today.

There had been hopes as far back as April 1910 that a site in the area might become a so-called 'Government aeroplane station'. But nothing transpired except for the Sanders episode, Beccles saw no World War One service, and only entered the next conflict as one of Britain's last batch of airfields. Opened on a C&M basis on January 1 1944, the mark two version was scheduled to fully burst into life on March 20. The Americans however could find no use for Beccles, nor Bomber Command, and not until August 14 did Coastal Command end this prolonged period of inactivity.

After such crippling indecision, what more appropriate unit should have come along than perhaps the most jinxed RAF element of all time. No 618 Squadron flew down from Wick in northern Scotland intending to use *Highball*, a weapon essentially developed from the 'bouncing bombs' No 617 Squadron's Lancasters took away from Scampton in May 1943 on their unforgettable raid against the Ruhr dams. This was an excellent device but target considerations chopped and changed; fears also remained about preserving secrecy. No 618's Mosquitoes were therefore relegated to practice dropping *Highballs* off the East Anglian coast, while a 'ship' painted on one of Beccles' runways as a target offered more training. Eventually the squadron boarded aircraft carriers on October 30 bound for Australia but official indecision again prevented use of this superb weapon. Daft as it may seem, *Highball* had suffered from the problem of being too good, like someone buying a Rolls-Royce and then never driving the car.

Other unusual visitors subsequently appeared as Nos 810 and 827 Squadrons made fairly brief stays until the war's end. FAA units based at British airfields were never operationally active to any tremendous extent during World War Two but these ones still gave Beccles its only taste of action, namely against enemy ships and submarines.

Most time was directed instead towards humdrum but necessary ASR work as several units dealing with this task also stayed at various times. Big Vickers Warwicks of No 280 Squadron arrived from Langham at the end of October 1944, going back there in November 1945. Another Warwick squadron, No 279, moved in on September 3 1945, while a Walrus detachment of No 278 Squadron stayed for the greater part of that year as well.

The somewhat awkward life of this airfield took a new twist during the ASR phase. Beccles had saved many people from a watery end but failed to stop one death from occurring in its own backyard. On November 9 1944 the body of a WAAF aircraftwoman was discovered in a ditch near the Station Sick Quarters. Soon the culprit was found, and Leading Aircraftman Arthur Heys of No 280 Squadron stood on trial at Bury St Edmunds from January 10 1945, charged with the murder of Winifred Mary Evans. A guilty verdict declared after a fortnight saw Heys eventually being hanged in mid-March. This wholly unsavoury episode looked bad enough but Beccles II had to suffer the further indignity of being Britain's only airfield before or since where a murder has been committed on site. Some of you might ask about Attlebridge earlier on in this book and its claim to this dubious feat too, yet the shooting incident there does not count as that crime happened away from the USAAF airfield.

THE AIRFIELDS OF BRITAIN

Matters of more long-term consequence began to hit Beccles in the summer of 1945. No 15 ACHU formed at this time on June 12 to hold surplus flying personnel. Such an event was always a bad sign for any airfield. Gradually the ASR squadrons filtered away elsewhere before Beccles officially closed to aircraft on October 30 and the ACHU disbanded on November 6. Twenty-four days later C&M started.

What exactly happened during the following months at this airfield remains confused; the mysteries involved can be partly solved but not entirely. Believe other aviation history publications and No 279 Squadron would seem to have held on, having Warwicks and a few Supermarine Sea Otter amphibious flying boat biplanes replaced in September 1945 by Lancasters. These aircraft are supposed to have served as a detachment in Burma, of all places, until the unit officially (that word again) disbanded on March 10 1946. The reality is that most of this information is wildly off target as No 279 Squadron's aircraft at Beccles only formed a detachment, HQ airfield being Thornaby since October 1944. Slow delivery of Lancasters and Japan's surrender in August 1945 severely affected this force meant to support RAF heavy bombers stationed in the Far East. Only one Flight reached Burma in late January 1946 and became No 1348 Flight on February 1. Lancasters never flew from Beccles, and No 279 Squadron was not renumbered No 38 as that unit in Malta never disbanded during 1946 in the first place.

The question marks multiply like wildfire as the C&M establishment is listed as having been cancelled on December 17 1945. An ex-member of No 279 Squadron has said that hardly any personnel remained by Christmas, local people being brought along to boost numbers for the station festivities. Thornaby's ORB nevertheless still mentions how No 280 Squadron aircraft made trips to Beccles in January 1946, while an Anson visited as late as February 25. So is the use of language to describe the C&M party misleading? Should cancelled really read suspended? Beccles certainly continued to be regarded as inactive in 1946 by Coastal Command, being parented by Langham and then Felixstowe from July 15. Equipment clearance proved painfully slow, and much still had to go by the summer.

After World War Two the FAA had also taken over the airfield. Satellite to surely the oddest Navy base of them all, Culham in deepest Oxfordshire, the Admiralty does not appear to have employed Beccles in any capacity unlike the days when aircraft lodged under RAF Coastal Command control. Naval involvement ended in 1946.

185

Beccles formally changed from RAF to Ministry of Works ownership on September 8 1946. This new owner apparently first appeared the previous January; another date quoted is infuriatingly March 10, the same day as No 279 Squadron disbanded. As you can appreciate, the base's history is a lethal minefield of confusion, though the military undoubtedly refused to go away: German PoWs could not for a start. By January 1947 it was proposed to give the airfield to Fighter Command from alternative Government departments. Declared a future permanent RAF station two years later, happy times looked possible given a break but aircraft units never did return and the Air Ministry relinquished Beccles for industrial purposes in the summer of 1960.

This tale of mystery, murder and general mayhem does have a qualified happy ending, for Beccles is still used for flying as a heliport stands on the east side. Copious natural resources under the North Sea and a need for helicopters to ferry rig workers back and forth ushered in BEA Helicopters in 1965. Beginning with a single Sikorsky S-61N, the first recorded flight from Beccles happening on December 29 after a heliport at Lowestoft had proved too small, more helicopters eventually joined in as British Airways just as gradually superseded BEA. That nice man Robert Maxwell in turn bought the BA operation in 1986 and called it British International Helicopters.

Even with the collapse of his business empire, this arm saved by a management purchase in October 1992, machines keep up appearances around one T2; another of these ubiquitous hangars in the industrial estate tells you that the Americans should have used Beccles. Go-karts do perform on the south-west side but nothing has come as of yet of a strange idea put forward in mid-1992 to have the ruinous control tower build full-scale Spitfire models, despite the industrial estate's developers cutting a path through undergrowth to the building.

The B1127 road crosses this site where only one of three runways is intact. Beccles' eastern perimeter track has also been torn up but this is still a very tangible airfield. Confusion no longer reigns either as in wartime days.
156/TM453882. 3 miles SE of town.

Bedford, Bedfordshire

Alternative Name: Thurleigh
This has become an extremely large airfield, made a fair stab

at rivalling Heathrow for acreage, is named after a major British town — and is virtually unknown. A lack of publicity has always remained intentional with Bedford forming part of the secretive Royal Aircraft Establishment. What makes this place even more unusual is that it was built on a World War Two site known as Thurleigh.

Approved for requisition in July 1940, more than a few finishing touches still had to be applied when personnel first occupied Thurleigh a year later on the 24th. Little really happened for over another year as the proposed opening date retreated into the autumn, obstructions being removed from the runways to let them be fit for use on October 22 1941. No 160 Squadron tried to make things happen by forming on January 16 1942 but the main party of this Liberator unit went overseas in February. The air echelon could not even train at Thurleigh, having to do so at Polebrook in Northamptonshire. There followed a mazy route to Wiltshire transport legend Lyneham on April 26, Nutt's Corner in Northern Ireland on May 7 for anti-submarine patrols and back to Lyneham on the 30th before No 160 Squadron's hapless airmen could at last leave for India via Palestine in mid-June.

No 18 OTU made a greater mark during the first half of 1942: its aircraft actually flew from Thurleigh. Wellingtons and their bomber trainees aboard were never intended to be long-term visitors as the OTU's home base was Bramcote in Warwickshire, quite a distance away, and inevitably left once more operationally suitable satellite airfields became available.

By now two years had gone by and construction workers still remained very much in view. Wartime life seemed to be one of stagnation for Thurleigh with relentless daily weather reports, a sure-fire sign of not much happening. A lot of agricultural notes featured too, records for August 21/22 1942 telling everybody the sensational news that cabbages had been pulled. More serious was the discovery in June of nails in wood chippings which camouflaged the runways; the shavings had to be burnt off in what became a long and surely soul-destroying job.

Fortunes changed for the better when the USAAF's 306th BG appeared in September 1942. Success awaited as B-17s gradually penetrated enemy territory, seeing more operational service than all other 8th Air Force Groups and receiving two Distinguished Unit Citations for their excellent work. Thurleigh represented World War Two heavy bomber airfields as they really were without having to resort to mass media hype as at Bassingbourn or suffer condescending visits by royalty or other dignitaries: a story of awesome raw power, hundreds of raids and many thousands of operational flights. These Americans became even more settled than usual as their Group spent the greatest period of time at one airfield in Britain of any US flying element. This static policy made sense with four squadrons in each Bomb Group and their positioning in a foreign, if friendly, country far from home.

Peacetime meant that the 306th BG had to go sometime. This it did in the first half of December 1945, flying unusually not for American climes but Germany, leaving No 3 Air Division Substitution Unit to take over Thurleigh on the 8th. One might have expected Maintenance Command to gain control in due course but Thurleigh's luck held out as it had already been chosen as a new research testing area in the autumn of 1944. While the plan was publicly revealed in February 1945, there still remained the little matters of finishing World War Two and getting out the 306th BG, so everything had to be put on hold indefinitely.

Only on January 2 1946 could the Ministry of Aircraft Production take over this airfield from Bomber Command, which had temporarily looked after affairs from December 22 1945. Major redevelopment work then began in the summer to create a much larger site known as Bedford but no sooner had building started than criticism came about the destruction of some wheat fields. A considerable closing or re-routing of public roads gave rise to more local groans.

Tremendously futuristic plans that would not look out of place even today were devised for the new experimental airfield. Easily the most incredible became a scheme to lay a five mile long runway between Bedford and noted World War Two Bomber Command station Little Staughton II, while a taxying track would run down to Twinwood Farm, Cranfield's satellite best known for being where American bandleader Glenn Miller took off from on his last flight. Isolated cases had occurred before of one airfield absorbing another but here was a unique example of three airfields in one. Planners feared that large jet aircraft or the even bigger but aborted Bristol Brabazon piston-engined airliner would need enormously long take-off runs: they should not have worried, and the proposed megarunway never saw the light of day. This has enabled Heathrow to continue holding the British runway length record of a 'mere' 2.42 miles or 12,800 feet.

Although Bedford's new east-west main runway finished up being over 2,000 feet shorter, certain other items created greater impact upon the surrounding landscape, if not always

THE AIRFIELDS OF BRITAIN

seeing use in their intended roles. The long taxiway plan was dropped but has left the land between Bedford and Twinwood Farm with various public roads and access tracks that are either cul-de-sacs, oddly-shaped or resemble unfinished stretches of motorway. Huge wind tunnels to the south towards Twinwood for aerodynamic testing were completed, though, and have proved their worth over the years.

The sheer scale and complexity of this project ensured that both planning and building would take a long time. Priority was initially given to the wind tunnels before a second wave of construction began in October 1951 to prepare the airfield for flying use. Two of the former Thurleigh's three runways were retained, the new big runway and a fourth one added, as well as a fresh control tower and hangars. Rebuilding duties had largely ended by the summer of 1954 but the airfield's official opening needed to wait until June 27 1957.

A variety of aircraft resided at Bedford once one machine effected a landing in June 1954. The Royal Aircraft Establishment sent sections from too cramped Farnborough in 1955, with the Blind Landing Experimental Unit coming from Martlesham Heath and Woodbridge in Suffolk during April/May 1957. Aircraft often had to be greatly modified for experimental purposes, as typified by those of the Royal Signals and Radar Establishment which arrived from Pershore in western England in 1977. About this time the 'ski-jump' device for FAA Sea Harrier fighters to take off more quickly from their aircraft carriers was first tested with great success. The rather less than glorious fellow British Aerospace Nimrod airborne early warning version could be seen at Bedford during the 1980s to show how testing can hit many problems too. Little change was left out of £1 billion for the taxpayer in costs when the politicians finally cancelled development work on this quite disastrous project after the radar systems in each aircraft failed to operate properly.

For its standard maritime patrol role, the Nimrod developed from the de Havilland Comet 4. Other airliner types have used Bedford for testing and flying training, and the airfield could have easily turned into an airport, given less complicated circumstances. Acreage was no problem but this hopeful third airport for London during the 1960s would have placed diabolical restrictions upon surrounding military airfields – and possibly have closed as many as eight of them! Bedford looked in danger of closing too in 1972/73 when the infamous Nugent Committee Report emerged publicly in July 1973 after two and a half years of research and recommended disposing of the site. While Nugent had singled it out for special attention, the primary worry about this investigation became Government plans to ditch closed service bases whose land still remained under Ministry of Defence control, all the more terrible as huge superstars such as Battle of Britain legend Tangmere were targeted.

It goes without saying that the average airfield or aircraft fan has never been actively encouraged to view Bedford at close range. But how much longer can these conditions continue? Government 'consultants' noticed alleged excess capacity at two MoD research airfields and planned to close them. Boscombe Down has taken over all experimental flying duties to leave Bedford and, as if this is not horrifying enough, Farnborough in the lurch. A few buildings of the old Thurleigh still stand, though not four wartime T2s, but perhaps even today's ultra-modern structures may go altogether now that the intended death sentence date – March 31 1994 — has passed.

The rot really set in when the word 'Aerospace' replaced 'Aircraft' in the RAE's title on May 1 1988 before this immensely great organisation, the RSRE and two others became known as the Defence Research Agency in April 1991. Faceless money men created a dull new name to make these now unidentified research and development units more profitable, a move which raised many eyebrows among those in the know. Concerns like RAE have always been speculative but they have to be – that is surely the whole point of their nature.

Already unsavoury complainants are creeping out of the shadows around Bedford. Some local people want a section of the airfield developed for commercial purposes; the remainder, according to environmental 'green at all costs' fanatics, ought to be made a nature reserve. Why not an airport for Bedfordshire? The Americans have shown recent interest, and such a realistic suggestion may be the only answer for turbulent times ahead. To just drop this unknown monster airfield without any progressive thinking would be nothing other than scandalous and a real waste of money.
153/TL042601. Take B660 N of town, turn left after 4½ miles on to minor road for Thurleigh village. Only real view of airfield from S side in this general area.

Beechwood, Hertfordshire

Alternative Name: Beechwood Park

Go south across the Bedfordshire border a short distance into Hertfordshire and you encounter another airfield sited relatively close to a large town. South-west of Luton lies Beechwood, also known as Beechwood Park after a preparatory school for boys which stands in private grounds, a former airfield about as far removed in every respect from mighty Bedford apart from being secluded. Tree-festooned countryside tries its best to dispel notions of past flying activity but an SLG did indeed exist during World War Two. The closest this area had come to airfield experience before then was a 1930s private civil airstrip at Studham Hall to the west.

Beechwood got off to a slow start like Barnsley Park, if not that slowly. By April 1942 it was still not ready for No 5 MU at Kemble on the Gloucestershire/Wiltshire border. This MU station which also eventually managed Barnsley sent along a Pilot Officer to Beechwood on May 19; a runway was thought to be '... usable in about six weeks' as he left on the 30th. All of No 5 MU's SLGs temporarily closed on September 1 but soon returned to action.

Aircraft from single-engined fighters upwards in size and weight to four-engined Stirlings landed at this airfield until after World War Two for storage. You discover that there is quite a steep climb out of Markyate in order to reach Beechwood, and nearby high ground forced pilots to be careful while arriving in the circuit. What now proves not so obvious is how far away the SLG stood from Kemble, 70 miles no less, though it has to be said that the parent airfield was most unlucky for long enough with supportive dispersal sites and glad to have somewhere reliable. Ownership later passed to purely Wiltshire MU base Wroughton and No 15 MU, closer at hand but still directly 60 miles from Beechwood.

The SLG closed on March 15 1946 and moved out of what little aviation limelight had shone upon the place; remaining records are not good at all. There were some RAF Regiment buildings available but the greatest survivor became a plain ridge flight hut used following World War Two to accommodate staff. This facility disappeared once the property gained different owners in 1980, although a bigger new house built on the same site continues to be called 'Flight Cottage'. Nothing else remains but at least one memory keeps going.

166/TL045146. SW of Luton, 2 miles SW of Markyate.

THE AIRFIELDS OF BRITAIN: VOLUME 1

Bekesbourne, Kent

Alternative Names: Bridge, Canterbury

A forgotten strategically important World War One airfield star and hardly used in the next conflict despite considerable civil use in between, little Bekesbourne is still easily evident. Amid farmland stands a Great War hangar employed as the East Kent Packers Limited (Bekesbourne) Depot, one of two sheds originally built. Some old supportive buildings alongside Aerodrome Road, which runs up to this fruit storage area, have even become perfectly inhabitable bungalows.

Bekesbourne's position in south-east England was responsible for the airfield's steady military development. The start of this tale is not completely clear as the authorities requisitioned a place called Bridge as an ELG in 1914. This was presumably the same site in the vicinity of Canterbury that the RNAS took over 'on or about' November 18 1915 as a night landing ground.

Already the governing powers had shown dissatisfaction with RNAS defensive operations over Britain. Shortly into 1916 the RFC was given an opportunity to see if it could do any better, and the service soon occupied Bekesbourne. From being a night landing ground by the end of March, a Home Defence Flight of No 50 Squadron later stayed prior to this whole unit being present from the early months of 1918, flying SE5As and then Camels from the summer until disbanding on June 13 1919. Squadron Leader Arthur Harris commanded No 50 after World War One, long before he turned his hand to another form of aerial warfare and acquired the sobriquet 'Bomber'. No 56 Squadron's fighters had also been here in 1917 from June 21 to July 5, rushing back from the Western Front in an attempt to counter enemy bombing raids on London. By November 1918 Bekesbourne had not scored any victories but without question played an important part as one of the many fighter airfields forming a defensive ring around Greater London.

The two aeroplane sheds built at this base bore considerably different dimensions. One measured 180 by 100 feet – official records state the width as 80 feet – and the other 135 by 120 feet. Within only a few years of peacetime after Bekesbourne closed in 1919 this first building remained on its own as a comparatively rare survivor in a Britain badly short of active airfields.

But not only had the hangar still lasted, the entire airfield fought back as aircraft once more returned. Single-handedly *(above left and right)* The control towers at Ballyhalbert and Banff can look to Bardney for some inspiration. From being a relative ruin not so long ago, this ex-Flying Control building is now employed as office accommodation.

(below) Barton's famous old hangar, still with the word 'Manchester' painted in large letters on both sides of the roof.

Two more Bartons: Marham's original satellite Barton Bendish *(above)* and SLG Barton Abbey *(below)*.

And another one, Barton-in-the-Clay, where no amount of trees can blot out this distinctive hangar *(above)*.

(below) The only approaches you will see close to Bassingbourn's main runway these days are not aircraft ones but those of the golf stroke kind.

One building at Beaulieu I still provides a public service *(above)*. But pitifully little is left of the main runway at Beaulieu III *(below)*.

The heliport at Beccles II uses this fine T2 *(above)*. Its roof was renewed in 1991.
(below) Secretive Bedford cannot entirely escape notice. To the right of a Vickers Viscount stands an immediately recognisable British Aerospace Nimrod AEW version with its bulbous nose, one of Britain's biggest ever aircraft flops.

World War One veteran Bekesbourne is still marked by a hangar *(above)* and support buildings such as this one *(below)*, now a private dwelling.

Bembridge is another survivor as the control building and hangars demonstrate *(above)*. No view of this Isle of Wight airfield can come without its most famous product, the Britten–Norman Islander *(below)*.

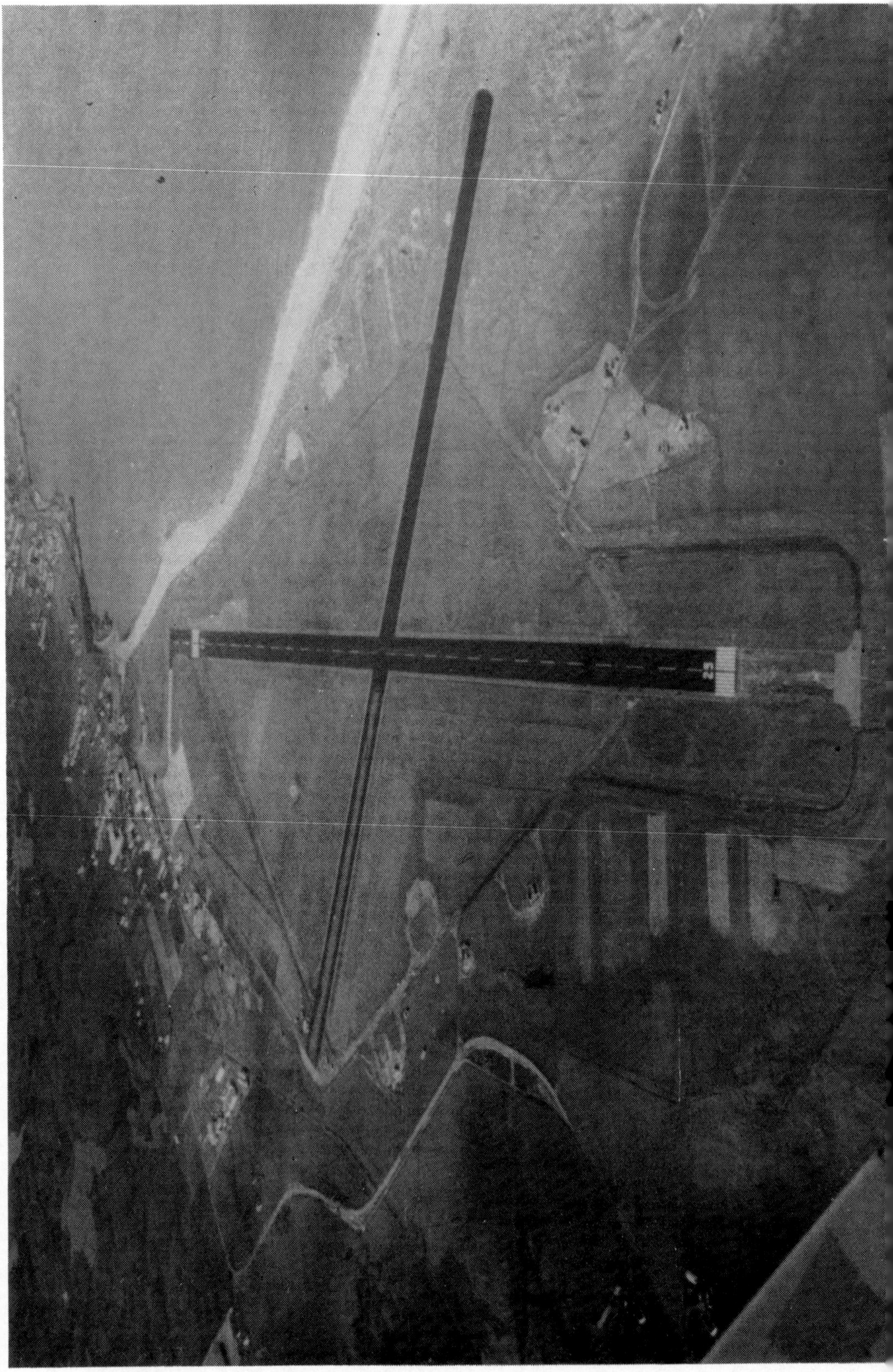

(opposite page) Benbecula today. Note the main runway's turning circle, large aircraft parking apron and complete lack of hangarage. *(Highlands and Islands Airports Limited)*

(above top) Benson's most recent control tower is typically detached from all other buildings.

(above) Wantisden Church mixes not altogether easily with a T2 hangar on the east side of Bentwaters. A quiet scene – and to become quieter still now that the USAF has gone.

A new boy amid the ranks, Beverley II *(above and below)*. The refuelling lorry saw service in the Gulf War.

(above) The guardhouse at Bibury.
(below) Biggin Hill – and not a Spitfire in sight. But this North American B-25N used to film classics such as *633 Squadron* was a familiar sight at the airfield legend in the 1960s, seen here on January 2 1964. *(C. Walker)*

(above top) Binbrook in the spring of 1991. Prominent are five C hangars, 'frying pan' and 'spectacle' hardstandings. Both subsidiary runways are closed. *(Milan Petrovic)*
(above) Barrack blocks at the base.

accountable was Edward Douglas Whitehead Reid, a Canterbury doctor who had learned to fly while on military service in Egypt during World War One and later often visited his patients by landing in nearby suitable fields. His name is typically unfamiliar to the average person today but this man merits much mention by being Britain's first private civil aircraft owner. All the Cessna, Piper and other lightplane pilots nowadays totally fail to recognise the magnificent pioneering work Whitehead Reid achieved all those years ago. It is hard to believe that by the end of 1924 only four private individuals owned civil aircraft in Britain; still only sixteen aircraft could be counted in 1925 but this total had risen to 333 by 1930.

The good doctor displayed a liking for flying war-surplus machines. After first turning up at Bekesbourne at the close of 1919, Whitehead Reid initially operated a DH6 and the only BE2c to see civil use. This unique type crashed in 1921, while an SE5A was also lost after a taxying accident, but a second SE5A lasted far longer until finally scrapped in 1930. Inevitably pure-bred civil aircraft had to be obtained for Whitehead Reid's professional and pleasurable needs, so single examples of Avro 548 and Westland Widgeon biplanes could be seen at Bekesbourne in the late 1920s. Sadly it was while using the latter type that he and a female passenger died from severe injuries on October 20 1930 after having tried to make a forced landing in poor weather at Detling, another of No 50 Squadron's old Flight Stations. The Widgeon never reached this redundant airfield with a great future and hit a tree at East Sutton Park, three miles south-west of Harrietsham, non-airfield HQ for No 50 Squadron before Bekesbourne accepted the task.

E. D. Whitehead Reid had undoubtedly managed to completely revive his own little unlicensed airfield prior to tragically leaving the scene. Already Bekesbourne had opened up for more public flying use when Kent Aircraft Services Ltd acquired the airfield late on in 1929, gaining an operating licence on January 9 1930. The company ran the Kent Flying Club which formed in 1931.

Ownership of the site significantly passed at the beginning of 1933 to a septuagenarian private individual named Robert C. Ramsay. Openly declaring that he had bought Bekesbourne to stop builders from grabbing the land, Ramsay learned to fly here and let the Kent Flying Club use his autogiro for flying instruction. Air Sales and Service Ltd was registered in 1935 with him as a director to manage the club and act as sales agents for Miles Hawk and Falcon light aircraft, CAG training

193

THE AIRFIELDS OF BRITAIN: VOLUME 1

occurring as well between 1938 and September 1939.

Bekesbourne had thrived right through the 1930s, being effectively known as Canterbury (Bekesbourne) from 1937, but World War Two changed everything as civil activities abruptly stopped. Air Sales and Service Ltd gallantly offered the airfield to the authorities on September 9 1939 for the duration of fighting out of duty. The Aerodromes Board declined to accept, though its decision was understandable with Bekesbourne's restricted acreage and position right beside a railway line taken into account. Military aviation – and especially fighter performances – had moved on by leaps and bounds since 1918/19 and the Sopwith Camel.

While considered too small for any major military use, Bekesbourne still played an albeit extremely limited part in the conflict. As our troops at Dunkirk needed all the assistance possible, No 2 Squadron's Westland Lysander army co-operation monoplanes flew covering patrols from this airfield in 1940 between May 20 and June 8, personnel conveniently finding 600 gallons of aviation fuel left behind by Ramsay and company in storage tanks on their arrival. Desperate bombing and supply-dropping missions to try and keep the Germans at bay made this brief encore all the more eventful.

No further military flying units stayed after No 2 Squadron had gone, nor did civil aircraft ever return. Sewer pipes had deliberately obstructed the landing area only days before the RAF moved in; similar devices were laid from time to time at Barton Bendish, according to a gentleman still living only yards away from Marham's satellite. Bekesbourne had to resort to letting the Royal Army Service Corps use its hangar, damaged with the airfield by the Luftwaffe in July 1940, from November 22 before transferring as a whole to the War Department in May 1943 and the Ministry of Works in April 1945 to serve as a post-war storage depot. Four civil aircraft found to be still there at that time were distressingly only worthless junk.

It would be an even greater tragedy if someone tried today to eliminate any remaining buildings. The hurricane of 1987 which blasted across southern England blew off the old hangar's original roof and destroyed its much admired supporting wooden trusses. Bekesbourne is one place which still looks as if having come straight out of World War One: a preservation order should be an absolute must. And such a declaration could happen, for in the village there is amazingly a standard modern road sign showing the way to 'Bekesbourne Aerodrome'. Who cares that the airfield has been closed for over half a century!

This endearing eccentricity hammers home the underlying message that airfield power is alive and well. How strange it is that most British airfields which served in both World Wars are better remembered for their participation in the second of them. For Bekesbourne, read the other way around.

179/TR205552. 4½ miles SE of Canterbury, easily viewed from an adjacent road to S.

Bellasize, Humberside

Bellasize resembled Bekesbourne in being an unrecognised veteran of both World Wars. They still greatly differed as the Kent airfield was an HD landing ground which eventually graduated to being an HQ. Its Yorkshire (later Humberside) counterpart never rose above landing ground status but did have the last laugh by seeing considerably more activity in World War Two.

First opened in April 1916, fighters of Nos 33 and 76 Squadrons originally called upon Bellasize, control switching between the two in October 1917. After little further use, the RAF relinquished it in May 1919 but this grass site enjoyed a revival when approved for requisition as an RLG for No 4 EFTS at Brough on November 28 1939. Blackburn B-2 biplane trainers arrived in the early days, two of them spectacularly colliding in mid-air over the River Humber on June 24 1940 with two fatalities, one body not being recovered for a month.

At this time Bellasize also turned into an unofficial scatter airfield or ELG as well as an RLG when EFTS aircraft hurriedly left Brough if an air raid alert sounded. A couple of small and ineffective Luftwaffe bombing raids on the Blackburn company's airfield did occur during the summer of 1940, so this precautionary measure proved totally worthwhile.

Tiger Moths replaced the B-2s mid-war and carried on with instructional duties throughout the remainder of World War Two before Bellasize was reduced to C&M on July 9 1945. Four Blisters and a few support buildings existed at this airfield but only a short hardened access track plus a small mound of broken concrete and bricks west of Bellasize Grange remain. Older local inhabitants still remember the place they called Gilberdyke – Bellasize is a locality – with affection; Brough acknowledged its wartime assistance too, although

flooding often featured in Bellasize's life. Agriculture has since obscured all other traces.
106/SE821274. Take A63 E of Howden to Gilberdyke. Turn first right at village and then second right on minor road.

Bembridge (landplane), Isle of Wight

Mention the name Bembridge and one immediately thinks of the Britten-Norman BN-2 Islander short take-off and landing transport, Britain's most successful commercial civil aircraft type ever built. Its birthplace possesses rather a subdued history for an airfield; while the Islander has admittedly almost entirely grabbed public attention, there is still more to Bembridge than meets the eye.

Flying in this part of the Isle of Wight goes back several decades despite an initial appearance of modernity here. An Avro 504K site was listed as being active alongside Bembridge Farm, across the B3395 road which forms Bembridge's southern boundary, from June 1921 until the following October. Farmowner E. U. Taylor retained his aviation tastes, further helped when the Automobile Association included Bembridge in its long civil landing ground list from October 1933. Within a year this small privately operated site became accepted as a fully qualified airfield but Spartan Air Lines had already made it an intermediate stop for the company's passenger route to and from Cowes/Somerton and Heston in western London since April 1933. Three-engined Spartan Cruiser monoplanes arrived to take care of this popular service. Private civil flying however continued to dominate proceedings during the 1930s.

Like most other Isle of Wight airfields, Bembridge had to close in September 1939 on the outbreak of war, not just because civil aviation was prohibited but that the island seemed far too vulnerable. For years it lay disused as deep trenches ran across the landing area and a compensation dispute tediously went on. Finally air taxi-cum-pleasure flying concern Morgan Aviation, previously at Cowes/Somerton, reopened Bembridge in 1948 and carried out extension work in the process. The Bembridge and Sandown Aero Club also arose in August and hosted a display on June 5 1949 which attracted an excellent total of 113 light aircraft. Sadly ex-ATA pilot Audrey Morgan's concern folded in the same year.

THE AIRFIELDS OF BRITAIN

Small firms mixed with airliners in the 1950s, notable among the former being charter, aircraft maintenance and aerial photography business East Wight Air Charter Ltd. Portsmouth, Southsea and Isle of Wight Aviation Ltd had joined Spartan Air Lines for services when demanded in the 1930s, and now twenty years on various independent operators such as BKS Air Transport and Starways flew summer holiday passenger routes to the airfield. Bembridge's landing area length almost doubled so that Bristol Freighters of Silver City Airways could transport tourists and their cars from Southampton after May 1953, this improvement enabling general airline traffic to briefly increase in the mid-1950s.

Another company was beginning to make a name for itself. F.R. John Britten and N. Desmond Norman had started their business association in 1951. From designing and building a one-off ultra-light monoplane, Britten-Norman became a limited company in August 1954 and took over the running of Bembridge in 1957 with the intention of promoting light aircraft use. The firm prospered by producing agricultural aerial spraying equipment through its subsidiary Crop Culture (Aerial) Ltd, well-known abroad with a vast fleet of 60 aircraft but not nearly as much once the prototype Islander first flew on June 13 1965.

Right from the word go this twin-engined monoplane looked a winner. Such was the Islander's potential that Britten-Norman opened a new factory at the end of 1966, away from Bembridge's old buildings on the south side, as orders poured in. Fitting a third engine to the tail produced the larger Trislander in 1970, and a militarised Islander version known as the Defender has become popular with smaller overseas air forces. Well over 1,000 Islanders have been produced alone and the type has a marvellous worldwide reputation.

The Britten-Norman story has still not proved to be an easy ride. Early mismanagement and some odd operating techniques — such as Islander manufacture in Romania — created severe problems, forcing Britten-Norman to call in the receivers in October 1971 with debts of over £5 million. The Fairey company stepped in as financial saviour in August 1972: aircraft production now began in Belgium, with Bembridge being relegated to design and sales duties. Worse was to come in 1977 when Fairey suddenly collapsed and made Britten-Norman once more rely upon Romania — not forgetting licence production in the Philippines. Founder designer John Britten also died in July to make it a miserable year all round; he had left the company in 1976 to pursue his own ideas but everyone felt sorry to hear of his premature passing.

Help had to appear during 1978 from another unlikely quarter of the world as Bembridge again staggered back from the brink. Pilatus of Switzerland has long been famous for its single-engined Porter monoplane, as renowned as the Islander in the short take-off and landing field of aviation, and at last brought much needed stability.

Although Pilatus Britten-Norman remains the major force at Bembridge these days, company flying has never excluded all other forms of aerial activity. Sailplanes of the Solent GC used to be present in the 1960s, while an Islander (naturally) gives pleasure trips to holidaymakers. The Vectis GC brought gliders back to the site in October 1993.

For years Bembridge tended to suffer as much as Bellasize from a suspect grass landing area, especially prone to flooding in winter. A tarmac strip did latterly exist but was tiny and only meant for Britten-Norman use. This stretch has gone by the wayside as a much longer hardened runway was installed during 1979. Along with three hangars, Bembridge is now more capable than ever of accommodating aircraft. Many lighter types indeed use the airfield as starting and finishing point for Schneider Trophy races, though these are not the high prestige and high pressure floatplane events of the 1920s and early 1930s but meetings now mainly for enjoyment. The times have changed at Britain's airfields: Bembridge has seen some pretty tough ones at that, yet has still lasted the course, even better than the Islander.

196/SZ632870. 4½ miles NE of Sandown.

Bembridge (seaplane), Isle of Wight

The Bembridge of today is not that town's first airfield, for seaplanes flew between the early months of 1915 and 1919 from a site used in more recent times by a short passenger ferry. Bembridge later saw No 253 Squadron form in the summer of 1918; a landplane detachment of *Scarecrow* DH6s stood close by at Foreland. One seaplane shed measuring 96 by 60 feet and a smaller square building 71 feet long on each side formed the hangarage.

This Short 184 marine base was put up for sale by the

utterly reviled Disposal Board in mid-September 1919 after No 253 Squadron had disbanded on May 5, having seen precious little in the way of action against U-boats like many other units. But it appears that water-borne flying lasted at Bembridge well into peacetime as local inhabitants are adamant civil seaplanes continued to visit until at least the early 1930s. The Supermarine company undoubtedly mounted a passenger service between Woolston in Southampton and various Isle of Wight towns during the summer of 1919. Finding other actual hard proof to corroborate such mostly verbal evidence however still remains a difficult job. Of course, when has British airfield research ever been easy?
196/SZ641887. NW side of town, on E side of Bembridge Harbour.

Benbecula, Western Isles

Alternative Name: Balivanich
Strange as it may seem, breezy Benbecula and the three big ELGs of Carnaby, Manston and Woodbridge on the eastern coastline of England all shared one thing in common. Each had a special type of runway, a mixture of bitumen and sand which produced a flexible surface easy to repair after any crash-landing. Only eight 1939-45 era airfields employed these unusual runways: like Benbecula, they have made particularly strong geographical and social impacts even by normal British standards.

Benbecula means in Gaelic 'mountain of the fords'. Not a good omen for an airfield, but this failed to deter Northern and Scottish Airways from first using this island site actually named after one at the other end of Britain from Bembridge. Merely a grassy field with a tiny hut and wind-sock for company in the days before World War Two, airliners arrived on request from March 1936 as happened at Barra. Licensing of highly rated Benbecula came in May 1938, four years after Midland and Scottish Air Ferries had originally tested it. Airliner flights stopped in September 1939 but restarted on May 14 1940.

The airfield was later prepared for RAF Coastal Command once into wartime because of obvious military potential. Service personnel began turning up from August 30 1941 but Benbecula did not fully open until April 28 1942 and only received its initial unit on June 30. No 206 Squadron had arrived from Aldergrove, converting to Fortresses which proved to have far greater ranges than Lockheed Hudsons.

This ability to reach further out into the Atlantic Ocean soon brought results as a U-boat slipped beneath the waves for good on October 27. Enemy submarine activity rapidly increased, with some of the fiercest fighting yet seen, but Benbecula easily moved up several gears to meet this latest challenge as No 206 Squadron sank another five U-boats in the first six months of 1943. No 220 Squadron appeared with more Fortresses in March to intensify the hunt, though the unexpected tactical U-boat withdrawal during the spring undoubtedly became a big factor in this new element scoring a duck while stationed in the Outer Hebrides. Soon No 220 was off on its travels again by departing with No 206 Squadron for the Azores in October to encounter a brand new U-boat threat and a brand new airfield built to counter them, their personnel facing a brand new climate too.

C&M held sway for just under a year as nobody could find any real use for Benbecula. There was hardly any flying, the most notable event being a small fire in the control tower on November 11 1943. This place only came alive again in September 1944 when Nos 179, 304, 838 and 842 Squadrons all transferred to the station. While No 304 became the sole example of this mixed RAF/FAA batch to remain any length of time, until March 1945, U-boats were becoming far more elusive as their numbers waned under constant Allied airborne and seaborne assaults.

Once another Wellington squadron – No 36 – had disbanded on June 4, Benbecula's military importance for the moment quickly dwindled. Not so RAF clearance as the airfield officially closed to flying on the 26th but its last resident aircraft – an Oxford runabout for No 36 Squadron – not going to Thorney Island until July 25; No 1680 Flight then still made communications trips to Benbecula and other Western Isles airfields afterwards. Theory clashed with reality a second time as C&M should have started on July 26, though an RAF party detailed for the task only arrived on August 22. Lined up for agricultural storage use in the autumn of 1945, a peculiar idea given that the harsh weather had not allowed unit gardens to flourish, Coastal Command held personnel at Benbecula right up to September 18 1946.

Service evacuation did not mean that all flying had stopped. Scottish Airways kept up its civil route to Benbecula after World War Two, having mounted a most helpful air mail function in the conflict. BEA took charge of civil duties in 1947, being succeeded as time progressed by British Airways and Loganair. Construction of a rocket range during the 1950s resulted in the airfield reverting to RAF supervision for a while, and it is now used by a mixture of civil and military aircraft, the latter also supporting an RAF radar station in the area. The shortest of Benbecula's three runways has closed to all visitors, a north-south stretch being worthy of note too because the northern half possesses no supportive perimeter track to aid taxying aircraft, simply a turning circle. You would think that this inhospitable area would be the last place to see gliders but the RAFGSA-aligned Greylag GC became a recent resident. Concerns have now grown about erosion threatening the landing area.

West of this extremely vital site in every respect stands the small settlement of Balivanich, by which name Benbecula is erroneously but almost inevitably known to the surrounding community. Local opinions of their airfield next door tend to vary greatly. Yes, they say, Benbecula provides tremendous employment and social benefits for the hard pressed islanders, but ... How they complain about the noise, rockets disturbing fishing boats, the 'shanty town' effect of Benbecula's modern support buildings. And let us not forget that hoary old chestnut they mention more about our disused airfields, missing the whole point as usual: the 'lack of beauty'. But they – exactly who are they? – forget that if Benbecula had never existed, the main road connecting South Uist, Benbecula and North Uist would never have been built and everyone still have to travel by ferry between islands.

What would the Netherlands' most famous airfield have done without this Hebridean site either? Two of its ten less standard ½T2 hangars were moved to Schiphol after World War Two: how on earth the Dutch got to know about their availability is anyone's guess. Some hangars have transferred great distances from their original airfield to a new one, but few this far. No ½T2s survive, though the control tower does in modified form.

Still more remarkable is how the famous Brahan Seer predicted centuries ago 'big grey geese' – presumably aircraft – on Benbecula. The Fortresses of World War Two indeed displayed a splash of grey, even if they were primarily coloured white. But did he, one wonders, predict their even bigger stone nest?

22/NF785558. Between North Uist and South Uist, NE of Balivanich.

THE AIRFIELDS OF BRITAIN: VOLUME 1

Benson, Oxfordshire

A good-looking twin-engined wooden aircraft flew into Benson on July 13 1941 for No 1 Photographic Reconnaissance Unit. *W4051* became the first de Havilland Mosquito in RAF service. This was an aircraft destined to be devastatingly successful, extremely versatile and greatly liked by crews. Few types have ever achieved such standards of near-perfection before or since. The Mosquito's inaugural operational base has not done badly as well.

Benson, the master PR airfield and massive British star, opened at the start of 1939. Sidney Cotton was still developing his aerial photography theories at Heston when Battle light bombers of Nos 103 and 150 Squadrons arrived in April. As soon as they crossed to France as part of the AASF on September 2, so more from Abingdon and Kidlington soon replaced them.

Nos 52 and 63 Squadrons joined forces in April 1940 to form No 12 OTU, receiving refugee Czech and Polish airmen as the summer progressed. New equipment was urgently required as Battle squadrons in France had suffered severe losses, and Wellingtons therefore appeared. Benson's satellite over four miles north-west at Mount Farm — as shattered now as the parent is preserved, just like Stanton Harcourt and Abingdon respectively used to be until 1992 — bore some of the pressure, strangely possessing hard runways while Benson still had a grass landing surface. No 12 OTU later moved to Chipping Warden in Northamptonshire during the summer of 1941 to give priority to PR aircraft. PR would really put Benson on the map.

Reconnaissance had become the first truly suitable role for military aircraft in the early days of flying. Its value rose as aircraft and cameras both improved in quality. As aircraft flew longer distances and at higher altitudes, strategic as well as tactical reconnaissance began to be feasible. Cameras meanwhile started producing photographs of increasingly greater definition, on film rather than plates, and work automatically instead of manually. Now No 1 PRU had necessarily come from vulnerable Heston, minus Sidney Cotton, at the end of 1940 with Spitfires and Blenheims. Benson lay not too far from London — but closer still was the Central Interpretation Unit at Medmenham, a few miles east of Henley-on-Thames, where sharp-eyed personnel meticulously examined photographs.

Speed became of the essence as aircraft touched down at

THE AIRFIELDS OF BRITAIN

Benson with roll after roll of film. As the Photographic Intelligence Section at the Old Mansion House in Ewelme, east of the airfield, dealt with immediate operational details, negatives would be speedily processed in a developing room. Prints were then whistled down the A423 by despatch-rider to Medmenham for instant evaluation.

No 140 Squadron joined No 1 PRU for this constant routine once having formed on September 17 1941. This unit also received Spitfires and Blenheims but shifted to Mount Farm in May 1942. Benson needed hard runways, having previously being extended for No 12 OTU's Wellingtons because the landing area had quite a downward slope. Such later reconstruction naturally reduced its performance for a few months, though probing flights still proved successful as distinctively coloured Spitfires and newer Mosquitoes travelled to all corners of Europe. The PRU quickly expanded with Flights at many airfields in Britain and overseas but their sheer dispersal required better organisation.

Squadrons were created as a result on October 19 1942, Nos 541, 542 and 543 operating Spitfires plus No 544 Mosquitoes in the long run. No 540 Squadron, which had formed instead at Leuchars in Fife with more Mosquitoes but maintained a detachment at Benson, came in full during February 1944. Unit movement co-ordination allowed films to pour in more than ever before as the photographic section set a new daily record on January 5 1944 by producing 6,483 negatives and 19,826 prints.

Although No 543 Squadron disbanded on October 18 1943, Benson's other units played a tremendous part in winning World War Two by always sending out usually unarmed aircraft, speed, height and manoeuvrability their only real defence. They watched enemy ports, kept a beady eye on the *Tirpitz*, discovered the V-1 at Peenemunde in November 1943 and monitored the subsequent *Noball* sites from where these missiles were launched. Some jobs never seemed like they would finish as Bomber Command had to be assisted both before and after raids for target location and bomb damage assessment. Tactical reconnaissance mixed with the strategic variety too when Benson aircraft scoured the French countryside prior to D-Day. Figures for May 1944 of 400 operational sorties, 185,376 negatives and 446,099 prints told their own story of the effort involved to make the Allied landings in Normandy a success.

These above achievements and many more Benson accomplished are too countless to mention. The airfield's brilliance was not affected by having to work increasingly

THE AIRFIELDS OF BRITAIN: VOLUME 1

alone in RAF circles, especially after the USAAF gained Mount Farm for its own PR aircraft in the early part of 1943. Detachments nevertheless continued to be as varied as in the days of No 1 PRU: apart from the other usual home-based airfield aides such as Leuchars and St Eval, Lossiemouth, Gibraltar and even airfields in Russia provided auxiliary help when range demands became impossibly great.

Benson had long since carved out an almost unique place in British airfield history when No 540 Squadron moved to France in March 1945. War was coming to an end but cameras aboard aircraft hardly let up by producing in that following month 126,691 negatives and 318,567 prints from 245 operational and 27 local sorties. Although No 540 came back to Oxfordshire in November, No 542 Squadron had already disbanded on August 27 and No 544 likewise on October 13 to leave Benson's PR element somewhat depleted. Such had been their strength in wartime that few other units then visited the airfield. No 618 Squadron of *Highball* fame stayed between September 1943 and June 1944 before its time at Beccles II, though only at cadre level while aircrews flew from Predannack in Cornwall to give them something to do. Benson had certainly been given a heavy work schedule but at least the station did not have to suffer a myriad of differing tasks as happened with many other World War Two airfields.

The Central Interpretation Unit moved from Medmenham to Nuneham Park, close to now doomed Mount Farm, in April 1946. Peacetime created some unusual jobs at Benson, notably mail-carrying, until Nos 540 and 541 Squadrons disbanded on September 30 1946. No 58 Squadron's Mosquitoes and No 82 Squadron's Lancasters immediately succeeded them next day and occupied themselves with survey duties at home and in Africa before going to Wyton in Cambridgeshire on March 25/26 1953. Their predecessors were revived at the end of 1947, eventually flying jets, No 540 Squadron also going to Wyton in March 1953. No 541 Squadron had been in Germany since June 1951.

This last unit had perhaps given a warning of events to come with the Cold War now in full flow. Aircraft required to be positioned further east instead of staying in central England, hence this sudden mass exodus to the Pathfinder Force's former HQ base. Wyton could always claim that Benson had stolen its thunder, for a Blenheim took off from there on September 3 1939 on the RAF's first PR sortie of World War Two. Nobody could dispute that it became the new PR airfield king after March 1953.

Out too had gone No 237 OCU. Formed in July 1947, the

THE AIRFIELDS OF BRITAIN

PR training unit made not for Wyton in October 1951 but Bassingbourn. Within three months there the OCU had become known as No 231 and started flying Canberras.

This massive overall clearance meant an unsettled life for some years. Benson became an aircraft ferrying base and even home for FAA fighter squadrons in the 1950s. No 21 Squadron later reformed on May 1 1959 as a Scottish Aviation Twin Pioneer light short take-off and landing transport unit but moved to Kenya in September.

A more defined role arose shortly afterwards for Benson to be the cradle for Armstrong Whitworth Argosy transport squadrons. The airfield needed considerable revamping for this task, and acquired among other items a new control tower in 1960. Eventually No 114 became the first squadron to operate Argosies when reformed on October 1 1961; Nos 105, 215 and 267 Squadrons plus No 242 OCU followed during 1961-63. All either travelled elsewhere or, in No 267 Squadron's case, stayed at Benson until disbanded on June 30 1970. The first in turn became the last, as the trail-blazing No 114 Squadron was forced to disband because of cut-backs on October 31 1971.

If not quite its busy self as in days of yore, Benson has kept and still keeps steadily active. No 72 Squadron's Wessex helicopters were present during part of 1981, replaced by Hawker Siddeley Andovers of No 115 Squadron for radar calibration work in January 1983. RAF airfields at home and in Europe had to have their navigation aids such as approach radars and Instrument Landing Systems constantly checked.

In addition to huge PR fame, Benson is also known for trifling royal use by holding a Flight for the reigning monarch. This element has maintained a presence since 1939 (excluding an absence for part of World War Two due to totally justified wartime economies) to use numerous fixed-wing aircraft and helicopter types. Gliders of No 612 Volunteer GS are still present too but not those of the Chilterns GC, badly crippled by a hangar fire in 1970 which destroyed all four club sailplanes and damaged the building.

Another graceful aircraft – the Mosquito – will always be best associated with Benson. But runner-up has to be the ungainly *Jupiter*, a silver-coloured monoplane with a propeller above the fuselage which for several years held the world record for a distance covered by a man-powered machine. Other British airfields had become involved in one of the greatest aviation dreams with varying success after an industrialist initiated the Kremer Prize for any craft to fly around a specified figure-of-eight course. Until the *Gossamer*

205

THE AIRFIELDS OF BRITAIN: VOLUME 1

Albatross finally won the large cash reward, no aircraft actually achieved this feat but *Jupiter* came closest by travelling 1,171 yards at Benson on June 29 1972.

The early 1990s, and particularly 1992, brought new faces and duties to the base. Abingdon's light aircraft trainers moved in when that airfield tragically and needlessly closed, while No 60 Squadron reformed with Wessexes after this ex-Andover transport element was pushed out of RAF Germany. No 115 Squadron's electronic Andovers remained until the unit disbanded in October 1993 and its aircraft contracted out to a civilian company at East Midlands Airport to carry on calibration work. Who would have ever thought that privatisation could touch the RAF?

Not much has been done over the years to radically change this great airfield's appearance. Easily recognisable are four C hangars, which were helped out during wartime by ten Blisters constructed from November 1943. Support buildings on the east side form a town in itself and have little altered either. Luftwaffe aircraft occasionally attempted to disfigure Benson but met with no real success, bar a raid by one Ju 88 on February 27 1941 that left one Wellington destroyed, five other aircraft and the control tower damaged plus one person dead.

You cannot somehow miss the unique atmosphere an airfield exudes. Look around and even surrounding buildings have airfield associations: to the north is Cottesmore Farm. Only the landing area has changed to any extent as the 06/24 runway lies closed of two mid-war period hard stretches built. The well-worn A423 used to run below Benson's southern boundary but runway extensions agreed with the Ministry of Transport in March 1941 closed the road at this point and resulted in having to turn a B class road into an A one with some ingenuity.

Close by stands the town of Wallingford which has enjoyed incalculable benefits from its neighbouring superstar. It might be said that a small private and AA-listed civil airfield of the same name owned during the 1930s by a Mr Frost indirectly helped create what became Benson a short distance north. Whether this is the case or not, more than adequate payment has been made by way of jobs and PR of the public relations variety. Maybe Benson is much quieter today, maybe the old PR aircraft have gone, but Benson will always be remembered for playing one of the most crucial roles of any individual British airfield since their inception.

164/SU627914. 2 miles NE of Wallingford. Good view of airfield from minor road on W side.

Benton, Northumberland

Virtually identical in name to airfield superstar Benson but totally different in purpose, Benton could not be more obscure in comparison. Houses and schools stand on this former landing ground controlled by No 36 (HD) Squadron from June 1917. Benton was still active at the Armistice in November 1918 but the RAF relinquished this site in June 1919, the same month as No 36 Squadron disbanded.

Various surrounding farms gave their name to the landing ground in its heyday. Suburbia relentlessly expanded after World War Two to so great an extent that Benton now forms part of the Longbenton residential area north-east of Newcastle. An RAF ground station named Long Benton however lasted for many years and held such diverse organisations as No 15 Balloon Centre, No 14 MU and No 64 RAF Reserve Centre.

88/NZ275695. NW of Wallsend, between A188 and railway line.

Bentwaters, Suffolk

Alternative Name: Butley
This major military airfield was noteworthy in two respects. While houses swamped and killed off Benton, an airfield wiped out just one building here in Suffolk, but far more important is how Bentwaters ranks in history as Britain's last active airfield of World War Two. While Culdrose is even younger, the Cornish military site did not open for business until 1947.

Wartime construction proved slow at Bentwaters after being requisitioned as an operational bomber base in July 1942 under an entirely different name. It was originally referred to as Butley, a title which possessed previous airfield links as a small experimental airfield known as such had supported Orfordness during World War One. Now for eighteen months in World War Two this name once again sufficed before Butley suddenly became Bentwaters on January 15 1944. Why this change took place is far from clear, for no other airfield in Britain sounded remotely like Butley; one can only guess that postal difficulties may have forced this alternative.

But such confusion, if that was the case, seemed minor when planners started hunting for a suitable replacement name. Every locality they traced threw up problems as Eyke and Rendlesham bore far too great a resemblance to fellow Suffolk airfields Eye and Mendlesham; Wantisden could be mistaken for famous Suffolk Expansion Period station Wattisham; and to the north stood Shepherd's Farm, alarmingly similar to Shepherd's Grove — yes, in Suffolk! This is why inspiration had to come from a solitary dwelling which stood on the proposed future landing area.

Yet another of Suffolk's apparently endless supply of airfields — Beccles II — entered the wartime arena with uncertainty as we have seen. Bentwaters did too, and mirrored early days at Beccles by being a rejected USAAF site passed to Bomber Command after opening on C&M on April 17 1944. The base lingered in this state for some more months as building work continued right through the summer and autumn while Britain's last batch of airfields thronged with activity. At last the FAA received true naval airfields after having to make do and mend as Crimond (later better known as Rattray) in north-east Scotland was commissioned on October 31. Culham, from where FAA fighters fled to Benson in 1953, then also opened next day. Bentwaters meanwhile stayed officially shut — but not for long.

Fighter Command recognised its potential three weeks later on November 22 by snatching this airfield from Bomber Command and fully opening Bentwaters. No 129 Squadron appeared during the second week of December, the first of many Mustang squadrons as Nos 64, 118, 126, 165 and 234 came in the same month with more examples of this tremendous American-built fighter. Most stayed until World War Two ended to escort RAF heavy bombers which now operated by day as Luftwaffe fighter opposition decreased.

The airfield may have opened terribly late but Bentwaters still gave everyone stationed there much lively activity, if on the extra-curricular and unintended fronts. Personnel experienced great difficulties in trying to create their own off-duty entertainment because of their airfield's particularly remote position, and 'Liberty Runs' to Ipswich therefore had to be approved. Despite being our last all-new World War Two site, airfield builders had still not entirely learned all the tricks of their specialised trade as the perimeter track showed signs of suspect construction techniques. The Drem lighting in this area first had to be raised as it had sunk to such an extent to be almost invisible; cracking and breaking then became noticeable in sections of the perimeter track by February 1945.

Bentwaters happily weathered these comparatively minor difficulties and carried on holding more RAF fighter squadrons into peacetime. No 234 Squadron made two further visits up to February 1946, this time with Spitfires, while Meteor jets of No 124 Squadron came in October 1945. This second unit became known as No 56 Squadron on April 1 1946, leaving in September to allow Meteor trainers of No 226 OCU be present prior to Bentwaters going on C&M in September 1949. The airfield closed down on February 28 1950.

Silence was only temporary as the USAF took over Bentwaters in early 1951 for the 81st Fighter Interceptor Wing. Another North American product after the Mustang now appeared in September: the F-86 Sabre, undoubted star of the Korean War and first foreign-manned aircraft ever to defend Britain. Following changes of name and aircraft types over subsequent years, the 81st Tactical Fighter Wing eventually settled upon McDonnell Douglas F-4 Phantom IIs in the mid-1960s. Some of the first examples of these excellent interceptors seen in Britain had earlier visited Bentwaters and greatly impressed all who watched them, a terrific advance upon the nuclear-armed Republic F-84F Thunderstreak fighter-bombers present in the 1950s.

The enormously strong Bentwaters fighter connection lasted for a while longer but yet another alteration as the 1970s ended saw a clean break as the Phantoms were replaced from January 1979 by Fairchild A-10A Thunderbolt II close support aircraft. Ugly, ungainly, not fast but structurally tough and fearsomely effective, this type best described as a modern day jet Ju 87 could savage enemy tanks or other armour with a devastating rapid-fire 30 millimetre cannon and underwing cluster bombs.

This airfield hugely altered both its own appearance and the landscape since 1944. A road which crossed Bentwaters originally required to be closed. The main runway was later extended at both ends to increase in length to 9,000 feet, half as much again as in World War Two when this place was a typical Class A airfield. Two T2s of that era survived but Hardened Aircraft Shelters lately tended to more catch the eye. Best place to view daily activities was from the tiny Wantisden Church on Bentwaters' east side, although supportive facilities crept up towards this building to limit opportunities for airfield and aircraft spotters.

Fighters tried to make a come-back here as the 527th Aggressor Squadron, formerly known as the 527th Tactical Fighter Training Aggressor Squadron, arrived from Alconbury in 1988. But General Dynamics F-16s did not stay long as swingeing US defence cuts announced a year later forced this element to disband. A heavy numerical superiority of A-10As however still confirmed that their late starter base had more than made up for lost time, showing the fallacy of government cut-backs by their brilliant collective performance in the Gulf War of 1991. Thunderbolts succeeded Mustangs, so in a way time stood still at Bentwaters.

Sad to say, events are happening too swiftly these days as the money-minded are back with a vengeance. The USAF was thanked for the Gulf War by being told to clear out by September 1993; the same applied to nearby Woodbridge where the 81st TFW also stayed. All 72 A-10As stationed at both airfields were to return to America, the Wing be inactivated or disbanded, and withdrawal of Bentwaters' approximately 4,500 military personnel to begin in 1992. These airfields would be handed to the Ministry of Defence once complete evacuation had been effected. In reality the last A-10As left not for home but Germany on March 23 1993.

Strong rumours persisted that RAF Harriers would move in from Wittering when the Americans left. Local residents expressed extreme regret as in August 1992 the MoD abandoned plans to take over Bentwaters and Woodbridge. No satisfactory reason was given but it is suggested that the RAF had overlooked one simple matter: the bases would have required total rewiring with different US amperage.

One shudders to think what will happen after Bentwaters finally closes in 1994. Will a higher education college for Suffolk be established, or a less imaginative industrial estate? Or will totally brainless yuppie housing win the day? We can safely bet that all the thousands upon thousands of people who have gained direct or indirect employment from a place which ploughed about £50 million per year into the local economy are deeply worried. Even an adjacent farmer has appreciated Bentwaters for all its worth. If the authorities do close down the airfield for good, there will be one almighty war. And we are not talking about the Russians...
156/TM352534. 7 miles NE of Woodbridge.

Berrow, Hereford and Worcester

Alternative Name: Pendock Moor
Airfields, by their very nature, have to exist in less populated

areas. Sometimes they appear in really remote places as Bentwaters has demonstrated. Berrow in western England can also be classified as one of the latter type, a hopelessly forgotten SLG ignored by even most local residents in this sparsely occupied piece of countryside dotted with tiny villages and hamlets such as Berrow to the west.

Perhaps Berrow's primary claim to fame was the abnormally long distance the SLG stood apart from each parenting storage airfield, almost rivalling Beechwood for remoteness. Nos 5 and 20 MUs at Kemble and Aston Down both resided over 25 miles south in Gloucestershire and made limited use of the airfield from the spring of 1941. The CO of No 20 MU visited Berrow on November 26 1940, which was stated as being ready to receive aircraft on May 16 1941 and in operation by the 15th. Four machines departed as bad weather forced the SLG to close on November 15 but orders received five days later kept it open.

Ownership passed in the summer of 1942 to No 38 MU – about 55 miles away in south Wales at Llandow. While this odd arrangement worked well enough until Berrow closed on May 31 1945, personnel must have felt the strain of two airfields in separate countries and Berrow transferred back to Aston Down on November 9 1944. No 38 MU still dispersed aircraft there, records not saying if No 20 MU did so as well. Apart from Blenheim and Spitfire storage, this airfield saw some auxiliary use like many other SLGs as communications aircraft of the Telecommunications Research Establishment a few miles north-east at Defford and (briefly) No 5 Glider Training School at Shobdon employed the grass site to a small extent.

Berrow's days looked distinctly numbered after No 38 MU closed its other SLG at Chepstow on March 31 1945. Activity here lasted but two more months exactly; soon a fairly empty field became available, although an odd support building around the ex-airfield has held on. To the south the M50 motorway makes a consistently greater noise than any aircraft, while north-east across the A438 is Pendock Moor, by which name Berrow was alternatively referred to. No nominal confusion would have occurred with Barrow in north-west England because of the official secrecy towards all SLGs in Britain. Ostensibly they never existed: today an airfield's presence seems equally unlikely. About the only people who know about this backwater are caravanners.

150/SO808340. 7½ miles W of Tewkesbury by A438.

Beverley I, Humberside

Racecourses normally tend to be in more inhabited areas of Britain: they have to be, or else business would dry up pretty quickly. The majority of British racecourses are also blessed with airfield links, one of the less obvious being Beverley.

No 47 Squadron formed as Beverley geared up on March 1 1916. 'C' Flight of No 33 (HD) Squadron was here too until October but No 47 Squadron had left a month earlier for Greece. This unit became famous in RAF circles for work in North Africa, India and the Far East before and during World War Two, and only returned to Britain and Fairford in particular during September 1946. Another new arrival in 1917 at Beverley to be established far more abroad was No 80 Squadron, equipped with the effective if unpredictable Camel fighter. It resided at the converted racecourse up to January 1918: Western Front service was followed by duties out further east like No 47 Squadron to ensure that No 80 – apart from a brief period in 1937 – did not permanently settle at home again until April 1944.

Real foreigners spent some time in the area. Several Canadian Reserve Squadrons had formed or gathered strength during 1917 until they were ready to leave and bring military aviation – and airfields – to their own part of the world.

The mix of training and secondary defence requirements lasted at Beverley for the remainder of World War One. No 72 TS arrived from Wyton in January 1918 to operate twelve Avro 504s and a similar number of Royal Aircraft Factory SE5s, while aircraft under the 6th Brigade retained the right to use this site as a 2nd class Home Defence landing ground. Activity was still evident by November 1918 but No 72 TS disbanded in 1919 and, after much uncertainty, Beverley moved to List E Disposal Board level in October. Flying may well have already stopped by the summer when the racecourse owners and Beverley Town Council agreed to alterations on part of the land. Final closure resulted in February 1920.

Although some areas were retained for military purposes post-war, racing soon resumed – in this case during June – as at Yorkshire's other racecourses-cum-airfields. The all-vital turf served as part of Beverley's landing area but this essential component also extended towards the north-west. Two hangars, an Aircraft Repair Shed and supporting facilities lay on the south-west side, though nothing can be seen of airfield relics today. Beverley hides a useful past all too well but the

town's Museum of Army Transport does deal with army aviation history, and aptly holds a restored Blackburn Beverley transport which was refurbished at Paull, a small disused civil site south-east of Hull. A hangar is badly needed to house the aircraft and an appeal has been started. Meanwhile, greater joy has occurred with a new Beverley airfield . . .
106/TA018399. On W side of town.

Beverley II, Humberside

Alternative Name: Linley Hill
Over 70 years had to go by until Beverley could receive another airfield. This replacement is quite a distance from the town, closer to the village of Leven, where you turn left and keep going west along a rough dusty road. The sight that greets you may not look impressive but Beverley II is licensed and has been since the summer of 1991.

Doubts increased about Brough's future when the Hull Aero Club was told to move out of the famous old Blackburn and now British Aerospace factory airfield. A farmer who already had a landing strip at Linley Hill on Leven Carrs saved the day by offering his land, and Beverley II was developed at a cost of £14,000, about twice as much as expected. Available at that moment were only a grass runway, portable club office and an ex-RAF refuelling lorry used in the Gulf War but more facilities are planned. These include a nearby barn turned into a hangar. We wish everybody well.
107/TA069462. Take A1035 NE of town 7 miles to Leven. Turn first left in village after church, airfield 3 miles to W.

Bibury, Gloucestershire

For our next piece of real history we stay in the wilds — and what an odd piece. The immediate scene is one of alleged 'temporary' buildings amid light woodland as you pass a small guardhouse to your right by a road running northwards. This must surely be an old Army camp. But it is not — and not just an airfield either, rather a Battle of Britain star. Bibury merits as much a mention as the Biggin Hills, Kenleys, Tangmeres *et al.*

Bibury's moment of glory came as the Battle reached its peak. Hurricanes and Spitfires of Nos 87 and 92 Squadrons detached here between August and December 1940 in order to fill up a defensive gap in central England. Their Flights often operated at night and gained some success against Luftwaffe aircraft but night flying did not suit the Spitfire in particular. This probably explains why No 92 Squadron's detached personnel only stayed during part of August and September. To add to their woes an enemy bombing raid blew away a Spitfire to smithereens on August 19. Only meant as an interim fighter airfield, Bibury said goodbye to these high-performance residents as soon as the Battle of Britain petered out.

Unspectacular efficiency otherwise marked Bibury's primary career as a training airfield. Nobody is quite sure when this glorified field first saw use. An RLG for No 3 SFTS at South Cerney from May 30 1940 anyhow, Oxfords of the succeeding No 3 (P) AFU further operated until November 7 1944. No 1539 BAT Flight, which arrived from the parent airfield in July 1943 with more Oxfords, lasted up to this time as well. Available hangarage gradually built up to the point where Bibury could call upon a T1 and five Double Blisters.

Aerial instruction stopped as Flying Training Command handed Bibury and a C&M party to Maintenance Command and No 7 MU on November 15 1944. A perimeter track which remains largely in place complemented two Sommerfeld Track runways but these metal stretches led to this relatively early closure to aircraft. Charmy Down near Bath duly replaced Bibury: that airfield lay over 30 miles south-west of South Cerney instead of just seven miles north-east but hard runways at Charmy Down easily compensated for the difficult travel arrangements No 3 (P) AFU would have to make from now on.

No 7 MU stored equipment at Bibury for a few more years. Criminality abounded in the early hours of October 6 1949 when items were stolen from the hangars. Five civilians received jail sentences in November – but so too did three airmen. All stores had gone by February 1950 for Bibury to close on the 28th, and South Cerney parented the inactive site from April 12 until August 1 1952.

Two Blisters plus some support buildings today stand sandwiched between a minor road and farmland to acknowledge the Battle of Britain's most unlikely hero. All those fussy villagers in Bibury would be well advised to spend some time promoting their nearby star than completely ignoring the airfield.

163/SP114093. 12 miles NE of Cirencester, 2½ miles N of village.

Bicester, Oxfordshire

Allowing for an uncertain existence in recent years, Bicester remains active and displays all the qualities of a mixed 1920s/1930s Expansion Period airfield. The prototype Handley Page Halifax heavy bomber made its first flight there on October 25 1939 too.

Aviation first hit the Bicester area when Lieutenant F.F. Waldron of No 2 Squadron popped in on February 19 1913 during his unit's epic movement from Farnborough to Upper Dysart near Montrose. Of course, no proper airfield as such was available to him then, and would not be to any aircraft at all until long after World War One started. Initial construction and occupation during 1917 enabled Bicester to become active but only in a lax sense, for builders still required to do much work. Not the least of their jobs needing attention was the erection of six 180 by 100 feet aeroplane sheds and an Aircraft Repair Shed with the same dimensions. This meant that little really happened for months afterwards, apart from No 118 Squadron being briefly present in the summer of 1918 before disbanding as one of the many prematurely born RAF elements of this era which never became operational.

At last Bicester appeared to be on the move when No 44 TDS and its trainers transferred from Oxford during October 1918. But World War One only had a month to go, so throwing this airfield back into the realms of uncertainty. No 2 Squadron oddly enough stayed after the Great War as a cadre unit during February-September 1919, succeeded by the mostly similarly grounded No 5 Squadron which disbanded on January 20 1920. Bicester could not realistically survive by holding such no-hoper forces and closed four months later as Britain's enormous anti-airfield assault gathered momentum.

Here became one airfield to see a quicker revival than most when reopened in January 1928 as a bomber station after the 1926 Air Estimates allowed £233,000 for reconstruction. 1928 proved a remarkable year all round for the general Bicester area, as archaeological excavations confirmed the existence of a Roman settlement near this old town best known for industry. No historical thought had been given towards saving the World War One hangars but Bicester was back to create more real history.

Nos 100, 33 and then 101 Squadrons passed through over the next few years, flying in turn good load-carrying Hawker Horsleys, speedy Hawker Harts and twin-engined Boulton

THE AIRFIELDS OF BRITAIN: VOLUME 1

Paul Sidestrands. This last unit switched to using a developed version of the Sidestrand known as the Overstrand, extremely notable for possessing a revolutionary power-operated nose gun turret. Nos 90 and 144 Squadrons later reformed in 1937, the first being given Blenheims along with No 101 Squadron in enough time before they moved east towards West Raynham in May 1939. Briefly breaking the bombers' dominance was the reforming No 48 Squadron in 1935. It evolved out of a Flight of No 101 Squadron but shifted to the fabled Manston without receiving Avro Ansons intended for use in a general reconnaissance role.

Although Battles of Nos 12 and 142 Squadrons arrived from Andover on May 9 1939, going to France on September 2, the Blenheims of Nos 104 and 108 Squadrons from Bassingbourn proved more portentous. These machines trained bomber crews instead under the guise of No 2 Group Pool until becoming known as No 13 OTU in April 1940.

Bombs often fell around Bicester in the second half of 1940, though usually not actually on the airfield. A decoy K site attracted many HEs and incendiaries, notably sixteen and 140 respectively on August 26. Later in the year on November 14 a Ju 88 strafed the real airfield but AA defences returned fire and shot down the aircraft near major Oxfordshire bomber OTU base Harwell.

As World War Two progressed, so Bicester's Blenheims churned out aircrews up to as late as February 1944 when these twin-engined types had long become obsolescent at the very least. Their roles had changed by then from daylight raids in 1940 to anti-shipping ones in 1941 and North African service during 1942/43. No 307 Ferry Training Unit formed in December 1942 to enable Blenheims to safely travel to these sunny climes, moving to the satellite at Finmere on March 18 1943.

Bicester suddenly became a ground station in all but name again as after World War One once No 13 OTU left for Harwell on October 12 1944. While busy with training and servicing right to the end, the airfield had slight limitations in not being suitable for night flying except in perfect conditions; even some trees and Bicester's shape did not help either. More modern light bomber types such as the Douglas Boston would have found it difficult to operate at length from the grass landing area which already was undergoing some punishment from aircraft undercarriages. These restrictions also made No 271 Squadron think again about coming from Broadwell near Brize Norton with Dakotas in late 1946.

But permanent buildings saved Bicester from the kind of

THE AIRFIELDS OF BRITAIN

fate brave Bibury started suffering at ironically almost exactly the same time. After Harwell had kicked its predecessor in the teeth by acting as parent for the rest of 1944, independence resumed on January 1 1945 as this airfield expanded an increasingly evident role as a supplier of general military equipment to the Second Tactical Air Force in Europe. No 246 MU carried on post-war up to April 1949 and dealt with RAF MT vehicles.

Administrative, instructional and technical duties made up for the scarcity of aircraft over the next three decades. No 71 MU became of note by attending to crashed or damaged aircraft and serviced preserved types of the Battle of Britain Memorial Flight, initially based at a place called Biggin Hill, of which more in a moment. Consistency still lacked with preserving historic types for years as the unit dismantled a Sunderland at Pembroke Dock in the early 1970s for display at Hendon's RAF Museum but had scrapped the last Hampden in 1955 only to save space.

While No 282 MU also stayed during 1952-54 to store explosives, powered aircraft had not disappeared. The Oxford University Air Squadron arrived in 1959 from Kidlington but, once its light aircraft departed to Abingdon, Bicester closed to flying with effect from September 30 1975 and totally along with other British airfield veterans in March 1976. Handed to the Army, the RAF regained this site two years later.

Now Bicester serves in a flying sense as the RAF Gliding and Soaring Association Centre. Service recreational activity of this type was noticeable for many years after World War Two, thanks to the Windrushers GC, until the RAFGSA absorbed the club. Light aircraft are evident too and exist in profusion with gliders at weekends. For all the airfield's diminutiveness, Bicester could take big aircraft in admittedly small doses, probably the largest visitor being not the first Halifax but the prototype Armstrong Whitworth A.W.27 Ensign civil monoplane airliner in 1938 which had to make a 'dead-stick' landing when all four engines completely failed during a flight.

Two 1930s C hangars, two smaller 1920s A types sited further into the technical area, a 'Fort' control tower and an old style circular instead of square topped water tower – Abingdon also has one – continue to distinguish Bicester from elsewhere as an airfield. Ground duties have ranged of late from holding the Army Central Ordnance Depot to storing American military equipment and accommodating USAF personnel and their families belonging to the 20th

THE AIRFIELDS OF BRITAIN: VOLUME 1

Tactical Fighter Wing at Upper Heyford. But Bicester's support buildings are a worry as some of them have been sold off. Demolition activities have occurred west of the A421 road, while a considerable acreage of land has been registered for sale. Shades of the desperate days after World War One? We must never let that horrifying situation happen again.
164/SP598245. 1½ miles NE of town, best viewed from NW side.

Biggin Hill, Greater London

Alternative Name: Westerham

Will there ever be a more popular airfield than Biggin Hill? Even before the Battle of Britain ended, it was already a living legend and resident squadrons went on to destroy some 1,400 enemy aircraft in World War Two. The Luftwaffe also tried phenomenally hard to obliterate this incredible place. It is only fair reward that not just our greatest ever fighter airfield but Britain's all-time favourite airfield is still active today, if in different branches of aviation.

The base you simply cannot run out of superlatives describing had about as humble a start as any airfield could have. By April 1916 Biggin Hill was in the process of being requisitioned as a Home Defence landing ground, given the secondary back-up name of Westerham after a town some distance to the south purely for postal convenience. Such titles were never meant to be quoted in correspondence as the official station name: just as well, for Westerham would never have created the same highly evocative effect as Biggin Hill.

Active from later on in 1916, the landing ground turned into a full airfield and opened in this role on February 13 1917 but its early days still stayed relatively quiet in contrast to World War Two. Biggin Hill scored a grand total of one kill during the first conflict, yet that victory over a Gotha biplane was one of six achieved in the rout of May 19 1918 which halted enemy fixed-wing bombing raids on Britain. The country could partly thank a Bristol F.2b of the recently arrived No 141 Squadron, a Home Defence unit which remained until March 1919. No 37 Squadron almost immediately came from Stow Maries in Essex to replace No 141 and operate Sopwith Camels and Snipes. Becoming No 39 Squadron on July 1, it had been reduced to cadre strength when transfer to famous RAF ground station Uxbridge followed in December.

THE AIRFIELDS OF BRITAIN

Involvement of any airfield with a non-flying military base always tended to sow seeds of disharmony and discontent. Slow peacetime demobilisation only enhanced general unrest. Popular though Biggin Hill was and always will be, here RAF technical staff mounted a short-lived mutiny in January 1919. Airfield uprisings reached nothing like the levels of the naval variety as Invergordon experienced in 1931 but this event became the first aerial one in Britain; Henlow in Bedfordshire transpired to be the scene of our only other airfield mutiny.

Biggin Hill's landing area, five mixed dimensions hangars and supportive buildings somehow managed to muddle through the immediate post-war period. The Instrument Design Establishment plus early photographic and wireless experimentation – all soon absorbed by RAE at Farnborough – kept the airfield alive but closure had come mightily close for comfort. By November 1920 aircraft movement levels had dropped so alarmingly that sheep could graze at the site from five o'clock in the evening to nine o'clock the next morning during weekdays, and without interruption on Saturdays and Sundays.

Such daily fear ended when Biggin Hill became available to RAF fighter aircraft again from July 1 1922. No 56 Squadron's Snipes bolstered up confidence by eventually arriving from Hawkinge in May 1923. Their latest home easily fitted into the newly devised Air Defence of Great Britain system as pilots changed to operating Gloster Grebes and then Armstrong Whitworth Siskins. But as No 56 had converted to this second fighter type in September 1927 than the squadron flew off to North Weald a month later. Biggin Hill was once more reduced to accommodating little more than a handful of specialised aircraft, a characteristic which had marked its early years of activity right from the beginning with the Wireless Telephony School, moved to Chattis Hill in Hampshire during April 1918.

A form of consolation could be found in the airfield becoming a familiar feature in the Greater London area, if not country-wide as a whole. An aerial lighthouse installed in March 1920 to assist airmen on the London-Paris route showed influence, further proof being inclusion with big stars Croydon and Lympne in an early attempt at safe aerial navigation by displaying a series of boards showing current weather conditions and the airfield's initial letter. Naturally Biggin Hill was 'B': one might have thought that a suitable *Pundit* two letter identification combination during World War Two would have been 'BH' but 'GI' lasted instead, possibly because the former code might have made the Luftwaffe's job

219

easier. 'BH' went to Barkston Heath.

Most surviving aircraft moved out in 1929 as Biggin Hill was deliberately put out of action until 1932. A fire on the morning of September 1 1925 in the Officers' Mess had caused some damage but everyone soon agreed by the late 1920s that the entire station badly needed refurbishing. Construction workers therefore more or less completely rebuilt it from top to bottom.

Only after they had finished could major flying resume when Nos 23 and 32 Squadrons settled in from September 1932. Bristol Bulldogs, Hawker Demons and Gloster Gauntlets all made an appearance during the mid-1930s as Fighter Command replaced ADGB. No 23 Squadron went to Northolt in December 1936 but No 79 Squadron reformed on March 22 1937, receiving Hurricanes as did No 32 from late 1938.

About this time in the last year or so of peace Biggin Hill often saw unusual aircraft fly across local airspace when German Lufthansa Junkers Ju 52/3m civil airliners made odd outward bound routes from Croydon Airport to the west. Nobody could complain as these transports were ostensibly doing nothing wrong but powers behind the scenes could help clear the area of friendly forces in order to make this site purely a fighter station.

The most obvious element to gently throw out was No 1 AACU. This unit had stayed at Biggin Hill ever since 1923, when known as the Night Flying Flight, with summer detachments at Lympne and subsequently Weston Zoyland from 1929. Changes of title in the 1930s to better reflect anti-aircraft co-operation involvement resulted in No 1 AACU forming on February 10 1937 before going to Farnborough in April 1938. The Air Defence Experimental Establishment meanwhile did not go to Christchurch in Dorset until 1939. This one-off night flying force could be traced back to the Searchlight Experimental Establishment, which came to Biggin Hill in 1923 and became the ADEE a year later.

Nos 32 and 79 Squadrons were present with Blenheims of No 601 Squadron as Britain entered World War Two. Both their personnel plus several other generations of past and future airmen always knew Biggin Hill as 'The Bump' because its raised geographical position enabled pilots to see the airfield from far-off. Few members of the general population outwith Greater London had still heard of Biggin Hill at the war's beginning: even fewer had not heard of it by the end.

Although all three of the airfield's initial wartime units soon left, both Hurricane squadrons came back in March 1940. Nos

THE AIRFIELDS OF BRITAIN

32 and 79 would be readily available at times over those critical summer months. Covering the Dunkirk evacuation alone proved a costly and wearing time for RAF fighters based here and at other south-eastern stations.

Having captured France, Germany turned its attention to Britain and started trying to knock out our airfields. By now Fighter Command had developed the Sector system into a fine art, whereby a major airfield controlled an area of territory and other airfields lying inside that area. Gravesend served as satellite to Biggin Hill, with Hawkinge, Lympne and West Malling all being advanced forward airfields to provide an even more immediate reply to enemy air attacks and help disperse fighters into the bargain. Military planning had reached completion after years of practice – and would be put to the test in spectacular fashion.

Luftwaffe aircraft made Britain's airfields their primary targets from August 1940 as they had previously done with those of other countries in Europe. The Battle of Britain resulted in our supersites receiving widely varying amounts of damage from enemy air attack: Hawkinge and West Malling stood devastated, Lympne almost obliterated, and yet Gravesend escaped virtually unscathed. But the Germans initially correctly realised that supportive sites such as these ones could still basically survive unless the controlling airfield in their Sector was completely knocked out.

The early afternoon of August 18 brought an eerie sight as 60 He 111s and 40 escorting Bf 109s droned over Biggin Hill to try and turn this theory into practice. This large force surprisingly caused comparatively little damage and only killed two personnel. August 21 proved a bad day but nothing compared to when a much smaller number of Ju 88s claimed 39 lives during one of five attacks on the 30th, most of the fatalities occurring when a lucky bomb hit a rudimentary trench shelter.

The period between August 30 and September 2 became a horrendous time for everyone concerned at Biggin Hill. A series of punishing Luftwaffe assaults brought a trail of carnage as bomb craters – often littered with bits of bodies – covered the badly struggling airfield. Hangars and support facilities were either destroyed or damaged beyond repair, and five Spitfires lost on September 1. Another fortunate enemy munition struck a pre-war design of operations block, inferior to its gloomy successor by being vulnerably situated among other airfield buildings and not built at least partly underground. Telephone communications were left in tatters too and meant an emergency replacement operations building

THE AIRFIELDS OF BRITAIN: VOLUME 1

had to be established in a butcher's shop at Biggin Hill village in a brilliant example of typical British improvisation. Such eccentric measures ensured that defensive fighter operations out of Biggin Hill never ceased altogether as units made pilgrimages from other airfields, including good old Bibury.

Biggin Hill just might have collapsed totally had raids of this ferocity carried on for a few more days. A big gap could have appeared in our aerial defences through which Luftwaffe aircraft would have ploughed towards London and elsewhere. But all of a sudden in stepped Hermann Goering, who ordered his air force to stop attacking Britain's airfields in strength and concentrate upon London. This catastrophic tactical error lost Germany both the initiative and the Battle of Britain, enabling Biggin Hill to be cleared of devastation, though the airfield lay ruinous for months afterwards well into 1941 with everything from no hangars to countless smashed windows. Flying continued as Spitfires of Nos 66, 72, 74 and 92 Squadrons all appeared in the autumn of 1940 but nuisance raids, especially by low-flying Bf 109 fighter-bombers, still gave trouble. Day and night snap raids varied in intensity but three barrack blocks were blown up on October 6, and bombing on the night of November 10/11 disposed of nine Spitfires belonging to Nos 66 and 92 Squadrons.

Many more Spitfires which survived to fight another day later stayed at Biggin Hill both in war and peace and perhaps became synonymous with this base than any other. Spitfires badly needed their friend 'The Bump' during the Battle of Britain as the airfield was one of only a handful to offer specialised servicing and repair facilities at that time. Squadrons equipped with the machine afterwards became extremely common, such as No 92 which lasted until September 1941, though other aircraft types naturally arrived. Among them were Defiant night fighters of No 264 Squadron, at Biggin Hill in 1941 from January to April.

1941 also saw RAF fighter units become more aggressive instead of sitting back to simply defend home territory. Biggin Hill had already started this offensive trend the previous year when No 66 Squadron's Spitfires flew the first *Rhubarb* sorties on December 20 1940. Pilots generally did not like these short-range low-level fighter-bomber sorties made in mediocre weather as they viewed *Rhubarbs* as both extravagant and rather ineffectual but attacks upon tactical targets in France often produced success. Even more important was how they kept considerable numbers of German armed forces tied down in western Europe. Other curiously named set piece operations — notably *Rodeo* fighter sweeps plus *Circus* and

THE AIRFIELDS OF BRITAIN

Ramrod day bomber escort duties – played their part in returning fire at the enemy.

Squadron after squadron came to Biggin Hill right through the mid-war period for these and related tasks as successive Wings relentlessly added to their airfield's fearsome kill tally. An increasing number of RCAF Spitfire units became noticeable at this period. British-manned Nos 72 and 124 Squadrons stayed long into 1942, No 611 Squadron being another Spitfire unit based at Biggin Hill from September 1942 to July 1943. It witnessed that momentous occasion on May 15 1943 when the Biggin Hill Sector bagged its 1,000th enemy aircraft and personnel triumphantly posed for the cameras at a dispersal. What a marvellous achievement – and the airfield superstar was far from finished.

Canadians of Nos 401, 411 and 412 Squadrons formed the last Biggin Hill Wing. Almost inevitably flying Spitfires, they arrived in October 1943 and left in April 1944. Their base would have been invaluable over the D-Day period which followed but unfortunately lay directly in the flight paths of V-1 missiles. Flying units were too much at risk if any flying bombs landed, so the Station HQ temporarily moved to Redhill on June 27 as No 22 Balloon Centre maintained a balloon barrage until September. Although this event became a minor tragedy for Biggin Hill, these lighter-than-air craft which generally terrified airfields still proved their worth in south-east England by destroying nearly 300 V-1s up to that month.

Despite the greatest of efforts by barrage balloon handlers, RAF fighter squadrons and AA gunners throughout southern England, many missiles still broke through this protective cordon. Three No 22 Balloon Centre personnel perished in a Nissen hut on July 1 after V-1s had rained down about the airfield in the second half of June. Two explosions happened near the married quarters on consecutive days but damage mostly proved negligible.

Several fighter units were able to come back from October onwards, most notable being No 154 Squadron. Having flown all around the Mediterranean area since the invasion of North Africa in November 1942, it reformed in Britain during November 1944 with Spitfires, switching to Mustangs in February 1945. These new aircraft moved to Hunsdon in Hertfordshire on March 1.

Soon World War Two ended – and what a hard but glorious war this by now massively changed airfield had experienced. By its own standards, Biggin Hill then held most unusual aircraft in RCAF Dakota transports over the next year. Where was the Spitfire? The airfield's favourite type returned in mid-1946 to equip Nos 600 and 615 Squadrons which had nominally reformed on May 10. Once Meteors replaced them in 1950, No 41 Squadron flew in with more of these jets during March 1951 before using Hunters from 1955. The Battle of Britain Memorial Flight of preserved World War Two aircraft types also formed in 1957 but the two RAuxAF units disbanded that year on March 10; No 41 Squadron followed suit on January 31 1958 as the historic Flight moved to North Weald and Fighter Command days at the airfield finished.

It was a most sad day when the RAF largely pulled out of Biggin Hill in 1959, thus ending over 40 years of terrific service. As said at the time, the place was 'wrong geographically' for fighter operations: this may have been true to an extent but really limited runways and ever-increasing suburbia served as the main reasons. The military did not totally desert their great haunt, for a personnel selection centre for officers and aircrews remained over a good number of years until this non-flying element also left in 1992 for Cranwell. RAF Biggin Hill closed on October 4 to inconceivably bring to a stop a legendary partnership. What a ring those three words uttered, and to have one title without the other is equivalent to mentioning Laurel without Hardy.

Service operations may now only be memories but civil aviation thrives today at this airfield which has an assured place in history. This particular activity began in earnest once Croydon closed in September 1959. Many former inhabitants needed another home and Biggin Hill gave them all they wanted. The Surrey and Kent Flying Club, as the Surrey Flying Club had been newly renamed, led the way by transferring across from Croydon the previous February as RAF aircraft left for the last time.

Flying club and executive aircraft abound today but conditions have not always run in their favour. New operators Surrey Aviation Ltd originally received only a seven year lease in 1959. Although the Ministry of Aviation acquired Biggin Hill's old southern military camp in October 1963 after the RAF had relinquished this area during 1962 to realise recreational aviation potentialities, by 1964 the runways and supporting facilities had all fallen into extremely poor condition. Carelessness in not putting water in an already badly maintained fire tender forced the airfield to lose its commercial operating licence in October 1966 and rely upon private users as Surrey Aviation wondered about the company's ownership arrangements. Would the local

THE AIRFIELDS OF BRITAIN

authority buy Biggin Hill? This Bromley Council did but only in the 1970s to stop people complaining about noise levels – the cheek, considering how aircraft engines so reassured them in 1940 – and has for years since considered selling the airfield.

The godfather of Britain's airfields has for long enough become a shrine to the vast army of airfield fans. Biggin Hill always scored the biggest attendance figures whenever the RAF held a Battle of Britain Open Day there and at other sites. Out of over one million visitors at 37 bases in 1957, 220,000 came to 'The Bump' alone; five years later the total was 185,000 out of 928,500 people at sixteen airfields. Pure military displays have since finished in another sad break with the past.

Part of Biggin Hill's charm can be explained by its looks. This is a rambling place, not least because of a strange layout with two runways and a taxiway which used to be a third stretch emanating from the same general area like the three middle fingers of a hand. The north-south runway was extended after World War Two and has assisted current operations. Standing out among other buildings is a large modern control tower: Biggin Hill has owned at least five such structures, which must be a record at British level. Four post-war T2s and fourteen other hangars also make quite a change from the second half of World War Two when Biggin Hill had to get by with a dozen Blisters and even a couple of World War One vintage canvas Bessoneaux, so devoid had it become of hangarage after bombing attacks.

Absolutely required viewing in your pilgrimage is the station chapel, which contains the names of 453 people killed in the Biggin Hill Sector during World War Two. One must never forget that more people paid the ultimate sacrifice at this one airfield than did the 'Few' during the entire Battle of Britain. Enough to say that these heroes will always be remembered.

The authorities would never dare close Britain's best loved airfield, so great would be the resultant uproar. Cavalcades of legends have passed through its gates over the years. Arguably the greatest resident became famous South African air ace 'Sailor' Malan, who during his spells at Biggin Hill graduated from a squadron to Wing leader and eventually station commander, being in charge as the 1,000th victory milestone was achieved. But perhaps the finest tribute you can pay Biggin Hill is that whenever the name is mentioned, you immediately think of the airfield and nothing else. Hundreds of our other supersites have provided great fame to otherwise

THE AIRFIELDS OF BRITAIN: VOLUME 1

unknown places. The tragedy is that, unlike Biggin Hill, they have not been accorded the same national reverence. However, now with an unfeeling MoD selling off the remaining RAF enclave to private developers in February 1994 amid howls of dismay from veterans and airfield supporters, even the king of them all is not sacred. You see, luvvies, only 'market forces' count today, not real history and achievement, heroism or paying the ultimate sacrifice.
187/TQ414603. 5½ miles NW of Westerham by A233.

Binbrook, Lincolnshire

Not quite such a huge star as Biggin Hill – but a big star nonetheless. Yet whether Binbrook transpires to be a fading star which disintegrates completely remains to be answered.

This noted if somewhat remote RAF airfield was a major bomber base which converted to fighters after some time. British military airfields have never been easy to view: Binbrook is no exception, even more so than usual as it lay upon a tableland. Flying Control personnel often had to endure a few anxious moments as aircraft left the main runway before disappearing temporarily from view and then revealing all was safe and well.

Virtually everyone accepted in World War Two that airfield construction could be a slow process. Binbrook overemphasised this trend to a degree. Building work had started in the early months of 1939 and gradually produced fine Expansion Period structures but the airfield did not open until June 1940.

Battle light bombers of Nos 12 and 142 Squadrons soon both moved in as an interim measure on July 3 while finishing touches were being added. Binbrook still struggled to come to terms with the daily rigours of airfield life, so the Battles left in August for Eastchurch – No 12 Squadron via Thorney Island – to give their Lincolnshire abode a break. The units also had less distance to travel while attacking German-held invasion ports in France but little realised how they were almost literally jumping out of the frying pan and into the fire as Luftwaffe aircraft savagely bombed Eastchurch during the Battle of Britain. Two enemy raids occurred in six days in August at Binbrook as the Battles stayed away, so no home airfield could be entirely safe.

Relief surely prevailed when Nos 12 and 142 Squadrons came back in September in order to receive Wellingtons.

THE AIRFIELDS OF BRITAIN

Bombing raids eventually started with the popular Vickers type until No 142 went to the brand new satellite station of Grimsby on November 26 1941. Still the Luftwaffe had prowled around by often flying about the airfield in late 1940 without usually making attacks. Three He 111s did however damage three friendly aircraft on October 27, and incendiaries hit the hangars to no adverse effect on April 7 1941. When No 12 Squadron later proceeded to yet another of Lincolnshire's emerging RAF bomber airfield contingent at Wickenby on September 25 1942, Binbrook was at last given three hard runways to facilitate operations.

Unlike the long time spent in building this base, runway construction proved fairly quick and enabled No 460 (RAAF) Squadron to come from Breighton in Yorkshire on May 14 1943. The Australians participated as much as anyone in Bomber Command's incessant night offensive against Germany and made themselves welcome in this part of Lincolnshire. A person of their own nationality had to be in charge as Station CO to fully co-ordinate affairs, and what better choice could there have been than Group Captain Hughie Edwards. Back in the summer of 1941 Edwards had won a Victoria Cross for leading a Blenheim force out of Norfolk on a daring daylight raid against Bremen in northern Germany. Now he stayed at Binbrook almost throughout 1943 and 1944; paperwork and other administrative matters inevitably took up the great majority of time but Edwards still managed to fly a number of operational sorties. Wartime life was generally happy here, and a unit memorial now stands in Binbrook village to honour the Lancaster force.

March 1945 brought intruders back to the airfield one last time. Several enemy aircraft flew low over Binbrook on the 4th as part of the Luftwaffe's infamous Operation *Gisela*. They made no direct attack but a No 460 Squadron Lancaster on a cross-country training flight was destroyed near Lincoln.

After No 460 Squadron had moved to East Kirkby at the other end of Lincolnshire in July 1945, No 12 Squadron flew back from Wickenby on September 24, just one day under three years since leaving Binbrook. No 101 Squadron joined it a week later, followed by Nos 9 and 617 during the spring of 1946. These last two highly distinguished units had previously resided in India for a few months but were now home once more in a pruned down post-war Bomber Command, hence the concentration of squadrons at this airfield instead of one or two as beforehand.

Over the next handful of years Avro Lincolns maintained a strong presence at Binbrook. But these 'super Lancasters' left the scene with fair rapidity when No 101 became the first RAF squadron to accept the English Electric Canberra. This delightfully unsophisticated twin-jet light bomber showed itself to be such an excellent design that No 101's sister units quickly phased out their Lincolns in 1952 to gain their quotas of Canberras.

The 1950s saw a considerable increase in regional conflicts all over the world: Binbrook went back to war again and had to deploy aircraft elsewhere twice in 1955 and 1956. First Communist guerrillas needed to be bombed out of their jungle hide-outs in Malaya, so Nos 101, 617, 12 and 9 Squadrons in that order stayed five months at a time at Butterworth between February 1955 and June 1956. Shortly afterwards the Suez crisis blew up into alarming proportions and sent the Canberras away again, this time to Malta, Nos 9, 12, 101, 109 and 139 Squadrons being there between September and December 1956. Once more Binbrook helped win a war – yes, Suez was a victory in a military sense. Only the politicians as usual somehow contrived to turn this necessary episode into a defeat. Airfieldpower, meanwhile, had emerged victorious as ever.

Although more Canberra squadrons had arrived at Binbrook in the 1950s as we have mentioned, in time they gradually faded away from here. Two disbanded on February 1 1957, while Nos 9 and 12 Squadrons left for Coningsby in 1959. No 139 Squadron also shut on December 31 of that year. With it ended the Binbrook bomber story.

Runway modifications meant this airfield kept mostly silent until June 1962 as Fighter Command prepared to move in. Two sections of the RAF Flying College from Strubby had briefly visited in the late summer of 1960 as Manby's satellite closed to have the main runway repaired. The more major alteration work at Binbrook changed local social life too as the minor road connecting Binbrook and Thoresway villages – across which Lancasters had dispersed on hardstandings – had to be closed and a new road fashioned to the south, complete with cuttings to protect vehicles. Once the main runway had been extended both south and especially north, No 64 Squadron's heavy Gloster Javelin fighters then stayed for a while. The noted Central Fighter Establishment experimental concern also finished its days at Binbrook in the mid-1960s.

Another new visitor was No 85 Squadron in April 1963 to begin fighter interception training with Canberras and Meteors. This became a useful unit up to January 1972, as No 5 Squadron reformed with English Electric Lightnings in

October 1965. Binbrook established itself as a major fighter station after almost two decades of accommodating bombers: the airfield was most certainly 'right geographically' as the Lightnings defended central Britain and fended off occasional intruding Russian aircraft over the North Sea. These fighters gained a reputation as 'guzzlers' but later versions with improved range and co-operation with Handley Page Victor air-to-air refuelling tankers conquered earlier difficulties.

More Lightnings of No 11 Squadron arrived shortly after No 85 Squadron's departure to bring a brace of fighter units to Binbrook; No 226 OCU from Coltishall increased Lightning strength during April to October 1972 as the Norfolk legend took a necessary short break like Strubby did in 1960. All continued to seem well but similar elements at Leuchars, Wattisham and foreign RAF airfields disbanded during the mid-1970s. Although a good type, the Lightning lacked the adaptability of successors such as the Harrier, Phantom and ultimately the Tornado which could take on other roles and not solely defensive duties.

Except for the period between April and October 1976 as Binbrook closed for runway re-laying, aircraft flying from Leconfield in Yorkshire, both Nos 5 and 11 Squadrons remained present for many more years. Age and inevitable servicing problems nevertheless gradually took their toll and No 5 Squadron ceased operations on November 1 1987. No 11 became the RAF's last Lightning squadron when disbanded on May 1 1988.

There are now increasing worries about this base's long-term future. Whether Binbrook enjoys happy times to come as Biggin Hill surely does is most questionable. When luck deserts anyone or anything, nothing ever seems to go right, and that old notion very much applies in this case. Take the example of an Australian trying to make a charity flight in a vintage Tiger Moth biplane to his homeland who had to force-land in Kent after taking off from Binbrook on March 3 1990.

Aircraft used to maintain flying levels on the main runway where one bright spark deposited several hundredweight of moth-balls during the 1950s in a crazy idea claiming to keep the landing area clear of birds for months. Closed as a fighter station in June 1988, Binbrook pluckily survived as an RLG for the Central Flying School at Scampton until closed in the late summer of 1992. Gliders have also used the airfield.

In the summer of 1989 a few B-17s arrived when the popular film *Memphis Belle* was shot here. Allowing for the dramatic licence of having a USAAF World War Two Bomb Group in Lincolnshire, good historical realism won the day, not least Binbrook's five C hangars — only one more than at Bassingbourn where the real *Memphis Belle* and company stayed. But bad luck struck again as one B-17 crashed during filming on July 25 by swinging on take-off, though none of the ten occupants met a premature fiery end. Screen stardom might never have happened at all had the local authority not rightly stepped in the previous February to reject a Government plan to turn this place into a prison.

A Lightning landed at Binbrook on July 23 1992 for preservation use elsewhere by a group of volunteers. Their highly laudable actions have not stopped officialdom from selling many acres of the site. As with Biggin Hill, current priorities are completely wrong as the Bomber Airfield Society was shabbily treated when recently refused to establish a memorial/museum after thinking it had acquired part of Binbrook. The sphere of military airfield operations has switched from southern England to Britain's entire eastern coastline. Fighters fly out of Coningsby in southern Lincolnshire and Leeming in North Yorkshire, and to close Binbrook permanently will leave a big hole in our air defence coverage. This would not only be a severe tactical mistake — it could be fatal.

113/TA190959. 11½ miles NE of Market Rasen. Turn left off B1203 at Binbrook village for airfield.

Binsoe, North Yorkshire

Alternative Name: West Tanfield

If Binbrook is remote, Binsoe can only be described as being right in the back of beyond. No 76 (HD) Squadron employed this landing ground amid hilly country after approved for requisition on December 16 1916 until the end of World War One.

Nothing now remains of this irregularly rectangular shaped field except farmland. An exceptionally narrow minor road forming the northern boundary leads to Binsoe, an incredibly tiny place that cannot even claim hamlet status but is still marked by a road sign. So unlikely are the surroundings you would never guess an airfield once existed here.

99/SE257800. 4 miles SE of Masham off A6108.

Birch, Essex

At last we head back to a truly flat area of Britain after Biggin Hill, Binbrook and Binsoe. East Anglia was where the Americans crammed their fighters and bombers into every available airfield during World War Two. Glamour and ostentation soon became obvious. Yet for every offensive airfield in USAAF hands, some others had to do the less attractive donkey work. One such place was Birch.

Records detailing the activities of World War Two airfields are on the whole not too difficult to find. Birch is a rare exception, a true enigma with no documents of its own and featuring next to nothing in official files relating to any other airfields or units.

So what do we know about this real baffler? Scraps of information that can be syphoned off tell us Birch was originally intended as an operational bomber station when approved for requisition in July 1942. The airfield opened on March 10 1944 but saw little activity for a long while with an RAF C&M party stated as still being present on July 29. American forces had moved in only for the 410th BG (Light) to stay in the first half of April and briefly assemble or store assault gliders. Even ATC gliders made far more use of Birch than the US 8th Air Force when No 145 GS resided for a period from early 1945.

The last big paratroop mission, Operation *Varsity*, brought a momentary spurt of considerable powered aircraft use – and official recording – to Birch as RAF and USAAF airborne forces elements flocked to various more advanced East Anglian airfields from further inland. A total of 48 Dakotas belonging to Nos 233 and 437 Squadrons at Blakehill Farm in Wiltshire, twelve more of No 48 Squadron from Down Ampney in Gloucestershire plus their 60 Horsas (each aircraft towing one glider) hence arrived: 'a phenomenal sight', declared No 17 Air Transportable Signals Unit in admiration. Birch's part in the operation on March 24 1945 went by with hardly a hitch but its role proved fleeting as next day the airfield emptied rapidly.

Ground units afterwards tried to keep the site busy. No 5355 Airfield Construction Wing stayed from late May until moving to Germany on September 8. On July 28 No 22 Supply and Transport Column formed as part of No 383 MU at Strubby to support the *Tiger Force* of RAF heavy bombers proposed to bomb Japan but was doomed with that country's capitulation in August. No 17 Air Transportable Signals Unit, whose personnel had come on March 13 from Melton Mowbray, could not even find Birch at first and discovered another C&M party in place when they did, lasted at the airfield for a reasonable period. Excitement brewed in October 1945 as everyone thought signalling facilities might be provided at Heathrow until the idea miscarried, and the unit left for Wormingford on December 11-14. Bomber Command did not require Birch any longer and put the station on C&M two days later.

Farmland has since reclaimed most support buildings and the two T2s which USAAF heavy bombers could have used but for planning vagaries. While every piece of runway and perimeter track has vanished on the east side, major sections of all three runways do survive, and the entire north-south one has turned into a minor road. Quite probably more vehicular traffic has run over this stretch than powered aircraft ever did: the last aircraft which tried to land at Birch was a light machine that crashed in mysterious circumstances one night in October 1989. Rumours circulated about illegal tobacco or other narcotic smuggling, alleged to go on at other disused airfields in East Anglia. Whether true or not, one of Britain's most unrecognised World War Two era sites still retains an allure of obscurity.

168/TL915196. SW of Colchester, 4 miles NE of Tiptree off B1022.

Bircham Newton, Norfolk

Castles? Stately homes? Historically insignificant, pretentious, worthless – and what an absolute bore. For real and exciting history, you have to visit Britain's airfields. One particular must on your list should be Bircham Newton, not least because it is this country's best preserved disused airfield. What a marvellous place this is with atmosphere you can almost reach out and grab. Whereas the vast majority of our other supersites have been cruelly defaced, old Bircham has had hardly any buildings removed or even damaged. The former guardhouse is now, of all things, a bank.

Bircham Newton's history has also transpired to be one of general excellence since first appearing on the landscape. Massively expanded to meet a proposed TDS requirement, No 3 Fighter School arrived in the spring of 1918 after forming as a nucleus at Eastburn (the future Driffield) in Yorkshire,

THE AIRFIELDS OF BRITAIN

but left again on the three mile trip west to Sedgeford in November.

Tremendously exciting days lay ahead for Bircham Newton. The Independent Force had already been bombing strategic targets in western Germany while based at airfields in eastern France. Aircraft mainstay was the Handley Page 0/400 heavy bomber but in mid-1918 military chiefs took the ambitious gamble of attempting RAF air attacks from British soil. No 166 Squadron therefore formed at Bircham Newton on June 13 to fly Handley Page V/1500s, developed from the 0/400 but much heavier, possessing a bigger wing-span and four engines in tandem instead of only two, while a bomb load capacity of 7,500 pounds easily outpointed the 0/400's 2,000 pounds.

Important as these facts counted, most spectacular of all was where planners scheduled the V/1500s to visit: Berlin. Crews would set out from Norfolk for the place Bomber Command in World War Two dubbed the 'Big City' as soon as reasonably possible and then try and make it back home; the V/1500 could travel well over 1,000 miles but diversions could be made to a neutral country or Czechoslovakia if any aircraft ran short of fuel. In many ways the whole idea sounded like a suicide mission but the thought of dropping a few bombs on Germany's capital bore huge propaganda value, in much the same way as Jimmy Doolittle's raid upon Tokyo in 1942.

This historical chapter disappointingly fizzled out in something of a whimper. By November 9 two V/1500s readied themselves for the big off after a few months of training. Bad weather postponed their departure for 48 hours, by which time the Armistice stopped this plan from ever reaching fruition, not to mention robbing Bircham Newton of even more glory. Whether in any case the airfield had been completely ready for this tough job was slightly doubtful, with eight Belfast hangars standing only 82 per cent finished towards the end of fighting and not expected to be fully fit for use until January 15 1919.

Peacetime swiftly cut short the V/1500's career. A hint of its potential was demonstrated on May 22 1919 when one machine with eight personnel on board stayed aloft for almost twelve hours on an 836 mile flight during which they passed over various towns and cities such as London, Birmingham and Manchester. The RAF however could see no real purpose in holding on to the service's first four-engined bomber. No 167 Squadron had formed back in November 1918 but disbanded with No 166 Squadron in May 1919; No 274 Squadron only lasted with V/1500s from then until January

233

1920. Nos 56 and 60 Squadrons also disbanded that month after having just arrived at Bircham Newton. These were fearful days without doubt.

Common sense won the day as the authorities retained this airfield because of its permanence. RAF squadrons still formed, No 207 doing so on February 1 1920 and being given Airco DH9A bombers. These machines later moved to Turkey in September 1922 to counter disorder there.

Bomber units thrived at Bircham Newton in the 1920s and early 1930s as the fortunes of Britain's airfields gradually picked up again. Among later 1920s squadrons here could be seen No 99, unique in solely operating Avro Aldershots between August 1924 and December 1925 as part of a stay lasting up to January 1928. These sturdy single-engined biplanes could carry a big bomb load for their day of 2,000 pounds but heavy bombers equipped with a solitary power plant soon fell out of official favour. Vickers Vimys of No 7 Squadron proved more durable: once this unit which had reformed on June 1 1923 departed for Worthy Down in Hampshire in April 1927, DH9As equipped the reforming No 101 Squadron on March 21 1928. This element was given Sidestrands in 1929 and quickly moved to Andover to allow Nos 35 and 207 Squadrons to appear as day bomber forces. Both stayed until 1935 before their Fairey Gordons flew off towards Abyssinia because of the troubles experienced in that country against the Italians. Eminent World War One Canadian air ace Wing Commander Raymond Collishaw also left Bircham Newton that year after a three year spell as Station CO. Three Hind light bomber squadrons which reformed at the turn of 1935/36 became Bircham's last bombers and left in the summer of 1936.

As the airfield stood near the sea, so policy changes made the RAF's new Coastal Command organisation acquire Bircham Newton in 1936. Ansons of No 206 Squadron headed what turned out to be a considerable line of coastal and maritime patrol units when they arrived from Manston in July/August. More, of the freshly created No 220 Squadron came along too, both forces monitoring surrounding watery stretches up to August 1939 in their reliable but offensively weak aircraft.

Even worse aircraft subsequently arrived as No 220 Squadron travelled north to Thornaby. Vickers Vildebeest torpedo bombers, as ancient and ugly as a biplane type could be, belonging to No 42 Squadron performed much the same job as No 206 until the newer Bircham resident returned to Thorney Island during April 1940. But more advanced aircraft had already started to appear and make a bigger impression. Nobody ever reckoned Blenheims to be great fighters, yet No 601 Squadron's machines at Biggin Hill were considered good enough to mount the RAF's first long-range fighter attack of World War Two against a German target on November 28 1939 when they staged through Bircham Newton en route to a Luftwaffe seaplane base.

Aggression further built up as the 'Phoney War' abruptly ended in the spring of 1940. No 206 Squadron was getting used to totally effective and modern Lockheed Hudson patrol bombers as the Vildebeests left, and No 235 Squadron's Blenheims joined them in June. While Fighter Command struggled over southern England to beat off the Luftwaffe, Bircham Newton's Coastal Command types scoured the North Sea for enemy aerial and naval targets, though some Blenheims made forward detachments to help out their fighter brethren. Obstinate determination paid off as No 206 Squadron sank a captured Dutch coastal defence ship on June 21 and shot down several Bf 109s during continuous convoy patrols. The Blenheims of No 235 Squadron meanwhile suffered some bad losses but still gamely fought back and scored a number of victories against Bf 109s and He 111s.

Luftwaffe aircraft started taking notice of this thorn in their side called Bircham Newton and targeted the airfield in the course of many effected or attempted bombing and strafing attacks. A decoy Q site foiled the Luftwaffe's opening raid during June by attracting enemy bombs; future raiders did reach their actual destination but never really posed a great threat as limited damage demonstrated. The worst assault on August 21 1940 as bombs fell on the married quarters brought considerable damage to both buildings and aircraft and injured 22 personnel, one of them fatally.

No 206 Squadron finally moved from Bircham Newton to St Eval in May 1941. Also leaving that month were early ASV radar-equipped Wellingtons of No 221 Squadron which had reformed on November 21 1940 and now gone away to Limavady. To emphasise how different changes of airfield could be for all RAF units in World War Two, No 235 Squadron departed a month later for Dyce. From Norfolk to Cornwall, Northern Ireland and north-east Scotland: our airfields had truly taken over every corner of Britain. Bircham Newton was certainly one place to be at for sheer variety.

Maritime patrol aircraft had become extremely active here but meteorological reconnaissance served as another important role throughout World War Two. No 521 Squadron formed for this task in the summer of 1942, later disbanding in March 1943. AA co-operation had been going on even longer since before the war. One wartime function to greatly increase in importance everywhere was ASR, so No 279 Squadron – the bugbear of Beccles II – arose on November 16 1941, joined by No 280 Squadron for a period mid-war. All this time Docking worked with Bircham Newton: not far away to the north, this satellite greatly helped with aircraft dispersal and had a great affinity with its parent, much like Stanton Harcourt did with Abingdon or Milltown with Lossiemouth II to take a couple of other examples.

Aircraft still heavily used Bircham Newton for maritime patrols despite such versatility, one later visitor being No 320 Squadron between April 1942 and March 1943. This unit flew Hudsons, common sights ever since 1940 and probably to this airfield what Spitfires were to Biggin Hill. No 407 Squadron kept No 320 company over the same broad period of time as fierce attacks continued against German shipping. These two Dutch and Canadian forces also enabled Bircham Newton to achieve its long-cherished ambition of strategically bombing Germany when Nos 320 and 407 Squadrons participated in the third thousand bomber raid against Bremen on June 25/26 1942, as RAF Bomber Command's Arthur Harris gratefully accepted every available aircraft that could carry bombs.

Eventually the Hudson became obsolescent as other types with better range and heavier offensive armament appeared. This still did not mean it was entirely finished in RAF service. Before No 279 Squadron's Hudsons moved to Thornaby in October 1944, they had achieved the distinction of being the first ASR force to use airborne lifeboats. On the operational front *Rover* anti-shipping patrols out of this base reached their final peak as Wellingtons of No 524 Squadron, Swordfish of No 819 Squadron and Fairey Albacores of No 119 Squadron carried out intensive searches for enemy submarines and E-boats. Just previously the RAF and FAA showed how they could co-operate when No 524 Squadron and Grumman Avengers of No 855 Squadron successfully dispatched a torpedo-boat on September 11. More general naval attacks – mainly at night – lasted into the early part of 1945.

By then No 695 Squadron had long resided at Bircham Newton, having formed for AA co-operation duties on December 1 1943 when these units replaced Flights. The airfield's last major squadron quietly proceeded with its job until transfer to Horsham St Faith near Norwich in August 1945. No 598 Squadron however did not have such a long life in East Anglia by disbanding earlier that year on April 30

THE AIRFIELDS OF BRITAIN

after coming south from Peterhead on March 12. This mixed Hurricane/Martinet/Oxford AA co-operation element displayed logistic capabilities to the bitter end with detachments as distant as Hutton Cranswick, Lympne and Peterhead itself.

Once more a war was over shortly thereafter as No 18 ACHU stayed from June 18 to September 22. What a brilliant campaign Bircham Newton had waged against the enemy but, despite a glorious performance and excellent facilities, the airfield suffered from the old fault of a grassy landing area. Vickers Warwicks had been present while on training duties but found the runways tight.

A second feeling of anticlimax therefore hit Bircham Newton in its second peaceful period with little further flying following World War Two. What aerial activity there was – such as No 1559 Radio Aids Training Flight's Oxfords in 1947 – effectively petered out in the autumn of 1948.

Ground training establishments dominated up to the airfield's closure on December 18 1962. During July/August 1946 the Aircrew Allocation Centre moved in from Catterick, renamed as the Combined Reselection and Allocation Centre in September and merged with the Combined Reselection Centre from Eastchurch in Kent. The Officers' Advanced Training School stayed from October 1948 to the end, witnessing a peculiar incident in May 1961 when 145,500 sandbags were stolen.

Although now officially disused, one or two special aircraft resided at the airfield in the 1960s. The sole Martin-Baker MB-5 lay in storage during its final days, a sad fate for this brilliant 460 miles per hour single-engined fighter resembling a Mustang whose only 'crime' had been to emerge slightly behind the times. A brighter future awaited a few Hawker Siddeley Kestrels – forerunners of the Harrier jump-jet fighter – which flew in 1965 from Bircham Newton instead of West Raynham.

A unique organisation which at the very least indirectly affects every one of us today uses this incomparable old base as the Bircham Newton (formerly Construction Industry) Training Centre gives instruction to all involved in the building trade. All those tens of thousands of people working throughout Britain illustrate yet again the devastating latent power of our airfields. The vast majority of buildings serve some sort of purpose, especially for accommodation and training, one example being an old style operations block which has lasted infinitely better than the doomed structure Biggin Hill once possessed.

So good is Bircham Newton's entire condition – it ought to be, considering who is now in charge – that casualties are restricted to ten Blisters and one out of three Bellmans removed. A 'Fort' type watch tower also stood in a moderately shabby state until the management wisely decided to spruce up the building. Cranes stand on the landing area but this is necessary, as was clearance of the eight Belfasts in earlier times to make way for three magnificent Cs which still survive. The 1930s Expansion era radically changed this station, though some support buildings dating prior to then remain in equally excellent states. And let us not forget that famous ghost in the squash courts!

Space simply prevents one going on and on in appreciation of the incredible Bircham Newton. Here is a place which has won Britain two World Wars, is packed with history, has revolutionised everyday society even more than most other airfields and is an architectural sensation. Nearly twenty RAF squadrons formed there, a tremendously high number for an airfield, perhaps telling you how the RAF knew a good site on finding one. You just have to visit Bircham Newton to absorb its magical atmosphere. Go on.

132/TF785345. 13 miles NW of Fakenham. Easy to view as B1155 road runs through site.

Bircotes, Nottinghamshire

Alternative Name: Bawtry

The grass airfield of Bircotes was unlike Bircham Newton in not being the best place for an airfield, often suffering from flooding or soft ground, though nowhere near as bad as painted elsewhere. While a satellite, in this case primarily for Finningley, facilities were at least reasonable. Farmland still contains one example each of a B1 and T2 – standard issue for a bomber OTU satellite – and now used for storage duties. Trees make the latter hangar surprisingly difficult to find.

Bircotes opened thanks to another airfield which lay opposite it on the south side of the A631 road. Bawtry was one of these little private airfields and AA-listed landing grounds that covered most of Britain during the 1930s, owned by Harald Peake, a businessman and commander of No 609 Squadron at Yeadon from formation in 1936. His AuxAF connections enabled Peake to reach a high rank in the Air Ministry during World War Two before returning to the commercial world as a bank chairman and company director. Plain Mr Peake was now Air Commodore Sir Harald Peake.

This information may look irrelevant but the landing ground surely had a say in events to come. The RAF knew Bircotes as Bawtry after it opened in November 1941 up to June 5 1942, having to alter the name because of confusion with No 1 Group's administrative ground headquarters at Bawtry Hall, where Harald Peake was raised.

Two Finningley OTUs stayed at Bircotes. No 25 used it once the airfield replaced superior but distant Balderton during November 7-14 1941. Earlier efforts to bring Bircotes into service in the spring had been thwarted by the landing area needing time-consuming regrading, and several enemy bombs dropped around Plumtree Farm near pre-war Bawtry on June 27 gave a fright. For real fear, though, nothing could beat the Avro Manchester with two shockingly unreliable Rolls-Royce Vulture engines. 'E' Flight flew in six of these aircraft from Finningley on November 17. They fortunately lasted not too long, Wellingtons of 'C' and 'D' Flights doing better until stopping instruction on January 7 1943. Bircotes had outlived No 25 OTU at Finningley by a week but both sites went on C&M on February 1.

Although Finningley only employed the satellite for accommodation purposes for much of 1943, the idea that Bircotes proved a decidedly so-so airfield is not at all true. No 16 (Polish) SFTS at Newton gladly sent over a number of Oxfords during February 19-21 to continue training as that Nottinghamshire base's grass landing surface was in a bad way. These machines left on August 17.

Finningley, which could not boast of having a good 1943 with runway problems of its own, continued to limp along as No 18 OTU arrived in October. The emergence of a superb new satellite at Worksop meant this second unit departed in August 1944 from Bircotes and the airfield fell back to C&M. Ossington in Nottinghamshire and Wymeswold in Leicestershire also saw their OTUs fly from here during 1943 and 1944 respectively, the rear party of Wymeswold's No 28 going on August 1.

For an airfield not supposed to have had the most distinguished of lives, the RAF showed a strange unwillingness to immediately toss away Bircotes. The ex-satellite transferred to No 61 MU on November 15 1944 as various equipment storage units prepared to check in, although Finningley maintained parenting responsibilities up to the spring of 1945. No 61 MU yielded room for other basically similar elements, No 66 holding MT engines and No 250 entire vehicles while this more important related MU stayed from July 1945 until disbanding on April 30 1947. Bircotes still kept going but No 61 MU closed its sub-site on July 13 1948: parenting however went on as no alternative Government department wanted to take up ownership of the now inactive airfield.

Wellingtons turned out to be Bircotes' most frequent aerial visitors. They maybe failed to remain any great length of time but their old satellite is architecturally highly tangible. Not all that many disused airfields can claim the same feat nowadays. 111/SK639937. 1 mile W of Bawtry, enter from S side.

Bishops Court, Down

The great airfield hunt in Northern Ireland during World War Two rapidly ran out of steam by mid-war as possible portions of suitable land dried up. Planners and builders had filled up the areas around Loughs Erne, Foyle and Neagh plus the Ards Peninsula: too many hills and uncertain atmospheric conditions ruled out about everywhere else in the country. But south-west of the last area and east of Downpatrick a thinly populated piece of countryside provided some hope as the proverbial last scrapings of the barrel. This land passed requirements, received approval for requisition in April 1942, and christened with the English-sounding name of Bishops Court as every other locality was Ballythis and Ballythat.

Over the next twelve months construction workers wove a merry path around farms and other obstacles to complete Northern Ireland's last all-new 'dry' wartime airfield to open: this it did on April 1 1943. Bishops Court looked a big site, easily capable for heavy bombers or the Americans had either party wished to use the base. The USAAF actually showed provisional interest but British aircraft of a more unexpected nature would become evident.

Two schools were based at Bishops Court in World War Two: one for navigational training, the other for teaching gunnery. Such a combination of diverse elements seemed an odd practice but their large airfield could easily accommodate both units. Bishops Court would have fitted in without any trouble in eastern England's 'bomber country', while a whopping hangarage total of four T2s and 35 Blisters resulted in this place becoming one of Britain's most numerically superior airfields for hangars ever.

No 7 AOS gathered here in the summer of 1943. The

THE AIRFIELDS OF BRITAIN

school had oddly reformed in mid-March before Bishops Court could even open. Visible signs took time but more Ansons, as well as Martinets, became evident when No 12 AGS formed on August 1. The Irish Sea's northern reaches already rippled with the sound of gunfire from aircraft based at Andreas, Barrow and Castle Kennedy. Bishops Court now occupied the western side of this major safe training area as No 12 AGS settled down like its separate colleague to a steady diet of instruction until World War Two ended. During this intervening period No 7 AOS was renamed No 7 (Observers) Advanced Flying Unit in February 1944 and then No 7 Air Navigation School in May 1945. This month marked the end of the AGS to significantly reduce activity at Bishops Court.

The incessant number of name changes which so many British training airfields had to be subjected to during wartime continued. Bishops Court's surviving school was yet again renamed in June 1947: now known as No 2 ANS, a dozen Wellingtons that had replaced the Ansons during November/December 1946 left for today's Teesside Airport at Middleton St George on October 1.

Planners suggested all sorts of ideas for this site now that aircraft had gone. One immediately arose for Flying Training Command to hand over the airfield to BEA on December 15 1947 for the airline to provide passenger handling facilities if Belfast's then airport Nutt's Corner experienced bad weather. The Ministry of Civil Aviation accepted some supportive buildings but nothing more apparently came of this alternative diversionary airfield scheme as far as one can gather, probably because of the marginally off-centre part of Northern Ireland in which Bishops Court stood. Officially resorting to inactivity, Flying Training Command passed the baton on April 12 1948 to Coastal Command, who might have earlier gained control had No 7 ANS flown out in June 1947.

Bishops Court would not give up the fight in its right to hold aircraft. A second spurt of activity occurred due to the Korean War once No 3 ANS was created in the spring of 1952. Time had changed little as Anson trainers returned to a place they knew well. The surroundings looked different in that a policy decided in January 1946 to dismantle fourteen Blisters had largely gone ahead, except for one hangar being kept for light aircraft and a few others for technical uses, but many features still lasted. New metal sheeting covered the T2s, while workmen refurbished the runways, perimeter track and lighting.

Allowing for general chaos around the airfield for long enough and very slow laying of connecting paths and roads,

241

THE AIRFIELDS OF BRITAIN: VOLUME 1

flying began in April 1952 and continued until No 3 ANS closed down on April 15 1954. C&M restarted on September 27 but constant efforts by local MP Captain L.P.S. Orr protesting about unemployment and Downpatrick traders feeling an acute loss of business paid off as Fighter Command ousted Coastal Command in March 1955. Bishops Court would be the first regular RAF fighter base in Northern Ireland since shortly after World War Two – or so everyone hoped.

September 1 1956 saw the once more reconstructed site's grand reopening for this exciting new phase. The military thought that fighter squadrons might use Bishops Court while their normal homes in England and Scotland temporarily closed for alterations, a reasonable assumption given Leuchars did so in the summer. Dreams suddenly turned sour with this airfield closing in late November, except for emergency landings, and an unclear operating routine during 1957 as a few aircraft called in each month. An exercise held in May brought 75 movements by Chipmunk trainers of the Queen's University Air Squadron and some Meteors but bitter disappointment greeted the news a month later that Fighter Command intended to send aircraft to Aldergrove and not Bishops Court, though the king of Northern Ireland's airfields never welcomed them regularly again either.

Resilience is a word one can readily apply to our airfields. Bishops Court proved an admirable example by managing with more than a little extreme improvisation to keep going since 1957. Particular thanks had to go to that great airfield ally: radar. From No 255 Signals Unit becoming operational in an air defence role from August 1956, a nearby radar station to the east at Killard Point developed to the point where the RAF and Ministry of Aviation established a new joint Air Traffic Control section on September 1 1959. Every civil and military aircraft flying above 25,000 feet was now being monitored. Early warning radar meanwhile fed vital information to the Sector Operations Centre at Boulmer in Northumberland, another airfield tenuously hanging on to its status.

Where Bishops Court fitted into this overall operation was to accommodate radar systems plus personnel and allow visiting aircraft to land on the main NE/SW runway. Communications might not be the most glamorous form of flying but without this duty every airfield would administratively seize up: Bircotes appreciated that basic fact, and so too did the radar staff in Northern Ireland. Occasional incoming military helicopters on exercises, such as a Wessex

THE AIRFIELDS OF BRITAIN

which crashed at the airfield on April 27 1990, and free-fall parachutists further held up movement levels, while gliders of No 664 Volunteer GS arrived in the 1980s. Engineless flight had occurred as early as the 1950s when No 203 GS and the civilian Shorts GC stayed. Even airport use was contemplated in 1970 until radar obstructions excluded that idea. In 1978 Killard Point closed but the Bishops Court end kept open, radar facilities there being upgraded in the 1980s.

Explaining airfield affairs is never easy. Bishops Court remained on C&M and ostensibly looked disused; the removal of every last one of its 39 hangars did not aid the cause either. But officialdom regarded this place as active and important. And the IRA did too: not known for attacks upon airfields if one discounts Sydenham near Belfast, this terrorist organisation made a mortar attack upon Bishops Court during the night of September 11/12 1989. The wonder is why it took so long, for RAF personnel had worried about possible raids in 1956.

To see Bishops Court in the autumn of 1991 was to see 'For Sale' signs up everywhere. The airfield stood deserted after having closed on December 4 1990 and modern two/three bedroom residential buildings lay empty for purchase at less than £13,000 each. Wartime supportive buildings around the technical site were in tiptop condition but would surely be harder to sell. Bishops Court's phenomenal run of good fortune had ended as, apart from government cost cuts, homing missiles fired from aircraft in profusion against Iraqi radar sites during the Gulf War showed how vulnerable were static stations. Smaller and more transportable tracking devices are now a must for any air force. As for Bishops Court, regardless of whether used as an established motor cycle racing circuit, one bally fight looms.

21/J578425. SE of Downpatrick, 4½ miles NE of Ardglass to W of A2. Most buildings on SE side of landing area.

Bishopton, Durham

While on the subject of Middleton St George before we forget about it for the moment, travel about five miles directly north of this airport to where No 2 ANS moved from Bishops Court in 1947 and you encounter an old World War One landing ground. No 36 (HD) Squadron employed Bishopton from October 1916 after the site was approved for development on August 18.

THE AIRFIELDS OF BRITAIN: VOLUME 1

Farmland now rules at this primitive airfield which the RAF eventually relinquished in August 1919. A minor road connecting Bishopton and Little Stainton villages formed the southern and eastern boundaries for those of you interested in establishing Bishopton's precise position.
93/NZ358208. W of Stockton-on-Tees, ¾ mile SW of village.

Bisterne, Hampshire

Just as anonymous, of considerably less duration yet thunderously active, Bisterne was a typical extremely temporary south of England Advanced Landing Ground.

It was March 1944 when the USAAF's 371st Fighter Group arrived with Republic P-47s to shatter the peaceful goings-on in this quiet area outside Bournemouth. Heavy aircraft in every sense, the Thunderbolts' sheer bulk became the reason why Bisterne made such a disastrous start to its airfield career. Nearly three years had to pass before everyone finally acknowledged that Bircotes possessed a 'could do better' landing area: the P-47s went many steps better by mashing their ALG's surface into a pulp in only a week during April. Admittedly the land here in Hampshire was soft but weak metal runways also had to take their share of the blame. Regardless of where responsibility lay, the 371st FG had to get out in the mean time for military construction personnel to strengthen Bisterne, and resided at RAF Ibsley on the other side of Ringwood.

Success at last prevailed at Bisterne once the P-47s flew back on May 1. The Americans made many highly effective fighter-bomber sorties around the D-Day period and soon eradicated all memories of initial difficulties. But these good times could not be expected to last for long due to the basic summer-only qualities of ALGs. As retreating German forces allowed available land abroad to see Allied flying use, so the 371st FG left for France towards the end of June on the 23rd; Bisterne closed as intended within a month.

As with Bishopton and so many other places, few today would believe that this farmland once contained an airfield. An odd scrap of metal runway is visible for fencing purposes but everything else has disappeared, including Bisterne's above average hangarage for an ALG of a transportable type and four Blisters. Both runways broadly formed an L shape, and the north-south stretch drove across a minor road to the

hamlet of North Kingston. Bisterne could have been called Kingston after other various surrounding settlements but quaintly-titled Oxfordshire RAF RLG Kingston Bagpuize ruled out that particular possibility.
195/SU155023. NE of Bournemouth, 2 miles S of Ringwood. Turn second left off B3347 once out of town for minor road to North Kingston. Old main runway straddles road, with secondary stretch to S.

Bitteswell, Leicestershire

Best remembered for post-World War Two aircraft production involvement with several companies, Bitteswell has like Binbrook generally suffered a savage downturn in fortunes during recent years. Again the fault lay not with the airfield but ageing aircraft and financial cut-backs.

Bitteswell arose on an area of fairly flat farmland west of the market town of Lutterworth. The town vied with Bitteswell village, towards which Lutterworth has ominously crept almost to the point of absorption, as a suitable name. A – well competed with a – worth – syllables, never mind whole titles, required extreme checking – and the smaller more distinctive locality triumphed.

This name first featured before any other development work beyond simply choosing a title had resulted when 30 incendiary bombs landed here shortly after midnight on June 25 1940. By then the site had only just been designated an emergency scatter airfield or ELG for newly-opened bomber station Bramcote, seven miles north-west of this crude place, which the Luftwaffe had tried to find.

Soon it became all too apparent that what is one of our few documented ELGs was wasted in this role. No 18 Operational Training Unit began night flying training on August 12 1941 as a watch office arose at the new promoted satellite airfield. 'D' Flight formed on the 18th but disbanded on December 18 as another ELG closer to Bramcote at Wolvey humiliatingly took over instructional duties. The Wellington detachment soon left while Bitteswell went under the scalpel again to have hard runways installed.

1942 passed by as something of a blur with no flying and some bad weather further affecting the landing area, though No 18 OTU retained a token occupation. A new year started and still the runways were unserviceable but everything changed on February 7 1943 as Bitteswell became an 'unbuilt'

THE AIRFIELDS OF BRITAIN: VOLUME 1

satellite to new Leicestershire airfield Bruntingthorpe, while Bramcote's unit prepared to move to Finningley. At long last regular flying could occur by No 29 OTU from June until Bramcote again regained control from November 1944 to July 1945. No 105 OTU initially used Wellingtons like its predecessors but as transport trainers and changed to Dakotas during 1945.

World War Two had transpired in the end to be a time of constant, if routine, work for this satellite. All that Bitteswell needed was some variety: it would soon be rewarded. Classed as closed and on C&M from July 17 1945 once 'B' and 'D' Flights had gone to No 105 OTU's other satellite at Nuneaton II, Bramcote continued as parent and loaned No 266 MU one T2 and one B1 for storing equipment from February 5 1946. Prior to the temporary sub-site being cleared in January 1947, Bitteswell altered Commands once more on July 1 1946 for Flying Training to appear and permit No 20 FTS from Church Lawford in Warwickshire to have a Relief Landing Ground. Harvards visited up to mid-1947 when the Ministry of Supply became the latest owner on June 3 after being delayed for around six months in its wishes.

This Government acquisition proved much more promising than at first glance, for Armstrong Whitworth could now employ Bitteswell with greater confidence. The company had held on since final assembling Lancasters from 1943, wisely performing aircraft maintenance duties post-war as activity ran down after World War Two. If partly only to keep Bitteswell in business, what really counted were the three hard runways, items that Armstrong Whitworth's primary operating base Baginton did not possess. Having fended off a 1948 proposal for the airfield to become a vehicular proving ground, this long-term planning worked a treat when aircraft final assembly/flight-testing restarted in 1952; Armstrong Whitworth then bought Bitteswell altogether four years later instead of only leasing the site. Experimental flying had ceased at Baginton in early 1954, leaving that airfield to deal with company liaison duties.

Apart from exotic aircraft already conducting engine tests for Armstrong Siddeley Motors Ltd, brand new aircraft types subsequently appeared in strength as the rejuvenated former bomber OTU satellite aided and eventually supplanted Baginton when the Coventry factory shut down in mid-1965. By now Hawker Siddeley was in charge and carried on the Armstrong Whitworth tradition for a while by sorting out its Argosy transport design. Hawker Hunter jet fighters also became frequent sights.

THE AIRFIELDS OF BRITAIN

The 1970s brought in British Aerospace as other types arrived for general overhauling. Shackleton maritime patrol aircraft and Vulcan V-bombers dominated but at this time the situation began to look serious for Bitteswell. Although both of these Avro designs had given excellent service, they were getting older and so stood a greater chance of retiring; money also became tighter as Britain's shrunken aircraft industry further thinned down. Eventually the RAF's Shackleton fleet was reduced to the 'Magic Roundabout' AEW element of No 8 Squadron at Lossiemouth II which had to start seriously considering approaching museums in order to keep these ancient contraptions going. Retiral of all Vulcans announced in 1982 spelt ultimate doom for Bitteswell, BAe supplying the coup de grace in March of that year by declaring an intention to close the site. Company flying finished on June 30.

Civilian servicing staff cleared out for life on the dole to leave their popular place of work utterly stranded. But as ever the weird and wonderful rules of airfield life bent severely to Bitteswell's advantage as it remained active of sorts, being best described as an (extremely) unlicensed site. A ray of hope later seemed to appear in the autumn of 1984 when aircraft enthusiast Doug Arnold bought Bitteswell for £3 million and planned to move in his Warbirds of Great Britain preserved aircraft collection from a place whose history immediately follows. Official snags sadly arose and industry purchased the airfield in turn from Arnold two years later to finally put an end to all active aviation expectations.

Bitteswell altered not too much architecturally after World War Two. The main workshop facilities stood at the northern and southern ends, with hangars dotted around the perimeter track. Four T2s mingled with three Ministry of Aircraft Production A1s and five B1s unusually standing together in a line. The runways were re-laid and strengthened during the late 1950s but never greatly changed shape either, despite all the jet fighters and Vulcans which visited.

For a time after 1986 this place looked totally lifeless: the body was there, though not the blood. A sign hanging pathetically alongside a road saying 'Bitteswell Airport' effectively summed up the tragic situation another fine airfield had been involuntarily allowed to get into. Soon developers dismembered the body with massive demolition to create Magna Park − not even Airfield Park, observe − as a warehouse/distribution centre area for companies such as Asda, Toyota and Volvo. The local populace who often complained about aircraft noise levels now intensely dislike the huge ugly modern block buildings standing on the overwhelmed landing area. We have to say serves them damn well right for not trying harder to save the airfield before closure.

Survey the business park today and little survives apart from the five B1s and one T2. The Government constantly moans about how Britain is losing manufacturing jobs, so why throw areas like Bitteswell upon the scrap-heap, even if service ones are being created instead? Political logic as ever defies description – but then our alleged great leaders have never understood Britain's airfields ever since 1909.

140/SP512845. N of Rugby, 2 miles W of Lutterworth by A427.

Blackbushe, Hampshire

Alternative Names: Hartfordbridge, Hartford Bridge Flats

Blackbushe and Hartfordbridge were and still are the same airfield: its name altered in late 1944. Of high military importance in World War Two, Blackbushe has had quite a rocky civilian existence since 1945.

One source has stated that Blackbushe first saw use as an airfield during World War One. In what role, whether as a landing ground or a duty involving greater permanency, is unknown and no other historical documentary evidence has yet been found to back up this unsubstantiated claim. We do know with cast-iron certainty how many years later in October 1941 the same site was approved for development as a satellite to Odiham. Built as a typical mid-war type airfield, it received the name of Hartfordbridge after a hamlet two miles to the south-west, although some military and local civilian residents alike also preferred to dub the base Hartford Bridge Flats in recognition of surrounding land.

Hartfordbridge opened on November 7 1942. No 171 Squadron came from Gatwick in December but soon folded on January 1 1943, though No 430 Squadron arose out of this defunct mixed Mustang and Curtiss Tomahawk Army Co-operation Command force before almost immediately going to Dunsfold in Surrey.

PR and light bomber types were destined to appear at this base surrounded by woodland during 1943 and 1944 as Hartfordbridge began to stand on its own two feet. Nos 16 and 140 Squadrons carried out the first job after arriving in the spring and early summer of 1943. These units operated Spitfires and Mosquitoes, and No 140 Squadron briefly flew

THE AIRFIELDS OF BRITAIN

some Lockheed Venturas as well. Their time at Hartfordbridge proved far from wasted as both elements examined large areas of Europe for future military use. This was a difficult task: as PR aircraft normally did not carry guns, so crews had to rely upon superior speed and height to escape enemy predators. Nos 16 and 140 Squadrons moved to Northolt in April 1944 to leave the way clear for bombers at Hartfordbridge.

Two Douglas Boston squadrons and No 21 Squadron, operating a few more of the RAF's unsuccessful Venturas, had already come along in August 1943. Professedly visiting to take part in the largely worthless spoof invasion of France's Pas de Calais area known as Operation *Starkey,* policy dictated that Nos 88 and 107 Squadrons – plus No 342 which arrived in September – should remain at Hartfordbridge. Operation *Crossbow* or the assault upon V-weapon targets started before No 107 Squadron was sent to Lasham in Hampshire during February 1944 to collect Mosquitoes, while No 226 Squadron's Mitchells moved in. Some RAF fighter activity also resulted at this time but top priority stayed with the light bombers as they kept German tactical forces at bay once the Normandy landings were effected.

It gradually became obvious how further away enemy targets seemed as Hartfordbridge's units required foreign bases for less taxing flights. A period of heavy airfield movements followed as No 107 Squadron returned from Lasham on October 23 with Nos 305 and 613 Squadrons. These visitors abruptly went back to Lasham two days later and then once more transferred to Hartfordbridge on the 30th due to 'a sudden change of programme' but all this airfield's residents, Bostons, Mosquitoes and No 226 Squadron's Mitchells alike, crossed to France in October and November.

Despite the thousands of tons of bombs plastered on opposition targets up until this period, November 18 1944 – the day before Nos 107, 305 and 613 Squadrons left Hartfordbridge – proved the most meaningful day in its wartime career. But why did the name of this airfield change to Blackbushe? Nobody has ever given a precise reason, yet we can offer a couple of good possible answers. The name of Yateley featured quite prominently in the vicinity with a village, a common and a wood but probably the factory airfield at Yate north-east of Bristol prevented use to stop any confusion. A much simpler explanation could of course be that Hartfordbridge looked too unwieldy for its own good: maybe even, if you recall what happened at Bitteswell, the last

249

syllable gave difficulties. There is nevertheless one major shortcoming with this second suggestion as several other Hartfords – and two literal Hartford Bridges in northern England – existed in Britain without airfield links whatsoever. About the only vaguest of vague connections was a village called Hartford near Pathfinder Force HQ station Wyton – and who could mistake that great base for anywhere else? Regardless of still elusive reasoning, a farm one and a half miles south of the airfield ensured Blackbushe would rule from the autumn of 1944 onwards.

While more Mosquitoes of Nos 418 (RCAF) and 605 Squadrons became later visitors, staying until March 1945, transports of No 167 Squadron moved in that month to start the next big phase of Blackbushe's life. Being situated not tremendously far west of London with the busy A30 right on the doorstep offered great opportunities but No 167's initial activities were dogged by problems as Dakotas and Ansons had to supplement engine-troubled Warwicks as World War Two drew to a close.

Although mail-carrying Mosquito transports of No 162 Squadron began to come in June too, a detachment of No 24 Squadron made real news by flying an evaluative all-weather freight/mail service to and from Prestwick. An airfield provided with an SCS 51 landing aid – the first Instrument Landing System or ILS – co-operated with another one possessing the only other example of this device at an RAF base and also arguably the best weather record in Britain: perfect ingredients for success. So brilliantly executed was this test route that it had an enormous effect in paving the way for safe future military and civil transport flying. Now absolutely no-one feared poor visibility or any other forms of bad weather.

The military shut down Blackbushe in November 1946 after Nos 167 and 162 Squadrons had earlier disbanded in February and July respectively and the pioneering No 24 Squadron ceased round trips to Prestwick in the autumn. Designated a civil airport in February 1947, a FIDO anti-fog installation was strangely retained for many years while all other British airfields except for Manston hurriedly dropped their fiery friends, though being Heathrow's main fog diversionary aide justified retention. US Navy transports used Blackbushe along with numerous small civil operators, typically Westminster Airways which in 1947 positioned maintenance headquarters here than Battle of Britain superstar Kenley and employed Croydon as an operational base but was wound up in November 1949.

No 622 Squadron met with as little success when reformed towards the end of 1950 in an ambitious attempt to create a RAuxAF transport force. It was attached to omnipresent British aviation company Airwork and used Vickers Valettas but ceased to function on September 30 1953. A different Vickers product, a Viking belonging to Aldermaston's last resident Eagle Aviation, later crashed on the night of May 1 1957 with 34 fatalities while on a trooping charter flight.

Blackbushe had won a war – perhaps even two if those reports about World War One are to be believed. But many locals bereft of gratitude and a sense of history disgracefully could not care less and played a key role in forcing the airfield to close in 1960; the US Navy was furious at having to leave. At first planned that closure should occur as the year ended, the Ministry of Aviation put this date considerably back to May 31. Blackbushe would be silenced – permanently.

Auctioned off in July, Hampshire Planning Committee wanted the airfield to revert to being common land. A Butler hangar built for the US Navy was proposed to be an athletics coaching centre but finished up under industrial ownership. This proved the sole constructive decision made at this terrible period as the enemy tried to visibly flatten Blackbushe. By mid-1962 only the American-designed hangar and an airport terminal building survived.

Heavy opposition to these scandalous actions was mounted by many airfield operators and tenants before their home had closed. Not least among them stood PFF creator and leader Air Vice-Marshal Donald Bennett, someone who most certainly knew the difference between Wyton and Blackbushe. He had come to the latter site during the late 1940s after a few personally unsettled years with his airline Fairflight, which merged with famous pre-war Croydon-based concern Surrey Flying Services in 1952 to become Air Charter Ltd. Now Bennett faced a massive battle against officialdom without a shot being fired. Grim determination marked the Ministry of Aviation's efforts to kill off Blackbushe – and who was in charge? One Duncan Sandys. The ultimate egomaniac helped local inhabitants reject a proposal for the construction of light aircraft hangars in August 1961.

Yet the marvellous Bennett refused point-blank to surrender. Astonishingly later assisted by the MoA – what a shambles on its part – in trying to reopen the airfield, he managed to do so in 1962 and won a crushing victory against Hampshire County Council on appeal. The Blackbushe Aero Club had used this eponymous base since early on in the year but initially could only give flying instruction at

Southampton's airport Eastleigh; not until October 6 did an official airfield opening ceremony happen.

While all doubts vanished in March 1963 with national and local government approval for continued activity, both these and affiliated Establishment institutions still picked away at planning technicalities. The courts told Bennett in 1965 that the main runway could not be extended for bigger aircraft to land on, and Hampshire County Council pettily continued objecting during 1966 about a go-ahead given three years before for three new hangars.

Ever since, Blackbushe has limped on for business and light aircraft use by organisations such as the Three Counties Aero Club and Blackbushe School of Flying: the original Blackbushe Aero Club closed down in 1977. The Warbirds of Great Britain Museum remained for some years too with various World War Two and vintage post-war types, joined by a few privately owned preserved aircraft until Doug Arnold sold out in October 1984 and moved to Bitteswell (see above). This character, who had replaced Donald Bennett as owner during the 1970s, was hindered as much by local vested interests while trying to develop the place.

British Car Auctions Group in turn bought this airfield for £7.3 million, and now Blackbushe Airport 85 Ltd (a subsidiary of ADT Auctions Ltd) has big plans in hand. But you only have to see that Blackbushe is a pale shadow of its old self with being territorially eaten away since World War Two. Only the main runway is open, all three stretches are reduced in length, the eastern perimeter track is missing and very few original buildings survive. Available hangarage in World War Two consisted of three T2s, six Blisters and two Bessoneaux but the major structures stood either close to or south of the A30. Aircraft frequently had to cross this road — often closed in wartime — for maintenance to an area which woodland has now obscured. Go-kart racing is now another activity but huge Sunday markets really draw in the crowds. The post-war Butler hangar met a strange end in the late 1980s when allegedly pushed over after gipsies had removed this building's steelwork.

While many British civil airfields have picked themselves up off the floor after a post-war fight for survival, Blackbushe looks to be caught in a time warp. How does a place like this in such a prosperous and heavily populated region of Britain have to survive so uncertainly? Its luck may improve at the expense of another if the unthinkable happens and Farnborough is forced to close, though let us not tempt providence in that direction. Whatever the future brings,

THE AIRFIELDS OF BRITAIN

Blackbushe deserves better.
186/SU807592. 5 miles W of Camberley on N side of A30. Large viewing area beside road.

Black Isle, Highland

Alternative Name: Blackstand
Greenery abounds around the former Black Isle airfield, unusually named after the peninsula above Inverness. This is surely one of Britain's most unexpected areas for airfields because of a hilly terrain and sheer isolation. Cromarty on the tip of Black Isle did see a faint combination of land and marine flying during 1913 and World War One but nobody could have ever guessed how any piece of countryside further inland would accept aircraft.

The apparently impossible occurred in 1941 as Kinloss and Lossiemouth II hunted for SLGs to help their busy Maintenance Units. Dornoch and Kirkton north of Tain came to their assistance but most surprising was the acceptance of a site on Black Isle by the road between Rosemarkie and Balblair. Inspected on May 19 for construction work to begin on June 9 and opened on August 22, No 46 MU at Lossiemouth found little or no trouble in using the SLG until it closed in October 1945, having outlasted both Dornoch and Kirkton. Several aircraft types touched down for storage amid the woodland but Beaufighters became particularly prominent.

Visit the Black Isle today and you encounter even more surprises. SLGs never possessed many buildings for secrecy reasons: this one was no exception, yet still has the odd minor support building scattered here and there. As if this is remarkable enough, a Super Robin hangar moved from Lossiemouth in 1944 miraculously looks down upon the A832 from a lofty position. Close to Black Isle on the north side is a farm called Blackstand, a name local residents sometimes still give to their little historical wonder. What a survivor!
27/NH717607. 4½ miles N of Fortrose, to right of B9160.

Blakehill Farm, Wiltshire

Alternative Name: Cricklade
Another airfield named after a farm. Even so, our top

253

historical stars did not have to be in such remote parts of Britain as Black Isle to give planners naming problems. Land in the vicinity of Cricklade approved for requisition in December 1942 bore this Wiltshire town's name. For a reason which like Hartfordbridge/Blackbushe is also unexplained and more impossible to interpret, the title changed not before long on May 29 1943. As a satellite for Aston Down called Chedworth already existed, this new airfield which opened as planned on February 9 1944 near Chelworth was named Blakehill Farm instead after a settlement on the south side.

Trying to open up this three runway base became something of a trial. Personnel encountered extremely difficult conditions with few essential buildings being ready. Every airfield also heavily depended upon MT for communications, ferrying, maintenance and safety duties but no vehicular transport at all was initially available. Difficulties lasted for a while too with civilian farmers working within Blakehill Farm's environs and all the resulting security problems involved. Secrecy here as at every other airfield was a must — and especially had to be with events to come.

No 233 Squadron appeared at Blakehill Farm in March as numbers of airmen and paratroopers plus their aircraft and gliders massively built up prior to D-Day. Having previously hunted for U-boats from Gibraltar, this unit which used to operate Hudsons seemed a strange choice for an airborne forces squadron but crews adapted to their new Dakotas and Horsa assault gliders. Intensive training culminated in these craft being towed over from Blakehill Farm to France as part of the D-Day operation, joined by a section of No 271 Squadron. This other unit spent June/July 1944 at Blakehill Farm as its main station Down Ampney on the opposite side of Cricklade found the going a bit tough. No 271's temporary refuge continued to have things not too easy either as MT failings with daily organisation and maintenance lasted until after D-Day.

The Dakotas began to resupply Allied paratroops and more conventional land forces once the bridgehead in Normandy had been secured. No 233 Squadron performed a shuttle service by ferrying in supplies and flying out the wounded. For a former maritime patrol unit, it had come on by leaps and bounds in only four months and registered a major first on June 13 when No 233 Squadron Dakotas became RAF Transport Command's earliest aircraft to touch down in post-D-Day France on landing at a British-controlled airstrip.

No 437 Squadron later formed at Blakehill Farm as September 1944 started just in time for that gallant failure called Arnhem. Both the Canadians and No 233 Squadron had far less to celebrate as enemy air and ground defences, bad planning and atrocious weather resulted in several Dakotas failing to make it back to Wiltshire. A happier day was March 24 1945 as Blakehill Farm's aircraft successfully transported Horsas across the River Rhine while briefly stationed at Birch.

World War Two was almost over and No 437 Squadron went to Belgium on May 6/7. When No 233 Squadron also departed in June, No 22 Heavy Glider Conversion Unit from Fairford took up the space at Blakehill Farm with Albemarles but glider towing had fallen out of fashion and the HGCU disbanded during October.

Dakotas made a come-back a month later as No 575 Squadron arrived. Normality apparently returned but was illusory as this transport force turned out to be Blakehill Farm's last major flying unit to wholly stay. From the second week of January 1946 transports took off for Bari in southern Italy until the last five moved out on the 29th as the airfield Operations Record Book stated 'The health of the station remains good'. Nothing could have been further from the truth, at least for the immediate future.

True, two Radio Aids Training Flights for navigational instruction did survive past the initial stages of 1946. No 1528 came in December 1945 and left for Fairford in early February to form No 1555 RAT Flight. This second small Oxford unit returned to Blakehill Farm on April 30 but regressed to Fairford on August 17, though still using its old base's Blind Approach Beam System (BABS) landing aid. Fairford did not at first have this facility which No 24 Squadron had also employed while flying between Blackbushe and Prestwick: the planners however preferred that airfield to Blakehill Farm's cost.

On a closing down basis from November 5 and C&M from December 1, some dispersed sites had already been abandoned for disposal when Transport Command gave away the airfield on January 31 1947. Flying Training Command now regarded Blakehill Farm as an unmanned RLG to South Cerney in Gloucestershire. Sections of the RAF tended to treat the term 'unmanned' differently, an unmanned satellite in Bomber Command being a euphemism to describe a closed airfield: that ghastly modern scourge called political correctness is not altogether new. Barkston Heath, though, was officially unmanned as trainers visited in the late 1940s and beyond, a new task destined for Blakehill Farm.

The Central Flying School (Basic) Squadron and No 2

Flying Training School used this site well into the 1950s. Piston-engined trainers such as the Percival Provost found how their RLG could be a handy assistant, especially as South Cerney only had grass runways; No 2 FTS needed to start operating at Blakehill Farm from December 15 1948 as the parent's landing area struggled. No 2 FTS disbanded into the CFS (Basic) element on May 1 1952 but the RLG and its useful landing aid equipment which caused so much envy in 1946 continued in service until the replacement training establishment ceased to exist in March 1957. As 'A' and 'B' Squadrons amalgamated in May and went to the main CFS base at Little Rissington, personnel removed Blakehill Farm's special radio apparatus to bring an end to flying.

What is described as an 'Experimental Radio Station' today straddles Blakehill Farm – that is what a sign anyhow says at the north-eastern entrance. The tops of some aerials can be spotted all around but no doubt there is more happening than we are supposed to know about, and as a result this old airfield is out of bounds to the average buff. It would seem that most tracks and structures – including two T2s and a Blister – have gone to leave only the northern perimeter track and a few support buildings. One structure certainly still remains: the original Blakehill Farm, as detached from the outside world these days as the airfield it helped to inspire. 163/SU078915. 1½ miles SW of Cricklade.

Blaston, Leicestershire

Alternative Name: Uppingham
During World War One the authorities pinpointed Blaston as one of Britain's multitude of Home Defence fighter landing grounds. Described as having been 'recently taken up' by November 17 1916, it had become active by the end of December to assist No 38 Squadron. Control passed to No 90 Squadron after No 38 moved to France in May 1918 and Blaston was under its jurisdiction at the Armistice six months later.

Although the Eyebrook Reservoir has since vastly altered the adjacent landscape, we can still track down this landing ground's position. Blaston's western boundary formed a crossroads south of Bolt Wood and southern limits a minor road down to Great Easton village. Nearby Great Easton Lodge has long outlasted this forgotten airfield alongside the B664. 141/SP830963. NW of Corby, 5 miles SW of Uppingham.

Two unlikely disused airfields: World War One landing ground Binsoe *(above)* and the north-south runway at World War Two enigma Birch *(below)*, today a public road.

(above) Guess what the former guardhouse at Bircham Newton now is?
Both main hangars at Bircotes remain. A B1 *(below left)* is easy to spot but not so a T2 *(below right).*

The guardroom *(top)*, World War Two era support facilities *(middle)* and modern housing *(bottom)* at a fading Bishops Court.

(above) Blackbushe and residents on December 29 1963 as the airfield resumed business after a period of closure *(C. Walker)*. Nearly 30 years on, the aircraft may be more modern but little else has altered *(below)*.

(above) No other original structures survive at Blackbushe apart from the terminal building.
(below) There never was much to mark Irish flying boat satellite Boa Island, and even less these days.

No Blenheims or P-51s at Bodney *(above)* today, only a control tower on the far right side.
(below) Many supportive buildings continue to stand at Bodorgan on Anglesey.

(above and below) Foundations give away unknown Bogton, World War One assistant to Britain's worst airfield, the disastrous Loch Doon.

The two hangars at Boston *(above)*.
(below) Odd man out: nine T2s outnumber this B1 at Bottesford, detached from the rest by a minor road.

A strange sight is this English Electric Lightning gate guardian *(above)* at Boulmer, which never landed at the site, as is Boxted's extremely welcome airfield memorial flanked by runway lights *(below)*.

Unlike the main runway, trees have spared the north-western perimeter track at Boxted *(above)*. How generous of them.
(below) Three of the World War One Belfast hangars at Bracebridge Heath.

The control tower at Bradwell Bay has turned into a house *(above)*. Follow the electricity cables behind, go past the NW/SE runway and you reach Bradwell nuclear power station *(below)*.

(above) Two C hangars and firing butts at Bramcote.
(below) Further away from the airfield stand several pillboxes such as this example beside a minor road.

Blidworth, Nottinghamshire

Certain so-called airfield historians unfortunately look down upon information supplied by people living close to a site. Can such disdain be explained due to a fear of unreliable sources or in-built literary snobbery? Praise be therefore for the residents around Blidworth as they have provided many more details – and consistent ones – than official records.

An ELG for Hucknall from 1940, No 51 MU at Lichfield in Staffordshire decided in 1941 to use the same airfield as an SLG after carrying out an inspection on March 21. An officer reported for duty on May 9, more personnel coming on August 1 as Blidworth prepared to open. The airfield temporarily closed in early February 1942, later reopened and then closed again for a time in October. Not exactly a thrilling life, but this is about all military recorders ever bothered to tell us.

Field research tells a more expansive story. Blidworth comprised of an area of farmland developed into an east-west runway, occasionally home to rows of poles to stop enemy aircraft landing, where friendly types flew in before dispersing under trees to the north-west in a field next to Blidworth Dale House called The Park. Everyone remembers Westland Whirlwind fighters being on view but also frequently mentioned are Tiger Moth trainers making touch-and-go landings. These biplanes belonged to No 25 (Polish) Elementary Flying Training School which stayed at Hucknall between 1941 and 1945. You would not know this fact by investigating official files: if you think No 51 MU's records are bad, details for the EFTS irritatingly do not actually mention Blidworth as such.

Ignorance for once became anything but bliss with regard to future historical research as individual and even Command records continued to overlook the SLG/RLG from 1943 onwards. Blidworth closed during 1945 for sure despite Maintenance Command strangely not giving an exact date as with other SLGs throughout Britain. Local knowledge tells us this was the case, and No 51 MU gives the game away by mentioning standard monthly aircraft holding tallies at Lichfield and its SLGs – Hoar Cross also being used – right to the end of World War Two.

Situated in hilly and wooded country, this airfield is not easy to either reach or find but a visit is well worth your while. On the south side is a private dwelling that used to be the combined administration and guardroom, though the house is heavily modified and only the centre section original. Behind it is a small separate building and, away to the east alongside Blidworth Lodge, a single Nissen hut. A compound for dogs guarding the site and a camouflaged hangar were also built in World War Two, the three feet concrete base still remaining. Pieces of concrete elsewhere around the airfield are still being dug up now and again.

Blidworth does not really deserve such an intricate description in proportion to the airfield's history. These facts should nevertheless be told to show how relentless persistence during the course of historical research can work if you just listen to people and go for the less obvious targets. Thanks, everybody.

120/SK575533. 7 miles SE of Mansfield off A60. Turn first left after B6020, airfield N of minor road once past Ravenshead.

Blyborough, Lincolnshire

One HD landing ground not to last the full course until November 1918 was Blyborough, half-way between big World War Two airfield stars Hemswell and Kirton-in-Lindsey II. Approval for developing this oddly shaped piece of land on August 18 1916 allowed No 33 Squadron to use it from October. But farmer R.J. Hutchinson's efforts meant that more official approval given on February 22 1917 restricted Blyborough to a roughly rectangular shape with the western section being rated valuable for agricultural purposes.

Such a severe handicap as this would have only one longterm end result. Although active by February 1918, the landing ground closed shortly afterwards. Blyborough had vanished when the first of two large-scale maps published in 1918 showing every airfield in Britain which will be familiar to major researchers attending the Public Record Office was issued in May of that year.

A minor road and a stream bound unlucky Blyborough. A private airstrip close by has no connections other than bearing the same name of this hamlet.

112/SK955938. 14½ miles N of Lincoln, 1 mile E of hamlet between B1398 and A15.

Blyton, Lincolnshire

Five and a half miles directly north-west of Blyborough is Blyton. Both airfields shared one similarity in being frustrated by landing area problems mostly throughout their flying lives. While in Lincolnshire, Blyton differed to a greater score from other airfields in the county as being a typical three runway base mainly employed by a bomber Heavy Conversion Unit. However, in the beginning this World War Two site did enjoy a front line role.

Requisitioned in November 1940 and opened on April 20 1942, there was some delay at Blyton before flying activities could fully blossom. A few Wellingtons of No 18 OTU from Bitteswell's parent Bramcote stayed briefly in late summer prior to No 199 Squadron forming on November 7. Wellingtons took part in some raids but moved on February 3 1943 to badly laid out Ingham near Scampton, something of a come-down as their new base contained only a grass landing area precariously positioned amid various obstructions. Blyton still could not claim perfection either as its hard runways proved troublesome for long enough.

No 199 Squadron's successor became No 1662 HCU, which operated a mixture of Halifaxes and Lancasters up to disbandment on April 6 1945. A considerable chopping and changing of types occurred as the two 'heavies' competed for supremacy. Blyton provided a stable home but the runways and perimeter track began wilting under constantly heavy aircraft movements. The main runway rapidly deteriorated in February 1944 and was only partly serviceable for a while. Repair work on all the airfield's tracks had been effectively completed by July, though the dispersals proved slow going in attending to as construction duties lasted into 1945. Aircrews meanwhile fretted about how best to stop ice forming on microphones in their aircraft. And what items solved this problem? Condoms ...

Work carried on at 'high pressure' during May 1945 to put Blyton on C&M, despite construction personnel continuing to re-lay drains among other jobs. Inactivity started on January 31 1946 after No 7 ACHU had coped with airmen in transit from June 4 1945 until five days earlier. Maintenance Command dithered for much of 1946 about whether to use Blyton, finally deciding not to, before No 202 Advanced Flying School's Wellingtons were granted the airfield as a satellite during 1947. How long the training unit required this extra assistance is not certain as daily records forget about

Blyton, apart from one mention of a standard bi-weekly inspection there in April. Most flying schools active in the late 1940s and first half of the 1950s usually adopted this practice.

Finningley had served as parent since January 1946 but Kirton-in-Lindsey II later looked after Blyton from October 27 1947. A reprieve came in September/October 1951 when the airfield turned into an RLG for No 101 Flying Refresher School (No 215 AFS from February 1952) stationed at Finningley. Bircotes had closed years earlier and Worksop now held its own training establishment but Blyton became a good enough substitute for the parent's former wartime satellites. Meteors mostly visited during this third period of existence until May 1954 as parent and RLG both closed, Finningley temporarily to later allow in V-bombers, Blyton for ever. American military aircraft never showed up at their proposed British reservist and it returned as inactive to Kirton-in-Lindsey II in November 1956 for further parenting.

Of note at Blyton used to be an unusual control tower, straddled by a building either side with a tiny observation top thrown in for good measure on the roof. This structure is now removed along with most support buildings, two T2s and a B1. Farmers handed the airfield retained all paved surfaces for years but the southerly runway and perimeter track sections are in a bad state and the NW/SE runway mostly gone.

Many of our disused airfields are suffering fearful maulings, and Blyton's distinctive outlines could go for good the way events are unfolding. Even electricity pylons along the western side hardly help but you can still stop Blyton and allies being possibly annihilated if more radical countermeasures are set in motion. Suspect runways or not, this place was and always will be recognised as a winner.
112/SK868957. 7 miles NE of Gainsborough, E of A159 and N of B1205.

Boa Island, Fermanagh

Alternative Name: Rock Bay
Northern Ireland's last airfield to open in World War Two – hence the 'dry' reference to Bishops Court – was Boa Island at the top end of Lough Erne. This busy waterway had already hosted Castle Archdale and Killadeas since 1941 but enough space remained to squeeze in a third marine base. As

Killadeas needed a satellite for No 131 OTU, so Catalinas and Sunderlands dispersed to Boa Island once an advance party arrived on May 31 1944.

Facilities at this fresh airfield were restricted to a slipway and a few Nissen huts nearby, with some more buildings grouped together away from the water across the A47 road. Flying use as a result proved limited and Boa Island later largely closed for a period: although fully reopened on February 19 1945, No 131 OTU soon pulled out on March 1 and left the satellite on C&M. Castle Archdale became parent instead of Killadeas from April 11 but only did so to acquire extra accommodation, and nothing was heard of Boa Island after May 22.

A number of relatively minor flying boat bases around Britain merit just a passing mention because of their negligible architectural presence and inconsistent aircraft use. Boa Island's structures and history save it from this fate, especially as the slipway and several huts still survive. A picnic lay-by makes this area a restful beauty spot even if − shame on you − anyone is not interested in airfield history.

17/H115632. On extreme N side of Lower Lough Erne, 7 miles W of Kesh on either side of A47. Picnic site at central point of airfield.

Bodmin II, Cornwall

Cornwall is as noted as Northern Ireland for not being particularly hospitable to airfields except around their coastlines. The climate and geography make sure that will always be the case. Yet there will inevitably be somewhere or other trying to beat the system, and Bodmin has achieved this feat with regard to Cornwall.

Bodmin Moor, full of rough terrain and prone to fog, is hardly ideal airfield territory. Flying nevertheless can be traced back to the 1920s when joy-riding aircraft passed by on short visits. A civil landing ground of which little else is known lay close to Bodmin during this decade. Pleasure flying moved further north-east out of the town in the 1930s towards today's airfield but one display on August 16 1935 ended in disaster when an Avro 504K of the Cornwall Aviation Company crashed and killed all three people on board. One of the fatalities happened to be the Lord Mayor's son: perhaps this fact turned officialdom against an airfield for Bodmin, and no site appeared for many more years. An ELG situated on the moors could have given service in World War Two, say for Davidstow Moor to the north, though planners ignored such possibilities.

Thoughts suddenly turned to establishing a proper airfield once another quarter of a century had gone by. In 1970 businessman C. Mike Robertson built Bodmin at a cost of £60,000, paying for it out of his own pocket. Flying began in the autumn and fully took off by 1971 to much interest from the local general public but the site lacked buildings. Worse still proved heavy opposition from the National Trust and national government, so bad that the Secretary of State for the Environment ordered Bodmin to close at once on February 3 1973 in spite of earlier political sanctioning. The situation remained up in the air in a way Robertson and friends did not want for nearly a year before the authorities issued an operating licence. Problems over planning permission however still made closure possible, Bodmin not securing a surer footing until 1976.

Mike Robertson's attempts at aircraft production met with even greater obstacles. Particular efforts were made to develop the small Trago Aircraft (named after his Trago Mills line of Cornish shopping areas) SAH.1 lightplane but a lack of British money being pumped into the project led to an ill-fated proposed idea to build the aircraft in Hungary. Any hopes of production there failed and Robertson was bought out in 1988, his company becoming known as Orca Aircraft.

Today Bodmin II still survives as home to the Cornwall Flying Club. Two grass runways and a row of small hangars are available to light aircraft visiting this pleasant little airfield with its neat clubhouse. Bodmin is a perfect example of how determination can overcome adversity.

(For Bodmin I see Other British Airfields)
200/SX111701. 6 miles NE of town to right of A30.

Bodney, Norfolk

Many parent airfields and their satellites up and down Britain such as Abingdon and Stanton Harcourt or Bircham Newton and Docking fostered great relationships in World War Two. Two more airfields which portrayed what one might call this fish and chips syndrome in being strongly connected were Watton and Bodney. From March 1940 until mid-1943 the latter acted as satellite to its more famous parent and saw as much action.

No 82 Squadron became familiar at Bodney between March 19 1940, when sending ten Blenheims with three more of No 21 Squadron on stand-by, and March 1942. Their supportive base consisted of not much more than a big open field in those days but took on abnormally heavy duties for a satellite by frequently dispatching Blenheims on dangerous *Circuses* and anti-shipping raids. Luftwaffe aircraft not unnaturally got to know about Bodney and made attacks during 1940/41 but not too seriously.

Other units to disperse at the airfield included No 90 Squadron with early Fortresses which never encountered much luck on operations, unlike later RAF marks used for maritime patrol duties at Benbecula and elsewhere. No 17 (P) AFU came on January 29 1942 but moved its Miles Masters out of Bodney and Watton to the far safer surroundings of Calveley in Cheshire on May 4 1943. Any training establishment in East Anglia at that time was extremely rare and rather inadvisable, if not downright dangerous, because of vast daily Allied aircraft movements and Luftwaffe intruders.

The only RAF unit to form – or more reform – at Bodney was No 21 Squadron on March 14 1942. This previous Watton-based visitor left in October for Methwold in Norfolk after having converted from Blenheims to Venturas. Bodney still faithfully served master Watton in the middle of World War Two, though when the Americans seized both airfields during 1943, the humble satellite became able to move in its own direction with spectacular results.

Whereas Watton held a depot, USAAF fighters became evident at Bodney from July 1943 as the 352nd FG's P-47s appeared. What was in mid-war an unsung airfield with only a solitary Blister registered as available hangarage soon blossomed into a respected independent station involved in constant action. In 1944 P-51s replaced the P-47s as at nearly every other American-manned British airfield but a freak accident happened during their stay when a Mustang swung on take-off – probably due to wrong power settings – and ploughed into the control tower on Bodney's west side, flattening it and killing the pilot. Bad enough – but this was the morning of D-Day! This episode could be put down to one of these classically unpredictable events at Britain's airfields but still slightly marred an otherwise marvellously successful 24 hours in their history.

The 352nd FG later had to leave Bodney for a while to help American ground forces under siege in Europe as German troops suddenly counter-attacked during the 'Battle of the

Bulge'. A detachment transferred to Belgium on December 23, the entire Group having gone as well by February 7 1945 before moving back as one on April 13. In a way the P-51s and their personnel had been fortunate in staying away when they did, despite the hassle required in leaving and then having to return again, for Bodney was raided during the Luftwaffe's Operation *Gisela* intruder extravaganza on the night of March 3/4.

Bodney passed to RAF Fighter Command at C&M level on November 1 1945 as the 352nd FG prepared to leave two days later with a Distinguished Unit Citation to its credit. Closed the same month on the 26th, by June 1946 agriculture prevailed as the planners did not want the area held back for more flying use.

The blocking off of tracks today means a good view of this airfield in Army country is restricted to that from an adjoining public road. A second control tower, built on the east side as if not to tempt fate to have another go, can just be seen peering over a slight rise in the fields. While Watton continues in a non-flying role, Bodney sleeps unnoticed, a dividing line of trees making the site look much smaller than it really was. A memorial commemorates the 352nd FG but metal runways, two T2s and five Blisters have sadly disappeared without trace.

144/TL840995. 6 miles W of Watton on N side of B1108.

Bodorgan, Gwynedd

Alternative Name: Aberffraw

Valley is by far the most prominent of Anglesey's airfields. Although not such a familiar name to the general public, Mona is remembered, if only for its long history which goes back to World War One. These two sites apart, who has heard of Bodorgan? Not many, but this airfield still provides worthwhile service and jobs to the Welsh island, and is in much better architectural condition than the gallant Bodney.

The main party of personnel destined to operate from this overlooked outpost arrived from Watchet in Somerset on September 11 1940. Valley would not open until February 1941 but a Tiger Moth flying from Bodorgan found suitable nearby fields for possible use as ELGs to obstruct extremely hard to come by in Anglesey. 'Z' Flight of No 1 AACU, using de Havilland Queen Bee pilotless gunnery targets, soon came

THE AIRFIELDS OF BRITAIN

in full in October and was joined the following year by 'J' Flight's manned light aircraft types. These two elements turned as a result of administrative reorganisation into Nos 1606 and 1620 Flights in October 1942.

A completely different activity which increasingly preoccupied Bodorgan between March 1941 and December 1944 was aircraft storage. There is a twist to this chapter of the airfield's life, for No 48 MU at Hawarden employed it as an SLG. Bodorgan stood out alone from the 50 or so other sites of this type by already being an officially acknowledged airfield but for that reason operated uncomfortably in this supposedly secret role. AA co-operation remained an easier job as No 650 Squadron's Hurricanes and Martinets further helped ground batteries with their training once the MU had departed. No 1606 Flight evaded late 1943 mergers or disbandments of similar units into squadrons and survived up to April 30 1945, going at the same time with the non-flying No 70 Gp Leaders School which had formed in the summer of 1943.

Not the greatest of airfields as the grass landing area suffered badly from poor drainage, Bodorgan lasted only a short while after World War Two. No 650 Squadron disbanded on June 26 1945, its second HQ base after Cark then closing to all air traffic on August 23 as Flying Control shut down. Valley gained responsibility as C&M started on October 1 before Bodorgan officially closed as a Fighter Command station on January 9 1946; the Air Ministry Works Department took over a fortnight later but the last few RAF personnel did not head for the parent until February. Even as late as July 1951 Valley displayed a long memory as members of the Paratroop Regiment deplaned from a USAF Fairchild Packet transport to use this airfield as a Dropping Zone during an exercise.

Agricultural estate concerns now mix with light industry and benefit from some of the many support buildings left standing but two Bellmans and a Blister which provided necessary hangarage vanished long ago. One odd structure evident nearby is a brick pillbox with an added section placed on top. Bodorgan notably endured nominal confusion with being called Aberffraw at first before logistic difficulties – and surely the sheer Welshness of this name – forced a change in May 1941. A few dwellings, a country house and a railway station substituted instead as inspiration for one of Britain's lesser known World War Two airfields. Mind you, Bodorgan could have been called Llangadwaladr...

114/SH382685. 9½ miles SW of Llangefni. Take B4422 to

A4080 before leaving road at crossroads and head straight on to minor road.

Bognor (landplane), West Sussex

Our many World War Two Advanced Landing Grounds in southern England proved so successful that some of them exceeded their expected lifetimes. One was Bognor, heavily dominated by Spitfires throughout its short career. The current Bognor Regis private airstrip which the Lec Refrigeration company has used for many years is a quite different site and lies on the other side of town.

The Norman Thompson flying boat manufacturing firm provided Bognor with an original taste of aviation before and during World War One. Flying of the drier variety however only materialised when Sir Alan Cobham held one of his famous National Aviation Days at Chalcroft Farm near the village of North Bersted, which now forms part of Bognor, on August 9 1932. This was a hesitant beginning, and any real fame would not come for over another decade.

What eventually became Bognor ALG stood just west of North Bersted. After Spitfires of Nos 19, 122 and 602 Squadrons had brought it up to semi-operational status during June/July 1943, a much improved ALG came alive again on March 31 1944. Nos 66, 331 and 332 Squadrons had travelled from North Weald for a steady round of offensive fighter and fighter-bomber sorties in their Spitfires through D-Day until leaving for Tangmere on June 21/22. Time had also been needed during this trio's stay for weaponry training, as No 66 Squadron showed by having to make short visits to Southend and even Castletown in the extreme north of Scotland while based at Bognor.

The airfield remained on the scene in an unexpected way and became busier than ever as No 83 Group Support Unit moved in until late September 1944 with yet more Spitfires, not forgetting Mustangs and Hawker Typhoons. The GSU acted as a back-up replacement force to cope with wartime attrition both in aircraft and pilots. Bognor held them in readiness until required as such.

The authorities later decided that they would dispense with the services of this excellent short-term airfield. Authority was

hence given for derequisitioning on November 6, the same day as at Appledram five miles west of Bognor, both ALGs having been requisitioned in December 1942. Nothing can be seen of Bognor's two Sommerfeld Track metal runways or four Blisters amid farmland, which could also disappear if more houses are built. 'Bugger Bognor!' a certain royal said of the town – and the town thought exactly the same of its heroic wartime airfield.
197/SU915005. On NW outskirts of town, to E of B2166.

Bogton, Strathclyde

Virtually unheard of Bogton was a temporary World War One airfield employed for flying between April 1917 and January 1918. It had a loose communications and training connection with the disastrous Loch Doon but, despite also being somewhat marshy, did see more landplane use than Britain's worst ever airfield as a few biplanes occasionally visited. Temporary though it may have been, Bogton did possess two hangars and their concrete bases remain in a field. These foundations are nevertheless so unremarkable any passer-by cannot be blamed for not taking a second glance at the surrounding historical scenery.

History has not treated World War One airfields well, and this site north of Bogton Loch comes off worse than most with differing documentary accounts. Records imply that military occupation lasted from January 1917 to August 1918 but 21 acres of land were acquired on October 1; certainly a few marine aircraft which flew at Loch Doon stayed in storage for most of 1918. Later on in December 1919 Mrs Charlotte Tilke McAdam of Craigengillan near Loch Doon made a claim for compensation in the Scottish courts. This redoubtable lady alleged that not only had £60-80,000 been spent on Bogton but it was also never used as an airfield: a bit of a fib there, and accordingly reduced her asking price from £40,698 8s. 3d. to £13,048 18s. 4d. On December 13 1922 the Government agreed to pay £14,500, less £5,000 already given to Mrs McAdam, on or before January 8 1923, though other records going into 1924 suggest she did carry out the option of paying back £3,750 for seven and a half acres. No wonder the law can at times be such a pain.
70/NS472059. Just W of Dalmellington at junction of A713 and B741.

THE AIRFIELDS OF BRITAIN: VOLUME 1
Bolt Head, Devon

ALGs such as Bognor really began to appear in the months preceding D-Day. Equipped with extremely few facilities, they served a purpose and no more. But this idea was far from new for, when opened during 1941, Bolt Head looked an ALG in all but name.

Bolt Head first came to prominence in 1928 as the National Trust claimed ownership of the land. How this headland attracted planners towards potential use as an airfield is unknown but across the Kingsbridge Estuary stands Prawle Point, scene of a similarly titled World War One airfield from where DH6 biplanes flew *Scarecrow* anti-submarine patrols. A different war now resulted in another geographical feature inspiring a more advanced airfield as the Air Ministry considered in August 1940 when best to start construction. Close to Bolt Head is Soar: as this settlement used to be known as Sewer, one can see why the former name provided more appeal.

RAF fighters, notably from Exeter, employed Bolt Head over a considerable period of time from the spring of 1941 for sweeps and bomber escort work. More facilities became available as the airfield turned from a glorified forward landing ground into a satellite in 1942, attractions including two Blisters and a couple of metal runways.

Another year passed and some RAF fighter squadrons even began permanently staying instead of moving forward for set piece operations. No 610 Squadron's Spitfires led the way by spending the second half of 1943 at Bolt Head. Turnover of units mainly equipped with Spitfires stepped up from mid-March 1944 as No 234 Squadron was succeeded on April 29 by No 41 Squadron. This newer unit had to attend an Armament Practice Camp firing course at Fairwood Common near Swansea during May 16-24, No 610 Squadron returning briefly to fill in the void at Bolt Head, but saw out D-Day and its immediate aftermath until June 19. Typhoons of No 263 Squadron temporarily broke the Spitfires' domination before No 611 Squadron carried on with the offensive tactical onslaught from mid-July to going to Bradwell Bay in Essex on August 30. All these fighters had been forced to operate one squadron at a time because of their airfield's generally limited nature but Bolt Head gave as good a performance as any British site at this vitally important time.

None of these squadrons could compete in terms of length of residence with No 276 Squadron as it maintained at least a token force of Lysanders, Spitfires and Walruses on ASR duties between October 1941 and August 1944. No 275 Squadron followed on and actually placed the unit HQ at Bolt Head instead of Dorset Battle of Britain star Warmwell; although centralised control shifted to ever-dominating Exeter in October 1944, a detachment stayed on until No 275 Squadron disbanded on February 15 1945.

By then Harrowbeer, an RAF fighter airfield north of Plymouth, had replaced Exeter as Bolt Head's parent. But more significant was how the fighting had drifted away from south-west England. The happy hunting grounds in northern France for fighters stood free, and fewer aircraft in trouble while venturing over the western English Channel needed help from ASR types; an impressed No 275 Squadron Miles Magister on November 18 1944 force-landed on a nearby derelict golf course in poor weather conditions which often affected the airfield. It was therefore only a matter of time before Bolt Head shut up shop. C&M started on April 25 1945, though the site did not close completely for another two years.

Compensation arguments between farmers/'landowners' and the authorities lasted for a further period of time. The first two parties unusually protested about the metal runways, Bolt Head having closed for extension work for about a fortnight in the early part of 1945 in what was possibly an unnecessary duty given the benefit of hindsight. A London firm had later on bought hundreds of these prefabricated sections at about 25 shillings a roll as nobody locally wanted them for fencing but farmers and the rest still felt outraged at being asked up to 60 shillings in the first place.

A Ground Controlled Interception (GCI) station distinctively stood close to Bolt Head. Hope Cove was named after a small bay four miles to the north-west: remembering Sewer, the only other choice was much closer Stink Cove! In use solely for weekend RAuxAF training by No 3513 Fighter Control Unit after having gone down to a caretaking basis on August 1 1946, No 926 Signals Unit revived this separate site by moving from Exminster on April 8 1953. A new technical area appeared at Bolt Head but living accommodation was kept apart by standing to the north at Malborough. The radar unit disbanded on September 9 1957 and became the School of Fighter Control until going to well-known GCI station Sopley close to Bournemouth in October 1958.

You have to follow a convoluted route along minor roads out of local watering-place Salcombe in order to reach Bolt Head. The journey ends in extreme disappointment as the

airfield has virtually disappeared and farmland these days contains hardly any buildings. A narrow track on the north side leads to the old Hope Cove radar station for directing fighters on operations. Local inhabitants insist that a civil light aircraft flew about this area in the early 1970s but otherwise Bolt Head is solely known nowadays as a popular cliffwalking route. As with Bogton, few people appreciate the real history in their midst.
202/SX715375. 3 miles SW of Salcombe, follow track S of Soar.

Booker, Buckinghamshire

Alternative Names: High Wycombe, Marlow, Wycombe Air Park

Many light aircraft can be viewed at Booker, or Wycombe Air Park as it has become known since the mid-1960s. This airfield looks much the same as in World War Two days, with four Bellmans in two rows of two by a wood for hangarage. A hard runway has been added but two grass stretches – one of them running parallel with the tougher surface – are also available.

Some notable privately-owned machines have resided here. A few replica World War One fighters among them add a slight touch of irony to this small airfield, for Booker saw hardly any Great War service and nearly did not see World War Two either. A Home Defence landing ground during 1917 for No 39 Squadron between February and July under the name of High Wycombe, Sir Alan Cobham later held a display at 'The Flying Ground', Marlow Hill on May 27 1932. The name Marlow held on when the airfield opened in June 1939 for civil use but Germany then invaded Poland. While a shattering blow by any standards, the right people behind the scenes had not failed to take notice of the site's potential.

Sure enough, barely embryonic Marlow had made a sufficient enough impression with a decision in March 1940 to form an EFTS there: No 50 E&RFTS never had the chance of arising pre-war as once proposed. What soon became referred to as Booker was expected to be ready after construction as the summer of 1940 ended but this assessment proved far too hopeful. Considerable redevelopment of the landing area stopped a skeleton staff and defence element from opening their base until April 7 1941.

At last No 21 EFTS formed on June 1 with Tiger Moths as

aircraft returned after the pre-war false start. Resident personnel had their doubts at first about Booker as many hollows and ridges surrounded their airfield to make take-offs and landings difficult. The grass landing area was considered to be very hard in dry weather, the entire site hard to spot, and camouflage treatment still had to be carried out even with all the trees nearby. Instructors and trainees however soon grew to accept such shortcomings and flying continued without much in the way of problems. About the worst accident seen at Booker during World War Two occurred on August 29 1942 as a 'cuckoo' Handley Page Hampden medium bomber overshot the airfield and badly damaged itself in the process. Eight Blisters assisted Booker's Bellmans for the wartime duration, while another of today's light aircraft airfield survivors at Denham acted as an RLG to disperse some of the Tiger Moths.

No 21 EFTS eventually closed on February 28 1950. The final school of this type, all future through training of Air Observation Post pilots would be conducted at Middle Wallop. Next day the airfield moved to Reserve Command for No 1 Basic FTS to arise in January 1951 and use Chipmunks. Something still had to be done to beat occasional waterlogging problems, so an all out effort from July 19 to August 20 resulted in the creation of a PSP metal runway measuring 800 yards in length across the north side and an accompanying taxying track made from the same material.

No 1 Basic FTS lasted until July 1953 but Booker now became mainly important as a local communications RAF station. Luck had it that High Wycombe stood close by, headquarters of RAF Bomber Command since World War Two and now where Strike Command directs business. Light transports bringing in and out high-ranking staff on necessary but prosaic liaison visits mixed with civilian recreational gliders and the High Wycombe Flying Group to keep Booker active over the following decade.

Suddenly only the sailplanes and light aircraft were left once the Bomber Command Communications Flight disbanded into the new Southern Communications Squadron at Bovingdon in August 1963. Booker militarily became disused but the civil fliers held their ground, aided by the then Wycombe Rural District Council gaining their base by way of a central government loan. Three gliding clubs were present when the 1930s style titled Wycombe Air Park came into being late on in 1965. Soon various small flying clubs joined the High Wycombe Flying Group, as did Personal Plane Services Ltd from White Waltham to deal with special aircraft

271

requirements such as those imitation Great War fighters.

High Wycombe really has taken over this airfield since: even Booker village has been swallowed up by the town. Today the Wycombe Air Centre and Booker GC, merged from two other clubs in April 1982 following a period of uncertainty regarding the site's future, ensure that pleasurable aviation thrives. Airways Aero Associations Ltd, a subsidiary of British Airways, runs daily affairs on a lease from Wycombe District Council. To think that flying at one time might never have started because of a war now seems hard to comprehend.
175/SU826910. Between M40 and B482, SW of High Wycombe.

Boreham, Essex

Millions of British vehicle owners should thank this airfield which has allowed their motors to sustain high levels of performance – but have never heard of it. This airfield occasionally features on television and in advertisements – and yet all but those few people who work there do not recognise the place. If this is not a classic example of our airfields' towering control over their country, then what is? Boreham, take a bow.

Look at the relevant OS map and you will see north-east of Chelmsford a place which is quite obviously a disused airfield. What is not mentioned is that this is a prohibited area as a proving ground exists for the Ford car company. To call Boreham disused is ridiculous, though in World War Two it perversely tried to look at least redundant for a supposedly active site.

Boreham was approved for requisition as a typical three runway bomber station at the same time in July 1942 as Essex's other highly enigmatic 1939-45 era airfield Birch. Its name posed no problems, unlike Little Waltham village to the west which would have created near-nightmarish complications. One big difference from Birch was that Boreham did have the pleasure of operationally holding bombers after opening on March 6 1944 when Martin B-26s of the 394th BG arrived. For over four months the Marauders fulfilled planning predictions while these medium types raided enemy tactical targets.

Initial life at Boreham had proved to be a case of so far, so good. Unfortunately, the base became just one of many casualties in East Anglia's southern sector to suffer from the

THE AIRFIELDS OF BRITAIN

US 9th Air Force's general withdrawal from that region. Operational range considerations forced this tactical air element's units such as the 394th BG to transfer to southern England, and the Group left for Holmsley South in Hampshire during late July. C-47s of the 442nd TCG later spent three days at Boreham in September in preparation for Operation *Market*.

What can one say about subsequent events? Not a great deal of any substance — for the simple reason that nothing much did happen in military spheres. Boreham switched from American to Bomber Command control on a C&M basis on February 15 1945 and then again to Transport Command on April 13. Less than a month previously C-47s of the 315th TCG from Spanhoe in Northamptonshire had called in to participate in Operation *Varsity* but no truly positive use could be found for the airfield. A small army of Staging Post and Forward Staging Post plus Transportable Signals Unit RAF ground forces to handle air traffic, personnel and freight or deal with radio communication respectively did stay for short periods, sometimes going abroad to newly liberated countries such as Denmark or Norway.

This rudderless life as a whole led to the Medical Officer claiming that station buildings were badly maintained and in urgent need of redecoration. Boreham's CO also stated in August how his base's uncertain future disturbed many and deteriorating living conditions affected morale. As the number of units fell away in the autumn, resident personnel were having to generally fiddle away their time as the airfield ORB recorded such less than thrilling activities as not even football matches between different airfields but school playground-type kickabouts involving opposing sets of Boreham staff. Their ailing airfield was almost begging to be put out of its misery: a couple of Air Transportable Signals Units survived to the year's end before a spell of C&M and closure on April 15 1946. There would not even be any bi-weekly inspections afterwards with total abandonment.

After such an unhappy wartime career following a promising start, things could only improve for Boreham — and they have. The vehicle testing role since the summer of 1955 owes a good deal to events of the early 1950s when the airfield served as a motor racing circuit. The West Essex Car Club mounted Formula and sports car meetings and the Chelmsford and District Auto Club some motor cycling events, an excellent crowd of 35,000 people turning up in terrible weather for the first car race meeting on March 26 1951.

Improvements were carried out to this three mile circuit for the successful 1952 season but the West Essex Car Club then had to declare on February 16 1953 that Boreham would see no racing in this year. The airfield's landowners had no objections to the WECC organising events, yet would not permit motor sport activity. This was like asking the human body to operate without blood, an impossible situation, and future motor car racing was held at former USAAF heavy bomber station Snetterton Heath in Norfolk. What is now known as Ford Motorsport however arrived in 1963 to create the company's rallying headquarters.

Viewing of current work practices is naturally disallowed as with all other disused airfields now serving as proving grounds. Sole obvious hint of past aerial history is a once dilapidated and recently spruced up memorial – a none too factually accurate one at that – outside Boreham's boundary, with a 'Danger – Keep Out' sign and massive concrete blocks alongside on a track leading to the airfield. Enquiries reveal all major tracks have kept complete, while Essex Police has used the control tower since July 1990 to hold a helicopter on site. One out of two T2s has also survived.

Although a gravel company threatens, this once most unlucky airfield which existed in the wrong place at the wrong time has become a great success without hardly a soul knowing about it. 'Our return trip today is one of the greatest highlights of my life', wrote a former American serviceman on May 2 1992. Says everything, doesn't it?
167/TL742120. NE of Chelmsford, on N side of A12 and 2 miles NW of village.

Boscombe Down, Wiltshire

Alternative Name: Red House Farm
Try as hard they might, the authorities have a tough job in attempting to preserve the secrecy of this Wiltshire airfield as much as Boreham. Boscombe Down is one of Britain's all-time greats with a long and distinguished history. Home to the most famous specialised British flying establishment for now over half a century, numerous prototypes of future renowned aircraft types have either first flown or undergone thorough evaluation here, notably the Lancaster, Mosquito and Hunter. Throw in the fact that a particularly noteworthy Victoria Cross was awarded to one occupant and you can see we are not about to relate the tale of an ordinary place – if any

THE AIRFIELDS OF BRITAIN

airfield in this country can be described as such.

The remarkable Boscombe Down story stretches right back to 1917. On October 1 this place opened for training duties — but not with its pleasantly distinctive name. For sixteen days until the 17th the title Red House Farm reigned before planners altered it along with several other airfields in the Salisbury Plain area which originally bore some astonishingly obscure names even by usual airfield standards. Various bi-plane types belonging to No 6 TDS then stayed for the rest of World War One before vast post-war cut-backs ended in flying training ceasing on May 15 1919. Later used for storage, Boscombe Down was ultimately disposed of on April 1 1920 and the buildings sold for £1,100. Many Royal Aircraft Factory SE5A fighters were eventually burnt at the officially inactive site.

How glad must planners of days ahead have been that this was one airfield to remain dormant and not be slaughtered like so many others, such as nearby Lake Down which endured far greater hardship during the 1920s. Boscombe Down rode out those dark days of 1921-24, the worst period in British airfield history, and had its land and buildings repurchased as this agonising time ended for the sum of £15,000.

Another £271,000 were put aside in the 1927 Air Estimates for reconstruction but this was a surprisingly largely untouched site which reopened on September 11 1930 to house RAF bomber units. No 9 Squadron first arrived on November 26 with Vickers Virginias after its new home's Station HQ had formed on the 3rd. These lumbering night bomber biplanes stayed until October 1935, other bomber squadrons coming in the next few years. Nos 150, 166 and 214 all reformed at Boscombe Down, as did a Coastal Command Anson squadron (No 217) on March 15 1937. The most unusual — though not as odd as at first sight — visitor here in this decade became the civilian Isle of Wight GC, present by the spring of 1931 to take advantage of Britain's 1930s gliding boom and named after a hill four miles south-east of Boscombe Down.

Battle light bombers of Nos 88 and 218 Squadrons, around since 1937/38, flew to France as part of the Advanced Air Striking Force when World War Two broke out. Now came the major turning point in Boscombe Down's life as the Aeroplane and Armament Experimental Establishment moved in. This had been a forced choice on the famous test unit's part as its residence of 22 years at Martlesham Heath in Suffolk became too exposed to enemy air attack. British and

American fighters later employed Martlesham to tremendous effect in World War Two but the A&AEE needed to shift inland, both for its own good and because of this concern's immense military importance.

Some operational RAF units still came to Boscombe Down in the early war years despite the appearance of A&AEE. Bomber Command Whitleys of No 58 Squadron temporarily transferred to Coastal Command control mounted maritime patrols in the opening months of fighting, a unit which had previously converted to these Armstrong Whitworth machines at this airfield during 1937/38. Fighters of Nos 56 and 249 Squadrons also stayed: the latter arrived on August 14 1940 and held in its ranks Flight Lieutenant James Nicolson. He won Fighter Command's sole VC for his actions two days later when, despite terrible injuries and his Hurricane ablaze, Nicolson shot down a Messerschmitt Bf 110 heavy fighter before bailing out. Fate eventually gained the upper hand by claiming the life of this hero in a Liberator crash over the Bay of Bengal in May 1945. Not quite as important an event in 1940, but one of considerable future aviation note, was the first air-to-air night refuelling procedure involving civil aircraft.

The A&AEE was left alone afterwards to conduct numerous tests at Boscombe Down for the rest of World War Two. A dazzling procession of aircraft types arrived for testing, evaluation and possible improvements in their performance: some passed the grade, others did not. Secrecy mattered even more here than at other airfields, and personnel were forbidden to simply name aircraft outside the site. Other A&AEE duties included testing of not prototype or special one-off but standard production aircraft, every hundredth RAF heavy bomber being thoroughly tested to ensure flawless levels of production.

The organisation spawned a number of elements under its control, especially in 1943 the Empire Test Pilots School which left for Cranfield in the autumn of 1945; back to Boscombe Down the ETPS came from Farnborough in 1968 and remains today. Another A&AEE offspring was the Beam Approach (later Wireless Interception) Development Unit, a particularly notorious force because of 'beam bending' activities, whereby Luftwaffe bomber crews could not enjoy the same degree of reasonable bombing accuracy which their own guiding radio beams provided. WIDU was again retitled as No 109 Squadron on December 10 1940 and left in January 1942.

For such an important airfield, Boscombe Down persisted without hard runways throughout World War Two. Civil aircraft had become much more prominent as in pre-war days by the time three stretches were ready. A&AEE staff who once thought Martlesham Heath a superior airfield now gave their new base a higher overall rating.

Reconstruction off the landing area also created in the 1950s Boscombe Down's famous weighbridge hangar. This massive structure with in-built weighing equipment was originally intended for the Bristol Brabazon, though this huge and ill-fated airliner born out of its time never came here as many had hoped. Abilities such as determining an aircraft's centre of gravity or c.g. position saved the weighbridge from becoming a similar white elephant. This function alone could have stopped 80 people from dying in then the world's worst air accident at Llandow in 1950 if only the building had arisen earlier.

Greater success greeted another extreme flying rarity that did reside at Boscombe Down and handed the airfield a second world record as a result. The Fairey Delta 2 delta-winged supersonic research vehicle was present in the mid-1950s, almost coming to a catastrophic end on November 17 1954 when suffering a fuel system failure and having to glide back to base, careering off the runway and just missing the control tower before stopping on some grass. Both the Delta 2 and pilot Peter Twiss fortunately survived to later set a closed course world speed record of 1,132 miles per hour on March 10 1956.

Boscombe Down had by now seen scores of highly interesting aircraft types. The publicity nobody wanted could not for once be avoided when in January 1952 a stricken USAF Convair B-36 – the world's biggest ever bomber – clattered through fields and hedges before halting near the runway. But for all the standardised Lancasters or unique visitors such as the Fairey Delta 2, a different rarity made the biggest impression of all, an aircraft with fantastic potential which became perhaps the unluckiest design in British aviation history: the fall-out still lingers in certain quarters today.

The English Electric TSR-2 was proposed for RAF use as either a strike bomber or reconnaissance machine. Longer than a Lancaster but with a tiny wing-span, the first pre-production example took to the air at Boscombe Down on September 27 1964. Apart from slight undercarriage retraction and structural vibration problems, the TSR-2 immediately looked a brilliant future prospect, and the military drooled at the thought of seeing it in service.

A tragic end however resulted as one of the world's most

advanced aircraft types was cancelled in an uproarious Parliament on April 6 1965 due to political and financial decisions. All blame lay squarely with the newly-elected Labour Government as it tried to justify a disgraceful pre-election pledge by claiming how the TSR-2 would be too expensive and that the American General Dynamics F-111 fighter-bomber offered better value. This swing-wing jet later a familiar sight in British skies never even entered RAF service but Labour doggedly refused to admit being wrong, becoming more stubborn than Duncan Sandys if that was at all possible, and cruelly let go of three completed TSR-2s as gunnery targets; other half-built examples were scrapped at Brooklands in Surrey.

Our airfields already knew all too well about such crucifying millstones round their necks. Think of this alleged 1960s economy move, yet four decades earlier the Government had bought back Boscombe Down for over thirteen times the price it had been sold only four years beforehand. No wonder politicians are not exactly regarded as the most consistent of people.

Away from such tremendously sophisticated aircraft as the TSR-2, a tiny number of humble World War Two vintage North American Harvard monoplanes of the A&AEE have operated from their most private base as the RAF's last surviving examples. An ex-Argentinian FMA IA58 Pucara twin turboprop-engined light attack type also flew around here in 1983. Spares came from two other cannibalised machines captured during the Falklands conflict of 1982. The civilian Bustard Flying Club has spent much longer at this airfield and/or nearby Old Sarum since the late 1950s.

Aircraft may vary but state of the art ones will always dominate, with the ETPS working in close support to create new domestic and foreign test pilots. The A&AEE now divides into A, B and C Squadrons to deal with fighters, bigger aircraft and helicopters, D Squadron – once Beaulieu III's Airborne Forces Experimental Establishment – no longer existing.

British participation during the Gulf War period illustrated how technological advances in aviation bound ever onwards. Urgent work was carried out to protect RAF Tornadoes from worrying electromagnetic interference (EMI) or garbled radio waves which could make their control systems haywire. Fighting had started only the night before when laser designation pod equipment to mark targets for air-launched missiles to hit with stunning accuracy first became airborne under a Tornado at Boscombe Down on January 18 1991.

Test flying looks set to increase in the future now recommendations to cease activities of this nature at Farnborough and Bedford have been followed through. Yet the legendary Boscombe Down continues to keep its light hidden very much under a bushel by being heavily fenced. Photography is strictly forbidden, and casual sightseeing not especially encouraged either.

Distant views do show the airfield's long history by way of varied hangarage. Seven World War One Belfasts, accompanying Bessoneaux, a 1920s era A, an uncommon B design and twelve World War Two Blisters have housed aircraft at different times. Some of these buildings remain, though the weighbridge hangar steals the show without doubt. More recent Hardened Aircraft Shelters were built to allow F-111s, of all aircraft, to use Boscombe Down now and again in the 1980s as a collocated airfield loosely available to the USAF should war have broken out. The landing area has meanwhile vastly extended southwards, with the main NE/SW runway today measuring well over 10,000 feet in length. Closure is clearly not on the cards for this reluctant superstar. 184/SU186400. NE of Salisbury and SE of Amesbury, between A345 and A338.

Boston, Lincolnshire

Alternative Name: Wyberton
About as far removed from mighty Boscombe Down is little Boston. Sir Alan Cobham used what he called the 'Boston Flying Ground' for one of his National Aviation Displays on June 15 1932. Other events followed but a proposed airfield and flying club or even an airport in 1937 never happened, and not until the second half of 1948 did a proper airfield emerge.

Civil light aircraft have steadily used it since, especially for agricultural purposes. Crop-spraying is a deceptively dangerous business with the large amount of low flying involved and Boston has witnessed a number of crashes in and around the airfield over the years. A hangar fire destroyed an Auster on April 6 1952 but two buildings remained available to a fair number of these monoplanes and later on Piper Pawnees. Their home has mostly stayed unlicensed, unlike at the beginning when the Boston Aero Club formed on October 21 1949 and lasted for a few years. Official opening of the organisation's clubhouse and airfield on April 7 1950 was marred by another aircraft crash implicating an Auster which killed three people.

A firm based at Skegness IV took over Boston in the mid-1950s but the Lincs Aerial Spraying Company in time performed an effective reverse take-over; a further change saw the word 'Spraying' replaced by 'Maintenance' to acknowledge increased aircraft overhaul work. Crop Aviation (UK) Ltd, a smaller agricultural support concern, eventually moved in as well but both businesses departed in the late 1980s.

Although still open to aircraft, courtesy of Boston Aviation Services, Boston is now much quieter and resembles more a private airstrip than an airfield. Nobody gives it any publicity, while unanswered requests for more information show how nobody really cares. And this is Lincolnshire, our number one airfield county: what a shameful advert for the rest of Britain. 131/TF296437. 2 miles W of town by A1121.

Bottesford, Leicestershire/Lincolnshire

Boston is alternatively known as Wyberton. Anyone exploring Bottesford on the Leicestershire-Lincolnshire border will be as confused if talking to local inhabitants as they call it without any official acknowledgement Normanton in recognition of a hamlet half-way between this disused airfield and Bottesford village. What no-one can dispute is that many buildings remain, including all the hangars.

Bottesford opened on September 10 1941 after a year of construction work and accommodated No 207 Squadron two months later. The squadron operated Avro Manchesters with their unbelievably dodgy two Rolls-Royce Vulture piston engines – one aircraft dared to test the runways on September 25 – and had to convert to the Manchester's four Merlin engined descendant the Lancaster in March 1942. No 207 became only the third RAF unit to receive Lancasters but left in September for a new bomber airfield with a separate county line running through it: Langar, split between Leicestershire and Nottinghamshire.

A brief lull ensued, this ending with the re-formation of No 90 Squadron on November 7. Before its Stirlings went south to Essex and Ridgewell at the end of 1942 without having flown any operational bombing sorties, they were joined by

THE AIRFIELDS OF BRITAIN

No 467 Squadron which came to Bottesford on November 24. The Australians became the established unit here until their Lancasters had to go in November 1943 to Waddington, Britain's second greatest ever bomber airfield and where No 207 Squadron had transferred from two years previously.

Australians made way for Americans as the 436th and 440th TCGs appeared during January and March 1944. These paratroop carrying forces were solely present for initial acclimatisation to Britain and a little training, both Groups moving to southern England after brief periods at Bottesford. Another lull started in April and this comparatively operationally rearward airfield lay quiet over D-Day. What Boscombe Down and the TSR-2 suffered from government incompetence and personal deceit, so Bottesford endured a whole new kind of officialdom in vacillation.

The airfield finally came to life again when No 1668 Heavy Conversion Unit arrived in July 1944. No 1321 Bomber Defence Training Flight soon formed to co-operate with the Lancasters but disbanded after a short while, although the HCU took on charge its fighters. Aircrew training continued not without incident for what remained of World War Two as Bottesford's hangars leaked during the winter of 1944/45, while the perimeter track needed much more attention than usual. An intruder attacked the base too on March 20 1945 but could do no more than damage a Lancaster.

No 1668 HCU left for Cottesmore on September 17 1945, with Bottesford passing to Maintenance Command on October 1. No 256 MU took over on the 29th to store military equipment as another airfield looked to have finished with aircraft. Not quite, for No 17 SFTS at Spitalgate was surprisingly allowed to employ Bottesford as an RLG from September 16 1946 – in theory. We have to make this qualification as records suggest that the site had not reopened to flying either by January 1947 or by April when an accident resulted. Undoubtedly serviceability problems here and Folkingham lying closer to Spitalgate made the SFTS, known as No 1 FTS from June, choose this ex-USAAF airborne forces airfield with effect from July 28.

Too much time had elapsed between these periods of actual (or intended) aircraft activity. Still, there was always No 256 MU, but this ground force disbanded on November 30 1948 once a Ministry of Supply sale of goods the August before had raised the sum of £13,515. Again uncertainty hovered over Bottesford until No 93 MU moved in on January 17 1949. Bombs came back to the station but solely for storage as this sub-site retained surplus HE devices.

281

Bottesford would give over another eleven years of useful RAF service. Control changed to No 92 MU on January 5 1959 and further munitions holding, though by then the number of sub-sites for bomb or any other form of storage was much reduced. This example finally closed on March 4 1960 to end its days as an inactive station in Technical Training Command and parented by Newton.

As already mentioned, many buildings still stand to make this an extremely well preserved disused airfield. All three runways and perimeter track are complete in length, and the control tower has been refurbished as offices after years as a ruin. Bottesford possessed an abnormally high number of hangars for a bomber airfield, yet every one has survived for storage use. There are nine T2s, eight of them grouped together on the north-east side, plus a single B1 positioned to the west across a minor road.

Landowners have for once made a better job of using an airfield to its full capacity – and that really is saying something these days. Fine, but as with Boston everybody from those in authority to the local library prefer to look away. Even when Bottesford raised £1,000 for a Nottingham hospital in February 1992, the mass media played upon the totally false sinister aspect of airfields as several people had to spend a night at this supposedly haunted place to collect their money. With publicity such as this, we should not be re-educating peoples' minds to change: we should be bludgeoning them.

130/SK820415. 11½ miles NW of Grantham, turn right off A52 at Bottesford village. Airfield 2 miles to NE by minor road.

Bottisham, Cambridgeshire

Who would guess that this largely flattened farmland revolutionised airfield runways in Britain? Quite so, for metal ones first saw active service at Bottisham during World War Two.

Landing areas had coped reasonably well enough with grass ever since 1909 but adverse weather never helped, nor did heavy aircraft movements. September 1939 and what followed showed up these deficiencies and brought about the downfall of grass in favour of concrete and tarmac. Both surfaces were always slow in installing, though, and metal offered a faster secondary alternative to combat soft patches of ground or the

THE AIRFIELDS OF BRITAIN

effects of undercarriage rutting.

While crude Army Track served at certain airfields, including Bottisham, Sommerfeld Track became the initial completely original type of metal runway designed with airfields in mind. This combination of wire mesh netting supported by lateral rods needed some months in perfecting but airfield construction engineers learned in time how they could build and picket a runway in well under a day. At Bottisham one Army Track runway had been removed during June 20-23 1942, still retaining its coconut matting undersurface, and Sommerfeld Track laying exercises carried out. The airfield briefly became unserviceable in July but 400 sappers used 400 tons of this new material to lay two runways in only nine hours on the 3rd. If 'Tin Lino' eventually proved a shade weak for long-term use at Britain's airfields, later products such as Pierced Steel Planking and Square Mesh Track turned metal runways into a total success. Far more prominent airfields than Bottisham had no qualms about employing any version of this artificial surface.

Tiger Moths of Cambridge's No 22 EFTS first used Bottisham as an RLG between mid-1940 and July 1941. The airfield was then a grass field before acquiring its pioneering runways, a T2 and seven Blisters, now all removed. Subsequently the scene of army co-operation training, No 241 Squadron arrived from Westley near Bury St Edmunds on July 1. Curtiss Tomahawks and North American Mustangs in turn replaced Westland Lysanders prior to No 241 going to Ayr II in May 1942. Nos 168, 652 and 654 Squadrons – the last two being AOP Auster units – also stayed at Bottisham in 1942 for a few months each.

While more Army Co-operation Command Mustangs of No 4 Squadron were present for reconnaissance sorties during 1943 between March 20 and July 16, their airfield suffered bouts of inactivity for general improvement work. One day a B-17 heavy bomber touched down – and official recorders were quick to add that the metal runway surface came through unscathed. USAAF P-47s of the 361st FG settled things down again in December, both they and their P-51 replacements flying many offensive missions until the Group went to Little Walden in Essex on September 26 1944.

The 361st's second British base possessed hard runways: Bottisham did not – and that reason proved ultimately harmful. It reverted to RAF control as satellite to the great North Weald from November 10 until playing a supporting role in assisting the expanding RAF (Belgian) Training School based a few miles away at Snailwell after switching on C&M to

Technical Training Command on June 1 1945. The RAF gave considerable assistance to European air forces as they tried to rebuild from virtually nothing, and the school's flying training and servicing elements changed to using Bottisham on November 23. Home however beckoned the Belgians and their mixed lighter aircraft types during March 1946, with the airfield shutting down in May.

In the late 1940s displaced persons stayed here to receive training for eventual employment in coal mines. A more unusual twist in Bottisham's post-war fortunes was a scheme for the control tower to be turned into private accommodation – not as a house, as can be seen with other buildings throughout Britain, instead flats. But the variable attitudes of landowners had already become noticeable, as did disused airfield vandalism when another British historical site was nearly wiped out in the 1950s. Metal runway creator Kurt Sommerfeld encountered as much strife after World War Two and had to struggle for years to gain adequate official compensation and recognition for his great invention.

The A45 and a minor road today plough through agricultural Bottisham, where only a little perimeter track and a few minor buildings remain. Hardly any people who especially participated in the D-Day landings, where metal runways proved so vital at airfields both in Britain and on the Continent, realise how much they owe to this shattered trailblazer.

154/TL540595. E of Cambridge by A45, S of village.

Boulmer, Northumberland

Few World War Two satellite airfields remain in RAF service. Boulmer has somehow survived against all the odds, if in a roundabout way, now a fairly familiar name due to its SAR helicopter role.

First inhabited by RAF personnel for AA defence duties on November 10 1942, Boulmer opened for flying on March 1 1943 as satellite to Eshott and No 57 OTU. Spitfires from the parent stayed largely in evidence until the OTU disbanded on June 6 1945 and C&M immediately began. Probably because of basic facilities, Boulmer received very few other visitors during wartime. Only some aircraft from noted Northumbrian fighter OTU base Milfield plus Fleet Air Arm Supermarine Seafires of No 808 Squadron which made a momentary stop in September 1944 bothered No 57 OTU's training syllabus.

The War Office acquired Boulmer on November 22 1945; under agriculture by the following summer, a Miles Martinet from Acklington later made a wheels-up landing because of engine failure on June 27 1949. This particular story should have ended but soon enough No 500 Signals Unit started forming on June 5 1953 to run one of Britain's many radar stations. A new GCI installation arose some distance away, though the HQ site was established on the disused airfield's periphery.

Flying and not just ground duties then began when Boulmer became an RLG for No 6 FTS at Acklington in the early 1960s. Long after the school had disbanded in 1968, a Flight of No 202 Squadron crossed from the doomed airfield superstar on October 2 1975, and helicopters are still present to assist everyone from oil rig workers to holiday-makers in whatever trouble they find themselves. The Flight's preceding letter changed on occasion to fit in with administration, Westland Sea Kings ousted their inferior Whirlwind stable-mates and in 1992 No 202 Squadron moved its HQ to Boulmer from Finningley in Yorkshire but SAR tasks operate on the same general pattern.

Less publicity has been directed towards the development of radar systems for air defence and traffic control in the area since the 1960s. Boulmer became one of three extremely important Sector Operations Centres to feed Fylingdales with early warning defensive information, and used to superintend the radar station at Bishops Court. The School of Fighter Control is another resident after having made the long trip from Bolt Head via Sopley. As with the SAR helicopters, the early 1990s heralded great changes with less vulnerable transportable radars replacing much older systems. One particularly big radar scanner known to everyone in the area was removed with not a little regret in August 1991.

We should technically view Boulmer as at least a redundant airfield despite such activity. The helicopter station reinforces this point by standing north-west of the airfield, not actually on the site itself. Where Spitfires once flew can be seen an empty field containing a largely intact perimeter track; most basic outlines have been retained but the north-south runway out of three usual stretches has disappeared.

This is a remarkable place in many respects which has achieved infinitely more than its nearby tiny village namesake: Boulmer's past reputation as a smugglers' paradise is hardly something to be proud of. A hangar for the SAR helicopters which has succeeded four wartime Blisters now stands out on a slight rise. Not far away has rested a most curious sight by a camp entrance: a Lightning, exceedingly odd considering that none of these supersonic jet fighters ever properly visited. An even more lethal Phantom has become a new gate guardian!

North-east England has been mainly stripped of airfields since World War Two. How Boulmer has held on is a near miracle. But there it is, a great public servant with a phenomenal growth record. The spartan ex-satellite has spectacularly outlived its neighbours, including the horrifically disfigured Acklington.

81/NU258130. 6 miles E of Alnwick, SE of Longhoughton.

Bourn, Cambridgeshire

Boulmer is naturally not the only British satellite airfield still able to accept aircraft. Bourn, hugely different in purpose and geographical position, has also returned to flying – albeit for civil needs. Although in the course of time declared self-accounting or independent, this East Anglian bomber base's master was initially Oakington which, like the more austere Eshott, has been taken apart more recently.

Approval for requisition of the land which became known as Bourn occurred in November 1939. Indirect influence may just possibly have come from Hardwick, a World War One civilian training airfield not far to the east once associated with Acton but closed in peacetime. The death of a North Weald-based fighter pilot flying an Armstrong Whitworth Siskin biplane which crashed and caught fire on March 19 1931 certainly made no instant difference.

Oakington was allocated its new satellite in the early months of 1941 and made considerable use of Bourn until mid-war, pleased to have on hand a supportive airfield already with three hard runways laid while the parent converted from grass to concrete after the tough winter of 1940/41. Short Stirlings and Vickers Wellingtons dispersed at Bourn but the Luftwaffe soon acknowledged their presence by bombing the airfield in April 1941. Worse followed one night in October when an intruding Ju 88 shot down a Stirling in the circuit.

Constant RAF bombing raids instead of the occasional one started in 1942 as No 101 Squadron's Wellingtons arrived from Oakington on February 11, becoming the first unit to be fully stationed at Bourn. When No 101 moved to Stradishall

THE AIRFIELDS OF BRITAIN

in Suffolk on August 11, No XV Squadron from Wyton replaced it but this unit's Stirlings had just settled in when they were off again to Mildenhall in April 1943. Several months earlier Bourn and this latest resident had been subjected in September 1942 to another nocturnal E/A attack, though belated revenge was achieved for previous inconvenience as a Mosquito night fighter later destroyed the offending Dornier Do 217 bomber.

Specialist friendly bomber units mainly operated at Bourn from the spring of 1943 as Bomber Command's assaults upon Germany and elsewhere reached new levels of intensity. Pathfinding Lancasters of No 97 Squadron marked enemy targets from arrival in April to a year later, going back to Lincolnshire and Coningsby. Operations were slightly affected during August/September 1943 due to runway repair work, and No 97's three Flights had to temporarily move to Gransden Lodge, Graveley and Oakington to keep up an operational momentum. Strange, is it not, how this trio of sites proved more prominent as bomber airfields than Bourn in World War Two but were later mauled beyond recognition?

Two Mosquito squadrons came in place of the Lancasters. No 105 arrived from Marham a month before No 97 Squadron departed and carried on the target marking task with great success, little troubled by the Luftwaffe's latest intrusion upon Bourn a fortnight prior to D-Day. The second Mossie unit became No 162 Squadron which reformed in mid-December 1944 as a late addition to the Light Night Striking Force. This combination of pathfinding and strategic nuisance bombing over Germany lasted throughout World War Two's final months, although No 162 Squadron took on a mail-carrying role after hostilities ceased. 'A' Flight was sent to Blackbushe as No 105 Squadron meanwhile went to familiar Cambridgeshire Bomber Command station Upwood, and the whole of No 162 left during July.

Operational notes had filled daily records – maybe too much, with not enough being said about the airfield. Even heavier daily weather reports now crammed every page by the end of 1945 as indecision dogged Bourn's post-war life under RAF control. Use was partly limited to the Bomber Command School of Pharmacy, present from May 17 1946 until going to Lindholme in Yorkshire on August 28, despite this base operating under Transport Command since January 1. A wholly appropriate user was No 1 Air Transport Depot which from November 1945 received and despatched airmen but the extensive overseas RAF trooping programme had already significantly reduced by March 1946.

Worries grew as Bourn fell away again to only a holding party basis from August 20. In July 1947 Maintenance Command took over and proposed to bring along No 54 MU until suddenly deciding to disband the unit. Back went Bourn to Transport Command on January 15 1948 as a result for another potential bout of non-achievement.

The airfield completely closed the same year – but solely in a military sense as civil flying had been noticeable since 1946. Gliders of the Cambridge GC had come from Cambridge and its wartime RLG Caxton Gibbet on May 19, lasting until going back to Cambridge as the Cambridge University GC in the middle of 1950. Club members greatly improvised by auto-towing their sailplanes and saved still more money by replacing towing ropes with piano wire.

By then Bourn had become involved in agricultural aviation circles as farmers finally realised how airfields could assist them with their working duties. Pest Control Ltd inaugurated a contract crop-spraying service from the airfield on June 11 1948 with a Westland-Sikorsky S.51 helicopter, seven years after the company had first undertaken experiments in this field. Performing good work in Africa, the firm's name changed in December 1954 to Fisons Pest Control Ltd, then combining with Airwork in 1955. Fisons proceeded to relinquish its half-interest in Fison-Airwork in 1960 so that this latest company could integrate with Bristow Helicopters to form the helicopter division of British United Airways but Fisons Pest Control Ltd continued to maintain crop-spraying interests.

Many early civilian helicopter types and fixed-wing Auster monoplanes used Bourn during the 1950s. The 'choppers' proved more durable as firms succeeded one another in future years, first Management Aviation in 1961 and then Bond Helicopters in 1984. Oil charter flights made since September 1972 reached such levels that this second company switched its centre of operations to Aberdeen's airport at Dyce as the 1980s wore on.

Flying at Bourn is split into two main areas, with helicopters based on the north-east side. Light aircraft of the Rural Flying Corps still operate from the north-south runway's southern half. All three runways – noticeably extended in World War Two to cope with aircraft advances – are pretty intact in length. Sections of perimeter track are missing and two T2s plus a B1 have gone but this is one airfield still making an indelible mark upon Britain. A brand new village called Highfields has however appeared out of nowhere to the east: combined with indistinct business or new town proposals, they have added to closure threats which have lasted for many years. One almighty near miss resulted on December 8 1993 when a plan to build 3,000 houses on the site was rejected against the local council's wishes, a secondary area of land at nearby Monkfield Farm being chosen instead.

What particularly strikes anyone who encounters Bourn is a row of three T2s later used by helicopters. Dispersal would appear to have been the last thing planners thought about but these buildings specially dealt with Stirlings. The Sebro company operated a repair depot a short distance away towards Cambridge, lorries taking aircraft to the hangars for final assembly before they flew off. Civilians mixed with the military: only the former remain now but Bourn will hopefully continue to display an air of versatility.
154/TL340594. 8 miles W of Cambridge on S side of A45.

Bovingdon, Buckinghamshire/ Hertfordshire

The decline of Bovingdon has been rapid and sickening. Flying only stopped altogether in 1970, not bad for a military airfield supposed to be one of the austerity breed, these 'temporary airfields' as once described by a certain distinguished television personality who should have known better.

Approved for requisition in April 1941, Bovingdon was accepted by the RAF when opened as scheduled on June 15 1942 and quickly given to the USAAF. The 92nd BG came from America via Prestwick during August and mounted a small number of fairly tentative raids but B-17 crews soon realised that their back-up facilities to cover losses were disorganised. This Group therefore became the first Combat Crew Replacement Center or broadly American-style RAF OTU element seen in Britain. When it moved in the space of a week to Alconbury in January 1943, a squadron held back created the 11th CCRC to firmly acknowledge how such a unit existed. Bovingdon proved a good airfield where to finalise training of 8th Air Force heavy bomber aircrews; the base anyhow lay somewhat far back from the East Anglia area where so many USAAF 'heavies' stationed themselves.

The 11th CCRC closed down in September 1944 after

having served its purpose. USAAF transports subsequently used Bovingdon for a long time as many servicemen passed through while on their way home. Less publicised visitors had been communications aircraft on hand for the 8th Air Force HQ at High Wycombe, and everyone wisely ignored the activities of personnel belonging to the Office of Strategic Services special forces espionage organisation.

Uncertainty resulted for a considerable number of months following World War Two about the possibility of civil transport operations as the USAAF would not release Bovingdon. Eventually the Americans gave in when they handed the airfield over to the Air Ministry in April 1946. BEA and BOAC notably gained access in due course as Bovingdon became a popular charter base, turning into a north-west of London Blackbushe.

For a fortnight short of ten years the more irregular cargoes always associated with charter flying shifted in and out of this officially recognised airport. Companies came and went in the same fashion, often because of business practices and planning ranging from the over-optimistic to amateurish, but certain others run on more professional lines survived. A major operator here was Hunting-Clan which in the 1950s mounted many service trooping flights with Vickers Viking airliners.

Earlier on in October 1949 Bovingdon had registered one of the more minor feats in British airfield history by welcoming the first Yugoslavian aircraft to land in this country since World War Two: today real ancient history without doubt. While worth mentioning, far more important was that the longer charter users stayed, the more anxious the Air Ministry became to regain ownership. Communications connections had remained in peace as in war with several Command HQs – both British and American – using what they considered a fine nearby site for speedy transportation of administrative staff. A Government White Paper published in 1953 declared that civil aircraft would have to leave, and airport status ceased from April 1 1956 as Bovingdon became in many ways a Booker for larger liaison machines.

This other airfield, positioned directly fourteen miles away to the south-west, gave a warning of future events to come when the RAF closed it in 1963. American employment had already ended a year earlier as assorted Bomber, Coastal and Fighter Command units at both places merged to form the Southern Communications Squadron in August 1963 but soon the RAF started contracting. Commands carried out more mergers or disappeared – and airfields in non-operational

THE AIRFIELDS OF BRITAIN

roles such as Bovingdon were suddenly under dire threat.

Years of unpretentious but unfaltering service counted for absolutely nothing when general flying ceased once the Southern Communications Squadron transferred to Northolt on January 1 1969. Another era had ended with the last RAF Avro Ansons being retired on June 28 1968 after 32 years of service, only gliders of No 617 GS lasting until the autumn of 1970 before going to Manston. And who would have dared to close that legend?

During these final few years of activity, Bovingdon was given a surprising but entirely welcome new role – that of film star. Both Mosquito films were shot here, plus (in relation to history) the more realistic *The War Lover* about a gung-ho B-17 pilot which amazingly received an X certificate in Britain. The better by far of the two former films, *633 Squadron,* finishes as we see Bovingdon's apron devoid of aircraft because every Mosquito has failed to return to base after successfully destroying a German rocket fuel factory in Norway. Somehow the end seemed eerily close to what actually happened at this airfield later on in the 1960s.

Many famous people stayed at or visited Bovingdon in its glory days. Everyone recognised Supreme Allied Commander General Dwight D. Eisenhower; other residents remained unknown until achieving fame in later life, such as popular American actor Walter Matthau who served as an instructor during World War Two. But people who merit infinitely less mention inhabit Bovingdon today as the site has become a prison. It is known as The Mount, an odd title, though the airfield did stand on high ground.

A facility of this nature was originally proposed as far back as 1970 but took an enormously long time to emerge. Vandalism and general neglect had already not gone without notice that year as buildings swiftly deteriorated, even with the military gliders still on site. Thoughts turned to demolishing all four T2s in 1972, positively criminal as these hangars had been reclad only in 1968 and still held emergency supplies in storage. Villagers did not want the prison built at all and ostensibly won against the authorities in November 1976 but in reality deferred construction on the old technical area on Bovingdon's east side. The Mount finally opened on March 15 1988 to hold young offenders, though it has since altered in policy to become a Category C training prison. Little more than one year to build the airfield, still less time taken to announce its closure and more than twenty years needed to reach this current prison role say much about differing human and social priorities. 'Yes please,' you can almost hear the rabble yell, 'we want to be saved but don't ask us for any assistance when our saviour needs some help.' Not that Bovingdon stands alone in this respect: oh, if only.

Merely two out of three runways, some perimeter track and the control tower now readily mark what used to be a major star in itself without the aid of top brass, future US presidents or film personalities. And just as if when anyone mentions Bourn they often spell it Bourne, so Bovingdon frequently has to suffer being called Bovington. A sad end to a highly fulfilling life – and heavy opposition to new light aircraft use proposals keeps that sadness coming.

166/TL008043. 3 miles SW of Hemel Hempstead by B4505.

Bowmore (landplane), Strathclyde

Alternative Names: Duich, Islay
Any island is always advised to have an airfield because of the communications, economic and social benefits involved. The Inner Hebridean island of Islay has held four since the 1930s.

Second was Bowmore, to where Midland and Scottish Air Ferries ran a passenger service from Glasgow's original airport at Renfrew. This route started experimentally in April 1933 to a beach closer to the village at Bridgend and fully from May when extended from Campbeltown, the company having effected an air ambulance flight from Bridgend on May 14, so pioneering this form of public service to the Western Isles. Shortly before the spring of 1934 aircraft changed to using Bowmore as their primary port of call.

M&SAF had a real go in trying to open up some of Scotland's remoter areas to aviation during its short existence. But the airline attempted a bus-stop style operation that was not too practicable for passenger air travel and technically ceased business in June 1934. Flights however went on a little longer until the end of September.

Civil transports returned to Bowmore on December 1 when Northern and Scottish Airways resumed the Glasgow-Islay route. This new company preferred to temporarily license its L-shaped landing ground bordered to the north by the Duich River to June 29 1935 and then to August 29: clearly it was looking for a better airfield. Two miles down the A846 stood Glenegedale, today's Islay Airport of Port Ellen, and flying changed again to there on August 30. Bowmore reverted to

being featureless rough grassland after this short period of social usefulness.
60/NR317545. 4 miles S of village by A846, immediately W of bridge at Duich.

Bowmore (seaplane), Strathclyde

Alternative Name: Islay

Bowmore held on to precious airfield links in World War Two by giving its name to a completely different type of site – but once more not a terribly good one. No hangars or even a slipway meant this was a very unsatisfactory flying boat base.

A unit known as 'G' Flight was born in Islay's Loch Indaal during September 1940. Reformed as No 119 Squadron on March 13 •1941, three impressed Short 'G' Class airliners – *Golden Fleece, Golden Hind* and *Golden Horn* – were employed in an anti-submarine role but their maintenance conditions proved far from perfect and had to be withdrawn in June. No 119 Squadron flew to Pembroke Dock in south-west Wales on August 4, though the 'G' Class types came back into service there for a short while. A couple of Short 'C' Class Empire flying boats so associated with Hythe in Southampton Water pre-war also served in 1941 at Bowmore. One of these ASV radar-equipped ex-BOAC machines was lost on operations when *Clio* flew into high ground nearby on August 22.

Fully militarised Empire flying boats came to Islay as No 246 Squadron reformed with Sunderlands in August 1942; this unit disbanded on April 30 1943. Bowmore would in addition hold No 422 (RCAF) Squadron from May 1943 but its extreme limitations forced the Canadians to leave for Northern Ireland on November 4 and C&M to begin. Closure to general flying occurred on January 15 1944.

General still did not necessarily mean absolute as the occasional flying boat kept visiting. Castle Archdale and Killadeas machines retained a faint link with Northern Ireland, though that was about all and Bowmore eventually completely, entirely and utterly closed down without any ambiguity on June 11 1945 – that is to aircraft! RAF motor boats had naturally gone about their duties to support flying boats as at any other base, and No 67 Marine Craft Unit's headquarters came to Bowmore in July from Port Ellen, where the MCU had formed in 1943. Exercises took place on a dwindling scale until the element closed by the end of March 1946.

While few hard traces are left, Bowmore can always say how it featured in a real war film, not fictitious ones like those shot at Bovingdon. *Coastal Command* was one of Britain's best documentary/propaganda films of World War Two and showed a Sunderland crew out on patrol. Wartime censorship meant Bowmore was called Port Ferry Bay and located on Lewis in the Outer Hebrides instead of Islay but the village's famous round chapel features at one point as the Sunderland comes in to land. The clergy in real life helped their local marine airfield by having a beacon light installed on top of this building to guide in machines.
60/NR311601. On N side of village.

Boxted, Essex

The three best remembered USAAF British airfields of World War Two – Debden, Duxford and Bassingbourn – all shared one factor in common by belonging to the 1930s Expansion Period. But plenty of austerity period sites with their humbler facilities became favourite American postings too. Top of this second category was Boxted.

This famous fighter station opened as late as May 1943. Boxted's first unit was ironically the 386th Bomb Group which arrived the following month. Once Martin B-26 medium bombers had crossed Essex to Great Dunmow on September 24, not long after a couple of nasty snap Luftwaffe bombing raids killed two personnel, the resultant gap was filled in November by the 354th FG from Greenham Common.

The air war changed significantly upon its arrival as this Group inaugurated operational missions with P-51Bs. These Mustangs little resembled earlier variants which RAF Army Co-operation Command and the Second TAF had used since 1942, primarily because the old Allison piston engine had been replaced by a Rolls-Royce Merlin, thanks to joint British-American development work. This superior power plant boosted the North American machine by making it considerably faster and not struggle at altitude; combined with the installation of underwing disposable fuel tanks to increase range the P-51B caused a sensation on appearing at Boxted. It was not quite the finished article USAAF and RAF pilots knew so well as lacking a 'bubble' cockpit canopy for improved vision but soon gave defensive Luftwaffe fighters an extremely hard time indeed over their own airspace while escorting USAAF heavy bombers on daylight raids. American B-17 and B-24 crews became glad to see their 'little friends' after having come off badly against enemy fighters on recent deep penetration raids such as those against Schweinfurt in the second half of 1943.

A form of retrogression happened at Boxted a day after the 354th FG left for Lashenden ALG in Kent on April 17 1944. The great 56th FG made an appearance here, known to all as the 'Wolfpack', the only Republic P-47 8th Air Force Group which did not convert to P-51s. Thunderbolts had not found operations over occupied Europe too easy but pilots learned that by flying at high altitude these heavily-armed fighters could overcome their performance limitations. Moreover, the 56th FG simply preferred P-47s to P-51s – and no-one was going to argue with a unit full of aces. But a sign of how the P-47 now fared not so well elsewhere in Britain was provided by the 5th Emergency Rescue Squadron, another Thunderbolt unit at Boxted and one of the USAAF's few second-line flying elements in this country. This ASR force arrived in May 1944 and went to Halesworth in Suffolk – the 56th's previous base – on January 16 1945.

Some of the personalities who assisted in creating the 'Wolfpack' legend abruptly left Boxted after only short periods of residence, though their departures had nothing to do with the quality of life at this station. The 56th FG's acclaimed leader Colonel Hubert Zemke transferred a few miles north to Wattisham in the summer of 1944 to command the 479th FG there. He was lost on a sortie and captured shortly afterwards, a fate which also befell Lieutenant-Colonel Francis Gabreski in July. Better luck favoured Major Robert Johnson, who shared the 8th Air Force record of 28 kills with Gabreski before finishing his operational tour of duty in May.

Other equally notable individuals filled their places at Boxted and maintained bomber escort and ground attack duties up to the end of fighting, eventually adding a second Distinguished Unit Citation award to the one received while at Halesworth. P-47Ms, fastest of all Thunderbolt production variants, operated from Boxted in the European war's last few weeks; despite engine trouble caused by corrosion, they even destroyed a number of Messerschmitt Me 262 jet fighters in diving attacks of the style which the 56th FG had turned into a fine art.

On September 9 1945, the 8th Air Force's top-scoring

THE AIRFIELDS OF BRITAIN: VOLUME 1

Fighter Group moved to Little Walden. More or less to the end of their stay American personnel defiantly made airfield life just that little different in relatively small ways. They had liked acquiring captured German aircraft as war booty, for a Heinkel He 111 crewed by US airmen and with P-47s as escorts arrived at Boxted after World War Two; a Focke-Wulf Fw 190 fighter once landed as well. Unfortunately, the USAAF not always left certain British bases on the best of terms, in this case coming in for criticism for being wasteful after burning two and a half tons of paper at the site on October 28.

At the same period in late October Boxted was left in RAF hands as a satellite to Duxford and then Castle Camps. Mosquitoes of No 25 Squadron came from this more unknown and now severely struggling Cambridgeshire station on January 11 1946, their stay punctuated by three short trips to Germany for firing practice.

Gloster Meteor jet fighter squadrons visited too in 1946 but the Cold War had started to freeze Boxted to death as sophistication showed up the flaws of austerity. No 263 Squadron moved to Church Fenton in June and No 234 Squadron became No 266 on September 1 as No 25 Squadron's Mosquitoes left. This new unit went off on another firing course to Acklington later on that month and returned on October 31 as Boxted notably lost its prestigious status as a Master Diversion airfield: the cracks had started to show.

Events moved swiftly as next day Boxted became satellite to Wattisham – an Expansion Period airfield. An AA co-operation detachment of No 695 Squadron, in place since July 1946, departed for North Weald on November 4 as No 56 Squadron's Meteors proceeded to Acklington after coming in mid-September, while the Meteors of No 266 Squadron apparently cleared out the same day for Wattisham. We have to use this vague adverb, because for some reason the unit had '... decided to finish flying at Boxted and fly from Wattisham': thus spake a Station ORB. A rather confused and messy end to major aerial duties for such a massive star concluded when the jets decided to go away during January 2-4 1947.

There was only one way for Boxted to go after that – downhill. Closed and termed an unmanned satellite to Wattisham on August 9 1947, RAF airmen made this indirect expression a joke as gliders of ex-Birch resident No 145 GS remained and had done so since at least late 1946. Bi-weekly inspections – if they really happened – could not stop over seventeen acres of land being inauspiciously relinquished during August/September 1947, and certainly did nothing to prevent squatters from invading by the autumn. The decline reached epidemic proportions early on in 1948 with the airfield proving very slow to clear up, more illegal tenants and even children extensively damaging unoccupied sites. Most incredible of all was an American named Murader who housed his Fairchild Argus 2 monoplane at Boxted without any permission. Everything had become an excruciating mess as the military tried to save the situation by officially abandoning the airfield on February 3. But they too botched their duties, for Murader was only thrown out in April and No 145 GS disbanded in the same month.

Could anyone come up with an inspired suggestion regarding Boxted's future employment? Of course not. People weakly mooted use as an airport for Colchester, while others were soon stopped from learning to drive on the airfield in the late 1940s. Airfield supporters are said to have encouragingly established close by a wooden memorial and commemorative seat dedicated to Boxted soon after World War Two but for whatever reason these items were quickly removed. The local council took the seat, claimed to have been lying in a scrap-yard when last heard of. My word, the huge army of modern airfield fans will make sure that some people are going to pay dearly for their disgraceful actions one day – and have already partly carried out revenge, as you will shortly find out.

Squatter evictions still occurred as late as 1953 but the Cold War refrigerator was put on hold for some years as more peaceful aircraft again used Boxted. Civil flying had started by at least 1950 and light aircraft could be seen from then on, a Tiger Moth crashing at the site in June 1959.

Although limited gliding featured in the 1960s, pride of place had to go to Airspray (Colchester) Ltd. This company performed crop-spraying duties and also ran the Colchester (later Colchester and East Essex) Flying Club. Austers and Tiger Moths were able to use two out of the three runways up to 1965 but their home never managed to achieve complete recognition as an active airfield. Both officialdom and farmers tended to regard recreational civil airfields and aviation with indifference or downright contempt for far too long after 1945. Boxted's runways provided proof of these mixed attitudes: by 1961 they were cracking up, becoming weeded and further weakened by farm vehicles. Add to all this an uncertain status and it is hardly surprising that closure came in the end.

No aircraft could hope to use Boxted today. An orchard has arisen on this truly great old airfield, taking over most of the runways and perimeter track. Trees reach out towards the village of Langham: despite being closer than Boxted, this name was not selected because of a station in Norfolk also called Langham. Those few buildings left include a Blister on Boxted's north-west side once for the ASR P-47s; two missing T2s provided main hangarage. The control tower, which survived into the 1960s, has vanished as well.

On July 15 1992 came the revenge of sorts mentioned earlier with a fine memorial surrounded by three runway lights being unveiled at the northern end of Boxted's main runway alongside a minor road. Promotional leaflets alas gave the name Broxted, and the story goes that a local female dignitary giving the usual patronising spiel on the appointed day wretchedly mispronounced the name of the 56th FG's greatest leader, at which point many airfield supporters shouted almost in unison: 'Zemke!' And what would Messrs Zemke, Johnson and Gabreski think of their former base in general now? Trees, not Thunderbolts? Probably they would not know whether to laugh or weep at the ludicrous sight before them.

168/TM015303. N of Colchester, turn first left off A12 after junction with A1232 for Langham. Best view of site from N end.

Bracebridge Heath, Lincolnshire

Not blessed with so dramatic a history but in remarkably better shape is Bracebridge Heath near Lincoln. This grass field opened during 1916 for use by several Lincoln-based companies as a convenient place where to flight-test their products.

Conditions improved when seven Belfasts and some Bessoneau hangars were built towards the close of World War One, being finished just prior to the Armistice. Two distinctive long but thin Handley Page sheds appeared too and did see 0/400 heavy bombers; other brand new types in view included Sopwith Camel fighters. Away from test flying, No 120 Squadron's diversity of aircraft stayed at Bracebridge Heath from August to November 1918 while on their way south between Cramlington and Wyton.

The enormous hangarage development had been intended to allow No 4 Aircraft Acceptance Park to move over from Lincoln's racecourse at West Common. This the AAP did in 1918 but World War One ended and the Government cancelled all aircraft production contracts to try and save money. These events left Bracebridge Heath with no option but to close in March 1920.

Despite Sir Alan Cobham holding one of his National Aviation Days on June 17 1932, this place lay quiet in a flying sense: a concurrent plan by Eastern Air Transport Ltd based at Skegness III to reopen the site failed to materialise. But Bracebridge Heath still kept in touch with aviation over many more years by acting as a ground repair and servicing depot for A.V. Roe, Hawker Siddeley and British Aerospace. Avro Lancaster and Vulcan bombers were notably attended to, aircraft being flown into Waddington a couple of miles to the south; there they were partly dismantled and taken by road to Bracebridge Heath for repair before the reverse procedure occurred. Aircraft factory connections only ended in 1984.

While some permanent and temporary hangars were gradually removed after World War One, five Belfasts – three of them in a row – still stand and are used mainly for storage. One hangar is in wondrously magnificent condition: a lick of paint can certainly work wonders. Now of late has come news that they may all be demolished . . .

121/SK987672. 3½ miles SE of Lincoln, on E side of A15 and 2 miles N of Waddington.

Braceby, Lincolnshire

Alternative Name: Grantham

Two Home Defence squadrons employed this inverted L-shaped field in very open countryside which served as a night landing ground. Used by No 38 from October 1916 after requisitioned on September 5, No 90 Squadron took over in mid-1918 and still controlled Braceby at the Armistice.

Like Bracebridge Heath, Braceby may well have also given indirect military assistance in World War Two. A site in the area became a decoy airfield for Grantham, the former Spittlegate and future Spitalgate, though a typical drought of information concerning this specialised subject means that no-one can be certain if the old landing ground was precisely involved or not.

130/TF016364. 9 miles E of Grantham by A52, N of village.

THE AIRFIELDS OF BRITAIN: VOLUME 1

Brackla, Highland

Whenever the Moray Firth area of northern Scotland is mentioned in an airfield context, Kinloss and Lossiemouth II almost invariably hog the attention. But there have been and still are plenty of other airfields along this coastal stretch, though not always as famous.

Aircraft first came to popular holiday and golfing resort Nairn before World War One. A BE2 of No 2 Squadron from Montrose once landed in the area to the delight of local children, while Captain G. W. P. Dawes – one of the pilots who flew from Farnborough to Montrose in February 1913 – arrived at Nairn in his Maurice Farman biplane on August 7 and stayed a day. A 1920s civil airfield existed to the east at Auldearn, and E. E. Fresson visited on joy-riding duties in the early 1930s, but not until World War Two did a fully-fledged airfield appear.

Brackla came to fruition in highly controversial circumstances. The airfield's opening in July 1941 resulted in Brackley, hundreds of miles away in Northamptonshire, having to change its name to Croughton (see *A Towering Control*, page 245). Admittedly the similarity in titles was obvious but an altogether more strange explanation recently suggested involves the adjacent village of Cawdor. Here in its castle Macbeth murdered King Duncan in 1040, and the suggestion – farcical as it may look – is that as actors talk about the 'Scottish play', so superstition again prevailed to forbid what became Brackla having any connections with Cawdor. Perhaps utter rubbish – but, as we will see much later on in this series of books, unproven supernatural beliefs had long before dictated the layout of Larkhill on Salisbury Plain.

One of Scotland's most forgotten airfields served largely as an RLG after this incredibly quirky beginning. Aircraft of No 2 Air Gunnery School from Dalcross used the site from the word go, No 19 (P) AFU being around in the winter of 1943/44, also more Oxfords of No 14 (P) AFU from Banff the following summer. A non-flying Aircrew Allocation Centre to hold temporarily resting personnel held sway too from the spring of 1944 but disliked Brackla's dispersed nature; Harrowbeer in Devon did not come up to scratch as a possible successor, and the AAC travelled to Catterick during January/February 1945 despite not finding this Yorkshire base perfect either. Flying overall proved erratic at the airfield: sometimes fairly busy, at other times being devoid of aircraft.

Another parent turned out to be Kinloss. Already that big star had despatched a few Whitleys belonging to No 19 OTU and officially opened Brackla as an 'unbuilt' satellite on June 14 1943. The OTU favoured Forres, though, and was ousted by the Aircrew Allocation Centre in April 1944.

Such general reluctance to use Brackla showed in a decision to remove 1,600 panels of Bar and Rod Track from the main runway in December 1944 and re-lay them on the troubled landing area at Lossiemouth's satellite Elgin II. Sommerfeld Track brought the missing width back from 46 to 50 yards but activity stuttered as ever prior to February 1945 when the other major resident at Kinloss, No 45 MU, moved in to accept its new supplementary storage site. If maybe impossible to visualise these days, many Halifaxes touched down at Brackla for storage. By June 1946 a total of 243 of these four-engined types could be seen – and there was still enough room left over for 89 Vickers Warwicks.

Aircraft had at last arrived in strength, although for the wrong reasons as emphasis soon changed to scrapping, a job that lasted for years. Some squatters moved into Brackla during 1947 before the airfield was abandoned in December and a C&M party provided by No 45 MU withdrawn on the 29th. A civil firm continued to break down aircraft into the late 1940s but the metal runways were entirely removed in just three days in July 1948.

Hardly anything now remains of this wartime airfield. To reach Brackla, turn off at Cawdor and you will find the perimeter track's north-western side is a minor road. An unusually high tally of four T2s considering the variable levels of activity here and most support buildings have long departed from this world to leave a field. If anyone does recall the name Brackla, it will be because of a distillery which dates back to 1812. The military requisitioned nearby Brackla House on February 1 1942.

27/NH855517. 4½ miles SW of Nairn, N of B9090.

Bradwell Bay, Essex

Somewhat detached from other airfields on a peninsula, Bradwell Bay seems to intrude out into the sea. And the imperative word is intrude, for Mosquitoes frequently probed German defences to wreak havoc and single-engined fighters escorted RAF heavy bombers when opposition decreased. Bradwell was a noted airfield and has not fallen from memory completely as a nuclear power station stands on the north side.

The 1937 Air Estimates announced when published early on in the year that air firing and bombing ranges would be built on Dengie Flats at a cost of £20,000; a facility could have been provided as far back as the mid-1920s but for protests by fishermen. A landing ground to the north-west used in a supportive capacity was under construction in 1938 and active by May 10 1939, though planners viewed it as too far away from North Weald to make a suitable satellite. Four years later the 'Magnificent Seven' megastar would prove everyone wrong by placing Bradwell Bay under its Sector control but initially another member of this supergroup – and one further away again – would dictate policy.

Hornchurch sent a Squadron Leader on July 11 1941 to look after affairs once the extremely basic grass site had been approved in October 1940 to become a far better equipped fighter airfield. Even allowing for this being a marshy area of Britain, construction workers performed well to build up Bradwell Bay reasonably quickly and let it open on November 28 1941.

Material shortages and poor weather made for a quiet winter. In April 1942 featured another round in the interminable series of rows during World War Two as to whether airfield building or food production should receive priority. Farmers could not care less about the general war effort, usually getting righteous come-uppance as a result, but on this occasion forced a 400 yard extension of the NE/SW runway to be delayed until after the harvest.

Douglas Bostons of No 418 (RCAF) Squadron nevertheless appeared during April and almost at once attacked targets at random for the next eleven months as the Canadians enhanced their reputation as one of the premier early intruder units. Defensive duties were not ruled out as No 29 Squadron's Mosquitoes came from West Malling on May 13 1943 in order to search for enemy aircraft over Britain until moving to Ford on September 3. More Mossies of Nos 488 (RNZAF) and 605 Squadrons arrived at Bradwell in turn; as they departed in April/May 1944, yet another squadron equipped with the wooden superstar flew in from Colerne in Wiltshire. No 219 went to Hunsdon at the end of August.

With this combination of taking the air war to Germany on *Ranger* sorties and sitting back at the same time, Bradwell Bay ran up a highly respectable score of kills over Luftwaffe aircraft. Intrusion was always the riskier of these two roles but also rated extremely profitable, especially whenever Allied aircraft appeared without warning to disrupt enemy airfields

THE AIRFIELDS OF BRITAIN

or aircraft flying about in their circuits. The loosening of restrictions as time went by on the use of AI radar over enemy territory further helped aircrews.

But as in line with that old saying about sowing and reaping, so the Luftwaffe returned fire at Bradwell, though the airfield was able to take care of itself as AA fire shot down a raider during one particularly eventful night in February 1943. A Ju 88 later crashed at this site on April 18 1944: ground personnel had fired off green flares to let the aircraft land after being told by Sector control it was friendly!

1944 saw fighter units posted in abundance to this wet and featureless landscape. Among those present became No 124 Squadron: at the end of August Nos 64, 126 and 611 Squadrons, which also flew Spitfires, were brought in from Bolt Head and Harrowbeer to form a Wing. Now started the Lancaster escort phase, a duty carried on until the close of 1944 when two of these units – now flying Mustangs – left for Bentwaters. By then air-launched V-1 missiles caused problems, so No 501 Squadron rushed to Bradwell Bay as its fast Hawker Tempest fighters could catch the flying bombs. With all these aircraft around, ASR cover was needed, No 278 Squadron therefore arriving on April 21 1944 to cope with coastal and long-range aircrew emergencies. The squadron's HQ switched to Thorney Island later on in February 1945.

The duties for which Bradwell Bay had become best known kept it fully occupied throughout the winter of 1944/45. To add to the congestion, Spitfires of three Czech-manned squadrons (Nos 310, 312 and 313) superseded the original Wing. A mass clearance in February 1945 saw them go as one to Manston on the 27th.

After No 501 Squadron also left on March 3, Bradwell Bay was never quite the same again, despite guns blasting away at a final flurry of V-1s and one missile exploding over the base on the 26th without doing any harm. Nos 151 and 456 Squadrons sent their Mosquitoes off on more prowling intrusive sorties until the war ended, No 456 then soon disbanding in June, followed by no other unit staying long here in peacetime. AA co-operation aircraft belonging to No 287 Squadron resided during June to September, symptomatic of the times by eventually transitting through from Hornchurch to West Malling, unlike Bradwell Bay in being of more permanent construction.

Once No 309 Squadron's Mustangs had taken a break from late Expansion Period Coltishall during October/November 1945, that was about it and Bradwell started on C&M on December 1. Parented by first Bentwaters and subsequently

THE AIRFIELDS OF BRITAIN: VOLUME 1

Boxted, closure resulted on October 31 1946 – except in the view of Wattisham. The Officers' Mess at what had become an unmanned satellite continued to hold a small party which operated the Dengie Flats ranges. Some farm fodder storage use also lasted into the 1950s.

Bothersome Labour MP Tom Driberg took an unhealthy interest in Bradwell Bay's fortunes after World War Two. This man who had the gall to declare before fighting ended how '... large parts of England, particularly East Anglia and Essex, are covered with airfields — far more than could possibly be needed permanently' and seemed obsessed by planning authorities often sniped at the star in his constituency. Driberg later quit his seat, only to become MP for Barking but finally still call himself Baron Bradwell in a classic example of sheer brass neck.

Everyone else almost inevitably completely forgot about usual airfield heroics for several years until an announcement came in October 1955 that a nuclear power station was planned to stand on the north side of this place. Local county council approval occurred in January 1956 and final official sanctioning six months later but this second action gave rise to heavy opposition from surrounding residents. Suddenly up cropped the Blackwater and Dengie Peninsula Protection Association to protest at rapidly unfolding events. This organisation and other individuals typically cared not at all about Bradwell Bay's fortunes, even though the moth-balled hero remained strongly evident with white crosses painted on the runway ends to prevent aircraft from landing. No mention of the redundant site featured whatsoever as media prominence was crazily given to how bird-watchers would be affected: these people deserved to fear the prospect of not one but two power stations as suggested at one point. The continued use of Dengie Flats for bombing practice still by the end of 1956 no doubt caused resentment too. In the end just one Magnox station slowly arose after construction work began in January 1957 and opened in 1962.

Having saved many distressed aircraft in World War Two on account of possessing FIDO, Bradwell Bay now requires some salvation. On reaching it after a tortuously twisted journey along various B-class roads from either Maldon or Burnham-on-Crouch, showing why Hornchurch was glad to get rid of the site in 1941, you encounter an area of land clearly once an airfield but one not marked by many historical artefacts. Driving along the mostly intact runway is done so at a snail's pace as the destructive effects of farming, poor drainage and moss have all taken a heavy toll. So too did

NIREX in the 1980s when this nuclear agency evaluated Bradwell Bay for possible atomic waste storage purposes.

You are far more recommended taking your vehicle around the southern perimeter track for, although few buildings have been retained, several interesting sights catch your eye. Leaving well aside poultry houses occupying what is left of the north-south runway and a useful area for HGV instruction, turn the corner past the tree-lined NW/SE runway and you discover in use for farm storage five Blisters out of an original twelve plus an equally missing Bellman. Here the road to Weymarks Farm is blocked off. Return the way you came to meet Bradwell's two prize exhibits: the control tower, turned to excellent effect into a private dwelling, and an airfield memorial fairly close by. This second item consists of a symbolic Mosquito flanked by plaques listing the names of 121 airmen who lost their lives while on operations. It really is a marvellous piece of work and only goes to show how dangerous intruder operations could be.

The control tower and memorial are beacons of hope for the future at this famous airfield which became famous for something else. But now the elderly Magnox station's days are definitely numbered as well, and once closed will presumably be eventually entombed in concrete. At least the local inhabitants who protested about it and then NIREX seem to at last have given the great Bradwell Bay some belated recognition. Duty demands them to do so.

168/TM005082. 14 miles NE of Burnham-on-Crouch off B1021, ¾ mile N of Bradwell-on-Sea. 'RAF Memorial' signpost leads to SW corner of airfield.

Bramcote, Warwickshire

Best remembered for involvement with the creation of four Polish bomber squadrons, though the scene of much more besides, Bramcote officially opened on June 5 1940. Wellingtons of No 215 Squadron had nevertheless already been present in September 1939 as part of the *Scatter Scheme* Bomber Command emergency withdrawal plan while the airfield was being built.

Poles started appearing in numbers at Bramcote when No 300 Squadron formed on July 1 1940, with No 301 Squadron doing the same on the 22nd. This former unit became the first Polish bomber force in RAF service, and both operated Battles as interim equipment. After training for operations they moved to Swinderby in Lincolnshire during August but two more Polish squadrons in Nos 304 and 305 formed as their predecessors left. Again Battles had to do initially before replacement by Wellingtons. These two newer squadrons did not overstay their welcome at Bramcote either by going to Syerston in early December.

Our Polish friends had gladly started afresh in this part of inland England after nine harrowing months of fleeing across Europe. The Germans had captured their country: now they were safe in Britain, yet invasion jitters tried to frighten Bramcote along with every home airfield in the summer of 1940. One day came a scary report about the arrival of enemy parachutists in the surrounding area, the 'paras' actually being bales of hay lifted by the wind. Everyone also greatly worried about Luftwaffe bombing attacks, though only three light raids materialised in the last quarter of 1940 and caused negligible damage. A Ju 88 indulging in some strafing left one or two holes in two aircraft on September 26 but the worst attack was saved for 1941 when enemy bombs destroyed two Wellingtons, a Magister and damaged a hangar on March 13.

Early wartime life did not confine Bramcote to bombers. BOAC held a handful of civil Armstrong Whitworth Ensign and de Havilland Albatross airliners here for storage and conversion purposes from late 1940 into 1941. Two Hurricane squadrons also visited during these years but Nos 151 and 605 principally stayed for night fighting operations only because Baginton was more or less incapable of defensive duties during hours of darkness.

Allowing for such variation, Bramcote was destined due to its rearward geographical position to remain a World War Two training base as No 18 OTU arrived from Hucknall on June 15 1940. More Polish aircrews appeared to carry on with training by mounting day and night exercises, *Nickelling* and some bombing raids. Satellites at Bitteswell, Blyton, Nuneaton II and even Thurleigh helped out at various times, 'A' Flight spending February-May 1942 at the future Bedford as the landing areas at Bramcote and Bitteswell were temporarily unserviceable. Blyton became the most notable of this supportive quartet as close by stood famous Lincolnshire bomber station Hemswell, where Nos 300, 301 and 305 Squadrons stayed during 1941-43. By installing a detachment at Blyton trainees could gain a feel of the front line service which in time they would have to face.

No 18 OTU left for Finningley on March 7 1943, No 105 (Transport) OTU forming in its place as this form of flying increased in importance. BOAC briefly returned that year to

THE AIRFIELDS OF BRITAIN

convert some Mosquitoes for company use but Wellingtons mostly remained at Bramcote until Dakotas replaced them as the European war ended and transports completely overtook bombers in planning priority. On August 10 1945 the OTU became known as No 1381 (T) CU and finally flew off to Desborough in Northamptonshire during October/November.

Throughout all this upheaval Oxfords of No 1513 BAT Flight had stayed in place at Bramcote. But worries again surfaced at the turn of 1945/46, this time about the airfield's future, and concern increased when the Flight left in the spring after a five year period of residence. Only equipment disposal unit No 266 MU essentially held the fort at Bramcote once formed out of No 254 MU at Balderton on January 1 1946 up to disbandment on June 30 1947.

The unpredictability which has characterised so many British airfields touched this one in December 1946 to end all woes. Another BAT Flight previously based at Melbourne in Yorkshire had kept flying activities in full view for a few months until the FAA decided to commission Bramcote as HMS *Gamecock* as part of its post-war plan to take on more inland bases. Unusual or not, the airfield would be grateful to the Navy for twelve more years of active service.

Seafires and Hawker Sea Furies of No 1833 Squadron resided between August 1947 and October 1955, as did Fireflies and Avengers of No 1844 Squadron from February 1954 to disbanding on March 10 1957. Other naval squadrons made fleeting visits, while the Gamecock GC – a branch of the Royal Naval Gliding and Soaring Association – formed in early 1954 after the first National Gliding Competition during June 21-29 1947 had recognised the return of recreational flying. Bramcote held several Open Days in its time under Navy control, to which the general public willingly responded in large numbers.

Despite such ostensible bliss, two abbreviations – GRS and RNVR – in time killed Bramcote as an airfield. Grass Runway Syndrome was back, that affliction haunting any site which did not convert to hard runways. Bramcote had only gone as far as equipping itself with three Sommerfeld Track metal runways in World War Two, near the war's end trying out the new Channel Track surface, and No 1833 Squadron had left in 1955 for Honiley simply because its old home could not accept jet-engined Supermarine Attacker fighters. Elimination two years later of the Royal Naval Volunteer Reserve, the Navy's RAuxAF equivalent to which both Nos 1833 and 1844 Squadrons belonged, became about the final straw.

Since being taken over by the Army in 1959, once a non-flying mechanical training school had gone to Arbroath to allow closure in Navy circles on November 10 1958, Bramcote has remained a familiar local feature in this new role. The M69 runs across what used to be the landing area but three out of five Cs and various other Expansion Period buildings still stand: their architectural style has saved Bramcote from a far worse fate. Several pillboxes survive too around the area.

So it is that a place which had to be named as such as Ryton to the south-west looked too much like Wyton carries on with an honourable life. By 1993 the Army barracks appeared to have a doubtful future with the generally uncertain defence situation in Britain but local interests are hard at work to resolve matters. Bramcote has always been popular as 15,000 people attended the Battle of Britain Open Day on September 15 1945, many people deeply regretting its closure in the late 1950s. Survival plans put forward then may save the day yet again, and seem to have with the operational signals regiment of the Royal Signals due to move in.

140/SP410880. NE of Coventry by M69, 4 miles SE of Nuneaton between B4114 and B4109.

Brancroft, South Yorkshire

Alternative Name: Finningley

Long before Bramcote's Polish OTU reached Finningley, a piece of farmland barely a mile to the south acted as a Home Defence landing ground in World War One. Brancroft was requisitioned on December 13 1916 and stayed under No 33 Squadron control at the Armistice of November 1918.

Nothing is naturally obvious of the humble Great War airfield just west of a farm namesake. Brancroft originally lay east of the A614 but, when Finningley's main runway massively extended southwards to hold V-bombers in the 1950s, this main road had to be diverted so the old landing ground now exists on its west side. Not that anyone really knows...

111/SK665971. 4 miles NE of Bawtry, on W side of A614.

Bratton, Shropshire

This airfield about as little-known as Brancroft had nearly as quiet a wartime career, this time of the 1939-45 variety. The future could have been very different — but was not to be.

Typically Bratton emerged out of nowhere. Its inspiration is barely a locality but other nearby settlements like Eyton-on-the-Weald Moors or Longdon-upon-Tern were impossibly long-winded. Another place not far to the north called Sleap would in time prove useless too when a Shropshire airfield of the same name opened in 1943.

Acquired shortly into World War Two in September 1939, Bratton first became active in October 1940 for Shawbury-based trainers of No 11 SFTS but had to close not long after due to poor landing area drainage. It reopened early in the following year for the SFTS (known as No 11 (P) AFU from April 1942) to fly Oxfords at this RLG until January 1944. The latter part of this school's stay was notable for FAA Oxfords of No 758 Squadron at Hinstock also lodging while on instrument flying instructional duties.

No 11 (P) AFU moved out as the HQ shifted to Calveley in Cheshire but Masters of No 5 (P) AFU then took over Bratton on January 28 1944. These aircraft remained up to this unit's disbandment in June 1945.

No more flying resulted once Bratton closed on July 9 and only empty farmland marked this forgotten grass airfield for years, although a farm has used a handful of minor support buildings. Ten Blisters once stood here as well. Under normal circumstances the site would have quietly slipped from memory but a most stunning plan was announced in 1992 to construct the Telford Skypark. This completely new idea as regards Britain, though common in America, consisted of 65 houses with their own hangars or 'garages' to hold individual aircraft up to executive size. Developer Skypark (UK) Ltd also proposed to build a control tower and terminal, a country club and even a hardened runway, which long before Bratton would have considered a real luxury.

Wrekin District Council held a public enquiry in July 1993 as to whether this private airfield should become reality or not. Telford Skypark would have greatly aided business and created jobs. There was nevertheless heavy local opposition to the scheme. 'We've a quiet cul-de-sac and we want to keep it that way': another recorded comment became 'Why can't they go to Sleap?', ignorantly forgetting how this oft-mispronounced airfield is in severe danger of closing. Plain daft were 'elitist' and drug trafficking fears, while intended landscaping took care of environmental freaks and RAF Shawbury being happy to share precious airspace.

Skypark (UK) Ltd deserved every possible support from the air-minded in Britain. The residential flying community should have done well when finally passed but little Bratton failed to make the most incredible come-back by a British airfield ever seen as the plan was rejected towards the end of February 1994. Local government said yes, national government said no after taking into account a few minority objections, so you know who to blame. Considering the extremely hard work and benevolent intentions involved, certain people should be utterly ashamed of themselves for blocking jobs and social improvement.

127/SJ635149. NW of Telford, 2½ miles N of Wellington between A442 and B5063.

Braunstone, Leicestershire

Alternative Name: Leicester
One of Britain's ill-fated 1930s municipal airports ceremonially opened on July 13 1935. An airport should be for airliners but, while Crilly Airways flew various passenger routes before British Airways absorbed the company in 1936, Braunstone's main pre-war use was as a centre for recreational light aircraft.

The Leicestershire Aero Club had held its first flying meeting not far away at Desford in September 1929. During 1930 the city council bought the land which would become their airport and hoped Braunstone would be ready for the summer of 1934. Flying club staff moved into the new clubhouse in November but a drought preventing grass on the landing area from growing had already put paid to aircraft use for the time being. Not until March 27 1935 did the airfield receive an operating licence.

Gradually Braunstone built up to mainly cater for the needs of the Leicestershire Aero Club. Facilities split into two sections kept well apart, with the clubhouse and a hangar for pleasure fliers on the west side and two more hangars to the east at what passed for the 'airport'. A Chance Light illumination device sited above the clubhouse provided night flying capabilities and Customs status began in mid-1937; the landing area was also earmarked for massive extensions in virtually every direction save to the west but nothing ever materialised. Too ambitious planning had hindered yet another municipal airport.

World War Two stopped No 58 E&RFTS from forming and silenced Braunstone but only for a short while. On November 11 1939 it was requisitioned as an RLG for No 7 EFTS:

THE AIRFIELDS OF BRITAIN

Desford, home for this training unit, had effected revenge for losing the Leicestershire Aero Club. Now Braunstone became the junior partner as Tiger Moths subsequently landed, as did those of No 6 EFTS from Sywell in Northamptonshire mid-war. Two Blisters augmented the civil hangars during wartime.

Straying aircraft — known throughout the RAF as 'cuckoos' — always arrived unexpectedly at airfields away from their normal homes. Frequently they did so none too safely, as a Wellington showed on February 1 1945 when overshooting Braunstone. An American Noorduyn Norseman single-engined transport monoplane did the same on June 21. Time then ran out for this airfield as the military closed the site on July 9 and reduced it to C&M as at Bratton. Officialdom still completely failed to follow through to achieve an instant end result as aircraft kept on arriving at Braunstone — and kept on coming to grief. A Tiger Moth crashed into a tree on October 9, while a Wellington force-landed on February 1 1946 and a Martinet suffered a taxying accident on the 22nd.

Flying Training Command gave Braunstone to the Ministry of Works on March 27 1946 before military derequisitioning eventually resulted in the early autumn of 1948. Some people immediately cast their minds back to pre-war days as provisional negotiations began to lease the airfield to a local charter firm: even the Leicestershire Aero Club seemed as if it might return. But all these plans fell through, especially as the club decided to stay at Ratcliffe for another eighteen months until moving to Leicester East in March 1950. This World War Two transport training base possessed three hard runways instead of grass, and this reason deprived Braunstone of any fast disappearing chance of ever reopening.

The whole west side of Leicester has since changed out of all recognition by being heavily built-up. Last remembered for a failed proposal to host the 1962 Leicestershire Agricultural Show, Braunstone is now submerged under an industrial estate, with the M1 and a golf course close by. Local officialdom had effectively killed off the airport by extending Leicester's boundary in 1935 to make it one of only a handful in Britain to lie within the limits of a city. While a couple of old hangars hang on, Braunstone has long left the airfield scene, a creation of the well-meaning but exceedingly aeronautically stupid.

140/SK538042. 3½ miles W of city to N of A47, on E side of M1 by minor road to Ratby.

Brawdy, Dyfed

Quite publicised as an RAF airfield because of a humanitarian SAR role helping all and sundry in distress, Brawdy opened on February 1 1944. Away back in July 1942 it had been requisitioned for employment as a bomber OTU station, at a stage in World War Two when all sorts of policy decisions were being made which both later and today look odd.

Reality proved entirely different once Brawdy immediately accommodated No 517 Squadron from St David's on the former's opening. Until November 1945, when the squadron went south to Chivenor, No 517's Halifaxes carried out meteorological flights over the Atlantic Ocean. This might not have been the most exciting of jobs but nevertheless tremendously important and far from easy. Although encounters with the Luftwaffe proved rare, foul weather often prevailed – Brawdy never enjoyed a good climatic record, though to what extent is open to debate – and several Halifaxes were lost without trace. These four-engined types also had a secondary role as anti-submarine aircraft just in case they spotted a U-boat while out gauging future atmospheric conditions.

Two other units stayed at Brawdy for short periods in 1945. 'A' Flight of No 8 OTU came with PR Mosquitoes and Spitfires from Templeton on the other side of Haverfordwest, moving with the entire unit based there to Benson's durable aide Mount Farm on June 21. An AA co-operation detachment of No 595 Squadron also briefly used Brawdy during that year.

On November 1 1945, Brawdy and St David's – the satellite and parent airfields respectively – switched positions, a wise move in retrospect as St David's had turned out to be the more inferior of these two stations. An even bigger event occurred soon after on January 1 1946 as Brawdy changed allegiance to the FAA and became known in Navy parlance as HMS *Goldcrest II* or satellite to Dale. A new career beckoned but the FAA made little use of the place. Apart from No 811 Squadron notably flying torpedo-carrying Sea Mosquitoes over the winter of 1946/47, not much else happened and their home went down to C&M status in August 1947.

Dale soon closed altogether and its tender further up the south-west Wales coastline lay inactive and more or less totally unnoticed. Being in a very sparsely populated area where there existed only one or two houses and a church to the south-east contributed to Brawdy's initial post-war condition. But things began to gradually pick up again after the civil Airwork company took charge of a Fleet Requirements Unit on January 5 1950 which acted as a Heavy Twin Conversion Unit to train FAA pilots.

The FRU's Sea Mosquitoes moved to St David's in September 1951, returning later on in the 1950s, by which time Brawdy had become infinitely more settled with being referred to as HMS *Goldcrest* since September 4 1952. Several Hawker Sea Hawk squadrons proceeded to form here during this decade, and some examples of this uncomplicated jet fighter went into action in the 1956 Suez crisis while operating from Royal Navy aircraft carriers.

Brawdy saw major rebuilding carried out upon its features in the 1950s and 1960s. After slow runway extension and support facility work had lasted into the summer of 1944, an overall poor condition made the airfield unusable for two months once officially reopened in September 1952. Further altering, extending and resurfacing of the runways and perimeter track began in October 1961 to keep the levels of flying activity in this area extremely uneven.

Not until 1963/64 did a steady routine appear when Nos 738 and 759 Squadrons arrived to offer advanced instruction on Hunters as Brawdy became the FAA's main pilot training base. Fairey Gannet AEW variants with their distinctive radomes slung underneath the fuselage also moved in as No 849 Squadron transferred from Culdrose in Cornwall where it had stayed for many years. Both these machines and the Hunters occupied Brawdy for another six years until they all cleared out in 1970, the pilot training squadrons disbanding, and left their airfield to close in the following year as the Navy had planned since 1969.

Events were far more settled than they seemed at Brawdy because the base was returning to its original owners. No 849 Squadron's Gannets had gone to Lossiemouth II: that great Scottish airfield soon spent a good part of the early 1970s undergoing massive modifications while switching back from FAA to RAF control, and the same basically applied to this Welsh counterpart.

Once again mainly in RAF hands, though not fully as the US Navy established an oceanographic research centre, No 228 OCU appeared in September 1974 and remained as No 1 Tactical Weapons Unit from July 31 1978 with British Aerospace Hawk trainers. Their home became busier than ever before, so busy that a second TWU was forced to form at

Lossiemouth in 1978. A notable later event saw the last two Gloster Meteors in RAF service retiring in the autumn of 1982 after use as target tugs. An incredible 38 years had passed since No 616 Squadron introduced Britain's first jet fighter into use at Culmhead in south-west England. November 1982 also brought the end of service for the Hunter as an operational trainer.

No 1 TWU dominated daily proceedings but No 202 Squadron's Flight of Sea King helicopters however tended to make the headlines with all their SAR heroics. Brawdy-based aircrews saved too many lives to mention, especially distressed mariners, requiring on occasion to stage through Eire to extend the ranges of their machines out past the Irish Sea into the Atlantic. One other minor resident was the RAFGSA Preseli GC which formed in December 1979.

If Brawdy's gallant Halifax meteorological crews ever took the chance to see their old home again in the 1980s, they would hardly have recognised it. Massive runway extensions stretched both north and south and forced a number of minor roads to either close or be diverted. Many new support buildings stood on the airfield's west side; T2 and naval Pentad hangars with their sloping sidewalls lay in this area, including an unusual trio all linked together along their sides and straddling the old NE/SW runway.

Public viewing of the numerous hangars and flying activities here was alas none too easy because of necessary security precautions and Brawdy's somewhat raised position on the landscape. Such major changes still turned this place from being a relatively late starter in World War Two into one of Britain's most important rearward airfields. No 517 Squadron's Halifaxes had a secondary purpose and so too did Brawdy much later on in serving as a major employer in a depressed area. Local unemployment rates played a key role in letting No 1 TWU stay in the 1970s, while the RAF base spent £2.5 million per year on surrounding goods and services by 1990.

This airfield can be compared to Bramcote in being a highly favoured local asset. An odd position and lack of fame as today failed to stop 32,000 people visiting when Brawdy was thrown open one day in July 1954. Even airline companies have called in at times, namely Morton Air Services which mounted a service to London in the late 1950s and early 1960s plus Air Anglia in the 1970s.

Station Hawks deployed to Coningsby in eastern England as an interim measure to cover for aircraft based in the Middle East once the Gulf crisis flared up in August 1990. The thoughts of both training aircraft defending our country and flying instruction being reduced to meet this emergency were terrible enough for Britain as a whole, though west Wales faced far worse trouble with an announcement on January 24 1992 that training would cease. No 1 TWU disbanded at the end of August as No 2 TWU – now at Chivenor – assumed increased responsibilities and Brawdy closed to flying.

Politicians told their voters to have no fears as the SAR helicopter Flight would stay on. The last Hawk however still had to fly out, and would not do so until December 1992, when two months earlier No 202 Squadron received notice to get out by July 1 1994. Government figures trotted out reasons of saving money and the old story about Brawdy's weather record to justify their actions. Temporary Army occupation from August until 1996 as proposed could hardly be viewed as fair compensation for this loss.

Conserving a few more pounds in defence spending has become more important than creating far greater wealth for the local economy, saving many lives of people in trouble and keeping a vital airfield open. Me and now have replaced society and tomorrow without doubt. With the US Navy lodger also scheduled to close in September 1995, such current ideals must make the future for Brawdy nothing short of alarming.

157/SM854251. 7 miles E of St David's to N of A487.

Bray, Berkshire

Alternative Names: Bray Court, Maidenhead

Bray, sometimes known as Bray Court, remains one of the least known airfields to have ever existed on the fringes of Greater London – or anywhere in Britain for that matter. No Brawdy this, for no hangars stood here, not even any support facilities, just a couple of grass runways. No doubt this general state of affairs has helped to fuel such an air of anonymity.

The Bray we are concerned with – and not a clergyman in sight – can boast of being active as an airfield for a lot longer than many of its brethren, if only spasmodically. Civil light aircraft touched down in the area long before World War Two as an engineer named Donald Stevenson had opened his Maidenhead Aerodrome on June 8 1929. Civil aviation never had a chance to prosper as surrounding complaints about noise and safety levels resulted in a court order forcing the site to close during October.

315

By May 1930 the AA asked pilots not to land as hay was being laid down, although at times the organisation did subsequently list a landing ground available for use. At this particular period two separate 'airfields' existed, one (probably in OS sector SU91?80?) north-east of the village across the River Thames and the other a large field one mile south of Bray.

This second area, marked by a gravel pit, eventually proved its case as a true and completely recognised airfield. No 13 E&RFTS at White Waltham started using Bray as a crude supportive landing ground after the Tiger Moth school opened for business in November 1935. Come World War Two every E&RFTS became an EFTS and No 13 sent over 'D' Flight on July 4 1940, though the detachment soon withdrew on August 29.

Bray thereafter shuttled between owners, in and out of use, as the planners tried to satisfy everybody. A change of unit came after a break — but not the aircraft, for more Tiger Moths of No 18 EFTS at Fairoaks were around by February 1941. Intended as a temporary RLG for No 21 EFTS at Booker from June 1, Bray remained unready by the 30th as the grass required mowing and no facilities stood on hand. The school's 'C' Flight still began making circuits and bumps from then until starting flying training proper on July 5. Activities ceased on November 18 when Denham became available to No 21 EFTS as a permanent RLG.

There followed a slightly strange turn of events on December 15 when Bray once again made a temporary transfer, this time to the Ministry of Aircraft Production to assist the Air Transport Auxiliary at White Waltham. While returned to Flying Training Command control on April 30 1942 and registered as only an ELG, original RLG status gradually resumed and Bray kept open for Fairoaks' No 18 EFTS for the rest of World War Two. Its general closure date is not recorded but probably happened in 1945.

General cessation of flying is one matter, an absolute end another. More often than not in the story of Britain's airfields you find military gliders are the reason for clouding the issue, and those of No 3 (later 123) GS were responsible at Bray. This school formed in August 1942 and gained a few craft on October 4. Trainees had to cope with appalling conditions, not least having to use an old wash-house as their 'hangar': a leading expert on ATC history being told how ' . . . the RAF had better things to do' illustrates the disdain felt regarding cadet activities as a whole in World War Two. No 123 GS still survived and only went to White Waltham in the early months of 1948.

Today the scene is one of farmland, a waste disposal centre, riding stables and a couple of small artificial lakes on or edging the old landing area beside the village of Holyport. In one of these trivial and surely unintentional quirks often seen in airfield neighbourhoods, a nearby public road is called Coningsby Lane. A world of difference exists between that great Lincolnshire bomber-cum-fighter station and unknown Bray. Little has really changed over the years in this historical but poorly recorded area.

175/SU905777. 4½ miles W of Windsor to left of A308, on S side of M4.

Brayton, Cumbria

Alternative Name: Brayton Park

Rule one in airfield research: always expect the unexpected. An off-beat track near the Cumbrian town of Aspatria leads to a derelict watch office and a couple of huts which lie on this disused storage airfield. Brayton or Brayton Park operated under the control of No 12 MU at Kirkbride and several aircraft types could be seen: these included many Wellingtons plus even Fortresses and Halifaxes. The SLG's detached position worked to its advantage by ensuring the secrecy which every site of this kind required to operate successfully.

In use from May 29 1942, by December 1945 only two Vultee Vengeance single-engined monoplanes and a Wellington had to be cleared from the fields where once hundreds of machines stood. They left soon enough for their home almost in the middle of nowhere to close on January 31 1946; Maintenance Command records disregard unit files and put down this event as taking place a day later.

Brayton is again farmland but its sole Robin still stands across the former landing area from the bungalow-type watch office and other buildings. Few SLGs throughout Britain are in a similarly good state. West of here on the other side of the A596 road is a building which has an even stranger link than Bray and Coningsby Lane, particularly considering past aerial visitors. Is Wellington Farm pure coincidence – or not?

85/NY171429. 2¾ miles NE of Aspatria, turn left off B5299 at crossroads on to minor road, then first left.

317

Breighton, Humberside

The three runways at Breighton, one of Britain's less well-known World War Two heavy bomber bases, have suffered some punishment despite being virtually intact in length. Light aircraft do use this airfield in strength but have to land on grass. These same runways are interesting in that they all share the same intersection, not recommended in the past as colliding aircraft or an enemy munition reaching this point could have instantly put every runway out of action.

Away from the landing area, everything else seems incomplete. Look at the perimeter track, a few scattered support buildings in use for light industry, firing butts where machine-guns were tested and a Braithwaite water tower to the west. Breighton's control tower which used to stand on the south-west side has vanished, while only one T2 remains to the north-west out of two and a B1 originally built and serves as a storage facility. Altogether a grim picture? Believe it or not, the answer is no.

Selected for development in July 1940, Breighton opened in January 1942 and soon accommodated No 460 (RAAF) Squadron. The unit flew Wellingtons initially but converted to Halifaxes. As became standard practice in 1942 at Bomber Command stations, a Squadron Conversion Flight formed in August to enable this change-over from twin-engined to four-engined machines and quickly left for Holme-on-Spalding Moor. On its return to Breighton the following month, there had been another rapid change of aircraft type with the Lancaster's introduction. Yet more alterations – no wonder Con Flights proved unpopular – saw No 460 Squadron Con Flight join forces with No 103 Squadron's sub-unit from Elsham Wolds in Lincolnshire to become No 1656 HCU on October 10. It left for Lindholme after little more than a fortnight and at last freed No 460 Squadron from months of administrative mess.

The Australians carried on with raiding Germany until posted to their best known wartime British base of Binbrook on May 14 1943. Most squadron staff departed in spectacular style by taking a ride in Horsa gliders towed by Whitleys of No 297 Squadron at Thruxton in southern England. This operation – not all that uncommon – served two purposes by speeding up unit movements instead of having to rely upon slow MT vehicle convoys and also gave the airborne forces squadron involved some valuable glider towing practice.

After a brief period without any flying units, Breighton

welcomed Halifaxes of No 78 Squadron from Linton-on-Ouse on June 16. Earlier examples of the Handley Page type had been given a raw deal at this airfield but successive aircraft more than made up for lost time by attacking many enemy targets until their last bombing sorties in April 1945. No 78 Squadron soon accepted a new transportation job as crews changed to Dakotas and left for the Middle East in September. These aircraft nearly went to Broadwell in Oxfordshire instead but the proposed move on August 31 was cancelled terribly late, so late that an advance party had reached there on the 29th.

The end looked close for one more airfield. Being too dispersed did not help either. No 35 MU still wanted Breighton from November 15 1945 to provide some hope, though, and began a chapter of frequently changing ownership. This ground element passed it to Flying Training Command on June 1 1951 for Meteors of No 103 Flying Refresher School to start using their new RLG from July 3. The Full Sutton-based unit became known as No 207 Advanced Flying School on November 21 but retained Breighton, if hardly mentioning the airfield in unit records, right up to the school's closure on July 1 1954.

On the same day parenting changed to No 91 MU at Acaster Malbis as another alleged anachronism became inactive. Transferred again in this state on March 6 1957 to the control of famous Yorkshire fighter station Church Fenton, still the military refused to leave as examples of Britain's two major post-war missiles lay in readiness afterwards. No 240 Squadron maintained Thor IRBMs here between August 1 1959 and January 8 1963, despite a raid on the incomplete launching area by pacifist students from Hull in June 1959. Bloodhound SAMs of No 112 Squadron joined these nuclear missiles in November 1960 and lasted at Breighton until disbandment on March 31 1964.

As you must have observed by now, no British airfield can ever be written off. This one may have been severely disfigured but has somehow achieved the impossible by returning to flying. It appears that the first civilian aircraft to operate from Breighton was a Grumman agricultural biplane which arrived about 1971. A small company named Hornet Aviation later stayed for a number of years before the Real Aeroplane Company moved in at the end of the 1980s. This concern flies various interesting and often quite rare aircraft for pleasure, and has mixed refurbishing with totally new construction around a small enclave for the benefit of members. More aircraft are coming in all the time.

Such perseverance, yet how has local officialdom rewarded the airfield? By installing a landfill site on the east side – the ultimate humiliation, and what an absolute disgrace. But never fear, for our disused airfields will never surrender to rabble like this: morality will eventually win. Now Breighton is ramming that message down their throats with gusto.
105/SE721350. 5 miles NW of Howden, to W of B1228. Enter from SW side, N of Breighton village.

Brenzett, Kent

One of Britain's more unusual ALGs became one of the small number to be first brought into action during 1943. This was however largely out of necessity due to repair work at Kingsnorth, No 122 Squadron's Spitfires only being detached from September 14 until the 16th. Almost inevitably, Brenzett underwent reconstruction work into 1944, receiving five Blisters in addition to its two Sommerfeld Track runways.

June 6 1944 passed by and still no fighters could be seen unlike at most other ALG contemporaries. Two similar sites each a short distance away were in the same boat but, whereas Lydd II and New Romney II never saw aircraft at all during 1944, Brenzett sprang back into life on July 8-10 when Nos 129, 306 and 315 Squadrons appeared. Their Mustangs had arrived to primarily mount anti-*Diver* patrols and proved quite successful in eliminating V-1s.

After this Wing left for Andrews Field on October 10 1944 to assist operating range while attending to a new daylight heavy bomber escort role, the authorities were given permission on December 13 to derequisition Brenzett and it soon returned to farming. These same agricultural interests nine years later opposed an idea for a new airfield in the general Romney Marsh area but arguably lost when Lydd Airport opened not too far away to the south in 1954.

All but nothing remains of efficient short-term Brenzett as is normal with our ALGs. To the south-west is a small museum – of no connection, despite appearances – which contains assorted aeronautical paraphernalia such as the nose section of a Dakota.
189/TR015282. 6 miles NW of New Romney. Turn left off B2070 at Ivychurch, then first right, airfield on W side.

Bridleway Gate, Shropshire

As anonymous today is Bridleway Gate. Secured for use on

(above) The watch office at Cumbrian SLG Brayton. A converted crew room at Breighton for the Real Aeroplane Company *(below)*, a new control building alongside *(bottom left)* and a T2 not too far away *(bottom right)*.

Being a World War Two ALG, Brenzett *(above)* has naturally vanished for good.
Bridlington III *(below)* has also closed. Seen here in better times is a Cessna F.150M with apt registration of the Hull Aero Club. This machine can also be seen in the line-up of aircraft at Beverley II.

(above) Like many other heavily paved airfields, Brize Norton had to additionally rely upon metal runways in World War Two. An Armstrong Whitworth Albemarle having a glider tow-rope fixed stands on PSP during April 3/4 1944. *(IWM)*

(below) A de Havilland Tiger Moth sits inside a T2 as Airspeed Horsas float over 'Brize' the same month on the 15th. *(IWM)*

The north-south runway at Broadwell *(above)*. In great condition – for the moment.
(below) Demolition is all too noticeable on Broadwell's NW/SE runway, except for the section which has become a minor road. We must have these golf courses at all costs …

(above) Square Mesh Track metal runway fencing is common at Brockton.
(below) This track leads past a Robin hangar to the Shropshire SLG's landing area.

(above) The famous domed clubhouse and other artefacts at Brooklands are being reduced to an enclave with massive industrial redevelopment. Jobs – but at what cost?
(below) Much more exists of Bruntingthorpe but this B1 is about the only item which can be easily noticed.

Pass the air raid shelter *(above)* at Brunton, open (and close) an entrance gate, go along part of the perimeter track *(below)* ...

... and you will reach the offices of the Border Parachute Centre *(above)*.

After all these years, the entrance board to Bungay during its time as sub-site to No 53 MU remains, thanks to the Norfolk and Suffolk Aviation Museum at Flixton *(below)*.

Three not too encouraging views of Burn: a runway section *(top)*, an access track *(above middle)* and the since demolished gymnasium *(above)*.

But the Yorkshire bomber base is fighting back, with this neat clubhouse and adjacent hangar for the Burn Gliding Club *(above)*. *(below)* Burnaston, only months before this great and highly historic airfield fell victim to the Japanese.

(above) The naval three storey control tower at Burscough has slipped into disuse again after limited civil aviation use.
(below) A parachute store building at Bury St Edmunds.

Two ex-SLGs, two converted watch offices/guardrooms. The building at Blidworth *(above)* is heavily modified but chez Brinklow *(below)* is just as genuine.

September 21 1940 and active from October, this grass airfield acted like Bratton as an RLG for Oxfords of No 11 SFTS/(P) AFU based at Shawbury.

Bridleway Gate closed extremely early for a World War Two airfield, on January 10 1944, though only in a flying sense. Whether it could have gone on for much longer was anyhow questionable, partly because of its overall crudity and circuit overlap with Shawbury. The parent's replacement resident for No 11 (P) AFU also became the Central Navigation School: Wellingtons and mixed four-engined types would have found Bridleway Gate nearly impossible to operate from. While aircraft such as these flinched at the thought of actually landing, 'heavies' stationed at airborne forces training airfield Tilstock discovered the ex-RLG to be a useful practice DZ where to drop parachute-attached items. No 245 MU became another employer and stored fuel at the site between January 15 1944 and October 25 1945.

Inactive once the MU closed, No 2 MU controlled Bridleway Gate but abandoned it in mid-1946. No relics survive today apart from some minor foundations. Hangarage consisted of ten Blisters, a larger Bellman planned at the outset never being built.

Shropshire has gained something of a reputation for vaguely named airfields, and this is one of them, owing its title to a farm. The name which Shawbury persisted in describing as Bridlewaygate had to suffice as Preston Brockhurst helped out Shawbury by storing some aircraft in the hamlet's vicinity and might have created confusion. Besford (remember Braunstone's neighbour Desford?) undoubtedly would have, while Stanton upon Hine Heath rivalled Holme-on-Spalding Moor for size. And if there existed a Stanton, could there be somewhere called Harcourt to clash with Abingdon's satellite? By uncanny chance this was indeed the case. How airfields in Britain acquired their names never ceases to fascinate: this tale within a tale for once almost makes more interesting reading than Bridleway Gate's history!
126/SJ538262. 3 miles SE of Wem, N of junction between B5063 and A49.

Bridlington III, Humberside

Alternative Name: Grindale
Many familiar towns throughout Britain have possessed long airfield connections, yet connections that can only be

described as weak. English holiday resort Bridlington is an excellent example.

The town first held an airfield in the 1920s. RAF flying boats moored alongside a decade later, while the Bridlington GC secured a site far inland by August 1930 at Fordon. By all accounts a licensed landing ground was made available at this place deep in wold country for visiting powered aircraft, although it does not count for the purposes of this or other books. Neither does a temporary airfield much closer to Bridlington at East Leys Farm where Sir Alan Cobham held one of his National Aviation Days on July 6 1932. A flying club airfield further north near the village of Speeton did gain such prized status for a dozen or so years after World War Two.

Bridlington's most recent airfield, alternatively known as Grindale, kept up tradition by maintaining a low profile but still proved the most durable to date. It lay less than a mile north-west of East Leys Farm and opened fairly late on in 1969 for flying club use but really made news on becoming Britain's first custom-built sports parachuting centre two years later. The Bridlington and Hull Aero Clubs also operated from two available grass runways, as did the North of England Microlight School during the 1980s.

Legendary RAF fighter ace 'Ginger' Lacey became a familiar face here until his recent passing. Another sad event that was narrowly avoided occurred in September 1989 when a young woman fell 3,500 feet to the ground after her parachute failed to deploy and miraculously only suffered some broken bones. She had passed out in mid-air: unconsciousness made her body limp and so cushioned her landing.

Bridlington III could point to an excellent safety record but had closed before the year was out. Local sources have brought forward a host of unconfirmed and confused tales as to why the airfield shut down, ranging from financial problems to even possible suggestions of arson. One person went as far to claim that eventually visitors were allegedly confronted with a shotgun and told in no uncertain terms to clear off. Certainly site ownership had constantly changed to prevent any sense of continuity, despite the parachuting function surviving under the Sport Parachute Centre and subsequently British Skysports, and the last owner – the East Coast Aero Club – received terribly short notice to leave in the end.

In happier days visitors were welcome to go along a rough track leading to a clubhouse. This is all that Bridlington III

consisted of prior to becoming a field again. A councillor declared as the East Riding Flying Club officially opened at Speeton on August 14 1947 how an airfield was '... essential to every town, especially to a seaside resort' but the town can no longer finally claim to have a steady site to call its own. So where now, Bridlington?
(For Bridlington I, II and (seaplane) see Other British Airfields)
101/TA145718. 5½ miles NW of town. Turn left off A165 for Grindale, then first right before village.

Brighton (seaplane), East Sussex

We head south for another famous holiday spot with not exactly immediately acknowledged aviation links. Brighton however is extremely noteworthy, for the town became home to Britain's first entirely recognised marine airfield. If Lake Windermere introduced water-borne aircraft to this country and created a base for them too, the general public at large perceived the south coast site as leading the way ahead.

One of Brighton's landmarks is Volk's Electric Railway along the sea front. After the Daily Mail newspaper had sponsored Claude Grahame-White to give demonstration flights at the resort in July 1912 while promoting flying in Britain, a semi-permanent seaplane station opened in 1913. Magnus Volk's son Herman had built a canvas hangar measuring 52 by 40 feet just west of the railway's Paston Place stopping point which allowed aircraft to operate from there for part of this year and the following one. American pioneer aviator Glenn Curtiss delivered one of his own flying boats to Brighton in October 1913 for his representative in Britain, the White and Thompson company at Bognor. Crowds always gathered in large numbers to watch whenever any flying took place.

Dismantled by the end of 1913 and re-erected for the 1914 season, the home-made hangar vanished for good on the outbreak of World War One when requisitioned for military service. Few now remember Brighton's little place in airfield history but Herman Volk provided one further service to this area of Sussex by becoming a director of the Southern Aero Club at Shoreham and helped build its famous terminal

323

building during the 1930s.
(For Brighton (landplane) see Other British Airfields)
198/TQ323036. 1 mile E of town centre by Paston Place railway station (middle one of three serving Volk's Electric Railway).

Brize Norton, Oxfordshire

Many bombers have landed at Brize Norton but the majority of aircraft at this distinctively named airfield have turned out to be transports. These aircraft may not be quite as attractive to the layman, so what does he think of the new occupants, gigantic air-to-air refuelling tankers? The story of one of Britain's greatest ever and most influential airfields is far from dull.

Other roles have naturally functioned here right from day one. Training and aircraft storage became initial duties, with No 2 SFTS arriving from Digby on September 7 1937. No 6 MU formed in October 1938 and these two units were present at Brize Norton on the outbreak of war. Mixing instructional and storage elements as occasionally happened at RAF airfields before World War Two usually proved too awkward for all concerned because of their sheer dissimilarity but this became one case where everyone got by.

More trainers joined the Harvards and Oxfords already around at Brize Norton in June 1940. They belonged to No 15 SFTS, formerly of Middle Wallop, another future Battle of Britain superstar like Digby shaking off a second-line past. These latest arrivals without knowing it had made the worst possible unit movement as their new airfield was blown apart on August 16 in the most devastating small-scale enemy bombing raid seen on any British base during World War Two. Just two Ju 88s wiped out 46 aircraft (mostly Oxfords) and wrecked two hangars; perhaps the Luftwaffe should have been more gainfully employed attacking Fighter Command stations but no-one could deny the effectiveness of this blistering assault. Unit records however tried to resort to typical British phlegm by stating the day's events broadly in the style of 'August 16, attack by enemy aircraft, 46 aircraft destroyed': no emotion, simply pure mechanical statement.

Feelings were nevertheless running high on other parts of Brize Norton after that amazing raid. No 15 SFTS could not wait to get out as fast as possible and left for Kidlington on August 19. Although the Luftwaffe did return to harass Brize

Norton, it essentially only created nuisance value on future visits. A bombing raid by two E/As during the evening of October 8 saw one HE bomb explode in front of a hangar's doors, while a single Ju 88 injured several personnel on the 14th.

Both of Brize Norton's original residents subsequently stayed on without much further trouble. No 2 SFTS became a (P) AFU in March 1942 before disbanding in July, having lasted long enough to witness runway laying beginning on September 16 1941. Builders finished the NE/SW stretch on May 14 1942 as the base remained open but only partly serviceable. Only two runways ever arose, though planners did think about creating a third one.

The station now stood clear for the Heavy Glider Conversion Unit to move in. Having just formed at Shrewton, a minor Wiltshire site light years removed from Brize Norton in appearance, this special establishment enabled Army pilots to fly Airspeed Horsa assault gliders towed by Whitleys and would be vitally necessary for any future airborne invasions. Gliders such as the Horsa looked fairly strong but these engineless craft could be surprisingly frail on occasion, in fact positively frangible if on landing hitting a tree or some other obstruction. Paratroops travelling to the front later discovered how they could be in even greater danger than their pilot should this happen as the Horsa's fuselage would severely twist on impact: death by mutilation frequently followed. Military gliders also tended to be not too easy to fly, being rather cumbersome, but for all their shortcomings made a highly important contribution to the winning of World War Two.

When the HGCU flew up to Leicestershire and North Luffenham in March 1944, operational gliders plus their Albemarle tugs of Nos 296 and 297 Squadrons acted as replacements at Brize Norton. Training was realised as D-Day loomed ever closer, then Arnhem later on during September, although this second operation proved nowhere near as successful. Brize Norton fortunately did not become directly involved in the Netherlands fiasco – the Albemarles positioned themselves further forward at Manston – and so avoided getting embroiled in the deadly resupply missions which claimed many Allied aircraft.

Arnhem's disastrous effects still caused various changes here over the next few months. Nos 296 and 297 Squadrons soon went away again to Earl's Colne in Essex at the end of September to allow the HGCU back from North Luffenham. It was immediately renamed No 21 HGCU and instructed

THE AIRFIELDS OF BRITAIN: VOLUME 1

badly needed replacement glider pilots for Operation *Varsity* in March 1945. The unit had re-equipped with Halifaxes on departing once more in December.

Transports, airborne forces types and the ever-present No 6 MU continued to inhabit Brize Norton immediately after World War Two. Among peacetime visitors could be counted No 297 Squadron which returned in September 1946 to now fly Halifaxes instead of Albemarles up to August 1947 as the numbers of RAF airborne forces squadrons fell away alarmingly. No 6 MU had meanwhile held too many friendly aircraft designs to mention in wartime but for a fair period afterwards looked after a large number of retrieved Luftwaffe types. Jets, oddities and more mundane machines came along as by the autumn of 1947 Brize Norton accommodated everything from 39 Junkers Ju 52/3m transports to nine of the ultra-advanced but equally ultra-dangerous to the pilot Messerschmitt Me 163 Komet rocket-propelled fighters. Smaller totals of so many other aircraft could be spotted as well – including, of course, Ju 88s.

A general evacuation of RAF forces later occurred in 1950/51 after a few trainers had again used this airfield and No 6 MU disbanded in December 1951. The Americans had arrived several months earlier but their heavy bombers did not come as such until well into 1952 to enable enormous modifications to take place. Boeing B-47s began staying in shifts as Wings consisting of 45 aircraft rotated every so often as became standard USAF Strategic Air Command practice. These six-engined jets were considered highly exciting machines for their time, what with their swept wings and tail assembly, graceful looks and unheard-of munition and aviation fuel-carrying capacities. Yet the distances B-47s would be expected to fly if the Cold War broke out into an actual conflict saw Boeing KC-97 air-to-air refuelling tankers having to also position themselves on stand-by at Brize Norton.

Other USAF types came to the airfield in far lesser numbers during the 1950s and 1960s. The first examples seen in Britain of Boeing's KC-135 tanker, developed from the popular 707 civil airliner, and the fabled B-52 heavy bomber brought much welcome publicity to Brize Norton. Home pacifists perversely viewed events in a completely different light and subjected the base to the first CND march upon a British airfield – discounting disused Aldermaston – in May 1958. Nobody rightly took any real notice of these whingers and B-47s in the main kept on flying in and out up to the spring of 1965 when the RAF regained Brize Norton.

Within a year B-47s had passed out of front line USAF

service. Their evacuated home across the Atlantic now lay unavailable to aircraft but still had a long life ahead of it. Vast reconstruction started once again as more transports were due in as scheduled since June 1964. Brize Norton owned a longer main runway than Lyneham but part of the £5.6 million spent on improving this site as a whole had to go towards establishing a modern automatic blind landing system, for which the airfield closed during parts of 1966 and 1967.

British Aircraft Corporation VC-10s of No 10 Squadron plus Short Belfasts of No 53 Squadron – both rare types in the RAF – came from Fairford as work finished in 1967. Other uncommon types in quiet turboprop-engined Bristol Britannias of Nos 99 and 511 Squadrons arrived from Lyneham in June 1970 but these units disbanded in January 1976. Brize Norton's ten strong Belfast force also ceased to exist on September 14 of that year, an exceptionally bad blow as they comprised the RAF's entire special heavy lift element. The Belfast bore major significance on the airfield side of operations too as it became the world's first front line transport to possess a fully automatic landing system, hence why the main runway had to close back in 1966.

Since those uncertain days of the mid-1970s when our politicians seemed determined to wreck Britain's whole military transport fleet, Brize Norton has experienced a mixture of change and steadiness. No 1 Parachute Training School is still around and has been for many years; so are No 10 Squadron's VC-10s. Other examples of this attractive British-built jet type, disastrous sellers in civilian airline service which have excelled in RAF hands, and its Super VC-10 offspring appeared in 1984 but these were refuelling tankers belonging to No 101 Squadron. Fortunately No 115 Squadron's radar calibration Hawker Siddeley Andovers had gone to Benson a year earlier after seven years at Brize Norton, for No 216 Squadron soon brought huge Lockheed TriStar militarised airliners for use as either tankers or transports.

Brize Norton has required to undergo even more structural modifications to let in these monstrous aircraft, though this superbly equipped base should now have a secure future. Until recently, that was unbelievably not always the case, especially in the late 1970s as numbers of empty service houses and married quarters dramatically increased. Civil authorities even went as far as considering taking over control from the RAF in order to create an airport. Airliners did land as Concorde testing switched from Fairford but local residents complained about noise levels.

THE AIRFIELDS OF BRITAIN: VOLUME 1

Still some doubt regarding the future lingered as many servicemen injured during the Falklands conflict landed in 1982. Nine years later brought terrible fears that many thousands of dead and wounded would come back from the Gulf War, especially if the Iraqis used their biological or chemical arsenals, but such was the remarkable success of this campaign casualties resulted in being the faintest of trickles. Like so many other airfields in this country, Brize Norton also played its part by sending out every available aircraft to Saudi Arabia and later Turkey, tankers being constantly on hand to refuel Coalition forces aircraft. The RAF had already wisely learned from the Falklands episode to acquire more air-to-air refuelling types.

Having helped win three wars and stave off a potential fourth one, Brize Norton richly deserves its present place as our joint top military transport airfield along with Lyneham. In World War Two Lyneham became associated with more specialised duties, while this place had to take on more run of the mill airborne forces flying, but now Lyneham does the mundane work. This is not to say it is ordinary, and this rival is no humdrum place either. To say that Brize Norton has affected the surrounding area is extreme understatement.

Proof of such an incalculable social effect can be seen in two ways. First is the local public road network, caused by post-war extensions to Brize Norton's landing area. The B4020 which originally ran north-south between Burford and the village of Clanford had to be diverted to the west; other minor roads closed as well. But yet more remarkable has become the rise of Carterton, a town for service personnel and their families which has expanded from nothing at all in earlier days. It contrasts with the airfield's Expansion Period features, somehow ignored by a newspaper during a meeting involving British and Russian political leaders here in December 1987 which described Brize Norton as '. . . a spartan place of barbed wire and old buildings, reminiscent of a German stalag.' Did the journalist who wrote this piece live on another planet?

Here is a big, big airfield, one strangely difficult to view. Brize Norton always was a large station, both runways stretching far beyond its initial perimeter track. Since World War Two the main runway has crept relentlessly further westwards – and on to another OS map for good measure. A total of 42 hangars – consisting of five Cs, two Ds, six Lamellas, five T2s, two B1s, three Bellmans, ten Robins, two Super Robins and seven Blisters – stood in wartime. Many of the larger examples remain in usually good states but have all been overshadowed by a cantilever hangar on the north-east side. This one-off building was constructed in the 1960s at a cost of £1.8 million, handed over to the RAF in August 1967, and is one of Britain's largest hangars at over 1,000 feet in length.

Many people will quote Brize Norton's name when asked to mention any British airfield. It shares with Biggin Hill the distinction of being a quaintly-titled, rambling and almost eccentric site once savagely bombed by the Luftwaffe but a phenomenally effective and successful site all the same. All perfectly good reasons why both of them keep healthily active today.

163-164/SP293059. SW of Witney, to W of A4095. Passable long-range views from various surrounding roads.

Broadford, Highland

Alternative Name: Skye

Skye is one British island which has never really come to grips with holding airfields. Perhaps a reputation as a misty and hilly place has had a lot to do with it. World War Two curtailed Glen Brittle's career, and Skeabost hardly so much as scratched the surface post-war. The most recent site to try and beat this hoodoo has been Broadford.

This tarmac airstrip was one of the several Army-constructed Operation Military Aid to the Community (OPMAC) airfields created in Scotland. Built over two years, plans to open Broadford in July 1971 had to be delayed as Royal Engineers personnel did not finish the runway until September. A formal opening took place in April 1972 but licensing problems briefly held up the new Loganair route to Skye.

The famous Scottish airline operated a passenger service to Abbotsinch before stopping in March 1988. Lack of business was responsible, and this action might be enough to kill off the raon adhair (Gaelic for airstrip). Only a few light aircraft and an occasional Loganair air ambulance machine now land at this unlicensed site where many visionaries once expected a functional terminal building to be fairly busy. Will the new road bridge to Skye be the last straw for its third airfield? Let us hope not.

32/NG694247. 4 miles E of village.

Broadwell, Oxfordshire

In the enormous shadow of Brize Norton lies a far more basic disused airfield which enjoyed much greater operational activity during World War Two. Broadwell became one of RAF Transport Command's many bases created in the months preceding D-Day.

Gradually opened up from November 15 1943, after only being approved for requisition as a proposed American-operated airfield the previous May, Nos 512 and 575 Squadrons later transferred from Hendon in February 1944 once Flying Control facilities began on January 31. For nearly the next four months exercises on friendly soil interspersed with probing *Nickelling* sorties over France. Both duties proved of great value as the days of preparation ended and the squadrons' Dakotas dropped paratroops in the early hours of D-Day, Horsa gliders soon following. Apart from a slight hitch when a No 575 Squadron machine crashed on the main runway during take-off and briefly held things up, this momentous day ran like clockwork.

Nos 512 and 575 Squadrons before long became able to land at crude French airstrips. The securing of foreign territory enabled Broadwell's aircraft to ferry out wounded troops after bringing in supplies in quantities that even the Gulf War would have been hard pressed to beat had Iraq resorted to more cynical tactics. Tens of thousands of soldiers would be grateful to Broadwell, Blakehill Farm and Down Ampney on touching down at these reception centres prior to entering a large military hospital at Wroughton.

The Dakotas based at this airfield resorted to towing gliders over to Europe in September at the start of the Arnhem campaign. Heavy enemy flak and poor weather did not ensure the same amount of success as in June. When airborne forces personnel on the ground started suffering severe reversals, Nos 512 and 575 Squadrons had to be detached to Belgium. No 512 further cemented links with that country from March 1945 while still officially stationed at Broadwell but finally went with its companion to Yorkshire instead in August.

After Nos 10 and 77 Squadrons spent short periods at Broadwell before going overseas, No 271 Squadron arrived from Odiham on October 5 1945 and continued the Dakota tradition here. It flew routes mainly to southern France and Italy until being redesignated as No 77 Squadron on December 1 1946. A former visitor returned of sorts but this second stay was equally brief and the unit moved to Manston the same month, resulting in Broadwell running down.

Once personnel had so packed this airfield that 400 bicycles needed to be delivered on May 1 1944 to reduce strain on MT vehicles: by early 1947 little more than the Transport Command School of Plumbing remained before Broadwell closed on March 31. Whether it could have continued indefinitely was anyhow debatable because of circuit overlap with Brize Norton; that airfield's runway extensions for American use would only have made the situation worse. Add Broadwell's two since demolished T2s – showing American links – and austerity period support facilities versus Brize Norton's 42 hangars and Expansion Period buildings and there was a terribly uneven contest as to which airfield would win. No 6 MU at Brize Norton did consider in November 1947 moving Horsa gliders held in storage at Market Harborough in Leicestershire but derequisitioning at Broadwell had already gone too far and the two T2s earmarked for dismantling.

Unlike Brize Norton, there are absolutely no problems as regards viewing this piece of history today as part of Broadwell's NW/SE runway is a minor road. Parts of all three runways and the perimeter track have been sacrificed for farming, though a Cessna 172N lightplane (*G-BHUJ*) has still operated from the old landing area. Elsewhere the control tower, water tower and some minor support buildings survive in reasonable states and have witnessed the Carterton Model Flying Club do its best to maintain aviation connections.

But will Broadwell remain in any shape or form whatsoever now golf courses and an hotel are to appear on part of the airfield? Runway removal slowly progressed during 1992/93, and the signs look far from good if one considers what has happened to Snitterfield in Warwickshire. Are there not enough golf courses in Britain anyway for yuppies? But then yuppies tend to turn a blind eye to places of extreme historical and social value . . .

163/SP249065. W of Brize Norton, 4½ miles S of Burford. Turn left off A361 for Kencot.

Brockton, Shropshire

The watch office, a Robin hangar and some other airfield relics such as metal runway sections now acting as fencing remain at this area of farmland and former SLG supplementary storage airfield named after a hamlet.

Brockton opened on June 30 1941 following an inspection on February 7, No 9 MU at Cosford holding many fighter aircraft types here, especially — and not surprisingly — Spitfires.

History has scantily treated this site whose entrance is marked by a public house on the edge of Kemberton village. Among the few items of information we are told is how staff built their own guard dog compound out of wood and steel mesh in August 1942. No 9 MU does not even bother mentioning when Brockton closed but most SLGs did so in 1945 and this one became no different, shutting on December 21. A passing thought is that remember to visit the correct Brockton, for Shropshire contains four such places.
127/SJ730038. 4 miles SW of Shifnal, turn first left off B4379, then first right to Kemberton.

Brockworth, Gloucestershire

Alternative Name: Hucclecote
And now to the first of three great aircraft production centres in fairly quick succession ... We begin on a sad note as anyone connected with the famous old Gloster company's main factory airfield would today find little other than increasingly depressing memories. One consolation is that a good number of people possess jobs by courtesy of an industrial estate.

Brockworth, originally known as Hucclecote for many years, first saw use in 1915 as a testing area for machines produced by H.H. Martyn and Company Ltd of Cheltenham, which became the Gloucestershire Aircraft Company on June 5 1917. Airco bombers, Bristol F.2b fighters and other designs were produced either whole or in partial component form during World War One. Eventually this good work resulted in an AAP appearing to better co-ordinate operations at the Hucclecote end, though the facility still stood unfinished in November 1918. Shortly before then five Belfast hangars had reached virtual completion but 21 standard storage sheds each measuring 200 by 60 feet were only half-finished. No 90 Squadron became Hucclecote's solitary RAF visitor in the conflict, one of these abortive 1918 Great War units that arrived in July and promptly disbanded after only a short while.

Effectively redundant during 1919/20, Gloucestershire still held on as a renter to make a fresh start in a difficult post-war climate for aircraft manufacturers and their airfields. Confidence was high enough for the firm to take over design rights when the Nieuport and General Aircraft Company at Cricklewood close to London closed in November 1920. For a few years the dice ran favourably as the successful Grebe RAF biplane fighter emerged, then later the Gamecock.

Another good omen was Hucclecote being bought for £15,000 by the new Gloster Aircraft Company Ltd later on in the 1920s. This nominal alteration had resulted on November 11 1926 through nothing more than sheer simplification as foreigners – particularly the Japanese – found Gloucestershire awkward to pronounce, and the firm had departed from its Sunningend factory within four years. So ended the greater inconvenience of taking aircraft by vehicle from works to airfield but Gloster already had worse matters to worry about as the company struggled into the 1930s with a procession of unsuccessful prototypes. For a period early in that decade non-aeronautical production had to mix with such unlikely activities as tennis just to keep the hangars occupied and maintain business. Fortunes improved beyond all recognition once Hawkers took over Gloster in May 1934, though, and the latter's own popular Gauntlet and Gladiator biplane fighters made everything even rosier.

World War Two bombing fatalities failed to stop Hucclecote/Brockworth from building Hawker products by the veritable barrow-load. While the site produced a total of 200 Henley AA co-operation machines, and later on some Armstrong Whitworth Albemarles under licence, far more notable proved construction of 2,750 Hurricanes and the entire 3,300 production batch of Typhoon fighter-bombers. Work-force staff found themselves able to settle into a steady routine with this last type as the Typhoon hardly ever changed in appearance, save slightly cutting down its rear fuselage as time progressed in order to install a 'bubble' cockpit canopy. What everyone knew as the 'Tiffybomber' gave marvellous service, not least following D-Day when running riot against German tanks, but was shamefully treated as World War Two ended by being rushed out of RAF use while Brockworth continued to build Typhoons up to November 1945.

A hard runway laid during the war helped in the long run to bring about this factory airfield's downfall. Although reasons of secrecy also played their part, a restricted landing area and surrounding houses forced Britain's first jet-engined aircraft – the Gloster E.28/39 – away to Cranwell from where it historically took off in May 1941. Well over 3,000

THE AIRFIELDS OF BRITAIN: VOLUME 1

Meteors and a number of bulky Javelin fighters emerged from Brockworth in peacetime but the landing area problem became progressively worse. Ever greater amounts of flight-testing therefore had to be carried out south-west of Gloucester at Moreton Valence, which Gloster had used since 1943. Yet Brockworth held out until closing as an airfield only in April 1960.

Gloster's factory survived a time longer in its accepted form, having to pitifully produce lamp-posts at the end to provide work. Precise ties ended on April 6 1964 but the industrial estate which has risen from this demise does not suffer from employment difficulties. An offshoot named Gloster-Saro Ltd also continued for many years to make highly worthwhile items such as aircraft refuellers, fire-fighting vehicles and insulation material. Here stood the main factory, not being affected like Beaumaris when Cammell Laird bought the Welsh site in 1967. Finally the Gloster-Saro title quietly disappeared in the late 1980s.

Numerous former factory installations still give their all, including the five Belfasts, and that somewhat controversial runway remains as well. Photography in the estate is not allowed but inside an office building is an excellent blown-up wall photograph showing Brockworth or Hucclecote – whatever one wants to call the airfield – in all earlier glory days. At last we have found some grateful people, a lesson which the yuppies at Broadwell would do well taking notice of. 162/SO883160. SE of Gloucester, on E side of M5 by A417.

Brooklands, Surrey

Alternative Name: Weybridge
While this and other books deal with Britain's airfields, one cannot forget the other Brooklands, that equally legendary motor racing circuit. The track with high banking to increase car speeds is dreadfully neglected, being hopelessly impassable in places. There is no airfield either but enthusiasts of both sects are slowly reversing the situation and restoring Brooklands to its wonderful glorious past.

Brooklands' airfield lay inside the circuit, opened on July 6 1907 and named in honour of an area on the other side of a railway line to the north. A.V. Roe brought along his first aircraft – which initially failed to fly – during the summer as the owners offered £2,500 for the first flight around their course. But Roe received no help from the clerk of course at

THE AIRFIELDS OF BRITAIN

Brooklands, a Pole and complete aviation philistine called Rodakowski, who hindered him constantly. Matters became so bad that life for the would-be flyer turned into a ritual of furtive operations at night and unorthodox alterations to fencing: such was the harshness of early British airfield days. The gallant Alliott Verdon finally achieved his dreams of sorts by 'hopping' at Brooklands on June 8 1908 but eventually left for Lea Marshes across London.

Certain other motor racing officials than Rodakowski thankfully saw the endless potential aircraft offered as Brooklands gained recognition as a true airfield by the end of 1909. About a dozen sheds had cropped up by then, Claude Grahame-White's great rival Louis Paulhan being a key figure, as were Helmuth Martin and George Handasyde of the Martinsyde company on becoming permanent tenants. Their place of work evolved into being better known as the Blue Bird Restaurant and later the airfield Officers' Mess in World War One until destroyed with some adjoining hangars in a fire on March 28 1917.

Other firms and individuals moved in as organised flying met with far less resistance after 1910 – even A.V. Roe, who showed how he had mastered the problems of flight when his world-beating Avro 504 first flew at the airfield in July 1913. Vickers appeared too in 1910 and with another young aircraft company by the name of Bristol saw further future profit in establishing important flying schools. Of course, for every winner there was a loser, many individuals failing to make their mark in this embryonic aviation world or doing well to simply survive on shoe-string finances. Airfields have never exactly been cheap items to run.

Brooklands turned into an exceptionally exciting place in these opening years with this mixture of flying and motor racing. Easily the outstanding highlight before World War One occurred on September 25 1913 when the pioneer of aerobatics, Frenchman Celéstin-Adolphe Pégoud, performed a dazzling display to spectators below and set the trend for future British stunt pilots to follow. Much less reported was how Noel Pemberton Billing learned to fly here in typically eccentric circumstances during 1912. The 'inventor' of Britain's airfields had bet with Frederick Handley Page as to who would not only pass instruction and receive a pilot's certificate first but do so within 24 hours: 'P-B' won the day and gratefully accepted the sum of £500.

None of our original airfield band came without their quirks either. At Brooklands the racecourse banking notably caused unusual wind effects affecting aircraft. And then there

335

THE AIRFIELDS OF BRITAIN: VOLUME 1

lay the unforgettably awful sewage farm nearby which Vickers in time disposed of by building over it as the company expanded. You may recall the running joke about aircraft crashing into a place of this nature featured during the popular 1965 film *Those Magnificent Men In Their Flying Machines*. This comedic scene was actually for once based upon fact.

Although best remembered as a factory airfield, other duties occupied Brooklands in the course of World War One. A proposed RNAS base pre-war, a few operational RFC squadrons present during fighting came in the early days. No 1 Squadron received aircraft towards the end of 1914 but No 8, formed on January 1 1915, was of more note as the first RFC squadron to open with only one aircraft type, namely the Royal Aircraft Factory BE2c. Nos 9 and 10 Squadrons arrived that year, while wireless instruction continued until a school left for Hursley Park in Hampshire in October 1917, though Brooklands now mainly became concerned with aircraft production and some pilot training. Vickers, Sopwith and Martinsyde all operated factories which turned out several thousand machines during World War One. In turn No 10 AAP stayed available to process these finished products prior to military acceptance.

The period after November 1918 proved terribly tough for Brooklands like every other home airfield. No end to this malaise seemed in sight despite the last vestiges of military connections having been cast off by April 1920. Familiar faces disappeared for good such as Martinsyde, desperately unfortunate as its F.4 fighter – a tremendous design and better than the Sopwith Snipe – arrived too late for World War One. T.O.M. Sopwith meanwhile decided to wind up his company and pay shareholders in full.

Even so, hope still lingered on the horizon. Vickers conversely kept going and indeed expanded once withdrawing from troublesome supportive production/flight-testing site Joyce Green and also bringing over the design office from Knightsbridge in 1919. Hawkers used Brooklands too to recondition Snipe fighters for RAF service after noted test pilot Harry Hawker had helped resuscitate the old Sopwith concern during 1920, as did Messrs Brand and Van Ryneveld when they left on their pioneering flight to South Africa on February 4 of the same year.

The motor racing circuit gradually got back into its stride once reopened in April 1920 but unfortunately became involved in an aerial tragedy on April 13 1922. Sir Ross Smith, one of two brothers who had made the first flight to Australia,

THE AIRFIELDS OF BRITAIN

crashed into the notorious banking and was killed. On a happier note the Brooklands Aero Club and a civil flying training school both arose in future years and duly thrived. Private fliers were greatly assisted by the first aero filling station – complete with newfangled petrol pumps – appearing here in 1927 specially for their use. All in all, this airfield turned into quite a fashionable place in the late 1920s and 1930s.

Brooklands' high social standing allowed it to head scores of other licensed British airfields which wanted in 1936 to introduce landing fees for privately owned aircraft. One sum would cover the cost of both pilot and machine, a lesser price being proposed for anyone else aboard. Landing charges are today an accepted part of airfield life but varied wildly in the 1930s: by 1937 Braunstone charged nothing, while to touch down at Yeadon in Yorkshire cost 4s. 6d. The whole idea was then a total mess and Brooklands wisely quickly withdrew, soon having to cope with a fire on October 24 1936 which destroyed two hangars and several aircraft. Not until 1938 did aerodrome fees really become standardised.

By now aircraft production at Brooklands had returned to much more like its old self. Vickers busily built cumbersome but reliable biplane bomber-transports and heavy night bombers such as the Virginia, and Hawkers the extremely successful Hart family of fast multi-purpose military types.

Two of Britain's greatest and best loved service designs later made their first flights at Brooklands in the mid-1930s. The immortal Hawker Hurricane fighter took to the air on November 6 1935, followed by the prototype Vickers Wellington medium bomber on June 15 1936. They differed in terms of construction, particularly Vickers' product which possessed a special geodetic fuselage layout whereby spars crossed one another and allowed the Wellington to absorb more than usual battle damage.

Over 2,500 Wellingtons were constructed at Brooklands, a fact the Luftwaffe could hardly have failed to notice. Now that Hawkers and the airfield's other aviation operators had gone, not to mention motor racing once more ceasing, Vickers was left alone to face up to the worst Germany could throw at this ultra-important target.

The onslaught started on July 24 1940 when a Ju 88 faked a landing and bombed some buildings. Another raid resulted on September 2 but these two incidents looked trivial in comparison to events two days later. At a stage of concerted Luftwaffe attacks upon factory airfields during the Battle of Britain, twenty Messerschmitt Bf 110 fighter-bombers raced across Brooklands and made a frighteningly successful job of heavily damaging various buildings, despite No 253 Squadron's Hurricanes from Kenley destroying six E/As. A total of 86 staff died, hundreds more being injured, while Wellington production stopped for several days: years afterwards in the mid-1950s one MP alleged that a German pilot involved had been taught to fly at the airfield pre-war. The Luftwaffe however failed to press home this advantage as more bombing raids on September 6, 9, 11 and 21 brought only inaccurate or ineffective results.

Other Vickers types built during and after World War Two included the troubled Warwick broad Wellington look-alike ASR/anti-submarine patrol aircraft plus the Viking, Viscount and VC-10/Super VC-10 airliners. These civilian types especially no longer had to compete with racing cars or light aircraft concerns as Vickers-Armstrongs Ltd (known as such since Vickers merged with Armstrong Whitworth in 1928, though everyone still only used the first name) bought Brooklands outright for £330,000 in January 1946. The sale was completed in July, despite the Royal Automobile Club strongly protesting and much gnashing and wailing in the mass media. These two parties should not have complained as plenty of disused or redundant military airfields such as Silverstone soon sorted out this lack of motor sport venues. The Brooklands Flying Club additionally merged post-war with the Southern Aero Club at Shoreham.

In 1960 the resident company became part of the British Aircraft Corporation: half a century and an era had passed since Vickers' arrival. But time was beginning to run out for Brooklands in the same way that 1960 marked the passing of Brockworth. In a flying sense, this airfield had not been renowned for size and even a runway built in the late 1940s finally proved too short for jets. Suburbia and an adjacent railway line did nothing to help, the River Wey further adding to complications by flowing straight through the site to dictate its landing area. These reasons therefore made Brooklands close to general flying in February 1970 once those attractive VC-10/Super VC-10 airliners were built and tested. British Aerospace remained to produce Concorde sections among other items but the Weybridge site was reduced to holding helicopters at the end.

An aircraft factory should always have an airfield close at hand. BAe did not here, and so the statement in July 1986 that production would cease at Brooklands perhaps came as little surprise. Although the factory had completely closed by early 1988, a year after a business park idea received planning approval, many people recognised the huge historical worth of this place in the aviation world and decided to establish a museum. The airfield's clubhouse has become a listed building in connection with this scheme. Already a Wellington once owned by No 20 OTU at Lossiemouth II that crashed into Loch Ness during 1940 and was fished out of the water over 40 years later is being fittingly restored.

One could argue how jobs are arising at the expense of history as the museum fits into a small corner. Among still obvious odd features are the access bridge over the River Wey across which factory employees used to push aircraft and an ostensible garden shed erected in 1911 as a flight booking office, still in daily use by the 1930s and reasonably claiming to be the world's first ever control tower. Brooklands would not be complete without cars either but conservation developments are occurring in this area too. This whole two-pronged preservation project is coming along nicely and offers exciting times ahead for an exciting arena of days past. 187/TQ066620. 5 miles NE of Woking by A245.

Broomfield, Essex

Alternative Name: Chelmsford
We temporarily break off from the realms of aircraft manufacture to mention two airfields called Broomfield. They existed in different counties but shared a second similarity in being World War One landing grounds later used for civil flying.

The RNAS selected a number of landing grounds shortly into World War One once given official clearance to aerially defend Britain. One site became an area north of Chelmsford known as Broomfield, provisionally earmarked for airfield use in October 1914 and listed by December. From May 1915 a few Caudron G.III biplanes flew anti-Zeppelin patrols with the intention of dropping bombs on these airships from above. As aircraft could not even reach an adequate altitude, pilots could offer no more than futile token resistance, and one Caudron suffered the grave misfortune of exploding on landing. Sorties continued up to February 1916.

The RFC succeeded its rival organisation in the air defence role with Broomfield being taken up as a night landing ground but lying not quite ready for use, according to official records for February 22. No 37 (HD) Squadron later controlled the airfield from October and stayed in position at the Armistice.

Relinquishment followed during peacetime in August 1919. But the old Great War landing ground had made a fair enough mark to unexpectedly reopen as a civil airfield in January 1932. Aviation Transport, Sales and Service Ltd set up shop, a typical jack of all trades joy-riding, transportation and instructional concern which managed the Chelmsford and District Flying Club. A large wooden barn fitted up in the south-east corner served as a combined hangar/workshop/offices, the airfield being licensed and officially opened on May 18.

Such a promising start deserved to be rewarded, yet disaster struck in Barrhead fashion on September 18 when a fire destroyed the hangar, clubhouse plus an Avro 504 and a much less familiar Vickers Type 142 Vivid biplane. So devastating proved the conflagration that Broomfield never again returned to flying. Consideration as an early satellite airfield for RAF fighters in the event of war brought brief hope in 1936 but the authorities understood the land would be sold for building development and interest quickly waned.

Maybe a carefully planned ploy to stop aircraft from returning had come into operation, for Broomfield is today still only a field. Nothing has lasted as architectural testimony but its L-shaped landing area continues to be fairly easy to trace out.

167/TL694112. 3½ miles N of Chelmsford, ¾ mile NW of village off A130.

Broomfield, Kent

Alternative Name: Herne Bay
Authorised for requisition on October 23 1916, No 50 (HD) Squadron had use of the Kentish Broomfield landing ground by the year's end. It seems that no confusion ever resulted between this piece of farmland and its Essex opposite number during World War One, although World War Two planners would never have given two separate airfields the same name. Mercifully nobody ever officially adopted the local name for Montrose either.

This Broomfield was relinquished in June 1919 but made a come-back in September as a licensed List D2 'Avro 504K' site — only the joy-riding aircraft based here turned out to be

an ex-military Airco DH6. One J. F. Stallard, who traded as Stallard Airways, employed the airfield while a licence lasted in 1919, from September to November 1920, then again from May 1921 to about April 1922. And in the same year that Broomfield/Chelmsford rose from the ashes, only to be burnt to a cinder, Sir Alan Cobham used this Kent field for a National Aviation Day flying display in 1932. No aircraft have since appeared: indeed you find it odd to believe while looking on how any aircraft ever landed.
179/TR204669. 2½ miles SE of Herne Bay on S side of A299.

Brough, Humberside

Solid land, good approaches, a fine weather record and development potential: four excellent factors in choosing an airfield. But the airfield always associated with the famous Blackburn aircraft company arose because of an altogether more eccentric reason...

An aide of Robert Blackburn discovered Brough in 1915. Mark Swann thought that its position looked right, yet the close proximity of two public houses seem to have influenced his final decision. His actions made the ill-judged military selections of some World War One airfields, especially landing grounds, almost look reasonable in comparison. A top Blackburn official even had the guts much later on to admit that adverse sea mist and tidal conditions were not uncommon in the general area. Did the demon drink therefore make Swann's judgement cloudy? Clearly the same could not have been said of his beer...

Water of the non-alcoholic variety gave real value for money as Brough became classed as a land and marine airfield for many years. No 2 (Northern) Marine Acceptance Depot took charge of newly-produced RNAS/RAF seaborne machines, and a slipway from where they were launched can still be seen. Construction of seventeen seaplane sheds began but these buildings remained only half-complete towards the Armistice and not scheduled to be finished until March 1919. A flight shed also built during the Great War and known as the North Sea hangar became one of Britain's best known individual structures.

On dry land, production orders for types such as Blackburn's pioneering Kangaroo maritime patrol bomber flowed for a while too until evaporating after World War One ended. For years Brough rolled out small numbers of civil and

341

military aircraft and tiny quantities of flying boats. Not until the 1930s did Blackburn create a noticeably successful new product, the Shark torpedo bomber/reconnaissance FAA biplane which could use either a wheeled or float undercarriage.

Necessary required diversification had already occurred with formation of a flying school in 1924 run by Captain Norman Blackburn, Robert's brother; seaplane instruction gave Brough a unique edge at this period. The school eventually became known as No 4 E&RFTS and No 4 EFTS in World War Two. Blackburn B-2 biplanes flew around Brough and an RLG at Bellasize until retired in February 1942 and passed to ATC units for cadet ground instruction. Magisters and Tiger Moths – which the B-2 closely resembled – appeared soon into World War Two but Brough's uncertain weather savagely reduced the Tiger population in early 1940 when a strong gale destroyed about 30 aircraft. A temporary policy of placing aircraft outside around the airfield and tying them down with pickets had gone disastrously wrong, so back went every survivor into the North Sea hangar.

A few months later everyone waited to see if the Luftwaffe would come and cause far more trouble than the weather. Air and ground personnel prepared for every possible emergency. Fortunately, unlike Brooklands and some other British factory airfields, the enemy decided to mostly ignore Brough. A couple of light bombing raids did come into being in the summer of 1940 but, apart from one crater on the landing area and telephone communications being temporarily cut, there was no hassle.

Brough became very busy during World War Two. Along with Blackburn producing its own aircraft and the training programme, several hundred Fairey Barracuda monoplane torpedo bombers emerged and thousands of American-built naval aircraft modified to suit British FAA standards. It is ironic how Blackburn's own aircraft never really made the grade within the FAA or RAF. One thinks of the mediocre Skua fighter/dive bomber or resemblant Roc, an abysmal gun turret-equipped fighter with a pathetic climb rate unable to even reach a top speed of 200 miles per hour. At least these two types gave good second-line service, something the twin-engined Botha anti-submarine design could not claim. Many people had placed much faith in this aircraft but the Botha was generally poor and became one of the most hated types ever held in the RAF's inventory.

Let us immediately state at this point that no-one considered

THE AIRFIELDS OF BRITAIN

Blackburn a sub-standard company; after all, previous products such as the Kangaroo and Shark proved great successes, while the firm made a terrific contribution to the war effort at other airfields around Britain, notably Abbotsinch and Sherburn in Elmet. Nor did Brough show itself to be a bad airfield either – despite boozy beginnings. But World War Two continued to jinx Blackburn at an indigenous level by putting the boot into its next great white hope after the Botha. Although first flown in 1942, the single-engined Firebrand torpedo-fighter only entered FAA service after World War Two had finished. Serviceability problems followed painfully slow development, the rocket projectile had by then largely ousted the torpedo for anti-shipping duties, and the 200 plus examples built were primarily relegated to non-operational naval squadrons like all the Skuas and Rocs before them.

Another disappointment for Brough became the Tiger Moth school's departure on February 1 1948 after No 4 EFTS had altered to serve as a Reserve Flying School in March 1947. Blackburn however kept going and joined forces with General Aircraft Ltd, makers of the Horsa assault glider, during 1948/49. Here brought one success story anyhow as Brough turned out the Beverley heavy transport which inhabited Abingdon in strength. Hawker Siddeley then absorbed Blackburn in the 1960s, the name ceasing to exist altogether in April 1965. Brough's single hard runway was far too short for jets such as the effective Buccaneer strike bomber, so flying of this type had to transfer to Holme-on-Spalding Moor.

Since the 1960s partial component manufacture of military and civil aircraft – among them the Harrier fighter and Hawk trainer – has dominated rather than actual flying but light aircraft arriving on company business have become common visitors at this airfield where British Aerospace now resides. The area is restricted, photography being prohibited, and only a footpath to the south alongside the River Humber provides any real view of the clubhouse, hangars and other facilities. Seven Blisters added to Brough's civil tally in World War Two.

As Holme-on-Spalding Moor closed in 1983, it should be interesting to see what happens in the future. Could Brough follow the same sorry path as Brooklands, Brockworth and their similarly vulnerable landing areas? Lately the site has gone down to a C&M basis; although flying club aircraft are still active, the Hull Aero Club moved to Beverley II in 1991. Brough has nevertheless not proved a bad airfield either and

343

more than held its own despite enduring such potentially severe problems since 1916. And all because someone liked a drink!
106/SE948256. 12 miles W of Hull.

Broxbourne, Essex

Alternative Names: Nazeing, Tatsford

Broxbourne should not have survived long in theory because of extremely small dimensions. Fine facilities made up for this shortcoming, and the airfield would be active for over twenty years.

Two brothers named Frogley brought Broxbourne into being. Stimulating life for them meant getting a kick not out of alcohol but motor cycle racing instead. While this activity had nothing to do with airfield selection as at Brough, the Frogleys spotted the additional possibilities of flying once their father allowed his land to be used as an airfield from 1930. Their Herts and Essex Aero Club duly fully started operations in Easter 1931, Broxbourne formally opening on June 14.

By the early 1930s five small wooden hangars stood on the south side of this site squeezed in between roads, rivers and housing, with its irregularly shaped landing area later noticeably extended to the north-east; further hangars built included lock-up examples. Another prominent occupant at the increasingly popular airfield became the London General Omnibus Company Flying Club for the use of busmen, 1,200 of them joining up as members to buy three aircraft out of subscriptions at 6d. a week. At one early stage this concern looked as if it might not last but developed to be known as the London Transport (Central Buses) Sports Association Flying Club by 1939. Vital Civil Air Guard training could be seen as well during 1938/39.

In the mid-1930s RAF Fighter Command's alter ego Air Defence of Great Britain viewed Broxbourne as a possible satellite base. ADGB considered it unsuitable but, although never designated a service station in World War Two, the authorities regarded Broxbourne as one ex-civil airfield far too good to close down for the duration of hostilities. Like other small 1930s recreational grass sites such as Barton and Horsey Toll near Peterborough to name but two, this place earned a more than decent keep by maintaining and repairing

THE AIRFIELDS OF BRITAIN

lighter types of military aircraft, a little appreciated job nowadays which then gave bigger factory airfields more valuable time to tackle duties needed on larger machines. The Luftwaffe even bombed Broxbourne during the Battle of Britain.

World War Two may have closed dozens of other British civil airfields with lightning speed in September 1939 but their return to peaceful pursuits proved a long drawn out process. While Broxbourne had luckily stayed open, Herts and Essex Aero Club personnel could only reopen the clubhouse on May 19 1946 once their home had been derequisitioned; the busmens' club restarted post-war at Fairoaks. A sad event resulted the following year when the Frogleys' father died.

Over the past seven years since 1939 aircraft had advanced beyond all recognition both in design and performance: more than ever before they highlighted the airfield's one shortcoming. Acreage – or rather lack of it – had to tell in the end, and the Herts and Essex Aero Club cleared out to head for North Weald's former satellite Stapleford Tawney on April 1 1954. As that airfield resumed activity after being disused for several years, so Broxbourne shut down and lay deserted by the summer.

Roger Frogley, the Chief Flying Instructor and more influential of the two brothers, might have carried on but gravel extraction and resultant artificial lakes have now radically changed the landscape of this area. Even the small town of Broxbourne – situated in Hertfordshire, unlike its nearby airfield – has been swamped by adjacent Hoddesdon. An electricity power line crosses the savaged site in what amounts to a form of overkill. On the south side past a car park at a distinctively acute bend where people once could look over a hedge and see activities close at hand later existed a furniture manufacturer but the more modern company premises were recently vacated.

Fate tried very hard to hasten Broxbourne's demise long before the diggers moved in when a fire on the night of June 22/23 1947 wiped out two hangars; eight Tiger Moths, three Percival Proctors and a pre-war Comper Swift biplane housed inside were also overwhelmed. A replacement hangar could not stop private fliers from deciding to evacuate a few years later but their airfield had given its all for far longer than expected with great success – and won a war into the bargain. Nobody could have asked for more.

166/TL384064. 3 miles SE of Hoddesdon, ½ mile W of Lower Nazeing by B194.

Bruntingthorpe, Leicestershire

One airfield which has never needed to worry about size is Bruntingthorpe. Being big not only counts but can provide an airfield with a long life.

RAF personnel arrived to start opening up the base on October 20 1942 after requisition in August 1941. 'A' Flight of No 29 OTU came from North Luffenham on November 6 to use Bruntingthorpe for flying and nothing else as the parent seemed likely to become unserviceable in wet weather, while another satellite at Woolfox Lodge was receiving repairs. The detachment returned to these two places on January 30 1943, February 1 becoming an extremely eventful day as this airfield gained administrative independence and fell victim to a violent gale which destroyed or damaged some support buildings at a cost of £870. Britain's unfathomable weather could strike its airfields at any time as Brough no doubt wearily acknowledged, and further strong winds here in Leicestershire on May 10 caused more material damage.

No 29 OTU had not forgotten about Bruntingthorpe by soon appearing as one between May 24 and June 1 once the airfield's runways resumed full flying fitness. Its transfer was necessary as North Luffenham had to close to undergo runway laying and other major reconstruction duties. Wellingtons stayed as before for bomber aircrew training at their former satellite, equipped with four T2s and a B1 for hangarage, joined on formation from June 5 by obsolescent affiliation fighters of No 1683 Bomber Defence Training Flight until they moved to Market Harborough on February 3 1944. A hangar fire on June 14 claimed two Wellingtons prior to the OTU being lessened to three-quarter aircraft strength status in October. Jet engine inventor Frank Whittle's own company Power Jets (Research and Development) Ltd also employed Bruntingthorpe in 1945 as the firm's factory at Whetstone existed only about seven miles to the north.

As quickly as World War Two ended Britain as usual decided to make life difficult for all-conquering airfields and progressive companies. Power Jets (R&D) Ltd was finally forced to carry on jet engine testing elsewhere at Bitteswell – once satellite to Bruntingthorpe from June 1943 to October 1944 – after the Flight Section departed on June 3 1946. The main runway and hangars at the former parent station had not received proper amounts of maintenance, allowing no

THE AIRFIELDS OF BRITAIN

blame to be attached to the firm for leaving.

Already officialdom thinking how it knew best in every sphere had bogged down Power Jets (R&D) Ltd, a factor which led to Whittle resigning from the company. As for Bruntingthorpe, immediate peace brought only confusion. No 11 ACHU held temporarily redundant flying personnel from June 7 1945 as No 29 OTU finished business in the same month. Bruntingthorpe kept busy at a surely still awkward period, No 1333 Transport Support Conversion Unit at Leicester East performing some training movements late that year, but the removal of night flying facilities in December hardly helped anyone. German PoWs cleaned up the airfield in April 1946, though obviously not enough to make Power Jets (R&D) Ltd stay much longer.

No 11 ACHU disbanded on October 21 1946 for C&M on a self-accounting level to begin; Church Lawford subsequently acted as parent before Wellesbourne Mountford took over. Now that an idea put forward over the summer and autumn of 1946 for a multi-engined training unit to form either here or at North Luffenham — with Bitteswell as satellite — had been dropped, over a decade had to pass by until Bruntingthorpe could declare itself an airfield again.

Only just having survived complete abandonment during 1956, the USAF swept in shortly into 1957 to replace previous RAF supervision. This was the second time American forces had arrived after momentarily staying in 1953/54, long enough to still push out civilian gliders of the Leicestershire GC. Now they proceeded to turn this area into something quite different by discarding the normal wartime three runway layout to make the main stretch much longer. Intentions to hold far larger bombers than Wellingtons meant that two minor roads on the east side had to be closed and diverted.

The considerable time, effort and money expended was justified when part of the 10th Tactical Reconnaissance Wing flew in during August 1959. Its appearance became a barely indirect consequence of France's decision to throw out the USAF on political grounds: finding refuge at Alconbury, the Wing immediately deployed a squadron each to Bruntingthorpe and Chelveston on the Bedfordshire/Northamptonshire border. Douglas RB-66s maybe could not match any jet heavy bomber but these aircraft longer, far heavier and infinitely faster than the dear old 'Wimpey' made a big enough impact in their own right. Noise complaints showed how both the world in general and attitudes in particular had changed since 1945.

THE AIRFIELDS OF BRITAIN: VOLUME 1

Heightened world tension ought to have ensured the lives of British USAF stations in the early 1960s. But for some of them the opposite happened, with uncertainty ruling from day to day. One minute Bruntingthorpe was running down: by October 1961 this process ostensibly received a temporary suspension. Clueless planners then scheduled the airfield to close in March 1962, when in reality this second phase of activity with the 10th TRW lasted for another six months. Even there the story had not totally ended as Bruntingthorpe's ultra-long runway proved useful enough after the last few Americans moved out in 1963 for the site to remain as an ELG until 1970.

The primary post-war asset of this airfield is still in place, as is the perimeter track, for Bruntingthorpe has since become a vehicular proving ground. Hinting in a way at this activity are the trees which heavily screen the original World War Two landing area. In 1968 Chrysler (UK) Ltd had initiated talks with the Ministry of Defence, begun more extensive negotiations two years later and purchased the airfield in 1972. The scheme nearly never got off the ground at all as it looked at one stage as if Chrysler might leave Britain altogether.

Peugeot followed Chrysler before private engineering contractor C. Walton Ltd bought Bruntingthorpe in August 1983. Cars are still tested or stored, the recent recession seeing many new vehicles than usual waiting in readiness, but best of all is how aviation has returned. While microlights have been built and transatlantic air freight airport plans not happened, working aircraft museum hopes are now being met. In 1993 a Lightning jet fighter landed on January 21 for preservation, and the last Avro Vulcan bomber in RAF service was sold to David Walton of his family business' British Aviation Heritage Collection on March 18. Five days later this machine which the authorities scandalously refused to maintain made an emotional flight from Waddington over other former bases to Bruntingthorpe to be housed in a specially built hangar. Elsewhere a Hawker Hunter stands on display.

Poor surrounding views fail to stop a B1, one T2 and a rare Butler constructed during American occupation from being fairly evident. An industrial estate lies on the east side which C. Walton Ltd bought in 1989. Once more work combines with pleasure at an airfield without any problems.

Today this remarkably big place and main runway of over 10,000 feet can still put many entirely active military and civil airfields to shame. Had Bruntingthorpe existed in East Anglia, Lincolnshire or Yorkshire, we could be talking about a major star but perhaps its time will come again. Absolutely anything is possible with our airfields.

140/SP598890. 6 miles NE of Lutterworth, follow minor roads to Walton and then Bruntingthorpe villages.

Brunton, Northumberland

Another so-called disused airfield in good overall condition with three runways and perimeter track all still complete, Brunton lasted throughout its short military life as satellite to Milfield. So closely linked were both sites that requisitioning of the land on which they would stand occurred simultaneously in March 1941. Before then aviation use in the surrounding area had remained restricted to RAF airship dispersal at Chathill late on in World War One and a 1930s private airstrip at Doxford run by one W. L. Runciman.

No 59 OTU arrived at Milfield and Brunton from Longtown in August 1942 as these two new airfields fully opened. Parent and satellite both had to continue accommodating their builders for a time, in Brunton's case three of four Blisters incomplete by September 21. Hurricanes and latterly Typhoons were eventually left alone to train fighter-bomber pilots until the OTU disbanded on January 26 1944. Following limited use for the rest of 1944 by an instant but more specialised successor, the Fighter Leaders School, No 56 OTU became the last wartime flying unit at Brunton. Back came more ordinary instruction as Typhoon and Tempest pilots completed their training here from January 1945. A Canadian airman died in a most tragic accident on April 9 when his aircraft swung on take-off and hit a windsock mast.

Ever since August 1942, Brunton had loyally stuck by Milfield's side and given perfectly satisfactory service. But as the Typhoon in particular soon discovered, spectacular victory in Europe would be rewarded with a spectacularly swift scything of operational RAF squadrons flying the type. Post-war cut-backs instantly began biting hard too as No 56 OTU staff held a meeting on May 18 1945 to discuss when best to relinquish their supporting airfield. The dastardly deed was accomplished three days later, despite the OTU staying at Milfield up to February 1946.

By that time Brunton had already become inactive before being closed and transferred to the War Office on November 22 1945 – the exact same day, incidentally, as Eshott's satellite Boulmer. Reversion to farming land would be but a matter of time and proved so by June 1946.

Any outsider will be hard pressed to find Brunton hamlet these days, let alone this old airfield: it must rate as one of the most secluded in Britain. The visitor's eye will be attracted by a distinctive clump of trees in the intersection between all three runways than the woeful lack of airfield relics. Among many buildings removed are the quartet of Blisters and the control tower which was demolished in 1974. The runways and perimeter track however are in excellent states, their survival attributed to builders being generous with tarmac after a decision made in July 1943 to entirely resurface the runways and re-lay their intersections.

Learner drivers have used Brunton since at least the early 1960s, and go-karts from 1971, but most noteworthy of all are parachutists. The first descent took place on May 5 1975 and continued until 1980; operations resumed under the Border Parachute Centre in February 1983. Popular Flying Association light aircraft activity is also a feature every August. The late Duke of Northumberland – on whose land Brunton stood – wanted the airfield to be retained and, although the electrification of a nearby railway line has affected aviation uses, further developments may include a flying school.

Unlicensed or not, this airfield has lasted longer as one than its more illustrious but today excavation-riddled overlord in a similarly respective way to Boulmer and Acklington. Sweet justice for horrendously curt treatment at the end of World War Two.

75/NU204257. N of Alnwick, 4 miles NW of Embleton to W of B1340.

Buckminster, Lincolnshire

A two-way split airfield like Broxbourne, with the airfield being in Lincolnshire but village namesake in Leicestershire, grassy Buckminster belonged to an earlier airfield era. Personnel having to initially occupy some stables showed how primitive early sites could be.

Approved for development on July 23 1916, 'B' Flight of No 38 Squadron flew Home Defence sorties from October until May 1918. Royal Aircraft Factory FE2b biplanes replaced BE2 variants in July 1917 but no success greeted the Flight Station despite constant hard effort as Germany's Zeppelin fleet mounted fewer and fewer raids; those that did result rarely reached this far north as World War One grew longer.

One mysterious night in April 1918 saw what may – or may not – have become the sole occasion in which a home-based pilot received wounds while in combat with a Zeppelin. Lieutenant C. H. Noble-Campbell certainly got into difficulty but friendly defences may have hit him. Even the airship's subsequent declaration how it never opened fire (since disputed) only brings more confusion to this baffling story, one of Britain's more obscure airfield mysteries.

Soon after this excitement the FE2bs were painted black and took off for France via Dover/Guston Road on May 29 to act as night bombers. Such an idea had started as the unit accepted these aircraft, suitable pilots and observers then being trained, but No 38 Squadron left behind personnel at Buckminster to help reform No 90 Squadron on August 14 as a Home Defence unit. Avro 504K fighters were given a peaceful time as Germany had completely refrained from bombing Britain and No 90 Squadron later disbanded on June 13 1919, that fateful day for various HD elements throughout this country.

Buckminster closed down the following October. During World War One it had developed from being a Flight Station equipped with one 130 by 80 feet hangar into an HQ site and proposed Aircraft Acceptance Park. Seven 180 by 100 feet aeroplane sheds intended for this last purpose were rated as 95 per cent complete and due for completion on September 15 1918. Yet much else around the airfield, where most support buildings stood across the minor road connecting Buckminster village and the A1, had to be finished and the AAP as a result never became entirely operational. A few foundations are all that remain in the fields.

One could say how World War One ended too quickly for Buckminster. Nobody really remembers it now but the name lives on of sorts, thanks to a gliding club based two miles north-west at Saltby, a disused World War Two RAF/USAAF airfield.

130/SK894235. Take A1 SW of Grantham and go W of Colsterworth. Site 1 mile NE of village.

Bucknall, Lincolnshire

Alternative Name: Horncastle
Also in Lincolnshire but under different ownership, No 33 (HD) Squadron had use of Bucknall. A now disused minor

road formed part of the western boundary of this night landing ground requisitioned on September 5 1916. Active from a month on and still around at the Armistice, Bucknall has gone back to being farmland. World War Two RAF Bomber Command station Bardney arose just two miles west of here over twenty years later.

121/TF170705. 8½ miles W of Horncastle. Turn right off B1190 at Bucknall village, then left at junction.

Bude, Cornwall

The extreme north-eastern part of Cornwall's northern coastline has always proved a barren area for airfields. Yes, World War Two AA co-operation base Cleave lasted right through the conflict but is about the only exception.

Earlier airfield experience had been confined to May-December 1918 when Bude served as a non-rigid airship sub-station for Mullion. This out of town site disappeared for ever amid the trees and undulating fields after World War One finished as usual with these simple dispersal places. A private civil airstrip is known to have later existed very close to Bude by the early 1930s on a big field used as a showground, while Sir Alan Cobham provided a display to the south at Whalesborough on August 22 1932. Nevertheless, these minor details and Cleave apart, flying in this area has since stayed strictly awol.

190/SS238013. 6 miles SE of town, turn left off A39 for Langford Barton.

Bungay, Suffolk

Alternative Name: Flixton

Did Buckminster help found Saltby? Or Bucknall Bardney? We will never know but a combination of dusty official files and long memories may have influenced the choices of these newer sites. The same could be said about Earsham, a World War One HD landing ground which perhaps subtly assisted in the creation of a World War Two USAAF heavy bomber station less than two miles to the south-east.

Liberators operated in great numbers at Bungay, approved for requisition in April 1941 and opened in October 1942. But first visitors became rare British-based USAAF North

THE AIRFIELDS OF BRITAIN

American B-25s belonging to the 428th Bomb Squadron of the 310th BG (Medium). This Group, mainly positioned at Hardwick a few miles away, was intended to see action in North Africa and left in November. Bungay lay nowhere near ready with only one T2 hangar under construction by the 1st for a start but still held B-24s of the 93rd BG's 329th BS between December and March 1943.

Slow workmanship in finishing off the airfield ensured that a complete Bomb Group would not arrive until November 1943 when the 446th brought in a full complement of four squadrons. Its B-24s soon fitted in at now fully-functioning Bungay while helping sustain the American daylight bombing offensive upon Germany. Their airfield also made an impression locally – even if civilians decided to name it after the nearest village instead. Flixton was probably never selected as Suffolk contains two places known as such; a third Flixton for the record stands south of Manchester's 1930s airport Barton.

The 446th BG's last remaining personnel left Bungay on July 5 1945. Already No 53 MU had arrived in June: now days later the airfield moved to RAF Maintenance Command but changed again in September to Royal Navy control and be known as HMS *Europa II*. The Royal Naval Patrol Service's Central Depot at Lowestoft needed an extra centre to handle large numbers of sailors being demobilised, and Bungay volunteered until the parent non-airfield closed down in mid-1946.

More ground duties continued into the 1950s. No 53 MU had stayed on during the short naval phase before No 94 MU took charge over the period between November 1947 and January 1948. The original unit at old airship station Pulham later absorbed its replacement in December 1949/January 1950, though Bungay still stored ammunition and other weaponry in what really amounted to little change. Eventually No 53 MU closed this sub-site on June 1 1956 but parented the inactive airfield afterwards while Duncan Sandys shamefully declared it surplus to RAF requirements in the hit lists of May 1957.

Reinstatement of farming has since seen the flattening of most buildings: two absent T2s showed this was an American airfield. Light aircraft, microlight and parachuting activities ended in the 1980s when the three runways and perimeter track were ripped up to leave behind stretches of pathetic access roads. Bungay once looked comparable to Brunton in recent architectural appearance and flying levels but the former place's future is nothing like as rosy. Now only the

Norfolk and Suffolk Aviation Museum in Flixton village remembers the Americans and their airfield to any degree. How do farmers and landowners get away with destroying such important history?

156/TM324808. 4½ miles SW of town off B1062, 1 mile E of Flixton. Another good view from minor road on E side.

Burford, Oxfordshire

If an airfield fails to be tangible, then try to find records. And if little or no material survives? This is why the 'Other British Airfields' chapter comes after this main section. Grouped together are a few sites of minor importance, though most other ones badly lack information. Burford falls into the borderline case with airfields such as Billesley near Birmingham or Bridlington II (Speeton). Technically this example should be held back but is included to give you a brief taster of the historical nightmares to come.

Burford started off as an ELG for Little Rissington in the summer of 1940. Few airfields of any type can beat ELGs for documental evasiveness, and about all we are told is how No 8 MU at the parent brought it into use as a dispersal field on November 21. Six Handley Page Hampdens and two Vickers Wellingtons landed to be stored, so Burford must have seemed reasonable enough at the time. When unofficial Satellite Landing Ground use ended is not quoted as one might expect but probably did so fairly quickly.

The next notes of substance we can find date from 1946. A company named Anglo Continental Air Services operated two (later three) Auster monoplanes from June of that year for charter and pleasure flying. While these aircraft used the same open fields on Upton Down and one local resident tends to recall field walls being removed, which begs the question how Hampdens and Wellingtons safely flew in, the trail again goes cold. The Gloucester Flying Club at Staverton between that town and Cheltenham hiring an Auster as Anglo Continental Air Services opened for business is the only known piece of work to have come the firm's way. Farmer and owner C. J. Silvertop therefore gave up near the end of 1950, although the same source earlier mentioned has suggested he may have retained a residual interest in aviation matters as late as 1953.

Airfields are almost chock-a-block in and around the Cotswold Hills area. Everyone has heard of Little Rissington,

and the older generations will always pass some curious tales about other places down the line, many folk in Windrush village still remembering the occasion one day in 1940 when an Anson trainer collided with an attacking He 111 bomber near their local airfield. Burford, three miles directly east, meanwhile remains blurred – unless you know better.
163/SP233119. 1½ miles W of town, immediately S of junction of A40 and A433 roads.

Burgh Castle, Norfolk

Go north-east from Bungay and you will reach another of Great Yarmouth's World War One RNAS/RAF sub-stations which opened in the autumn of 1915 as a night landing ground. Flight Lieutenant Egbert Cadbury proceeded to assist in destroying Zeppelin LZ.21 on the night of November 27/28 1916.

Sopwith Camels of No 273 Squadron's Nos 485 and 486 Flights latterly used Burgh Castle to escort patrolling anti-submarine aircraft belonging to this unit once formed in August 1918. Movements of RAF elements previously under RNAS control are not always clearly defined but by September No 273 Squadron recognised this 'satellite' as its HQ base and not Great Yarmouth. Being the closest assistant and upgraded during 1918 to take some weight off the parent airfield, three 66 by 42 feet aeroplane sheds also meant Burgh Castle was better equipped than other contemporaries: Covehithe only possessed two examples of this design, while Bacton and Holt had to make do with one each.

Depriving No 273 Squadron of aircraft in mid-March 1919 gave a manifest sign of what lay in store. A cadre moved to Great Yarmouth in June and left Burgh Castle up for military relinquishment but flying did not end there for the airfield became licensed for Avro 504K use in August, and an ex-RAF Armstrong Whitworth FK8 biplane did fly about this area in the summer. Fields now give virtually nothing away of this largely rectangular-shaped site.
134/TG485049. 5 miles SW of Great Yarmouth, S of village.

Burn, North Yorkshire

Even though they continue to be easily evident on OS maps, vast quantities of our disused airfields are not officially recognised for their glorious service. The less noted World War Two heavy bomber base of Burn ranks as just one example. And all the more shocking as here a particularly courageous Victoria Cross was won ...

Burn could be described as Yorkshire's Bungay because of slow development. Liberators came along too: RAF ones of No 1653 CU, a short-lived unit thrown out of Polebrook in Northamptonshire to allow in the Americans which disbanded in October 1942 after only having appeared in June. Times were hard, and again the Bungay factor could be seen with incomplete hangarage by September 21. But Burn managed to formally open in November, 'only' 26 months after initial land requisition as opposed to the 31 months its Suffolk counterpart needed to move into top gear, for No 431 (RCAF) Squadron to form. Wellingtons took part in some bombing operations until moved on in July 1943 to Tholthorpe, another Yorkshire airfield with a lengthy building history.

So few visiting aircraft and still fewer resident personnel forced Bomber Command to place Burn on C&M from November 10. Machines decided to stay again on December 31 when Nos 658 and 659 Squadrons moved in, despite their latest temporary home retaining an official inactive air up to January 14 1944. These Auster units saw in the New Year but mainly stayed away on exercises as No 658 spent over a fortnight in January at Doncaster IV, returning as No 659 left for good to York.

Any airfield always appreciates flying activity, however unlikely, yet in early 1944 Burn really wanted bombers and not little artillery spotter aircraft. No 578 Squadron's Halifaxes therefore obliged by coming on February 6 from Snaith, where the unit had formed a month previously. This odd arrangement of one heavy bomber and one AOP squadron lasted a while longer until No 658 Squadron moved on March 14 to Wittering's close aide Collyweston.

Later the same month on the night of March 30/31 occurred an event which ought – note that word ought – to have set up Burn for life. The Nuremberg raid has gone down in history as RAF Bomber Command's most disastrous single operation during World War Two. A planned assault upon the city centre ran headlong into problems as questionable flying tactics, a clear moonlit night and pathfinding aircraft not only giving incorrect meteorological information but arriving over three-quarters of an hour behind schedule enabled German night fighters and flak to massacre the attacking force. Of 795 participating 'heavies', 95 were shot down, thirteen more lost in crashes at home and dozens damaged.

One member of the second category became a Halifax based at Burn with Pilot Officer Cyril Barton in charge. Although his aircraft suffered extremely severe damage en route when Luftwaffe night fighters attacked, Barton bombed the target and somehow flew back across the North Sea but crashed in north-east England. A posthumous VC followed for his heroism in about the only good point to emerge from this night of unmitigated failure. Coupled with another very heavy loss rate of 73 aircraft during a raid on Berlin a few nights earlier on March 24/25, Nuremberg forced Bomber Command to temporarily shy away from long-range targets and concentrate upon pounding France in readiness for D-Day.

No 578 Squadron carried out many other attacks with far greater success up to March 1945. Burn rapidly faded into the wings after its main occupant prematurely disbanded on April 15 before war in Europe had come to a stop. Jammed in between a main road and a railway line, with the landing area, dispersals, bomb dump and support facilities utilising every available space, this airfield could never have developed postwar into another Bruntingthorpe but a lack of esteem was obvious. Imagine officialdom telling a major airfield to go on C&M from March 19 1945 before a squadron has even wound up, and inactivity in force as everyone else celebrated victory during May.

No thanks could be expected in peacetime either. Bomber Command gave Burn to Transport Command until taking it back on June 1 for No 10 ACHU to stay up to October. After reverting to C&M on a self-accounting basis from December 31, the War Office acquired the site on January 15 1946 to store tanks and other military transport types for some time. Lindholme served as parent from May 23.

The situation changed from no thanks to tanks and then thanks but no thanks when a plan to dump power station powdered coal residue on Burn was rejected. World War One airship production centre Barlow became the unlucky victim instead as the local authorities received a much more acceptable proposal for alternative use. Many British airfields have seen unusual 'lodgers' in their time, especially Burn and those AOP Austers, and now sailplanes are present. The Doncaster GC had conferred with everyone from the Central Electricity Generating Board to nearby villagers over a prolonged period in an attempt to replace Doncaster IV, and opened as the Burn GC in 1983 on moving. Members afterwards belatedly wondered why they had not called their organisation the Selby GC to make it more readily recognisable.

The name Burn may have survived but, apart from the three runways and perimeter track, not much else. Agriculture has overpowered two T2s, a B1 and most other buildings to leave only the water tower and a few small supportive facilities. A new clubhouse and hangarage for the Burn GC have countered such vandalism.

Glider pilots did not casually toss aside this airfield, unlike ruthlessly selfish politicians and businessmen, farmers and landowners. The sheer fact that flying has not ceased has given unsung Burn rightful revenge. Home of a VC winner but mostly ignored and forgotten – unbelievable...

105/SE603284. 3½ miles SW of Selby, just E of village by A19. Gliding club premises on W side, also views from two minor roads on N and S sides.

Burnaston, Derbyshire

Alternative Name: Derby
The municipal airport was a good 1930s idea that quickly failed to live up to expectations. Airliners never even visited some of them, while others proved poor sites: one caustic wit went as far as saying how municipal airports often tended to have their control building, hangars and restaurant on the wrong side of the airfield. Certain examples such as Barton still became successful in less ambitious roles, as did Derby's original supportive aerial representative Burnaston for many years, a place destined for a ghastly death at the hands of foreigners.

June 17 1939 saw Burnaston become the second-last pre-war municipal airport to officially open in Britain, only being succeeded on July 8 by Elmdon, today still faithfully serving Birmingham – and a real airport at that. Flying had nevertheless happened in Derbyshire since the spring of 1938, shortly after construction work started in December 1937. No 30 E&RFTS later formally arose on September 29 1938. Not directly of note, but perhaps influential in its own way, was how Sir Alan Cobham held a National Aviation Display at a temporary airfield near the village of Stenson on May 11 1932: wherever this site lay, it stood at most only two miles east of what became Burnaston. Can the great Cobham who

THE AIRFIELDS OF BRITAIN

discovered so many other airfields all over Britain therefore be credited with finding this one as well?

As usual the airy-fairy ideas associated with municipal airports literally never got off the ground to leave instructional and recreational flying. Soon only training duties remained when war broke out as Burnaston's school became No 30 EFTS and then No 16 EFTS on May 10 1940. Right through World War Two and beyond into the 1950s the airfield unpretentiously taught trainee pilots with no hindrance from any other military flying units. Burnaston had to expand to meet this new challenge and added seven Blisters to help out two civil hangars and a single Bellman. Magisters were very common in this area until Tiger Moths began replacing them mid-war.

Service flying training continued up to the summer of 1953. By this time the wartime school had been renumbered yet again as No 16 RFS in 1947. No 3 Basic FTS accompanied it at Burnaston during 1951-53 until political cut-backs forced both of them to disband.

1953 was a bad year for airfields in Britain with the closing of all fourteen Reserve Flying Schools, leading to bitter protests from the secretary of the influential Aerodrome Owners' Association. Burnaston had already gone back to relying upon civil activities as the pre-war Derby Aero Club restarted, ceasing in 1957 before being known as the Derby Air Centre from 1959 and Midland School of Flying after April 20 1960.

A newer visitor named Derby Aviation now ran the show at Burnaston and the flying club side of daily affairs. Formed in January 1949, this firm steadily graduated from charter to scheduled seasonal transportation services on various routes to domestic and foreign destinations. Douglas DC-3s replaced de Havilland Dragon Rapide biplanes from May 1955 prior to vital Customs facilities being created at the start of 1959 to allow this airline's operating base to call itself a true airport. Alongside stood Burnaston House, the Officers' Mess in World War Two and in peacetime HQ for Derby Aviation and a mess for flying club personnel.

All seemed well by the late 1950s. Yet Burnaston owned a grass landing area, a type of surface that proved to be a harmful shortcoming. While Dakotas and other piston-engined airliners could operate with no problems at all, an inability to hold jet types made the commercial grass airfield as obsolete as its military equivalent. Striking changes could be seen at places such as Gatwick able to convert their runways as comparative strugglers turned into great successes. Burnaston was a good airfield but like Burn neatly slotted into a confined area, the adjacent A38 main road to Derby in particular ruling out any plans for expansion.

A previously little-known World War Two bomber/transport OTU satellite base called Castle Donington looked more appropriate for future requirements and opened as East Midlands Airport in April 1965. Derby Aviation instantly moved to this greatly altered runwayed site under its recent new guise as British Midland Airways or BMA. So too did the Midland School of Flying in August as Burnaston prepared to close.

You can never keep our airfields out of action as the last three places described in this book have demonstrated. Derby's ex-airport followed the same trend by being disused but never wholly closed to aircraft, still retaining an auxiliary connection with BMA. Two decades later it gained a new operating licence for light aircraft use in 1987: a sensational return, all the more so as a revived Derby Aero Club moved in along with another organisation bearing a famous name of old – Airspeed Aviation Ltd.

The scene at Burnaston towards the end of the 1980s was one of happy recreational flying with at least one Tiger Moth present to remind people of past activities. This airfield had helped beat Germany – but in then came Japan to suddenly announce on April 18 1989 that Toyota would be constructing a car factory on the site. First Battle of Britain star Usworth near Sunderland, now here plus Wiltshire factory airfield South Marston and Scotland's Turnberry as well: how anyone could have the cheek to give any airfield not just to the enemy but, worse still, the Japanese shows beyond doubt the frightening lack of respect given to our top historical stars. Local officialdom had much to answer for, and the selling price of £18.3 million for Burnaston's acreage to Derbyshire County Council raised allegations of buying on the cheap as valuers thought the land could be worth six times as much.

Flying defiantly carried on for as long as possible until closure came at the end of March 1990. Contractors A.F. Budge moved heavy plant on to the airfield in May in readiness for building to formally start on June 4, the first car rolling off the production line in December 1992. All aeronautical traces ranging from the hangars to Burnaston House have been demolished save – big deal – a pillbox.

You may wonder why we should be complaining about the creation of new employment. There is a simple answer: any types of fresh job are welcome but not those which breach the rules of basic morality and principle. Already Burnaston is

only a visual memory. It is now a sobering thought that Derbyshire does not have a single old-time active airfield to call upon at all.
128/SK290305. 7 miles SW of Derby by A38, 1½ miles SE of Etwall.

Burnfoot, Cumbria

Close to the Metal Bridge landmark familiar to travellers going between Scotland and England is an unremarkable field which assisted in World War Two's flying training effort. First discovered in July 1940 and in action from September, Burnfoot served as an RLG for No 15 EFTS at nearby Kingstown until 1945 and the July 9 massacre of these sites. Magisters and later on Tiger Moths appeared as at Burnaston.

The seven Blisters which once stood in this very unpopulated countryside disappeared long ago. Only agriculture marks what used to be a busy airfield, considered respectable enough to be officially regarded as a more superior satellite on opening as such on October 24 1942. A short distance away is Longtown but the town possessed an airfield of its own, so a farm had to give Burnfoot a suitable name.
85/NY372660. 2 miles S of Longtown, turn right off A7 on S edge of town. Take right fork in road and then first right on to unclassified road.

Burnham-on-Crouch, Essex

Burnham-on-Crouch is known as a major recreational sailing centre. Yachts have become far more familiar than aircraft but an airfield has existed in the past, and indeed shares a common link.

Near the end of 1914 the RNAS registered a landing ground by the town for fighters to use on defensive sorties if need be. Noted as 'being taken up' on April 21 1916, No 37 Squadron of the RFC maintained Burnham-on-Crouch from October while continuing Home Defence duties. The landing ground kept open past the Armistice and was relinquished in August 1919.

Involvement with boats can be traced to the 1930s as another vital abbreviation replaced RNAS, RFC and RAF:

AA. The Automobile Association included Burnham-on-Crouch as one of its many civil landing grounds, employing the same site, allowing for available grass landing runs being more limited in length. Pilots who once had to look out for menacing enemy aircraft or airships now only had to worry about an odd errant corn stack. On July 28 1934 the Duchess of Bedford opened Burnham-on-Crouch for the town's Royal Corinthian Yacht Club to use whenever members arrived or departed by air.

The field which could be still counted as active at September 1939 has not altered all that much. A sewage works stood in the south-west corner and a farm to the east: wind your way not too far north-east and you will reach the old Dengie Flats bombing range associated with Bradwell Bay. Yachts might rule but Burnham-on-Crouch infiltrated their cosy system in one more way as the Air Ministry acknowledged the River Crouch as an alighting area for civil seaplanes during the 1930s. No doubt about it, wherever you go in Britain, you cannot avoid airfields.
168/TQ960957. 1 mile E of town.

Burscough, Lancashire

For an idea of what the old type of British naval airfield looked like, go to Burscough, as reasonably preserved as any disused site in this country. A control tower stands amid farmland and light industry in quite good condition. Light aircraft and microlights used to operate from the landing area containing four runways which are great in certain sections, while the perimeter track retains some durability too.

The FAA could rightfully claim to have been given short shrift with regard to available airfields in the first half of World War Two. About all choice cuts went to the RAF, leaving the poor old Navy to get by on often pretty poor scraps. But fairness belatedly prevailed as more suitable bases fitted out with four shorter runways two-thirds the width of standard RAF stretches and different hangars designed to house folding wing aircraft began opening. What Admiralty officials dredged ornithological tomes to name as HMS *Ringtail* became one place to help proclaim the approach of genuine naval airfields when Burscough was commissioned on September 1 1943.

Although many squadrons soon found their latest grounded 'ship' a handy place where to stay away from aircraft carriers

THE AIRFIELDS OF BRITAIN

docked off Liverpool, various units arrived with more specific ideas in mind. Early visitors became six Supermarine Seafire squadrons belonging to the 3rd and 4th Naval Fighter Wings which both formed on October 25 1943. Four of these units alternated late on in the year between Burscough and RAF Andover in Salisbury Plain country where they could work up on tactical reconnaissance training. The 4th NFW's Nos 807, 809 and 879 Squadrons left for North Africa in 1944 but Nos 808, 886 and 897 Squadrons of the 3rd stayed on in Britain and performed vital gunnery bombardment spotting duties for Allied forces at D-Day while stationed at Lee-on-Solent in Hampshire. If never firing a shot in anger, Burscough could still easily claim how it made the Normandy landings a complete success.

Other first and second-line squadrons present at this airfield brought along the usual diversity of aircraft. British FAA bases were primarily intended for training duties, and Burscough fitted the bill perfectly, being highly rated by the naval authorities. It acted as birthplace to some units during 1944 and 1945, notably No 707 Squadron which gave radar training on Barracudas and Swordfish, Nos 1772 and 1790 with Fairey Firefly fighters and Grumman Hellcat fighters of Nos 888 and 1840 Squadrons.

The FAA's sole Curtiss Helldiver squadron also appeared in the second half of 1944. General British disfavour of dive bombers continued as No 1820 suffered several crashes and other bad luck: the average dive bomber was not meant to fly straight into the ground. Accepting 26 examples of a successful American aircraft used extensively in the Pacific which had still required thousands of design changes after the prototype crashed and held up production for months somehow seemed unpropitious to make disbandment come as a form of relief in December. This hiccup apart, Burscough's latest residents kept up attacking the enemy on its behalf by hitting both German and Japanese military targets with great results.

While still busy for a time after World War Two, squadrons increasingly began to depart or disband rather than arrive, such as No 1791 folding as a Firefly force in September 1945. Second-last to go in April 1946 – only marginally beaten by an FRU – was No 735 Squadron, an ASV radar training unit equipped with Ansons and Barracudas which had arrived in March 1944 and become the most durable resident at Burscough.

Responsibility for the airfield's enforced silencing lay entirely with the farming community. A school having to be necessarily removed niggled certain people in general but farmers fiercely opposed plans to extend Burscough in 1945 and actually forced the Government to submit to their wishes. The local agricultural fraternity had put forward one of the oldest excuses in the catalogue of anti-airfield objections, namely that this Lancashire land was among the most fertile in Britain; no airfield would have arisen had this false argument won every time.

Closure on June 15 1946 came with strings attached. The Navy recognised the value of this site by keeping it under inactive status for more than another decade. An important aircraft engine holding unit present until 1957 or so ensured that nobody wasted available facilities. Cheshire FAA airfield Stretton was ordered to look after Burscough, a more typical World War Two naval airfield of earlier origin which should have gone to the RAF and thus possessed a number of limitations. Finally the Admiralty relinquished both bases in 1961, Stretton to immediately become a prison, Burscough having to wait quite a while until industry emerged.

You will find not much has changed here once having discovered the somewhat unobtrusive entrance. Hangars survive en masse: Burscough was listed as holding 32 Mainhills and two Pentads by the end of 1944 but further building occurred as a greater number of Pentads can be seen. Not every last hangar has however kept its place as a short distance up the A59 at Burscough Bridge can be found perched on a rise beside a bridge another Mainhill – how did it get there? But the biggest quirk of all awaits any outsider who tries to pronounce Burscough's name, for you should never say the second syllable as if talking about a sound emitted from the mouth but what bread is made of!
108/SD425112. 2½ miles NE of Ormskirk, take first left off A59 after junction with B5242.

Burton-on-the-Wolds, Leicestershire

Alternative Name: Loughborough
Today's East Midlands Airport and successor to Burnaston at Castle Donington may well owe much to this little World War One HD landing ground approved for development on September 5 1916. Perhaps not directly, but in World War Two Castle Donington's parent was Wymeswold, which still

lies in fine disused condition like Burscough only a mile north-west of Burton-on-the-Wolds. So once again can be argued the case of one airfield through convoluted ways and means spawning a second nearby site.

No 38 Squadron controlled this mirror L-shaped place with a small wood on the east-west leg's edge from October 1916. Aircraft could land at any time if they wanted to at the 2nd class day but 3rd class night landing ground, obstructions being sufficient to downgrade this rating system applied to all similar World War One airfields. Later on in 1918 No 90 Squadron at Buckminster assumed control and supervised Burton-on-the-Wolds at the Armistice. Horse Leys Farm continues to stand on the north side to mark the position of this prototype Holme-on-Spalding Moor.
129/SK610212. 6 miles E of Loughborough, 1½ miles E of village to S of B676.

Burtonwood, Cheshire

Not all that far away from Burscough stands a far more strategically than tactically important disused airfield which has seen a massive clearance of buildings more recently. Burtonwood was huge in comparison with its tiny naval cousin but that has not stopped the local authorities from doing their best to wipe out another of our premier historical sites. The scene now can only be described as a real shocker.

Why should we protest so much about an airfield most Britons have never heard of? No bombers ever started raids from the runways, or fighters flamboyantly take off to defend the area. But where Burtonwood really scored was in allowing British-based USAAF/USAF flying elements to function day after day during the 1940s and 1950s by looking after aircraft and other equipment. Without this support America's 8th Air Force of World War Two in particular would have virtually ground to a halt. As Burscough again showed, an airfield did not necessarily have to shoot down countless enemy aircraft or bomb targets into dust to win a war.

One of Europe's, if not the world's, busiest airfields once upon a time started up in business under RAF ownership; C hangars gave away pre-war Expansion Period planning thinking. Political minds had certainly markedly shifted since 1935 when one MP almost begged the Government to allow the RAF to set up camp in Lancashire, in which Burtonwood then lay before county border tinkering, because of the area's

THE AIRFIELDS OF BRITAIN: VOLUME 1

industrial importance. The astonishing reply that our questionable leaders doubted whether the scheme would be feasible soon bore considerably risible overtones.

No 37 MU formed on April 1 1940 to store aircraft until the Americans arrived in 1942. Great plans were being drawn up for Burtonwood's future development even then, and an already large acreage increased rapidly. Little inconvenience resulted in surrounding civilian life with the area being negligibly populated to give airfield builders a relatively free run in getting on with their work.

Burtonwood became a perfect site for the Americans, not least for the two facts of being near Liverpool and as the RAF had processed many US-built aircraft during 1940-42. By the beginning of 1942 this airfield was definitely earmarked for American use as the 8th Air Force prepared to fly across to Britain now that country had entered World War Two. An agreement also arose how there would be shared control with Britain until the new visitors became fully settled in, though this amicable co-operation continued a lot longer than at first expected.

From the summer of 1942, once the first USAAF Boeing B-17 heavy bomber had landed in Britain at Prestwick, Burtonwood turned into a tremendous hive of activity. It is impossible to do justice in the limited space available in this book to describe just how much the airfield contributed to Allied victory. Many thousands of familiar American types arrived in every possible way to be assembled, ferried out to operational USAAF stations, modified, repaired and serviced. All sorts of individual aircraft components were dealt with as machines packed the dispersals solid. The 8th Air Force's fighters and heavy bombers almost inevitably gained most notice but aircraft of the more tactically-orientated 9th Air Force also received attention, as did the 12th Air Force before this element flew out late on in 1942 for the invasion of North Africa.

Burtonwood rejoiced in this role as the 1st Base Air Depot and made the biggest contribution of three home airfields allocated to primary USAAF aircraft back-up. Both the 2nd and 3rd BADs at Warton near Blackpool and Langford Lodge in Northern Ireland gave great value too but the former needed time to get into its stride, while Langford Lodge opted out of the task in 1944.

A fantastic run-down commenced at Burtonwood after World War Two as the USAAF bolted out of Britain. America only had to give up Honington in Suffolk when No 276 MU joined No 37 from January 7 1946 to hold American equipment. But our foreign friends decided to come back in strength during the second half of 1948, asking on September 29 for an additional 500,000 square yards of covered accommodation – immediately. No 37 MU had to surrender all six of its hangars and clear nearly 450 aircraft at the same time, including 291 North American Harvards to be dismantled and taken by road to Shropshire. This unit went down to 'number only' basis on March 1 1949 but No 276 MU did not disband until September 23 1950 after a proposed move to Cheshire RAF ground station Handforth near Wilmslow had been suspended in September 1949 due to possible heavy unemployment in the Burtonwood area. Certain politicians must now have felt severely ashamed about their past predictions.

The American revival brought a change from before as maintenance and repair duties now mixed with supplying British USAF airfields in all areas of their operation, right down to seemingly trivial knick-knacks. Transports had largely replaced bombers and other operational types as Burtonwood got down to this slightly altered post-war role.

The first stage in Burtonwood's descent into clinically devastating oblivion could be said to have started in 1954. USAF financial savings policies then drafted in 2,000-2,500 British civilians to work at the airfield. Proposed closure plans in 1957 were soon denied but not too convincingly, and soon came an announcement that the Northern Air Materiel Area – as Burtonwood had become known – would cease to exist on June 30 1958. The work-force reduced in number by 1,000 to 3,500 people as the Americans preferred to adopt a direct supply system from home. As a result that year's Open Day exuded a sad and subdued air.

So suddenly did USAF aircraft go that Burtonwood remained under Air Ministry control before anyone could really appreciate what had happened. Numerous surrounding local councils twice voiced a suggestion in August 1958 and March 1959 for the airfield to be converted into an international airport but nothing resulted. At this second date total closure became official as Mildenhall in Suffolk replaced Burtonwood in the transport role before Boeing WB-50s of the 53rd Weather Reconnaissance Squadron, which arrived from Bermuda in November 1953, moved to Alconbury during April 1959. General flying almost instantly ceased to permit transfer to RAF Maintenance Command on C&M level on July 1.

The USAF had not completely evacuated Burtonwood in order to man their Dry Food Storage Depot, a few aircraft

THE AIRFIELDS OF BRITAIN: VOLUME 1

visiting for this purpose. No 635 GS also formed as an ATC glider unit on November 1 1959 but the airfield's future became doubtful for several years. What could be achieved with a site of this size? Transfer to Bomber Command ownership in October 1960 made no difference, despite later brief use as a diversionary airfield for RAF V-bombers, and further airport hopes fared no better. Lancashire County Council still tried hard by May 1965 after Parliament had announced at the end of 1964 that the USAF would be leaving but the Ministry of Aviation emphatically ruled out any airport ideas in early 1966. Ringway and Speke for Manchester and Liverpool respectively supposedly made Burtonwood unnecessary, an opinion which today is still open to question.

Residual USAF and absolute RAF control ended and began on June 30 1965 before the US Army appeared on January 2 1967 for more logistic purposes. The French were at it again, ejecting American forces from their country, but this aloof policy proved Burtonwood's gain as Bruntingthorpe had found out back in 1959. Helicopters frequently visited and partly compensated for the general lack of fixed-wing aircraft.

In mid-1983 the world's first flying model wheelbarrow took off from Burtonwood. The ATC gliders ceasing activities later that year in September and departing further north to British Aerospace factory airfield Samlesbury sadly and ominously countered this lighter moment, though, as many parts of their old base succumbed to authoritarian pressure. No 635 GS had encountered one obstacle too many after having to work around one more obstruction after another and then the land being sold in 1982. One significant problem became subsidence caused by coal workings, which the airfield had first been warned about in November 1955.

Furious protests by airfield fans in newspapers, magazines and even a national radio news programme failed to halt demolition teams methodically wiping out the site bit by bit. Already a motorway and supportive service station had plonked themselves on where the main runway used to be; the 1980s sped up the destructive process as most other tracks and buildings – including a distinctive column-shaped postwar control tower – fell one by one. Burtonwood was fitted with a large and wide variety of hangars, spearheaded by three Cs, but only a handful of structures on the north side still hang on. Houses make most other parts of the airfield completely unrecognisable and make it very easy to become lost in this featureless yuppieland.

Further south in what survived of RAF Burtonwood stood

the airfield's most famous individual building. The Americans had used a huge warehouse almost from the beginning for equipment supply between World War Two and the Gulf War. In May 1992 the US Army was finally told to get ready to move out and officially did so on June 2 1993, although not in reality until October. Now this part of Burtonwood is being developed to become a business park from April 1994, with past events intended to help bring American companies to Britain.

Not every aircraft which landed at Burtonwood was military. DC-3s of Scottish Airways flew via here from June 9 1951 to February 14 1953 on their Prestwick-Northolt route, while BOAC kept Atlantic services away from Manchester during 1957/58 to allow Ringway to have its main runway extended. The USAAF and USAF however brought fame to this place. Many older local inhabitants still remember with awe the massive quantities of aircraft types that passed through both in war and peace. B-17s, P-51s, varied transports and B-47s are probably the best recalled; not far behind are B-36s, so big they made people in Manchester protest while landing at Burtonwood in 1956. Today you have more chance of seeing a Lancaster on the moon than finding an aircraft at this disused airfield of great repute, once home to 18,000 Americans and arguably the greatest single contributor to the passive winning of World War Two. Is there any concrete sign of appreciation? Now where's that Lancaster . . .

108/SJ566905. NW of Warrington, M62 runs through site. Alternatively take a minor road S of Burtonwood village which goes over motorway.

Bury St Edmunds II, Suffolk

Alternative Name: Rougham
One airfield which directly benefitted from Burtonwood like scores of others was this Suffolk B-17 bomber base. Other social advantages have since allowed many people to hold down a decent job.

Unlike of late Warrington, one has to say, Bury St Edmunds has appreciated aviation far more. On June 18 1920 the Central Aircraft Company – a small Northolt-based firm – sent over two of its own Centaur IV biplanes for joy-riding purposes east of the town, expecting to stay ten days or so and in the event remaining for three weeks. Nothing at first glance different there, but Bury St Edmunds had unusually asked Central to visit, instead of it or any other joy-riding concern just dropping in at short notice.

This area of marginally indeterminate background became rediscovered a generation later when requisitioned in June 1941. Initially called Rougham to distinguish it from a pre-war flying club and now army co-operation airfield across town first known as Bury St Edmunds and then Westley, this intention lasted until January 1942. Planners agreed to drop the Rougham title as Westley – really too small for anything other than AOP Auster squadrons – decreased in importance but the original name would not entirely bow out gracefully as the military still tended to use it by 1944.

Although many local people persisted in describing their airfield next door as Rougham, and still do, this locality some distance away needed to suffice in the interim as nearer villages and settlements could never have gifted their names. Both syllables ruled Blackthorpe out, Great Barton resembled umpteen other airfields, Cattishall looked and sounded a dead ringer for Coltishall, and to the west there even remains a place bearing the same name as Benson's satellite: Mount Farm.

The replacement – and maybe also relieving – Bury St Edmunds was first occupied on August 29 1942 and became self-supporting on September 10. Accommodating the 322nd BG from December 1, B-26 medium bombers did not start to appear until after March 7 1943 and a bad winter at the 'airdrome' which left much snow and some gale damage. These aircraft resided both here and briefly also at Rattlesden, another new USAAF bomber airfield seven miles to the south-east, for low level attacks. Quite unsuited for these duties, they transferred to Andrews Field on June 12 1943.

Next day B-17s of the 94th BG came over from Earl's Colne to succeed the Marauders. This Group had suffered heavy losses while in Essex but under new command results improved so greatly that the 94th went on to win two Distinguished Unit Citations during its stay up to December 12 1945. The man responsible for this change of fortune, Colonel (later General) Frederick W. Castle, sadly failed to see his Fortresses proudly leave Bury St Edmunds as he had been killed in action a year earlier.

Bury St Edmunds II has enjoyed in the main a better fate since then, far better than the town's MP presumably wished. Without naming any places, Lieutenant-Colonel G.B. Clifton-

Brown craved farming land so much he said on February 25 1946 that '... no effort has been made to rip up the tarmac, which should be done with mechanical implements.' Such drastic measures thankfully did not happen as Bomber Command took over control of the airfield on C&M a few days after the Americans departed. Abandoned in August 1946 and derequisitioned during 1948, a small research establishment bred house mice at the site in the 1950s in a peculiar task which assessed their behaviour in grain stores and how to control these creatures in similar circumstances.

Now transformed into an industrial estate called Rougham, sections of two out of three runways plus the perimeter track remain. Light aircraft have indeed never really gone away. Among plenty of other relics are the control tower which Luftwaffe intruders damaged on the night of March 3 1945, many support buildings and two T2 hangars.

Come to Bury St Edmunds today and you will see the factors which characterise so many other British airfields. Here is a real winner and piece of real history creating lots of real jobs and real social impact. What more could we ask for in the face of such brilliance?

(For Bury St Edmunds I see Other British Airfields)
155/TL890642. 4½ miles E of town, on N side of A45.

THE AIRFIELDS OF BRITAIN: VOLUME 1

Other British Airfields

Mystery, uncertainty and a general lack of information: the three factors which all too often dog the story of Britain's airfields. Not every site could be a Biggin Hill or Scampton, hence the inclusion in this section of some fairly minor airfields, but they are heavily outnumbered by places whose histories are largely unknown or incomplete. All can in the main be divided into eight categories:

(1) Civil airfields active before World War One. Records for certain sites belonging to this era tend to be patchy. Military airfields, incidentally, enjoy good documentation because of their novelty value at the time. Supportive landing grounds did not then exist as aircraft in transit or participating in small exercises could use about any field they pleased, though by March 1914 pioneering airfield advocates Colonels J. E. B. Seely and F. H. Sykes wanted proper service landing grounds, as did Winston Churchill.

(2) World War One airfields, especially landing grounds for Home Defence purposes. To try and track down both the histories and exact positions of these sites can be achieved. By employing a mixture of mileages from railway stations, acreage figures, landing run lengths and even telephone numbers in indoor and outdoor research can bring results. But this is a desperately slow process, not helped by little official evidence about how or how often landing grounds were used. One would think that places in East Anglia plus central and southern England would be best detailed, unlike the rest of Britain, yet strangely the opposite situation occurs. Surviving records tend to display albeit crude diagrams of landing grounds on the whole more outwith these three areas, leaving the rest as vague symbols on large general maps or not even marked at all.

Great War landing grounds pose further difficulties for researchers and writers. It is noticeable that the earlier one travels in the conflict, the less information there is about landing grounds. RNAS sites are worse in this respect than RFC/RAF ones, and the 1917/early 1918 period when some landing grounds prematurely closed is not clearly expressed. The worst aspect is trying to find out closure dates after World War One ended: 115 HD landing grounds were still active at the Armistice but, even using published figures (see *A Towering Control*, page 316), little help is given. All we can

OTHER BRITISH AIRFIELDS

say is that by May 1 1919 the casualty list mostly consisted of landing grounds.

Other types of World War One era airfields mentioned include a few places never completed. Again they lack general detailed information; indeed, the names of certain airfields are known and nothing else.

(3) Joy-riding and charter airfields of 1919 and the early 1920s. Such sites, mainly used for the first task and involving the Air Ministry List D2 or 'Avro 504K' variety, have proved notoriously awkward to trace. Being licensed does not always necessarily mean aircraft visited but this often brief permit ensures that every airfield merits a mention.

There seem to have existed about 55 joy-riding concerns in Britain after World War One. The year 1919 became their most profitable time, over 30,000 people being carried without a single fatality in four months by the Avro Transport Company from detached bases around the country. By 1920 firms preferred more to travel from town to town, staying usually between ten days and a fortnight, and greatly popularised aviation. Hundreds or thousands of people attended each temporary airfield; many of them took a quick flight, with sometimes thousands more 'hedgewatchers' looking on from the outside.

The problem with retelling what happened in these days is that information tails off after 1920. Reports about joy-riding reflect a general attitude: 1919 exciting, 1920 fairly noteworthy, 1921 ho-hum and 1922 not really worth mentioning. Attributable factors were poor weather in 1920, the financial crash of a year later and pleasure flying losing its curiosity. The most famous and influential company is also the best documented, Berkshire Aviation, but by 1921 pilots Fred Holmes and O. P. Jones had to split up into separate sections and travel in different directions to keep business up. Although a small number of firms continued pleasure flying afterwards, 1922 is the last year in which their airfields receive a substantial mention – and where we draw the line.

(4) 1920s civil airfields. British civil airfield operations in their entirety have proved difficult for historians to unearth but records are extremely uncertain and/or rare for this decade. A de Havilland Moth biplane could take off from a field in only 100 yards, so while some 1920s sites might be better described as private airstrips, everyone acknowledged them as full airfields and therefore count as much as any List D2 type.

(5) 1930s civil airfields, inter-war RAF landing grounds and Automobile Association civil landing grounds. Occasionally of

THE AIRFIELDS OF BRITAIN: VOLUME 1

relatively minor importance, though limited records again play a big part. Landing grounds coming under the AA's umbrella frequently became ephemeral affairs because of their tenuous existences upon farmland, crop rotation even forcing these places to shift fields from time to time. Many AA airfields lasted to the outbreak of World War Two.

(6) Lesser World War Two airfields, notably ELGs, unused SLGs, flying boat dispersal areas and AOP Auster HQ ALGs.

(7) Civil airfields existent during the first twenty years or so after World War Two. These sites, as before the conflict, either lack information or are of minor importance. Expendable post-war flight information publications (unlike before September 1939) hardly help.

(8) Minor active civil airfields, particularly those used in more recent times for recreational gliding.

One question may have entered your mind while reading these categories: when is an airfield not an airfield? For the purposes of this book and future volumes, the following do not register as proper airfields:

(a) The countless private airstrips and 'farm strips' that have existed or still do exist. Unlicensed, usually unmarked, frequently used by only one individual and/or one aircraft, of negligible historical note and little architectural impact, all are simply not worth mentioning. This category has always been a tricky one to assess, right from the days of personal 'aviation grounds' prior to World War One. Just how private is private? Eyebrows may be raised on not seeing certain airstrips being featured but the above guide-lines are strictly adhered to.

(b) 1920s and 1930s RAF army co-operation landing grounds. Squadrons dealing with this role made innumerable small detachments to temporary 'airfields' between the wars for Army exercises and manoeuvres. To give a brief mention of examples, we can include places such as Cheriton and Old Alresford in Hampshire during 1925; Somerton in Somerset, where No 13 Squadron's Bristol F.2bs stayed during September 22-24 of the same year; or the Hampshire sites of Newman's Farm and Oxney Farm for No 4 Squadron and Preston Candover for No 13 Squadron in 1935. The RAF regarded all of them as Advanced Landing Grounds, long before that term achieved its true meaning, but these landing grounds were only convenient grass fields for momentary use and not real airfields.

(c) Sir Alan Cobham's 'National Aviation Day' 'airfields' of 1932-35. From April to October during these years Cobham and his aides travelled around Britain to make millions of people more aware about aviation in general and give them a

OTHER BRITISH AIRFIELDS

good time. Displays were often held at recognised airfields or occasionally disused ones such as Alloa but frequently also on fields close to towns; events never lasted longer than two days. While only the itinerary for 1932 is reasonably documented, some of Cobham's grounds are worth mentioning in passing as they influenced the development of future airfields.

(d) Gliding 'hill' sites. These places abounded after gliding finally gained widespread popularity in Britain from 1930. Gliders of this period became airborne with the help of two groups of people holding a tow-line. Powered aircraft were never seen at these launching areas — and should never have been seen at them, as the Air Ministry belatedly recognised in November 1938 by introducing a triangular sign at gliding 'airfields' to warn off powered aircraft if they wanted to land except in an emergency.

ATC Gliding Schools of World War Two similarly employed 'non-airfields' until gradually switching more to true airfields from late 1944 as active British strength started to wane, and their civil gliding club counterparts did the same during the late 1950s/early 1960s as they began flying from disused military airfields abandoned by the Air Ministry. There are now few 'hill' sites, thanks primarily to powered aircraft tugs, vastly improved sailplanes, more stringent safety procedures and better financial grants allocated to clubs. Hardy examples nevertheless remain, such as Carlton Moor in North Yorkshire, the Newcastle and Teesside Gliding Club's base since 1960.

(e) RAF/Army AOP Auster and US Army Grasshopper 'airfields'. Such were the short take-off and landing capabilities of the Auster during World War Two and after until succeeded by helicopters in the 1950s that this type could emulate the pre-war de Havilland Moth by using just about any small field while on exercises. Detachments or individual aircraft flew briefly from places now too frivolous to mention. Auster ALGs acting as squadron HQs should be counted as airfields for this reason, however, as for their prolonged existences and important collective status in the months preceding D-Day.

The term Grasshopper covered several tiny single-engined monoplane designs which the Americans used for light liaison and observation duties while in Britain. Most common type became the Piper L-4, developed from the pre-war civil Cub. L-4s, Taylorcraft L-2s and others appeared like Austers at many airfields in World War Two but also frequented improvised areas. Usually only one or two aircraft stayed at each of these airstrips.

THE AIRFIELDS OF BRITAIN: VOLUME 1

(f) Current or recent Army-operated airstrips.

(g) Heliports and helipads. A helicopter can land at an airfield – but have you ever seen a fixed-wing aircraft land at either of them? Therefore, whether in civil or military use, no, no, a thousand times no!

It must be emphasised that all bar a minute handful of the airfields listed below and in sections to come today show no traces of past activities; many were anyhow lucky to have even a few tents, let alone a hangar, for supportive facilities. Exact Ordnance Survey positions are quoted where possible after each airfield's county but geographical sources are so poor on the whole that often only the relevant map number can be given.

Please note how years of ultra-deep penetration detective work have still left countless questions unanswered. The author has looked through a veritable mountain of records, tried to at least 'area target' or narrow down potential site locations, spoken to people on the ground and communicated in person or by letter with hundreds of County Record Offices, libraries, organisations and private individuals. Results have been mixed, from the odd tactical success to people not even having the decency to reply, and illustrate the urgent need for a real British airfield history book that this title has fulfilled.

You may recall that *A Towering Control* stated how over 1,700 airfields have existed in this country. Further research has incredibly resulted in even this total being surpassed to bring the figure to over 1,800. Several World War One airfields continue to evade detection; the inter-war civil airfield and military landing ground stories are surely incomplete; World War Two RAF ELGs remain swathed in mystery, right down to being deliberately unmarked on maps; and, of course, new airfields will always keep opening. If we included all those private airstrips and other 'non-airfields' throughout the years, we would not be talking about 1,800 or even 2,000 British airfields but certainly 2,500 of them – and probably well over 3,000. Some civil airfields active after World War One are lumped together to be considered here as one site because no OS positions are known, though it is more likely that flying occurred at separate places. All of these following airfields are listed alphabetically as in the main section except for airfields in what is now Eire and kite balloon bases, which will be featured in the final volume. Decoy airfields and their histories will be referred to in this book as well, although how far one can unravel this enormously complicated subject has yet to be fully evaluated.

OTHER BRITISH AIRFIELDS

A lack of basic information about this general subject also ensures that on occasion educated guesswork has to prevail with opening and closing dates, particularly in categories (2)-(5), so dates might vary from a few days to a month. Remember, as said earlier, an airfield being licensed does not inevitably equal being used by aircraft. Witness how Britain was officially listed as having 377 licensed civil airfields of all kinds at January 31 1933: the real total was at best little more than half, presumably artificially boosted by sites holding short-term licences and not a single permit for a whole year.

Space restrictions mean that a slightly abbreviated writing style and five special terminologies have to be used. WW1, WW2, LG, RS and Tel. denote in turn both world conflicts, landing grounds, plus railway stations and telephone numbers whenever World War One Home Defence landing grounds are mentioned.

Hopefully this introduction gives you an idea of the phenomenal complications encountered in trying to prepare this section. We could go on virtually ad nauseam: what about for a start the 64 exceptionally vague fields licensed by Scottish Motor Traction Co Ltd during the 1930s? Apart from a small number of exceptions, these places are deliberately excluded, as are some other airfields of dubious historical value. While this following list is the most expansive detailed survey of Britain's airfields ever attempted, it goes without saying that the author would be most grateful for any further information.

ABERAVON, West Glamorgan 170.
Used by the Welsh Aviation Company joy-riding concern at least in the first half of 1921.
ABERDEEN (WEST SEATON FARM), Grampian 38.
1920s civil airfield, licensed from May 1922.
ABERGAVENNY (LLANFOIST), Gwent 161/SO298134.
1920s civil airfield, S of town, licensed from May 1922. Joy-riding known to have occurred during Bank Holidays, and licensed by the Air Ministry in 1926 for mail-carrying purposes during the General Strike. The local authorities purchased this land in 1929 but Sir Alan Cobham's assessment of the general Abergavenny area for possible airfield development in 1931 did not favour any particular site, the one at Llanfoist being too small with bad approaches and alongside the River Usk. Although Cobham used a field at Racecourse Farm (the same place) for one of his air displays on August 27 1932, a municipal airfield plan laid out that year died a quiet death. In World War Two the US Army operated

THE AIRFIELDS OF BRITAIN: VOLUME 1

a Grasshopper airstrip north-west of Abergavenny town across the county boundary in Powys at Cwrt-y-Gollen but, as said in the introduction, it was not a real airfield. The Llanfoist site is now a golf course.

ABERYSTWYTH, Dyfed 135.

Joy-riding individualist H. V. David flew an Avro 504K from here after August 7 1919. The biplane crashed near the LG on the 28th, David and two passengers being injured.

ACCRINGTON, Lancashire 103.

Berkshire Aviation Company joy-riding airfield, used from January 16 1921 for a fortnight. On NE side of town, by A679 road to Burnley.

ACKLAM, Cleveland 93/NZ492164.

Tenant farmer Samuel Huddlestone and local motor trader Frank Elliot provided weekend pleasure flights with civil Austers from Sandy Flatts Farm *circa* 1947-52. Middlesbrough Corporation owned the farm. Houses and schools mostly surround what remains of this field, ¾ mile N of A1032/A174 roundabout and directly E of the distinctive Avenue of Trees.

ADDERLEY PARK, West Midlands 139.

Factory airfield for Wolseley Motors during 1915-18, many Royal Aircraft Factory SE5A fighters notably being flown. E of Birmingham city centre.

ADDINGTON, Greater London 177.

Aircraft sales agent Henly's wanted to establish a flying training and maintenance airfield here by late 1929. In 1930 this plan refused, then allowed after an appeal, but the company was at Heston instead by 1931. A 1930s LG for Croydon aircraft, also used by August 1933 for training by British Air Transport Limited once instructional activity banned at Croydon. Pleasure flights provided too but Addington always considered temporary, pending Redhill's opening, and BAT Ltd went to Gatwick in readiness at the end of 1933. Addington closed 1936 to allow for housing development. 2 miles SE of village and W of Biggin Hill, this airfield had a wooden hangar and an office available.

ALDERLEY EDGE, Cheshire 118/SJ83?77? (N side).

Manchester Aviation Company joy-riding airfield *circa* November 1920. Licensed again by November 1921. Farmland SSW of Chorley Hall, 1 mile SW of town.

ALTRINCHAM (WOODLANDS PARK), Greater Manchester 109/SJ776885.

Avro 504K site, licensed from November 1919 but not by early 1920. Probably this same area used as a 1920s civil LG. One secondary source claimed that an airfield still existed in the Altrincham area by 1931. This is a total mystery as

OTHER BRITISH AIRFIELDS

Ringway did not open until 1937 and Barton lay too far away; maybe Wythenshawe is being referred to but Manchester's interim airport had closed in 1930. Housing certainly covered Woodlands Park by the 1930s.

ALVA (KING O' MUIRS FARM), Central 58.
1920s civil airfield, 1 mile S of town, licensed from June 1922.

AMESBURY, Wiltshire 184.
1920s civil LG. Confused with Boscombe Down?

APPERLEY BRIDGE, West Yorkshire 104.
Northern Automobile Company of Bradford had made arrangements for an airfield here by December 1909 while 'doing a good business' in selling Bleriot monoplanes. J.W. House of the Northern Aero Syndicate flew a Bleriot and endured some accidents, notably a serious crash when he hit a stone wall. House was still at Apperley Bridge in July 1910 but had gone to Filey Sands by August. The Bradford GC temporarily operated later on from Apperley Bridge by October 1930 due to difficulties with the owners on its permanent site at Baildon Moor to the north-west. Today's Leeds/Bradford Airport at Yeadon exists only 3 miles directly NE of Apperley Bridge, which could call upon a hangar at this early airfield's peak.

ARDROSSAN, Strathclyde 70.
Foreshore of town licensed as an Avro 504K site from June 1920.

ARMAGH, Armagh 19/H876418.
WW2 RAF ELG, listed as active 1940. A field 2½ miles S of town, between A29 and B31 roads.

ASHGATE (CAUSHOUSE FARM, CHESTERFIELD), Derbyshire 119.
Alan Cobham, while working for the Berkshire Aviation Company, organised a flying week from September 22 1919. This Avro 504K site was not licensed by early 1920 but again from November 1921 to February 1922. W of Chesterfield.

AYLESBURY (RACE MEADOW), Buckinghamshire 165.
Avro 504K site, licensed from September 1919 but not by 1920. Alan Cobham performed joy-riding at Aylesbury in the summer of 1919.

BALLYCASTLE, Antrim 5.
Airfield being built for the RAF during 1918. Still unfinished at the Armistice but used as a landing ground during the RAF's time in Ireland. On edge of town.

BALLYMENA, Antrim 9.
WW2 RAF ELG, listed as active 1940. On NE outskirts of town.

BALLYWALTER I, Down 15/J619703? (unconfirmed).

Like Ballycastle, a proposed full airfield only used during 1918 and afterwards into the early 1920s as a landing ground by RAF aircraft. Presumed OS reference deduced by assessing general maps; if correct, site 1½ miles NW of village.

BALMAIN, Grampian 45/NO64?72?

WW2 RAF LG for No 8 SFTS at Montrose from 1940 (or earlier), and practice forced landing ground for No 2 FIS at same airfield during the 1942-45 period. 2 miles N of major MU station Edzell II.

BALTASOUND, Shetland 1/HP634090.

WW1 advanced mooring-out base for Catfirth flying boats, active from *circa* October 1918. Also used by RAF and FAA flying boats during WW2. On island of Unst.

BANBURY, Oxfordshire 151/SP429431.

The Northamptonshire Aero Club held a small flying meeting at Banbury on September 27 1931, the town's first link with aviation. 'Banbury Flying Ground', by the A41 road to Warwick, used for a Cobham display on April 26 1932. Another flying meeting on July 10, the airfield then being listed as an Automobile Association civil LG from February 1933. Temporarily withdrawn from AA register in June 1934 – the LG normally stayed closed between mid-May and mid-July each year for agricultural purposes – but certainly still active in a private capacity by September 1939. A field 3 miles NW of town, SW of Hanwell. Not directly relevant, but worthy of note, is that the town's Secondary Modern school building for boys was built of old military hangars from surrounding airfields after WW2. Even more disturbing is how the local history section at Banbury Library contains not one jot of airfield material.

BANGOR (GROOMSPORT), Down 15/J538831.

1930s AA civil LG, stated as active from August 1930 in connection with the Isle of Man TT races. E.E. Fresson used this place around the period. Pleasure flying in first half of 1930s, and very limited RAF use. S of Groomsport, housing and altered A2 road now occupy N half of site.

BARMBY (POCKLINGTON), Humberside 106/SE767497.

WW1 HD LG, taken up by March 17 1916 and in use from April. Used by Nos 33 and 76 Squadrons, still active at Armistice. Farmland ¾ mile NW of Barmby Moor on N side of A1079, not to be confused with WW2 bomber station Pocklington on opposite side of village.

BARROW-IN-FURNESS (airfield), Cumbria 96.

O.P. Jones of the Berkshire Aviation Company gave joy-rides from February 19 1920 for a fortnight. Business proved

OTHER BRITISH AIRFIELDS

excellent overall, despite frequent fog towards the end. Airfield at Rating Lane, near Furness Abbey railway station, 2 miles NE of town.

BARTON-UPON-HUMBER, Humberside 112.

Berkshire Aviation Company joy-riding airfield December 1921.

BASINGSTOKE, Hampshire 185.

Berkshire Aviation Company present for ten days in December 1922. Basingstoke also vaguely mentioned as a 'municipal civil airfield' *circa* 1933 but this is impossible as the town had only reserved a site for an airport (which never materialised) by 1932, the position not having altered by December 1933. The nearest active airfields at that time were the civil landing ground of Ecchinswell towards Newbury and Odiham, then only a military LG, though both of them stood well away from Basingstoke and therefore this fabled airfield is inexplicable.

BATTERSEA PARK, Greater London 176.

One of several very early WW1 ELGs established in October 1914 on London's parks, equipped with landing lights and intended for aircraft on night defence patrols (especially the pioneering RNAS machines flown from Hendon by Claude Grahame-White and others) if involved in accidents or damaged in action. All these sites were extreme stopgaps and none lasted in use for any length of time.

BAWTRY, Nottinghamshire 111/SK646921.

1930s private civil airfield for Harald Peake, raised at Bawtry Hall and who had learned to fly in 1929, owning a de Havilland Puss Moth monoplane from *circa* 1930 and later a Hornet Moth stable-mate from 1936. For a time Peake frequently flew to more isolated waterways to check their states while a director of the Sheffield and South Yorkshire Navigation Company. Bawtry also an AA civil LG from February 1933, still listed by September 1939. A field with a hangar on extreme E side 1 mile SW of town, on opposite side of A631 to WW2 bomber OTU satellite Bircotes, itself known as Bawtry until June 1942. The RAF used Bawtry Hall as HQ for No 1 Group from 1941 until moving to Upavon in the mid-1980s. For more about Peake's career, see Bircotes.

BEAULIEU II (BROCKENHURST), Hampshire 196/SU377015.

AA civil LG, active from late 1920s. A small field ¾ mile SW of village and immediately N of Swinesleys Farm. Still active by mid-1938 but not by start of WW2.

BEAUMONT, Essex 168.

WW1 HD LG, approved for requisition June 20 1916. No

37 Squadron had gained a replacement site to the south at Plough Corner as the summer of 1916 ended.
BEDFIELD, Suffolk 156/TM223672.
WW1 HD LG for No 51 Squadron from October 1916. Given to No 75 Squadron September 1917, and still active at Armistice. 1½ miles from Worlingworth RS, 38 acres, runs of 500 and 300 yards, Tel. Framlingham (not Framlington as quoted in records) 5. 8 miles NW of Framlingham, on E side of village.
BEDWORTH, Warwickshire 140.
Berkshire Aviation Company joy-riding airfield April 1922.
BEESTON, Nottinghamshire 129.
Berkshire Aviation Company joy-riding airfield May 1922.
BELFAST (MALONE, TAUGHMANAGH), Antrim 15. ·
Belfast Corporation approved on February 22 1924 the acquisition of 54 acres of land at a cost of £14,000 for a proposed airfield. Officially opened on April 30 as a Liverpool (Aintree)-Belfast service started. Northern Air Lines stopped flights from that destination in mid-June, later mounting short-lived routes from Carlisle and Stranraer into 1925. The Malone site was a disaster as an airfield because of excessive waterlogging and apparently closed about November/December 1925, though it may possibly still have been active as a civil LG by August 1927. Midland and Scottish Air Ferries approached Belfast Corporation as late as 1933 about the chances of gaining an operating lease. Off Malone Road and in Finaghy district, on SW side of city, today an area of housing S of a hospital.
BELFAST LOUGH, Down 15.
A Saro Cloud of British Flying Boats Ltd mounted an experimental air service between Greenock and Belfast during August 15-22 1932. Short flying boats common in area once a slipway built for production purposes at Queen's Island, W of Sydenham, in early 1941. Sunderlands still came in for overhauls at the works well into the 1950s.
BELHAVEN, Lothian 67/NT655792.
Sandy site and forward airfield on W side of Dunbar, where Sopwith Cuckoos from East Fortune deployed to between July 1918 and the Armistice to have torpedoes fitted on during tests. A Bessoneau hangar and limited support facilities available.
BEN FEALL (COLL), Strathclyde 46/NM152543.
Island airstrip used late 1940s and 1950s for air ambulance and occasional charter flights. Closed towards end of 1950s following an aircraft accident and replaced by Totronald. W

OTHER BRITISH AIRFIELDS

of Coll's current airstrip at Ballard Farm, and named after a hill.

BERNERAY, Western Isles 18.

WW2 RAF ELG. Occasional Loganair use since then at various points on island. Between Harris and North Uist.

BEXWELL, Norfolk 143.

WW1 HD ELG for RFC aircraft during 1915. Thought to have existed S of village. WW2 bomber airfield Downham Market, a short distance to the north, was locally known as Bexwell.

BIDFORD (BICKMARSH), Hereford and Worcester 150/SP106489.

Recreational gliding airfield in use since May 1964. Various club name changes (Worcestershire GC, Dowty GC, Avon Soaring Centre etc) and now known as Bidford Gliding Centre. Some parachuting activity too in the past. A busy place equipped with a grass landing area, hangarage and other facilities. 2½ miles S of Bidford-on-Avon across Warwickshire border.

BIDSTON (BIRKENHEAD), Merseyside 108/SJ28?91? (S side) (probable position).

Opened as civil airfield March 31 1920, heavy rain making the landing area become boggy and badly hindering this day. The Great Northern Aerial Syndicate concern operated Bidston and had extremely ambitious plans but ceased business at the end of 1921. Further information about Bidston is vague, though it may have remained active as a civil LG as late as 1927. Three hangars available at the beginning. Very close to Bidston railway station.

BIGGLESWADE, Bedfordshire 153/TL205472 (probable position).

WW1 HD LG, stated on February 22 1916 as 'being taken up' as a night LG, though not quite ready for use. Site cancelled as unsuitable on April 20 but then employed by No 75 Squadron from October. Given up by that unit in September 1917 but still active at the Armistice. Tel. Biggleswade 45. 2½ miles NE of town, to W of B1040, OS position deduced by combining official records saying that four farms existed ½ mile from this LG and markings on large-scale maps.

BILLESLEY (BIRMINGHAM, KING'S HEATH, YARDLEY WOOD ROAD), West Midlands 139/SP088805.

Early airfield with a somewhat patchy history, starting with limited Birmingham Aero Club glider and model flying prior to WW1. Home of Midland Flying School, flying with Bleriots began July 23 1915 but gales in early 1916 considerably damaged the airfield. The Horace Wright Aviation Company had taken over the Midland Flying School by June, one G.H. Bettinson then having opened a flying school in April 1917. Billesley known as King's Heath when an HD LG for No 38 Squadron from October 1916, and still listed as a Day LG for RFC aircraft on February 1 1918. After WW1 an Avro 504K licensed civil airfield from November 1919, upgraded to civil airfield status in February 1920 until January 1921. During August 19-24 and 30/31 1919 three Avro 504Ks of the Vickers company had drawn great crowds for joy-riding, while the Berkshire Aviation Company appeared in October 1920 among other pleasure users that year. Billesley is now a southerly suburb of Birmingham.

BILLING, Northamptonshire 152.

Small private civil airfield in use from *circa* 1951. Reportedly finally closed March 1983. Part of Aquadrome pleasure facility created by Mackaness family, which also had strong connections with the airfield. E of Northampton.

BIRCHWOOD PARK (SNELSTON), Derbyshire 128/SK15?40?

WW2 ELG for No 16 EFTS at Burnaston. 1½ miles SW of Ashbourne's satellite Darley Moor.

BISHOPS HATFIELD, Hertfordshire 166.

WW1 HD LG for No 39 Squadron, 'being taken up' by April 21 1916. Approval given to relinquish this site on October 22 as prone to fog and mist, replaced by Ware. In vicinity of famous factory airfield Hatfield.

BISHOPS WALTHAM, Hampshire 185.

1920s civil LG.

BLACKBOYS (UCKFIELD), East Sussex 199/TQ511202.

WW1 HD LG for No 78 Squadron from end of December 1916 until given up on August 21 1917. A field 1 mile W of village. Tel. Uckfield 10.

BLACKBURN (FENISCLIFFE BRIDGE, WITTON PARK), Lancashire 103/SD65?27?

Joy-riding here from September 13 1919 for one month. Charles Kingsford-Smith, later the first man to fly across the Pacific Ocean, served as a pilot. 1½ miles W of town in park.

BLACKHEATH (COLCHESTER), Essex 168/TM009217.

HD LG for No 37 Squadron from March 1917. Relinquished August 1919. Proposed in June 1925 to establish an airfield for Colchester in the area, the Berechurch Hall Estate being purchased by the War Office before the year ended. Still in use as a private civil LG during late 1920s. A field on S edge of town, to S of rifle ranges.

OTHER BRITISH AIRFIELDS

BLACKHEATH COMMON, Greater London 177/TQ39?76? (W side).
WW1 ELG for RFC fighters during 1915.

BLANDFORD, Dorset 195/ST893078.
1920s and 1930s civil LG, certainly active by August 1927 and in use as an AA civil LG by February 1933. Still listed at September 1939. On NE edge of town, housing and diverted A350 road on site. Uncertain whether Bryanston School to the west followed through with plans of June 1934 to build an airfield in nearby grounds known as the Gallops. A gliding club bearing the school's name was certainly active by March 1938, and an aeroplane (the same?) club in 1939, but no actual airfield mentioned.

BLARIS (LISBURN), Antrim 20/J227649.
WW2 LG for RAF aircraft being used on Army-related duties. A tested but rejected SLG after an Anson became stuck in muddy conditions during April 1941. ATC gliders of No 201 GS on-off users afterwards, known to have been present at least during May 1943, May-September 1945 and January-June 1946. On this last date the school moved to Long Kesh, having previously resided at Newtownards by May 1944 and Maghaberry during March/April 1945. 2½ miles W of Lisburn, N of B104.

BODMIN I, Cornwall 200.
Berkshire Aviation joy-riding in the area during 1924 at least. A civil LG certainly active 1 mile NE of town by August 1927. An Avro 504K of the Cornwall Aviation Company crashed during a flying display at the 'Three Chimneys' site not far from the current Bodmin airfield on August 16 1935 with three fatalities.

BOGNOR (seaplane), West Sussex 197.
Flying boat production base (to E of town at Middleton) for the White and Thompson Company, which changed its name to the Norman Thompson Flight Company on October 4 1915. Firm established 1910 and, after a sticky spell before WW1, notably produced in the conflict over 50 N.T.4/4A patrol flying boats and over 150 of the successful N.T.2B training machines; a distinctive and at that time unusual trade mark of Norman Thompson designs were enclosed cockpits. Other marine types and landplanes (tested at Bognor beach) such as Short S.38 trainers for the RNAS built in smaller numbers, also a builder of Felixstowe F.2a flying boat hulls. Handley Page took over Norman Thompson in early 1919 but soon brought to an end manufacturing activities in this area.

BOGNOR REGIS, West Sussex 197/SU946012.
Durable airstrip on NE side of town used by Lec

THE AIRFIELDS OF BRITAIN: VOLUME 1

Refrigeration; the former Longford Engineering Company has operated its own business aircraft since 1946. One or two other private companies use Bognor Regis as well. From being a field shared with cows and devoid of facilities, it expanded to receive hangarage, and the landing area was extended in 1957. A hard runway laid in the first half of the 1980s finally solved winter flooding problems.

BOLDON, Tyne and Wear 88.

Early pre-WW1 airfield, sited on a racecourse, and scene of limited flying by the Northumberland and Durham Aero Club. Although the airfield and some sheds were being erected in April 1910, flying still occurring in August, the club thought Boldon a poor site. A boy died there that year following an accident. Boldon much later on after WW2 heavily promoted as an airport for the area into the 1950s. S of South Shields.

BOLTON, Greater Manchester 109.

Cobham and Holmes Aviation Company joy-riding with an Avro 504K during April 1-14 1920. Alongside A58 road to Bury.

BOTCHERBY, Cumbria 85/NY42?55? (W side).

Avro 504K site licensed for the single machine belonging to the Border Aviation Company (later known as the Ingham and Little Aviation Company) from May-November 1920 and again during June-December 1921. This aircraft flew to Scarborough for joy-riding duties on June 5 1920, returned in October and finally crashed in early December 1921. Possibly, though probably not, still in use as a civil LG later on in 1920s. 1½ miles E of Carlisle, now partly housing.

BOUGHROOD, Powys 161/SO128398.

1930s AA civil LG, operated by Sir Laurence Philipps. Still listed at September 1939, and a WW2 ELG according to official maps. On N side of hamlet between roads. Farmland.

BOURNES GREEN (SHOEBURYNESS), Essex 178.

WW1 LG, short-lived in an HD capacity and only used during May 1917 by No 37 Squadron. Noted as serving in same month as an Aerial Gunnery Practice Ground for artillery co-operation with elements at Shoeburyness but lasted little longer in this role. On E edge of Southend.

BRADFORD, West Yorkshire 104.

1920s private civil LG. Stated as being 2 miles E of town, which places this site quite close to WW1 HD LG Farsley. Certainly Berkshire Aviation Company joy-riding in the same general area in November 1919.

BRADING, Isle of Wight 196/SZ612897.

WW1 Day LG for Gosport's gunnery school, active from

OTHER BRITISH AIRFIELDS

beginning of 1918. Two DH6 anti-submarine Flights of No 253 Squadron stayed from June 7, going to more advanced Foreland on August 8. Brading remained active by September but it is uncertain whether this airfield was still open at the Armistice, not least as some official maps and records make no mention of the place. 2 miles SE of Ryde and a short distance SE of what later became Ryde Airport.

BRAINTREE, Essex 167/TL74?22? (S side).

WW1 HD LG for No 37 Squadron from start of 1918, still in use at Armistice. Tel. Braintree 85. 1 mile SW of town where bypass now lies.

BRAMHALL, Greater Manchester 109/SJ87?83? (probable position).

Manchester Aviation Company joy-riding airfield for a fortnight in November 1920. 1 mile SW of town.

BRAMPTON, South Yorkshire 120.

WW1 HD LG for No 33 Squadron from October 1916. Approval given for relinquishment on March 24 1917 due to the food shortage situation in Britain and tactical reasons. The full name of this hamlet immediately E of the junction of the M1 and M18 motorways is Brampton en le Morthen.

BRANSTON, Staffordshire 128.

Berkshire Aviation Company joy-riding airfield by September 1921, firm there to 9th.

BREACHACHA (COLL), Strathclyde 46/NM162537.

Used by Scottish Airways 1936-39. Extremely poor sandy site by loch of same name.

BREAN DOWN, Somerset 182/ST312595.

Beach site on SW side of Weston-super-Mare, licensed for Avro 504K use from August 1919. The Avro Transport Company carried over 3,000 people here over the summer period. Flying stopped in November because of fierce opposition from local residents and golfers on an adjoining course but airfield licensed again during June-November 1920. Also a civil LG later on in 1920s. Taxiplanes Ltd performed joy-riding at Brean Down in the summer of 1928 but slight confusion as (backed up by photographic evidence) that machines may have flown instead from a field.

BREDON, Hereford and Worcester 150.

1920s civil LG.

BRENTINGBY (MELTON MOWBRAY), Leicestershire 129/SK783183.

WW1 HD LG for No 38 Squadron from October 1916. Quickly discovered to be too dangerous, narrow and low-lying, therefore approval given for relinquishment on November 25 and succeeded by Scalford to the N of Melton

THE AIRFIELDS OF BRITAIN: VOLUME 1

Mowbray. 3 miles E of town, S of hamlet across River Eye.
BRESSAY, Shetland 4.

E. E. Fresson landed on this island October 1933, after which occasional Highland Airways flights into 1934. Listed on official maps as a WW2 LG for FAA aircraft. E of Lerwick.
BRIDGEND (ISLAY), Strathclyde 60/NR311601.

Airliners used this Islay beach site on occasion in the 1930s, particularly from when Midland and Scottish Air Ferries began a service to the island in April 1933 until Bowmore took over in early 1934. The first air ambulance flight from the Western Isles also left Bridgend for Glasgow on May 14 1933.
BRIDGWATER, Somerset 182.

1920s civil LG, 1 mile W of town. As late as 1938 local authorities in the town hoped that Weston Zoyland could be used in a joint RAF/civil capacity in the future.
BRIDLINGTON I (SANDS LANE), Humberside 101.

Licensed for Avro 504K use during May-November 1921, a licensed airfield from May 1922.
BRIDLINGTON II (SPEETON), North Yorkshire 101/TA165747.

Lockwood Flying Services Ltd provided flying training and pleasure flights with mainly Austers from July 1946, additionally running the East Riding Flying Club. Airfield officially opened on August 14 1947. Butlin's held some air rallies for residents of the nearby holiday camp. This airfield remained active in June 1957 but the East Riding Flying Club had moved away south to North Frodingham, SE of Great Driffield, by October. A field shows no traces of Bridlington II, 7 miles N of the town and ½ mile E of Speeton village.
BRIDLINGTON (seaplane), Humberside 101.

1930s mooring site for RAF flying boats.
BRIGHOUSE I (STONEY LANE), West Yorkshire 104.

The Gun Club Field at Lightcliffe, on N side of town, scene of some joy-riding after WW1. Local man Herbert Sykes provided flying weeks here in 1919, as did two machines of the Central Aircraft Company from October 26 1919.
BRIGHOUSE II (THORNHILLS LANE), West Yorkshire 104/SE15?23?

Herbert Sykes gave joy-rides at this alternative place for a fortnight in August 1920 as the Lightcliffe site was not available in that year. People taken up included a woman of 100 – with 70 grandchildren! Licensed as an Avro 504K site during September/October 1920. Sir Alan Cobham later gave displays at Thornhills Lane in the 1930s. Available facts indicate that this airfield lay 1 mile NE of Brighouse, N of the A643 road.

OTHER BRITISH AIRFIELDS

BRIGHTON (landplane) (LADIES' MILE), East Sussex 198.

Four Avro 504Ks gave joy-rides from July 12 1919. On N outskirts of town, between Patcham and Stanmer Park, busy but too inconvenient and flying switched to West Blatchington in October. One hangar available.

BRIGMERSTON DOWN, Wiltshire 184/SU20?47? (probably E side).

WW1 LG, 2¾ miles directly SE of Netheravon. Other details obscure but probably an aide to either this airfield or Upavon.

BRIMS MAINS, Highland 12/ND044700.

WW2 ELG for Castletown. 7 miles NW of Thurso, S of Brims Ness. Named after a tiny locality to the north. A typical rudimentary airfield with no remains which never received any mention in Castletown's ORB. Rough grassland in a harsh environment, the author having visited at the peak of a fierce thunderstorm as rain hammered down. Brighton Brims Mains ain't!

BRINKLOW (BRETFORD), Warwickshire 140/SP436781.

Another puzzler, this time a WW2 SLG for No 29 MU at High Ercall near Shrewsbury, about 55 miles directly NW. Opened October 16 1941 but few further details. The landing area rolled by March 1942 and the airfield temporarily closed on August 25; still occupied at November 23, as on March 22 1943 when the Ministry of Aircraft Production took over seven Nissen huts from the War Department. Stated on November 4 1944 that Brinklow to be derequisitioned. Some aircraft did land for storage purposes, as did training types from nearby Ansty and Church Lawford. Biggest question marks of all concern No 48 GS, whose ATC gliders stayed from the school's formation in either October 1943 or April 1944 (disputed) until going to Castle Bromwich in September 1945. Powered aircraft trainers at SLGs were unusual though accepted sights, but the presence of No 48 GS makes one ask when aircraft storage duties finished at Brinklow as such a task needed considerable levels of secrecy. E of Coventry, 1 mile S of village by B4029. The watch office/guardroom is now a house but even many local inhabitants have never heard of the airfield.

BROAD SALTS (SANDWICH), Kent 179/TR343591.

WW1 night LG, active from September 1916, passed to control of No 50 (HD) Squadron January 1917. Still active during 1918 but uncertain whether it lasted right up to the Armistice. 1 mile NE of Sandwich, New Downs Farm on E side of LG still stands. Broad Salts is named after an area of land.

THE AIRFIELDS OF BRITAIN: VOLUME 1

BROADWAY, Hereford and Worcester 150.

1920s civil LG. A 'Flying Flea' field called Broadway Air Park later existed by 1936, a rally being held there on May 2/3.

BROOM, Hereford and Worcester 139.

WW1 HD LG for No 38 Squadron from October 1916. A poor airfield as sited on a very narrow plateau and aircraft capable of using only one runway, hence approval given for relinquishment on November 25. Tel. Hagley 58. S of Stourbridge, village now known as Broome.

BROOM HALL (PWLLHELI), Gwynedd 123/SH410375.

Lieutenant W. P. O. Evans, a landowner and private pilot based at the residence of this name, owned a hangar in the 1930s and flew a handful of de Havilland light aircraft types. He died on April 9 1937 when his Puss Moth crashed in Surrey. Main use of this airfield after WW2, primarily in connection with Butlin's holiday camp to SE which opened in 1947. Broom Hall in use from end of June, officially opened September 20-22. Butlin's used a Southern Martlet biplane for aerobatic purposes during 1947-49, and a Percival Q.6 monoplane based at Speke with a joy-riding firm crashed on May 6 1949. Cambrian Air Services bought the airfield in 1949, other minor charter operators flying seasonal services to Broom Hall in the early and mid-1950s, notably Dragon Airways from Liverpool and Manchester in 1953/54. Later history of site erratic: seemingly closed 1954, reopened 1956, closed again either 1961 or 1962, then once more reopened *circa* 1964. Butlin's continued with pleasure flying, Chrisair Aviation Services (based at Sywell) later taking on this task about 1966 before Broom Hall closed for the last time, probably in 1967. Local inhabitants claim that post-war this airfield, 3½ miles NE of Pwllheli, apparently only consisted of an open space with two runways and nothing else. But surely some hangarage must have existed?

BROUGHTY FERRY, Tayside 54.

Scene of occasional flying by RNAS Dundee aircraft in 1914, after which supportive use until 1919. E of Dundee.

BRYMON HILL, Greater London 176.

Following London County Council's recommendation in May 1927 that parks and other open areas in the city be used as ELGs for Home Defence operations, a policy very similar to that of 1914 which created sites such as Battersea Park, six places were established for RAF night fighters for use during exercises. Flares marked out these airfields. Brymon Hill and company were made ready by mid-December 1933 and lasted until 1935. This particular airfield existed at Parliament Hill,

OTHER BRITISH AIRFIELDS

just E of Hampstead Heath, typically crude as a biplane with the Marquess of Londonderry aboard which had to make a forced landing on November 10 1935 interrupted a football match.

BRYNMILL SANDS (SWANSEA), West Glamorgan 159/SS638918.

Avro 504K site, on SW edge of town, licensed from July 26 1919 and again from May 1920. A popular joy-riding airfield in that first summer season with the Avro Transport Company in charge but the Welsh Aviation Company did not encounter similar success once created in November 1920. A local bookmaker named Evan Williams acquired this firm and its four Avro biplanes in February 1922 but drowned with his pilot and another passenger when an Avro 504K crashed in the sea nearby on October 2. South Wales Airways later provided joy-riding flights at Brynmill Sands in the late 1920s.

BUDLEIGH SALTERTON, Devon 192.

1920s private civil LG. Sited on The Warren.

BUILTH WELLS, Powys 147.

Welsh Aviation Company joy-riding airfield during 1921.

BURNLEY, Lancashire 103.

Joy-riding airfield, used during first half of September 1919. Charles Kingsford-Smith and associates moved from here to Blackburn. On E side of town at Brunshaw.

BURRELTON, Tayside 53/NO20?36?

WW2 RLG for Tiger Moths of No 11 EFTS. 2½ miles SW of Coupar Angus by A94.

BURTON-UPON-TRENT, Staffordshire 128/SK252225.

A flying meeting held at Bass' Meadows during September 12-17 1910, followed by a second one at same site on August 1/2 and 4/5 1913. A civil LG active in the Burton-upon-Trent area later on in the 1920s but municipal airfield proposals in this decade and the next one failed to happen. Pre-WW1 airfield on main island in River Trent dividing two halves of town.

BURY ST EDMUNDS I, Suffolk 155.

Registered as an ELG for RNAS fighters from October 1914. Taken up by RFC about March 17 1916 for No 51 (HD) Squadron but closed before the year had ended. Thought to have lain on W side of town.

THE AIRFIELDS OF BRITAIN: VOLUME 1
Alternative Airfield Names

Many of Britain's airfields have held different names ever since 1909. Everything from airports to landing grounds have been given completely separate titles for a variety of reasons. In the following list, secondary names come under five categories:

(1) Original titles later replaced by new ones.
(2) New and more accepted titles.
(3) Alternative titles, primarily more localised but officially accepted ones.
(4) Generalised airport titles.
(5) Generalised World War One titles. Strictly speaking, these names should not be included as they were only meant for postal purposes, but personnel did recognise them in a semi-official capacity.

Localised names bestowed upon especially World War Two airfields by surrounding civilian populations are in the main not included below. However, as one can vouch for today, persistence can sometimes pay off and give an essentially false title – Boyndie for Banff, to take but one example – a certain respectability.

Secondary Name	Primary Name(s)
Abbots Ripton	Alconbury
Aberdeen	Dyce, Seaton
Aberffraw	Bodorgan
Abergele	Foryd
Affleck Farm	Huntly
Aghada	Queenstown
Aldenham	Elstree
Aldridge	Walsall
Alexandra Park	Didsbury
Alnwick	Rennington, Stamford
Alton Park Road	Clacton I
Ampthill	Flitwick
Anglesey	Mona
Apethorpe	King's Cliffe
Apse	Shanklin
Ardleigh	Colchester
Ards	Newtownards
Arlington	Wilmington

ALTERNATIVE AIRFIELD NAMES

Armthorpe	Doncaster III
Ash	Guilton
Ashbourne	Roston
Ashfield	Great Ashfield
Ashford	Lympne
Aston Rowant	Lambert Arms
Atherstone (-on-Stour)	Stratford II
Atlantic Park	Eastleigh
Auchterarder	Strathallan
Auldearn	Nairn
Aylestone Lane	Leicester
Aylsham	Saxthorpe
Badgeworth	Cheltenham
Baldock	Therfield
Baldoon	Wigtown
Balivanich	Benbecula
Ballycassidy	St Angelo
Baltasound	Unst
Barassie	Gailes
Barnstaple	Chivenor
Bath	North Stoke I
Bawtry	Bircotes
Bea Ness	Sanday II
Beck Row	Mildenhall
Beddington	Croydon
Bedford	Kempston, Lavendon, Little Staughton I
Beechwood Park	Beechwood
Belfast	Aldergrove, Nutt's Corner
Belfast Harbour	Sydenham
Berridale	South Ronaldsay
Berwick-on-Tweed	New Haggerston, Winfield
Bexhill	Hooe
Bexwell	Downham Market
Biggleswade	Old Warden
Birkdale Sands	Southport
Birkenhead	Bidston
Birmingham	Billesley, Elmdon, Great Barr, Northfield
Bishops Tachbrook	Leamington
Blackpool	Squires Gate, Stanley Park
Blackstand	Black Isle
Blaenannerch	Aberporth
Blagraves Farm	Caversham
Blue Barns	Colchester
Blundell Sands	Waterloo Sands

393

THE AIRFIELDS OF BRITAIN: VOLUME 1

Blythe Bridge	Meir
Bobbington	Halfpenny Green
Bogs of Mayne	Elgin II
Bohune Common	Manningford
Borras	Wrexham II
Boston	Willoughby Hills
Bourne	Swinstead
Bourne End	Cock Marsh
Bournemouth	Ensbury Park, Hurn, Southbourne
Bowldown Farm	Leighterton
Bowness	Windermere II
Boyndie	Banff
Brackley	Croughton
Bradford	Farsley
Brafferton	Helperby
Bramham Moor	Tadcaster
Brattleby	Scampton
Bray Court	Bray
Brayton Park	Brayton
Bretford	Brinklow
Bretton	Hawarden
Bridge	Bekesbourne
Bridge of Waithe	Stromness
Bridlington	Carnaby
Bridport	Toller
Bristol	Filton, Lulsgate Bottom, Whitchurch
Broadfield Down	Lulsgate Bottom
Brockenhurst	Beaulieu II
Brome	Eye
Brooklands Farm	Sale
Broomhill	Wombwell
Broughton	Hawarden
Brown's Farm	Alton Barnes
Bungay	Earsham
Bures	Wormingford
Burgh Road	Skegness I
Burrow Head	Kidsdale
Burton-upon-Trent	Lullington, Tatenhill
Bury	Upwood
Bury St Edmunds	Westley

ALTERNATIVE AIRFIELD NAMES

In Volume 2 of *The Airfields of Britain:*
A whole cavalcade of Battle of Britain superstars, including Coltishall, Debden and Duxford ... the world's most famous training airfield, Cranwell ... ace U-boat killer Chivenor ... the airfield flop now a household name ... Calshot, a story of glamour, durability – and potatoes ... the airfield built on rubbish and always treated as such ... and the overlooked minor airfield in the Rudolf Hess mystery.

A few selections from the second part of the most thorough British airfield account ever written. *The Airfields of Britain:* our real history.

Information? Photographs? Up to the minute developments? Send them to:

> K. P. Bannerman
> c/o IS Enterprises
> PO Box 379
> Clarkston
> Glasgow G76 8AD.

All photographs will be returned if requested.